B-BJ

Philosophy
Psychology

Library of Congress Classification
2012

Prepared by the Policy and Standards Division
Library Services

LIBRARY OF CONGRESS
Cataloging Distribution Service
Washington, D.C.

This edition cumulates all additions and changes to class B-BJ through List 2012/04, dated April 16, 2012. Additions and changes made subsequent to that date are published in weekly lists posted on the World Wide Web at

<http://www.loc.gov/aba/cataloging/classification/weeklylists/>

and are also available in *Classification Web*, the online Web-based edition of the Library of Congress Classification.

Library of Congress Cataloging-in-Publication Data

Library of Congress.
Library of Congress classification. B-BJ. Philosophy. Psychology / prepared by the Policy and Standards Division, Library Services.
pages cm
Includes index.
ISBN 978-0-8444-9542-2
1. Classification, Library of Congress. 2. Classification--Books--Philosophy.
3. Classification--Books--Psychology. I. Library of Congress. Policy and Standards Division.
II. Title. III. Title: Philosophy. IV. Title: Psychology.

Z696.U5B1 2012
025.4'61--dc23

2012023668

For sale by the Library of Congress Cataloging Distribution Service,
101 Independence Avenue, S.E., Washington, DC 20541-4912.
Product catalog available on the Web at **www.loc.gov/cds**

PREFACE

The first edition of subclasses B-BJ, *Philosophy and Psychology*, was published in 1910, the second in 1950 (reissued in 1968 with supplementary pages), the third in 1979, and the fourth in 1989. Editions published in 1996, 2000, and 2008 cumulated additions and changes that were made during the periods 1989-1996, 1996-2000, and 2000-2008. This 2012 edition cumulates additions and changes made since the publication of the 2008 edition.

In the Library of Congress Classification schedules, classification numbers or spans of numbers that appear in parentheses are formerly valid numbers that are now obsolete. Numbers or spans that appear in angle brackets are optional numbers that have never been used at the Library of Congress but are provided for other libraries that wish to use them. In most cases, a parenthesized or angle-bracketed number is accompanied by a "see" reference directing the user to the actual number that the Library of Congress currently uses, or a note explaining Library of Congress practice.

Access to the online version of the full Library of Congress Classification is available on the World Wide Web by subscription to Classification Web. Details about ordering and pricing may be obtained from the Cataloging Distribution Service at:

<http://www.loc.gov/cds/>

New or revised numbers and captions are added to the L.C. Classification schedules as a result of development proposals made by the cataloging staff of the Library of Congress and cooperating institutions. Upon approval of these proposals by the editorial meeting of the Policy and Standards Division, new classification records are created or existing records are revised in the master classification database. Lists of newly approved or revised classification numbers and captions are posted on the World Wide Web at:

<http://www.loc.gov/aba/cataloging/classification/weeklylists/>

Janis L. Young, senior subject cataloging policy specialist in the Policy and Standards Division, is responsible for coordinating the overall intellectual and editorial content of subclasses B-BJ. Kent Griffiths and Ethel Tillman, assistant editors of classification schedules, create new classification records and their associated index terms, and maintain the master database.

Barbara B. Tillett, Chief
Policy and Standards Division

May 2012

OUTLINE

B1-5802	Philosophy (General)
B69-99	General works
B108-5802	By period
	Including individual philosophers and schools of philosophy
B108-708	Ancient
B720-765	Medieval
B770-785	Renaissance
B790-5802	Modern
B808-849	Special topics and schools of philosophy
B850-5739	By region or country
B5800-5802	By religion
BC1-199	Logic
BC11-39	History
BC25-39	By period
BC60-99	General works
BC171-199	Special topics
BD10-701	Speculative philosophy
BD10-41	General philosophical works
BD95-131	Metaphysics
BD143-237	Epistemology. Theory of knowledge
BD240-260	Methodology
BD300-450	Ontology
	Including being, the soul, life, death
BD493-701	Cosmology
	Including teleology, space and time, structure of matter, plurality of worlds
BF1-990	Psychology
BF38-64	Philosophy. Relation to other topics
BF173-175.5	Psychoanalysis
BF176-176.5	Psychological tests and testing
BF180-198.7	Experimental psychology
BF203	Gestalt psychology
BF207-209	Psychotropic drugs and other substances
BF231-299	Sensation. Aesthesiology
BF309-499	Consciousness. Cognition
	Including learning, attention, comprehension, memory, imagination, genius, intelligence, thought and thinking, psycholinguistics, mental fatigue
BF501-505	Motivation

OUTLINE

	Psychology - Continued
BF511-593	Affection. Feeling. Emotion
BF608-635	Will. Volition. Choice. Control
BF636-637	Applied psychology
BF638-648	New Thought. Menticulture, etc.
BF660-685	Comparative psychology. Animal and human psychology
BF692-692.5	Psychology of sex. Sexual behavior
BF697-697.5	Differential psychology. Individuality. Self
BF698-698.9	Personality
BF699-711	Genetic psychology
BF712-724.85	Developmental psychology Including infant psychology, child psychology, adolescence, adulthood
BF725-727	Class psychology
BF795-839	Temperament. Character
BF839.8-885	Physiognomy. Phrenology
BF889-905	Graphology. Study of handwriting
BF908-940	The hand. Palmistry
BF1001-1389	Parapsychology
BF1001-1045	Psychic research. Psychology of the conscious
BF1048-1108	Hallucinations. Sleep. Dreaming. Visions
BF1111-1156	Hypnotism. Suggestion. Mesmerism. Subliminal projection
BF1161-1171	Telepathy. Mind reading. Thought transference
BF1228-1389	Spiritualism Including mediumship, spirit messages, clairvoyance
BF1404-2055	Occult sciences
BF1444-1486	Ghosts. Apparitions. Hauntings
BF1501-1562	Demonology. Satanism. Possession
BF1562.5-1584	Witchcraft
BF1585-1623	Magic. Hermetics. Necromancy
BF1651-1729	Astrology
BF1745-1779	Oracles. Sibyls. Divinations
BF1783-1815	Seers. Prophets. Prophecies
BF1845-1891	Fortune-telling
BF2050-2055	Human-alien encounters. Contact between humans and extraterrestrials
BH1-301	Aesthetics
BH81-208	History
BH301	Special topics

OUTLINE

BJ1-1725	Ethics
BJ71-1185	History and general works Including individual ethical philosophers
BJ1188-1295	Religious ethics
BJ1298-1335	Evolutionary and genetic ethics
BJ1365-1385	Positivist ethics
BJ1388	Socialist ethics
BJ1390-1390.5	Communist ethics
BJ1392	Totalitarian ethics
BJ1395	Feminist ethics
BJ1518-1697	Individual ethics. Character. Virtue Including practical and applied ethics, conduct of life, vices, success, ethics for children
BJ1725	Ethics of social groups, classes, etc. Professional ethics
BJ1801-2195	Social usages. Etiquette
BJ2021-2078	Etiquette of entertaining
BJ2139-2156	Etiquette of travel
BJ2195	Telephone etiquette

	Philosophy (General)
	For general philosophical treatises and introductions to philosophy see BD10+
	Periodicals. Serials
1.A1-.A3	Polyglot
1.A4-Z	English and American
2	French and Belgian
3	German
4	Italian
5	Spanish and Portuguese
6	Russian and other Slavic
8.A-Z	Other. By language, A-Z
	Societies
11	English and American
12	French and Belgian
13	German
14	Italian
15	Spanish and Portuguese
18.A-Z	Other. By language, A-Z
20	Congresses
	Collected works (nonserial)
20.6	Several languages
20.8	Latin
21	English and American
22	French and Belgian
23	German
24	Italian
25	Spanish and Portuguese
26	Russian and other Slavic
28.A-Z	Other. By language, A-Z
29	Addresses, essays, lectures
	Class here works by several authors or individual authors
(31)	Yearbooks
	see B1+
35	Directories
	Dictionaries
40	International (Polyglot)
41	English and American
42	French and Belgian
43	German
44	Italian
45	Spanish and Portuguese
48.A-Z	Other. By language, A-Z
	Terminology. Nomenclature
49	General works
50	Special topics, A-Z
51	Encyclopedias

	Historiography
51.4	General works
	Biography of historians
51.6.A2	Collective
51.6.A3-51.Z	Individual, A-Z
51.8	Pictorial works
	Study and teaching. Research Cf. BF77+ Psychology Cf. BJ66+ Ethics Cf. BJ66 Ethics
52	General works
52.3.A-Z	By region or country, A-Z
52.5	Problems, exercises, examinations
52.65.A-Z	By school, A-Z
	Communication of information
52.66	General works
52.67	Information services
52.68	Computer network resources Including the Internet
52.7	Authorship
	Philosophy. Methodology. Relation to other topics
53	General works
54	Electronic data processing
56	Relation to theology and religion Cf. BL51 Philosophy of religion
59	Relation to civilization Cf. CB19 Philosophy of civilization
61	Relation to history Cf. D16.7+ Philosophy of history
63	Relation to social sciences. Relation to sociology Cf. HB72 Relation of economics to philosophy
65	Relation to law and political science Cf. JA71+ Theory of political science
66	Relation to literature Cf. PN49 Philosophy of literature
67	Relation to science Cf. Q174+ Philosophy of science
68	Curiosa. Miscellanea Cf. GV1507.P43 Philosophical recreations
	General works Class translations of foreign works with originals except when largely rewritten
69	Latin
	English and American
71	Early through 1800
72	1801-

General works
English and American -- Continued
(73) Addresses, essays, lectures
see B29
74 Elementary textbooks
75 Outlines, syllabi, etc.
French and Belgian
76 Early through 1800
77 1801-
79 Elementary textbooks. Outlines, syllabi, etc.
German
81 Early through 1800
82 1801-
83 Addresses, essays, lectures
84 Elementary textbooks. Outlines, syllabi, etc.
Italian
86 Early through 1800
87 1801-
88 Addresses, essays, lectures
89 Elementary textbooks. Outlines, syllabi, etc.
Spanish and Portuguese
91 Early through 1800
92 1801-
93 Addresses, essays, lectures
94 Elementary textbooks. Outlines, syllabi, etc.
99.A-Z Other. By language, A-Z
Under each:
.x *Early through 1800*
.x2 *1801-*
e. g.
Dutch and Flemish
99.D8 Early through 1800
99.D82 1801-
103 Elementary textbooks, outlines, syllabi, etc. for Catholic students
104 Collective biography
105.A-Z Special topics, A-Z
For philosophy of specific disciplines, see classes BL-Z, e. g.
GV706+ Philosophy of sports
105.A3 Absurd
105.A35 Act
105.A44 Affiliation
105.A55 Animals
Anticipation see B105.E87
105.A75 Astronautics
105.A8 Authenticity
105.A84 Autonomy

	Special topics, A-Z -- Continued
105.B64	Body, Human
	Body and mind see B105.M53
	Brain-mind identity theory see B105.M55
105.C45	Children and philosophy
105.C455	Color
105.C456	Comic, The
105.C457	Common sense
105.C46	Communities
105.C47	Compensation
105.C473	Complexity
105.C477	Consciousness
105.C48	Construction
105.C5	Continuity
105.C54	Contrast
	Creative ability see B105.C74
105.C74	Creativity. Creative ability
105.C75	Crises
105.C9	Cycles
105.D37	Depth
105.D4	Description
105.D44	Desire
105.D47	Determinism
105.D48	Dialectic
105.D5	Difference
105.D56	Disposition
105.D57	Dissymmetry
105.D58	Distraction
105.D64	Dogs
105.D78	Drunkenness
105.E46	Emotions
105.E5	Engagement
105.E65	Essence
105.E68	Europe
105.E7	Events
105.E75	Exact
105.E77	Exaggeration
105.E78	Excess
105.E8	Existentialism
	Cf. B819.A1+ Modern philosophy
105.E87	Expectation. Anticipation
105.E9	Experience
105.E95	Expression
105.F29	Face
105.F3	Facts
	Feelings see B105.E46
105.F66	Food

Special topics, A-Z -- Continued

	Freedom see B105.L45
105.F75	Friendship
105.G63	Goal
105.H32	Habit
105.H37	Harmony
	Human body see B105.B64
105.H8	Humanism
105.I28	Idea. Ideas.
105.I3	Ideals
105.I44	Illusion
105.I47	Image. Images
105.I49	Imagination
105.I52	Immaterialism
105.I53	Indivisibles
105.I533	Ineffable, The
105.I535	Infinite regress
105.I54	Innate ideas
105.I56	Intentionality
105.I57	Interest
105.J87	Justice
105.L3	Law
	Left and right see B105.R54
105.L45	Liberty. Freedom Cf. JC585+ Political theory
105.L54	Listening
105.L65	Loneliness
105.M4	Meaning Cf. B840.A1+ Modern philosophy
105.M53	Mind and body
105.M55	Mind-brain identity theory
105.M57	Mixing
105.M6	Monism
105.M65	Movement
105.N33	Need
105.N34	Negativity
105.N4	The new
105.N65	Norm
105.O67	Opportunity
105.O7	Order
105.O74	Organism
105.O75	Origin
105.P35	Participation
105.P4	Peace
105.P47	Perplexity
105.P53	Place
105.P54	Play

	Special topics, A-Z -- Continued
105.P6	Positivism
105.P62	Preferences
105.P64	Presentation
105.P7	Principle
105.P73	Priority
105.P8	Purity
105.Q3	Quality
105.Q34	Quantity
105.R23	Recognition
105.R25	Reference
105.R27	Reflection
105.R29	Reification. Verdinglichung
105.R3	Relevance
105.R37	Repetition
105.R4	Representation
105.R47	Resistance
105.R54	Right and left
105.S25	Salvation
105.S43	Seeds
105.S45	Sense
105.S55	Simplicity
105.S59	Sound
105.S63	Specialism
105.S64	Spirit. Spirituality
105.S66	Spiritual exercises
	Spirituality see B105.S64
105.S68	Strategy
105.S7	Style
105.S79	Suffering
105.S85	Surfaces
105.T43	Techne
105.T47	Terrorism
105.T52	Theory
	Thinking see B105.T54
105.T54	Thought and thinking
105.T66	Topic
105.T7	Tradition
105.T74	Triads
105.U5	Universals
105.V33	Vagueness
	Verdinglichung see B105.R29
105.V5	Violence
105.V54	Vision
105.V64	Voice
105.W24	Waiting
105.W25	Walking

Special topics, A-Z -- Continued
105.W3 War
105.W5 Wisdom
105.W59 Women
105.W6 Women philosophers
105.W65 Wonder
General history of individual countries see B790+
Ancient (600 B.C.-430 A.D.)
108 Collected works (nonserial)
General works
110 Latin
111 English
112 French
113 German
115.A-Z Other. By language, A-Z
e. g.
115.I7 Italian
118 Nature philosophy of the ancients
Orient
121 General works
123 General special
Including special aspects of the subject as a whole
By region or country
Including ancient and medieval to ca. 1600, unless otherwise indicated
For modern Asia see B5000+
China
125 Collected works (nonserial)
126 General works, collective biography, etc.
127.A-Z Special topics, A-Z
127.C48 Cheng
127.C49 Chi. Qi
127.C65 Confucian philosophy
127.C68 Cosmology
Dao see B127.T3
127.F58 Five agents
127.H4 Heaven
127.H8 Humanism
127.I2 I ching. Yi jing
127.J4 Jen. Ren
127.L35 Language and languages
127.L43 Legalism
127.L5 Li
127.L55 Life
127.L64 Logicians
127.M3 Man
127.M38 Materialism

Ancient (600 B.C.-430 A.D.)
Orient
By region or country
China
Special topics, A-Z -- Continued

127.M48 Metaphysics
127.M65 Moism
127.N3 Nature
127.N4 Neo-Confucianism
Qi see B127.C49
127.R37 Rationalism
Ren see B127.J4
127.S47 Senses and sensation
127.T3 Tao. Dao
Yi jing see B127.I2
127.Y56 Yin-yang
128.A-Z Individual philosophers, A-Z
Subarrange each by Table B-BJ5
Class here individual Chinese philosophers from the ancient period to 1600
128.C26-.C264 Chan, Jo-shui, 1466-1560. 湛若水 (Table B-BJ5)
128.C28-.C284 Chang, Shih, 1133-1180. 張栻; 张栻 (Table B-BJ5)
128.C31-.C314 Chang, Tsai. 張載; 张载 (Table B-BJ5)
128.C33-.C334 Chao, Jui, 8th cent. 趙蕤; 赵蕤 (Table B-BJ5)
128.C346-.C3464 Ch'en, Hsien-chang, 1428-1500. 陳獻章; 陈献章 (Table B-BJ5)
128.C347-.C3474 Ch'en, Liang, 1143-1194. 陳亮; 陈亮 (Table B-BJ5)
Chen, Xianzhang, 1428-1500. 陳獻章; 陈献章 see B128.C346+
128.C358-.C3584 Ch'eng, Hao, 1032-1085. 程顥; 程颢 (Table B-BJ5)
128.C359-.C3594 Cheng, Hsüan, 127-200. 鄭玄; 郑玄 (Table B-BJ5)
128.C36-.C364 Ch'eng, I, 1033-1107. 程頤; 程颐 (Table B-BJ5)
128.C377-.C3774 Cheng, Xuanying, fl. 631-655. 成玄英 (Table B-BJ5)
Ch'eng, Yi, 1033-1107. 程頤; 程颐 see B128.C36+
128.C385-.C3854 Chi, K'ang, 223-262. 嵇康; 嵇康 (Table B-BJ5)
128.C3857-.C38574 Chia, I, 200-168 B.C. 賈誼; 贾谊 (Table B-BJ5)
128.C4-.C44 Chou, Tun-i, 1017-1073. 周敦頤; 周敦颐 (Table B-BJ5)
128.C5-.C54 Chu, Hsi, 1130-1200. 朱熹 (Table B-BJ5)
Confucius
Cf. BL1830+ Confucianism
Confucian Canon see PL2458+
128.C8 Biography and criticism
Deng, Xi, 545-501 B.C. 鄧析; 邓析 see B128.T39+
Dong, Zhongshu, 2nd cent. B.C. 董仲舒 see B128.T82+
128.F3-.F34 Fan, Zhen, ca. 445-ca. 510. 范縝; 范缜 (Table B-BJ5)

	Ancient (600 B.C.-430 A.D.)
	Orient
	By region or country
	China
	Individual philosophers, A-Z -- Continued
128.F82-.F824	Fu, Xuan, 217-278. 傅玄 (Table B-BJ5)
	Gongsun, Long, 3rd cent. B.C. 公孫龍; 公孙龙 see B128.K87+
	Guan, Zhong, d. 645 B.C. 管仲 see B128.K83+
	Guiguzi, 4th cent. B.C. 鬼谷子 see B128.K837+
	Han, Fei, d. 233 B.C. 韓非
128.H3	Original text. By date
128.H32A-.H32Z	Translations. By language, A-Z, and date
128.H335	Selections. By date
128.H336A-.H336Z	Translations. By language, A-Z, and date
128.H34	Biography, criticism, etc.
128.H48-.H484	He, Xinyin, 1517-1579. 何心隱 (Table B-BJ5)
128.H49-.H494	Heguanzi. 鶡冠子 (Table B-BJ5)
128.H523-.H5234	Hsü, Ch'ien, 1199-1266. 許謙; 许谦 (Table B-BJ5)
128.H525-.H5254	Hsü, Heng, 1209-1281. 許衡; 许衡 (Table B-BJ5)
	Hsün-tzu, 340-245 B.C. 荀子
128.H65	Original text. By date
128.H66A-.H66Z	Translations. By language, A-Z, and date
128.H67	Selections. By date
128.H68A-.H68Z	Translations. By language, A-Z, and date
128.H7	Biography, criticism, etc.
128.H86-.H864	Huan, T'an, ca. 40 B.C.-ca. 32 A.D. 桓譚; 桓谭 (Table B-BJ5)
128.H95-.H954	Hui, Shi, ca. 370-ca. 310 B.C. 惠施 (Table B-BJ5)
128.J44-.J444	Jen-tzu, 545-469 B.C. 任子 (Table B-BJ5)
	Ji, Kang , 223-262. 嵇康; 嵇康 see B128.C385+
	Jia, Yi, 200-168 B.C. 賈誼; 贾谊 see B128.C3857+
128.J83-.J834	Juan, Chi, 210-263. 阮籍; 阮籍 (Table B-BJ5)
	Kuan, Chung, d. 645 B.C. 管仲
128.K83	Original text. By date
128.K832A-.K832Z	Translations. By language, A-Z, and date
128.K833	Selections. By date
128.K8332A-.K8332Z	Translations. By language, A-Z, and date
128.K834	Biography, criticism, etc.
	Kuei-ku-tzu, 4th cent. B.C. 鬼谷子
128.K837	Original text. By date
128.K8372A-.K8372Z	Translations. By language, A-Z, and date
128.K8373	Selections. By date
128.K83732A-.K83732Z	Translations. By language, A-Z, and date
128.K8374	Biography, criticism, etc.
128.K84-.K844	K'ung, Chi, 483-402 B.C. 孔伋 (Table B-BJ5)

	Ancient (600 B.C.-430 A.D.)
	Orient
	By region or country
	China
	Individual philosophers, A-Z -- Continued
	Kung-sun, Lung, 3rd cent. B.C. 公孫龍; 公孙龙
128.K87	Original text. By date
128.K872A-.K872Z	Translations. By language, A-Z, and date
128.K873	Selections. By date
128.K874A-.K874Z	Translations. By language, A-Z, and date
128.K88	Biography, criticism, etc.
	Lao-tzu. 老子 see BL1900.L25+
128.L45-.L454	Li, Chih, 1527-1602. 李贽 (Table B-BJ5)
128.L456-.L4564	Li, Gou, 1009-1059. 李覯; 李觏 (Table B-BJ5)
	Li, Zhi, 1527-1602. 李贽 see B128.L45+
128.L57-.L574	Liu, Chi, 1311-1375. 劉基; 刘基 (Table B-BJ5)
128.L58-.L584	Liu, Chou, 514-565. 劉晝; 刘昼 (Table B-BJ5)
128.L586-.L5864	Liu, Hsiang, 77?-6? B.C. 劉向; 刘向 (Table B-BJ5)
	Liu, Ji, 1311-1375. 劉基; 刘基 see B128.L57+
128.L59-.L594	Liu, Tsung-chou, 1578-1645. 劉宗周; 刘宗周 (Table B-BJ5)
	Liu, Xiang, 77?-6? B.C. 劉向; 刘向 see B128.L586+
128.L64-.L644	Liu, Yin, 1249-1293. 劉因; 刘因 (Table B-BJ5)
	Liu, Zhou, 514-565. 劉晝; 刘昼 see B128.L58+
	Liu, Zongzhou, 1578-1645. 劉宗周; 刘宗周 see B128.L59+
128.L81-.L814	Lu, Chia, ca. 216-ca. 172 B.C. 陸賈; 陆贾 (Table B-BJ5)
128.L83-.L834	Lu, Chiu-yüan, 1139-1193. 陸九淵; 陆九渊 (Table B-BJ5)
	Lu, Jia, ca. 216-ca. 172 B.C. 陸賈; 陆贾 see B128.L81+
	Lu, Jiuyuan, 1139-1193. 陸九淵; 陆九渊 see B128.L83+
128.L85-.L854	Lü, Kun, 1536-1618. 吕坤 (Table B-BJ5)
128.L87-.L874	Lü, Zuqian, 1137-1181. 呂祖謙; 吕祖谦 (Table B-BJ5)
128.L94-.L944	Luo, Qinshun, 1465-1547. 羅欽順; 罗钦顺 (Table B-BJ5)
	Mencius
	For his work, Meng-tzu see PL2461+
128.M324	Biography, criticism, etc.
	Mo, Di, fl. 400 B.C. 墨翟
128.M76	Original text. By date
128.M77A-.M77Z	Translations. By language, A-Z, and date
128.M78	Selections. By date
128.M79A-.M79Z	Translations. By language, A-Z, and date
128.M8	Biography, criticism, etc.

Ancient (600 B.C.-430 A.D.)
Orient
By region or country
China
Individual philosophers, A-Z -- Continued

	Renzi, 545-469 B.C. 任子 see B128.J44+
	Ruan, Ji, 210-263. 阮籍; 阮籍 see B128.J83+
	Shang, Yang, d. 338 B.C. 商鞅
128.S47	Original text. By date
128.S472A-.S472Z	Translations. By language, A-Z, and date
128.S473	Selections. By date
128.S4732A-.S4732Z	Translations. By language, A-Z, and date
128.S474	Biography, criticism, etc.
128.S51-.S514	Shao, Yong, 1011-1077. 邵雍 (Table B-BJ5)
128.S54-.S544	Shen, Dao, 350?-275? B.C. 慎到 (Table B-BJ5)
128.S58-.S584	Shi, Jiao, ca. 390 B.C.-ca. 330 B.C. 屍佼; 尸佼 (Table B-BJ5)
128.T34-.T344	Tang, Zhongyou, 12th cent. 唐仲友 (Table B-BJ5)
128.T39-.T394	Teng, Hsi, 545-501 B.C. 鄧析; 邓析 (Table B-BJ5)
128.T74-.T744	Tseng, Shen, 505-437 or 6 B.C. 曾参 (Table B-BJ5)
128.T82-.T824	Tung, Chung-shu, 2nd cent. B.C. 董仲舒 (Table B-BJ5)
	Tzu-ssu, 483-402 B.C. 孔伋 see B128.K84+
	Wang, Bi, 226-249. 王弼 see B128.W286+
128.W25-.W254	Wang, Chong, 27-97? 王充 (Table B-BJ5)
128.W265-.W2654	Wang, Dao, 1487-1547. 王道 (Table B-BJ5)
128.W267-.W2674	Wang, Fu, ca. 76-ca. 157. 王符 (Table B-BJ5)
128.W277-.W2774	Wang, Gen, 1483-1541. 王艮 (Table B-BJ5)
128.W28-.W284	Wang, Ji, 1498-1583. 王畿 (Table B-BJ5)
128.W286-.W2864	Wang, Pi, 226-249. 王弼 (Table B-BJ5)
128.W33-.W334	Wang, Tingxiang, 1474-1544. 王廷相 (Table B-BJ5)
128.W34-.W344	Wang, Tong, 584?-618? 王通 (Table B-BJ5)
128.W36-.W364	Wang, Yang-ming, 1472-1529. 王陽明; 王阳明 (Table B-BJ5)
128.W73-.W734	Wu, Cheng, 1249-1333. 吳澄; 吴澄 (Table B-BJ5)
128.W82-.W824	Wu, Tinghan, 1490?-1559. 吳廷翰 (Table B-BJ5)
128.W85-.W854	Wunengzi, 9th cent. 無能子; 无能子 (Table B-BJ5)
	Xu, Heng, 1209-1281. 許衡; 许衡 see B128.H525+
	Xu, Qian, 1199-1266. 許謙; 许谦 see B128.H523+
	Xunzi, 340-245 B.C. 荀子 see B128.H65+
	Yan, Hui, 6th/5th cent. B.C. 顏回; 颜回 see B128.Y3664+
128.Y23-.Y234	Yan, Jun, 1504-1596. 顏鈞 ; 颜钧 (Table B-BJ5)
	Yan, Ying, d. 500 B.C. 晏嬰; 晏婴 see B128.Y393+
128.Y25-.Y254	Yang, Jian, 1141-1226. 楊簡; 杨简 (Table B-BJ5)
128.Y36-.Y364	Ye, Ziqi, fl. 1378. 葉子奇; 叶子奇 (Table B-BJ5)
128.Y3664-.Y36644	Yen, Hui, 6th/5th cent. B.C. 顏回; 颜回 (Table B-BJ5)

	Ancient (600 B.C.-430 A.D.)
	Orient
	By region or country
	China
	Individual philosophers, A-Z -- Continued
	Yen, Ying, d. 500 B.C. 晏嬰; 晏婴
128.Y393	Original text. By date
128.Y39313A-.Y39313Z	Translations. By language, A-Z, and date
128.Y3932	Selections. By date
128.Y393212A-.Y393212Z	Translations. By language, A-Z, and date
128.Y3933	Biography, criticism, etc.
128.Y55-.Y554	Yin, Wen, 350-284 B.C. 尹文 (Table B-BJ5)
128.Y8-.Y84	Yulingzi, 4th cent. B.C., 4th cent. B.C. 於陵子 (Table B-BJ5)
	Zengzi, 505-437 or 6 B.C. 曾子 see B128.T74+
	Zhan, Ruoshui, 1466-1560. 湛若水 see B128.C26+
	Zhang, Shi, 1133-1180. 張栻; 张栻 see B128.C28+
	Zhang, Zai, 1020-1077. 張載; 张载 see B128.C31+
	Zhao, Rui, 8th cent. 趙蕤; 赵蕤 see B128.C33+
	Zheng, Xuan, 127-200. 鄭玄; 郑玄 see B128.C359+
	Zhou, Dunyi, 1017-1073. 周敦頤; 周敦颐 see B128.C4+
	Zhu, Xi, 1130-1200 朱熹 see B128.C5+
	Zisi, 483-402 B.C. 子思 see B128.K84+
128.Z9A-.Z9Z	Anonymous works, A-Z
	India
130	Collected works (nonserial)
131	General works, collective biography, etc.
132.A-Z	Special topics, A-Z
132.A27	Acintyabhedābheda
132.A3	Advaita
132.A34	Śaktiviśiṣṭādvaitavedānta
132.A35	Viśiṣṭādvaitavedānta
132.A43	Ahankara
132.A5	Akṣara
132.A53	Analysis
132.A8	Ātman. Anātman
132.A83	Atomism
132.A9	Avidya
132.B7	Brāhmaṇas
132.C38	Causation
132.C52	Change
132.C6	Consciousness
132.C67	Cosmology
132.C73	Creation

Ancient (600 B.C.-430 A.D.)
Orient
By region or country
India
Special topics, A-Z -- Continued

132.D48 Desire
132.D5 Dharma
132.D6 Dialectic
132.D78 Dualism
132.D8 Dvaita (Vedanta)
132.E45 Emotions
132.E77 Errors
132.E9 Evolution
Freedom see B132.L53
132.H37 Harmony
132.I3 Idealism
132.I5 Individuation
132.J58 Jiva
132.K6 Knowledge
132.L53 Liberty. Freedom
132.L54 Life
132.L6 Lokāyata
132.M27 Man
132.M273 Manas
Materialism see B132.L6
132.M3 Maya
132.M5 Mīmāṃsā
132.M54 Mind and body
132.M62 Moha
132.M64 Mokṣa
132.N3 Naturalism
132.N8 Nyaya
132.O47 Omniscience
132.P37 Pariṇāma
132.P38 Perception
132.P39 Perfection
132.P4 Personalism
132.P73 Prakṛti
132.R3 Rationalism
132.R4 Realism
132.R415 Reasoning
132.R42 Reincarnation
132.R43 Relation
132.R45 Renunciation
132.S25 Sādhanā
Śaktiviśiṣṭādvaitavedānta see B132.A34
132.S26 Samavāya

Ancient (600 B.C.-430 A.D.)
Orient
By region or country
India
Special topics, A-Z -- Continued

132.S3 Sankhya
Cf. B133.K38+ Kapila
132.S356 Self-knowledge, Theory of
132.S4 Semantics
132.S43 Sensuality
132.S55 Soul
132.S57 Space and time
132.S6 Spirituality
(132.S83) Śuddhādvaita
see BL1289.5+
132.T54 Time
132.T78 Truth
132.U54 Universals
132.U62 Upamāna
132.V2 Vaiśeṣika
132.V24 Values
132.V3 Vedanta
Viśiṣṭādvaita see B132.A35
132.W47 Whole and parts
132.Y6 Yoga
Cf. BP605.S35+ Self-Realization movement
Cf. RA781.67+ Exercise
133.A-Z Individual philosophers, A-Z
Subarrange each by Table B-BJ5
Class here individual Indian philosophers from the ancient period to 1600
(133.A2-.A24) Abhedānanda, Swami, 1866-1939
see B5134.A24+
133.A35-.A354 Abhinavagupta, Rajanaka (Table B-BJ5)
(133.A633-.A6334) Ānandatirtha, surnamed Madhvācārya
see BL1286.292.M34
133.B47-.B474 Bhāskarācārya, 8th cent. (Table B-BJ5)
133.C35-.C354 Cārvāka (Table B-BJ5)
133.D48-.D484 Dharmakīrtī, 7th cent. (Table B-BJ5)
133.D65-.D654 Dignāga, 5th cent. (Table B-BJ5)
133.G42-.G424 Gaṅgeśa, 13th cent. (Table B-BJ5)
133.H37-.H374 Haribhadrasūri, 700-770 (Table B-BJ5)
133.J35-.J354 Jayarāśibhatta, 8th cent. (Table B-BJ5)
133.J37-.J374 Jayatīrtha, 14th cent. (Table B-BJ5)
133.K38-.K384 Kapila (Table B-BJ5)
133.M16-.M164 Mādhava, d. 1386 (Table B-BJ5)
133.M18-.M184 Madhusūdana Sarasvatī (Table B-BJ5)

Ancient (600 B.C.-430 A.D.)
Orient
By region or country
India
Individual philosophers, A-Z -- Continued
Madhva, 13th cent. see BL1286.292.M34
133.M34 Maṇḍanamiśra (Table B-BJ5)
133.R366-.R3664 Rāmānuja, 1017-1137 (Table B-BJ5)
Śaṅkarācārya
Collected works
133.S46 Original texts. By date
133.S47 Partial editions, selections, etc. By editor or date
133.S48A-.S48Z Translations. By language, A-Z, and date
133.S49A-.S49Z7 Separate works, A-Z
Biography, autobiography, criticism, etc.
133.S49Z8-.S49Z99 Dictionaries, indexes, concordances, etc.
133.S5A1-.S5A19 Periodicals. Societies. Serials
133.S5A3 Autobiography, diaries, etc. By date
133.S5A4 Letters. By date
133.S5A5 Speeches. By date
133.S5A6-.S5Z General works
133.S64-.S644 Śaṅkaramiśra, 15th cent. (Table B-BJ5)
133.U29-.U294 Udayanācārya (Table B-BJ5)
133.V264-.V2644 Vācaspatimisra, fl. 976-1000 (Table B-BJ5)
133.V37-.V374 Vijñānabhikṣu (Table B-BJ5)
(133.V4-.V44) Vivekananda, Swami
see B5134.V58+
135-138 Japan (Table B-BJ15 modified)
137.A-Z Special topics, A-Z
137.E46 Emotions
137.P45 Philosophical anthropology
Korea
139.1 Collected works
139.2 General works, collective biography, etc.
139.3.A-Z Special topics, A-Z
For examples of topics, see B398 , B491
139.4.A-Z Individual philosophers, A-Z
Subarrange each by Table B-BJ5
Class here individual Korean philosophers from the ancient period to 1600
140-143 Egypt (Table B-BJ15 modified)
142.A-Z Special topics, A-Z
142.C6 Cosmogeny. Creation
Creation see B142.C6
145-148 Assyria-Babylonia (Table B-BJ15 modified)
147.A-Z Special topics, A-Z

Ancient (600 B.C.-430 A.D.)
Orient
By region or country
Assyria-Babylonia
Special topics, A-Z -- Continued
147.C68 Cosmology
Armenia
149.2 Collected works
149.21 General works, collective biography, etc.
149.22.A-Z Special topics, A-Z
For examples of topics, see B398 , B491
149.23.A-Z Individual philosophers, A-Z
Subarrange each by Table B-BJ5
150-153 Iran (Table B-BJ15)
By religion
Cf. BJ1188+ Religious ethics. The ethics of the religions
Cf. BJ1188 Religious ethics
Judaism
Cf. B755+ Medieval Jewish philosophy
Cf. B5800+ Modern Jewish philosophy
154 General works
155-158 Before Christian era
157.A-Z Special topics, A-Z
157.C65 Cosmology
162 Buddhism
162.5 Jainism
162.6 Shinto
162.65 Sikhism
162.7 Taoism
Occident
162.9 General works
163 Dictionaries. Encyclopedias
Greece
At the Library of Congress the distinction in use between Classes B and PA in classifying philosophical works by Greek and Roman writers is as follows: In Class B: 1) Translations with or without original text, except translations into Latin (PA); 2) Original text with commentaries, if editor's purpose is interpretive. These are classified with the criticism of the work or works. In Class PA: 1) Original Greek and Latin texts (except as noted above); 2) Latin translations; 3) Texts with textual criticism.
165 Collected works (nonserial)
General works
Classic writers

Ancient (600 B.C.-430 A.D.)
Occident
Greece
General works
Classic writers -- Continued
168 Greek
169 Latin
171 English
172 French
173 German
175.A-Z Other. By language, A-Z
Philosophy. Methodology. Relation to other topics
177 General works
178 Relation of Greek philosophy to Greek life and literature
Cf. PA3015.P4 Philosophy in classical literature
178.5 Relation of Greek philosophy to Egyptian philosophy
179 Relation of Greek philosophy to Oriental philosophy
180 Relation of Greek philosophy to Phoenicia and/or the Middle East
181 Influence of Greek philosophy on modern thought
185 Nature philosophy
187.A-Z Other special topics, A-Z
187.A6 Antinomy
187.A66 Aporia
187.A8 Ataraxia
187.A85 Avarice
187.C38 Causation
187.C62 Color
187.C65 Contemplation
187.C7 Cosmology
187.D47 Determinism
187.D5 Dialectic
187.D73 Dreams
187.D8 Dualism
187.E5 Envy
187.E6 Equality
187.E9 The exact
Falsehood see B187.T7
187.F3 Fatalism
187.F67 Forgiveness
187.F68 Form
187.F7 Free will
187.F75 Friendship
187.H3 Happiness
187.I43 Imagination
187.I45 Immortality
187.I48 Individuation

Ancient (600 B.C.-430 A.D.)
Occident
Greece
Other special topics, A-Z -- Continued

187.I5	The infinite
187.K7	Knowledge
187.L47	Liberty
187.L5	Life
187.L6	Logos
187.M25	Man
187.M26	Mania
187.M28	Materialism
187.M3	Matter
187.M4	Medicine
187.M55	Mind
187.M6	Motion
187.N4	Necessity
187.N49	New and old
187.N66	Not being. Non-being. Nothing
187.O2	Objectivity
187.O5	Ontology
187.P55	Play
187.P57	Pleasure
187.P8	Psyche
187.R35	Reason
187.R37	Reference
187.R4	Religion
187.S32	Science and philosophy
187.S34	Self-reliance
187.S4	Seven wise men of Greece
187.S5	Silence
187.S6	Soul
187.S7	Space
187.S8	Substance
187.T5	Theology
187.T53	Theory
187.T55	Time
187.T68	Tragelaph (Mythical animal)
187.T7	Truth
187.V57	Vision
187.W64	Women philosophers
187.5	Pre-Socratic philosophers
	By period
	First period
188	General works
	Special topics
193	Atomism

Ancient (600 B.C.-430 A.D.)
Occident
Greece
By period
First period
Special topics -- Continued

196 Eleatics
199 Pythagoreanism
200.A-Z Other special topics, A-Z
200.E5 Enthusiasm
200.J8 Justice
200.K45 Knowledge
200.M45 Metaphysics
200.O5 The one
200.P45 Philosophical anthropology
200.S68 Soul

Individual philosophers

204 A - Anaxagoras
Subarrange each by Table B-BJ5
205 Anaxagoras (Table B-BJ4)
206 Anaxagoras - Anaximander
Subarrange each by Table B-BJ5
208 Anaximander (Table B-BJ4)
209 Anaximander - Anaximenes
Subarrange each by Table B-BJ5
211 Anaximenes, of Miletus (Table B-BJ4)
212 Anaximenes - Archytas
Subarrange each by Table B-BJ5
213 Archytas, of Tarentum (Table B-BJ4)
214 Archytas - Diogenes
Subarrange each by Table B-BJ5
215 Diogenes, of Apollonia, 5th cent. B.C. (Table B-BJ4)
216 Diogenes - Empedocles
Subarrange each by Table B-BJ5
218 Empedocles (Table B-BJ4)
219 Empedocles - Heraclitus
Subarrange each by Table B-BJ5
220-224 Heraclitus, of Ephesus (Table B-BJ3)
224.A-Z Special topics, A-Z
224.H37 Harmony
224.I43 Identity
224.L6 Logos
224.T56 Time
224.5 Heraclitus - Leucippus
Subarrange each by Table B-BJ5
225-229 Leucippus (Table B-BJ3)

Ancient (600 B.C.-430 A.D.)
Occident
Greece
By period
First period
Individual philosophers -- Continued
235 Leucippus - Pythagoras
Subarrange each by Table B-BJ5
235.M3-.M34 Melissus, Samius (Table B-BJ5)
235.O3-.O34 Ōkellos, ho Leukanos, 6th cent. B.C. (Table B-BJ5)
235.P2-.P24 Parmenides (Table B-BJ5)
235.P37-.P374 Pherecydes, of Syros, 6th cent. B.C. (Table B-BJ5)
235.P4-.P44 Philolaus, of Croton, b. ca. 470 B.C. (Table B-BJ5)
240-244 Pythagoras (Table B-BJ3)
For symbolism of numbers see BF1623.P9
248 Pythagoras - Thales
Subarrange each by Table B-BJ5
250-254 Thales, ca. 634-ca. 546 B.C. (Table B-BJ3)
258 Thales - Z
Subarrange each by Table B-BJ5
258.T4-.T44 Timaeus, of Locri (Table B-BJ5)
258.X3-.X34 Xenophanes, ca. 570-ca. 478 B.C. (Table B-BJ5)
258.Z3-.Z34 Zeno, of Elea (Table B-BJ5)
Second period
265 General works
271 Eclecticism
274 Elean-Eretrian school
279 Hedonism (Cyrenaicism)
285 Megarian school
288 Sophism. Sophists
Individual philosophers
293 A - Democritus
Subarrange each by Table B-BJ5
293.A2-.A24 Alcidamas, 4th cent. B.C. (Table B-BJ5)
293.A25-.A254 Anonymous Iamblichi, 5th/4th cent. B.C. (Table B-BJ5)
293.A26-.A264 Antiphon, of Athens (Table B-BJ5)
293.A3-.A34 Antisthenes, ca. 445-ca. 360 B.C. (Table B-BJ5)
293.A7-.A74 Aristippus, 435?-356? B.C. (Table B-BJ5)
295-299 Democritus (Table B-BJ3)
299.A-Z Special topics, A-Z
299.A58 Anthropology
299.A86 Atomism
299.C47 Chance

Ancient (600 B.C.-430 A.D.)
Occident
Greece
By period
Second period
Individual philosophers
Democritus
Special topics, A-Z -- Continued
299.M37 Materialism
305 Democritus - Socrates
Subarrange each by Table B-BJ5
305.D2-.D24 Diagoras, of Melos (Table B-BJ5)
305.D4-.D44 Diogenes, d. ca. 323 B.C. (Table B-BJ5)
305.E8-.E84 Euclid (Table B-BJ5)
305.E9-.E94 Eudoxus, of Cnidus, ca. 400-ca. 350 B.C. (Table B-BJ5)
305.G3-.G34 Gorgias, of Leontini (Table B-BJ5)
305.H57-.H574 Hippias, of Elis, 5th cent. B.C. (Table B-BJ5)
305.P4-.P44 Phaedo, of Elis (Table B-BJ5)
305.P7-.P74 Prodicus, of Ceos (Table B-BJ5)
305.P8-.P84 Protagoras (Table B-BJ5)
310-318 Socrates (Table B-BJ2)
318.A-Z Special topics, A-Z
318.D53 Dialectic
318.E8 Ethics
318.H84 Humanism
318.I7 Irony
318.K5 Knowledge, Theory of
318.M48 Methodology
318.R45 Religion
318.V57 Virtue
320 Socrates - Z
Subarrange each by Table B-BJ5
Third period
335 General works
338 The Academy
341 Peripatetics
Individual philosophers
350-398 Plato
350 Periodicals. Societies. Serials
351 Dictionaries, lexicons, etc.
Collected works
Greek texts
General see PA4279.A2
Editions with commentary
Interpretive commentary see B394
Textual criticism see PA4288+

Ancient (600 B.C.-430 A.D.)
Occident
Greece
By period
Third period
Individual philosophers
Plato
Collected works
Translations
Subarrange by translator or editor
Including translations accompanied by original text
Latin see PA4280
358 English
359 French
360 German
361 Italian
362 Spanish and Portuguese
363.A-Z Other. By language, A-Z
Separate works
365 Apologia Socratis (Table B-BJ7)
366 Charmides (Table B-BJ7)
Convivium see B385
367 Cratylus (Table B-BJ7)
368 Crito (Table B-BJ7)
De legibus
see class K
De republica see JC71
369 Euthydemus (Table B-BJ7)
370 Euthyphro (Table B-BJ7)
371 Gorgias (Table B-BJ7)
372 Ion (Io) (Table B-BJ7)
373 Laches (Table B-BJ7)
Leges
see class K
375 Lysis (Table B-BJ7)
376 Menexenus (Table B-BJ7)
377 Meno (Table B-BJ7)
378 Parmenides (Table B-BJ7)
379 Phaedo (Table B-BJ7)
380 Phaedrus (Table B-BJ7)
381 Philebus (Table B-BJ7)
382 Protagoras (Table B-BJ7)
Respublica see JC71
384 Sophistes (Table B-BJ7)
385 Symposium (Table B-BJ7)
386 Theaetetus (Table B-BJ7)

	Ancient (600 B.C.-430 A.D.)
	Occident
	Greece
	By period
	Third period
	Individual philosophers
	Plato
	Separate works -- Continued
387	Timaeus (Table B-BJ7)
	Spurious and apocryphal works
391.A2	Collected works
391.A3-Z	Separate works
391.A5-.A53	Alcibiades (Table B-BJ21)
	Amatores see B391.E9+
391.A8-.A83	Axiochus (Table B-BJ21)
391.C5-.C53	Clitophon (Table B-BJ21)
391.E5-.E53	Epigrammata (Table B-BJ21)
391.E8-.E83	Epistulae (Table B-BJ21)
391.E9-.E93	Erastae (Table B-BJ21)
391.H3-.H33	Hipparchus (Table B-BJ21)
391.H4-.H43	Hippias major (Table B-BJ21)
391.H5-395.H53	Hippias minor (Table B-BJ21)
391.M4-.M43	Minos (Table B-BJ21)
391.T4-.T43	Theages (Table B-BJ21)
391.Z5A-.Z5Z	Other, A-Z
392	Indexes, outlines, paraphrases, etc.
393	Biography
394	Early criticism
395	Criticism and interpretation
398.A-Z	Special topics, A-Z
398.A25	Abstraction
398.A3	Act
398.A4	Aesthetics
398.A5	Age
398.A6	Analysis
398.A8	Asceticism
398.A85	Atlantis
	Axiology see B398.W6
398.B65	Body, Human
398.C3	Causation
398.C34	Cave allegory
398.C6	Cognition
398.C63	The comic. Laughter
398.C64	Contemplation
398.C66	Cosmography
398.C67	Cosmology
398.C69	Courage

Ancient (600 B.C.-430 A.D.)
Occident
Greece
By period
Third period
Individual philosophers
Plato
Special topics, A-Z -- Continued

398.D47 Desire
398.D5 Dialectic
398.D58 Division
398.E3 Economics
398.E45 Emotions
398.E8 Ethics
Evil see B398.G65
398.F57 Forms
398.F6 Fortune
398.F7 Free will
398.F74 Friendship
398.G55 Glory
398.G6 God
398.G65 Good and evil
398.H5 History
Human body see B398.B65
398.H85 Human rights
398.I27 Idealism
398.I3 Ideas
398.I6 Immortality
398.I65 Individuation. Particulars
398.I7 Irony
398.J87 Justice
398.K7 Knowledge
398.L42 Language. Terminology
Laughter see B398.C63
398.L43 Learning
398.L85 Logos. Reason
398.L9 Love
398.M27 Man
398.M3 Mathematics (Greek)
398.M35 Matter
398.M38 Medicine
398.M4 Metaphysics
398.M67 Movement
398.M77 Mysticism
398.M8 Mythology
398.N66 Nothing
398.O47 The One

Ancient (600 B.C.-430 A.D.)
Occident
Greece
By period
Third period
Individual philosophers
Plato
Special topics, A-Z -- Continued

398.O5 Ontology
398.O64 Opinion
398.P3 Participation
Particulars see B398.I65
398.P45 Philosopher-kings
398.P54 Play
398.P56 Pleasure
398.P6 Poetry
Political science see JC71
398.P7 Progress
398.P75 Proportion
398.P9 Psychology
398.R3 Rationalism
Cf. B398.L85 Logos
Reason see B398.L85
398.R4 Religion
Rhetoric see PN173
398.S45 Self
398.S6 Sociology
398.S7 Soul
398.S73 Spirit
398.T4 Techne
Terminology see B398.L42
398.T53 Theory
398.T55 Time
398.T7 Transcendentalism
398.T78 Truth
398.V57 Virtue
398.W42 Whole and parts
398.W55 Women
398.W6 Worth. Axiology
398.Z63 Zodiac

Aristotle
400 Periodicals. Societies. Serials
401 Dictionaries, lexicons, etc.
Collected works
Greek texts
General see PA3890.A1+
Editions with commentary

Ancient (600 B.C.-430 A.D.)
Occident
Greece
By period
Third period
Individual philosophers
Aristotle
Collected works
Greek texts
Editions with commentary -- Continued
Interpretive commentary see B485
Textual criticism see PA3902+
Partial editions, selections, etc. see PA3890.A3

406.82-412 Translations
Subarranged by translator or editor
Including translations accompanied by original text
Latin see PA3895.A23+
407 English
408 French
409 German
410 Italian
411 Spanish and Portuguese
412.A-Z Other. By language, A-Z
For translations into the lesser known languages, see the language

Separate works
415 De anima (Table B-BJ7)
De coelo see QB41
De coloribus see QC494.8
De generatione animalium see QL41
De generatione et corruptione see Q151
De incessu animalium see QL41
422 De moribus ad Eudemum (Ethica Eudemia) (Table B-BJ7)
De partibus animalium see QL41
427 De philosophia (Table B-BJ7)
De poetica see PN1040
De republica Atheniensium see JC71
430 Ethica (Ethica Nicomachea) (Table B-BJ7)
Ethica Eudemia see B422
Historia animalium see QL41
432 Magna moralia (Table B-BJ7)
434 Metaphysica (Table B-BJ7)
Meteorologica see QC859
Oeconomica see HB77

Ancient (600 B.C.-430 A.D.)
Occident
Greece
By period
Third period
Individual philosophers
Aristotle
Separate works -- Continued
Organon
437 Complete (Table B-BJ7)
438 Categoriae (Table B-BJ7)
439 De interpretatione (Table B-BJ7)
440 Priora analytica (Table B-BJ7)
441 Posteriora analytica (Table B-BJ7)
442 Topica (Table B-BJ7)
443 Elenchi (Sophistici Elenchi) (Table B-BJ7)
444 Parva naturalia (Table B-BJ7)
Physica see Q151
Poetica see PN1040
Politica see JC71
Rhetorica see PN173
Scolion in Hermiam (Hymnus in virtutem see PA3891.C2
Spurious and apocryphal works
458 Collections
Separate works
Chiromantia see BF910+
De audibilibus see QP306
463 De innato spiritu (De spiritu)
De lapide philosophico see QD25
465.3 De Melisso, Xenophane, Gorgia
De mirabilibus auscultationibus see Q151
De motu animalium see QL41
465.8 De mundo
De perfecto magisterio see QD25
De plantis see QK41
467 De pomo (De pomo et morte; De morte)
467.3 De virtutibus et vitiis
De Xenophane, Zenone et Gorgia see B467.3
467.6 Diaireseis
468 Epistolae
Mechanica see Q151
Physiognomonica (De physiognomia) see BF840+
469.7 Problemata
Rhetorica and Alexandrum see PN173
Secreta secretorum see JC71

Ancient (600 B.C.-430 A.D.)
Occident
Greece
By period
Third period
Individual philosophers
Aristotle
Spurious and apocryphal works
Separate works -- Continued

472	Theologia
475	Indexes, outlines, paraphrases, etc.
481	Biography
485	Criticism and interpretation
491.A-Z	Special topics, A-Z
491.A24	Accident
491.A27	Act
491.A4	Aesthetics
491.A52	Analogy
491.A7	Art
491.C26	Categories
491.C27	Catharsis
491.C3	Causation
491.C58	Consciousness
491.C6	Continuity
491.C65	Contradiction
	Contrariety see B491.O64
491.C67	Courage
491.C7	Creation
491.D44	Definition
491.D5	Dialectic
491.E23	Ear. Hearing
491.E7	Ethics
491.F63	Forms
491.F68	Free will
491.F7	Friendship
491.G63	God
491.H36	Happiness
	Hearing see B491.E23
491.I2	Ideas
491.I3	Immortality
491.I35	Individuality
491.I4	Infinity
491.I55	Intellect
491.J87	Justice
491.K6	Knowledge (Theory)
491.L3	Language
491.L5	Life

Ancient (600 B.C.-430 A.D.)
Occident
Greece
By period
Third period
Individual philosophers
Aristotle
Special topics, A-Z -- Continued

491.L8 Logic
491.M27 Man
491.M3 Matter
491.M36 Mean
491.M365 Medicine
491.M37 Memory
491.M38 Metaphor
491.M4 Metaphysics
491.M45 Methodology
491.M5 Mind and body
491.M6 Motion
491.M8 Mysteries
491.N3 Nature
491.N43 Necessity
491.N68 Nothing
491.O5 Ontology
491.O64 Opposition. Contrariety
491.P3 Parousia
491.P38 Perception
491.P4 Perfection
491.P66 Possibility
491.P73 Predication
491.P75 Priority
491.P8 Psychology
491.R4 Reason
491.R44 Refutation
491.R46 Religion
491.S62 Sociology
491.S64 Soul
491.S65 Space
491.S8 Substance
491.S9 Syllogism
491.T4 Teleology
491.T5 Time
491.T78 Truth
491.V57 Virtue
491.W6 Worth

Ancient (600 B.C.-430 A.D.)
Occident -- Continued
Greco-Roman philosophy
For the distinction in use between classes B and PA, see the note in the record for B165+
504 Collected works (nonserial)
505 General works
507 Consolation
508 Cynicism
511 Dogmatism
511.5 Emotions
512 Epicureanism
513 Meaning
514 Moralists
517 Neo-Platonism
Cf. B350+ Plato
Cf. B645 Alexandrian and early Christian philosophy
519 Neo-Pythagoreanism
522 Peripatetics (Greco-Roman)
525 Scepticism (Pyrrhonism)
526 Self
528 Stoicism
531 Syncretism
Cf. B271 Eclecticism
532.A-Z Other special topics, A-Z
532.M48 Metaphysics
Individual philosophers
535 A - Apollonius
Subarrange each by Table B-BJ5
535.A2-.A24 Aenesidemus, of Cnossus (Table B-BJ5)
535.A25-.A254 Aëtius, 1st/2nd cent. (Table B-BJ5)
535.A3-.A34 Agrippa, Marcus Vipsanius (Table B-BJ5)
535.A4-.A44 Albinus (Table B-BJ5)
Alcinous see B535.A4+
535.A5-.A54 Alexander, of Aegae (Table B-BJ5)
535.A6-.A64 Alexander, of Aphrodisias (Table B-BJ5)
535.A68-.A684 Amelius, Neoplatonicus, 3rd cent. (Table B-BJ5)
535.A7-.A74 Andronicus, of Rhodes (Table B-BJ5)
535.A8-.A84 Apollodorus, of Athens (Table B-BJ5)
536 Apollonius - Carneades
Subarrange each by Table B-BJ5
536.A2-.A24 Apollonius, of Tyana (Table B-BJ5)
536.A3-.A34 Apuleius (Table B-BJ5)
536.A4-.A44 Arcesilaus (Table B-BJ5)
536.A47-.A474 Aristocles, of Messene (Table B-BJ5)
536.A5-.A54 Ariston, of Chios (Table B-BJ5)
536.A6-.A64 Aristoxenus (Table B-BJ5)

Ancient (600 B.C.-430 A.D.)
Occident
Greco-Roman philosophy
Individual philosophers
Apollonius - Carneades -- Continued

536.A7-.A74 Aspasius (Table B-BJ5)
536.A75-.A754 Athenaeus, of Naucratis (Table B-BJ5)
536.A8-.A84 Atticus, Titus Pomponius (Table B-BJ5)
Aurelius Antoninus, Marcus see B579.2+
537 Carneades, 2nd cent. B.C. (Table B-BJ4)
538 Carneades - Chrysippus
Subarrange each by Table B-BJ5
538.C2-.C24 Celsus, Platonic philosopher, fl. 180 (Table B-BJ5)
540-543 Chrysippus, ca. 280-207 or 6 B.C. (Table B-BJ3a)
545 Chrysippus - Cicero
Subarrange each by Table B-BJ5
550-553 Cicero, Marcus Tullius (Table B-BJ3a)
557 Cicero - Epictetus
Subarrange each by Table B-BJ5
557.C2-.C24 Cleanthes, 331-232 B.C. (Table B-BJ5)
557.C4-.C44 Crantor (Table B-BJ5)
557.C5-.C54 Crates, ca. 360 B.C.-ca. 280 B.C. (Table B-BJ5)
557.D2-.D24 Damaskios, ca. 480-ca. 550 (Table B-BJ5)
557.D28-.D284 Demetrius, the Cynic (Table B-BJ5)
557.D3-.D34 Demetrius, of Phaleron, b. ca. 350 B.C. (Table B-BJ5)
557.D345-.D3454 Dicaearchus, Messenius, 4th cent. B.C. (Table B-BJ5)
557.D35-.D354 Dio, Chrysostom (Table B-BJ5)
557.D4-.D44 Diodorus Cronus, 4th cent. B.C. (Table B-BJ5)
557.D56-.D564 Diogenes, of Oenoanda (Table B-BJ5)
557.D6-.D64 Diogenes, the Stoic (Table B-BJ5)
560-563 Epictetus (Table B-BJ3a)
565 Epictetus - Epicurus
Subarrange each by Table B-BJ5
570-573 Epicurus (Table B-BJ3a)
577 Epicurus - Marcus
Subarrange each by Table B-BJ5
577.E5-.E54 Eudemus, of Rhodes (Table B-BJ5)
577.F2-.F24 Favorinus, of Arles, ca. 81-ca. 150 (Table B-BJ5)
577.G2-.G24 Galen (Table B-BJ5)
577.H3-.H34 Hermarchus, of Mytilene (Table B-BJ5)
577.H4-.H44 Hierocles, the Stoic, 2nd cent. (Table B-BJ5)
577.H5-.H54 Hieronymus, of Rhodes (Table B-BJ5)
577.L2-.L24 Labeo, Cornelius (Table B-BJ5)
577.L4-.L44 Libanius (Table B-BJ5)
577.L5-.L54 Lucian, of Samosata (Table B-BJ5)

Ancient (600 B.C.-430 A.D.)
Occident
Greco-Roman philosophy
Individual philosophers
Epicurus - Marcus -- Continued
577.L6-.L64 Lucretius Carus, Titus (Table B-BJ5)
577.L8-.L84 Lyco, of Troas (Table B-BJ5)
Marcus Aurelius, Emperor of Rome, 121-180
Meditations
Original text see PA3939
English
580 Complete editions. By translator
581 Selections. By compiler
582.A-Z Other languages, A-Z
583 Criticism, interpretation, etc.
Biography see DG297
585 Marcus - Maximus
Subarrange each by Table B-BJ5
588 Maximus, of Tyre, 2nd cent. (Table B-BJ4)
589 Maximus - Nicolaus
Subarrange each by Table B-BJ5
591 Nicolaus, of Damascus (Table B-BJ4)
592 Nicolaus - Numenius
Subarrange each by Table B-BJ5
593 Numenius, of Apamea, fl. ca. 150 (Table B-BJ4)
594 Numenius - Panaetius
Subarrange each by Table B-BJ5
595 Panaetius (Table B-BJ4)
598 Panaetius - Plutarch
Subarrange each by Table B-BJ5
598.P3-.P34 Philo (Philon), of Larissa (Table B-BJ5)
598.P4-.P44 Philodemus, ca. 110-ca. 40 B.C. (Table B-BJ5)
600-603 Plutarch (Table B-BJ3a)
605 Plutarch - Posidonius
Subarrange each by Table B-BJ5
605.P5-.P44 Polystratus (Table B-BJ5)
Pomponius, Titus see B536.A8+
607 Posidonius - Pyrrho
Subarrange each by Table B-BJ5
607.P2-.P24 Posidonius (Table B-BJ5)
610-613 Pyrrhon, of Elis (Table B-BJ3a)
614 Pyrrhon - Seneca
Subarrange each by Table B-BJ5
614.S4-.S44 Secundus, of Athens, 2nd cent. (Table B-BJ5)
615-618 Seneca, Lucius Annaeus, ca. 4 B.C.-65 A.D. (Table B-BJ3a)
Cf. BJ214.S3+ Ethical philosopher

Ancient (600 B.C.-430 A.D.)
Occident
Greco-Roman philosophy
Individual philosophers -- Continued

619 Seneca - Sextus
Subarrange each by Table B-BJ5
620-623 Sextus, Empiricus (Table B-BJ3a)
626 Sextus - Z
Subarrange each by Table B-BJ5
626.S2-.S24 Speusippus (Table B-BJ5)
626.S3-.S34 Staseas, of Naples (Table B-BJ5)
626.S5-.S54 Straton, of Lampsacus (Table B-BJ5)
626.T25-.T254 Tauros, b. 105? (Table B-BJ5)
626.T3-.T34 Theophrastus (Table B-BJ5)
626.T5-.T54 Timon, of Phlius, ca. 320-ca. 230 B.C. (Table B-BJ5)
626.X3-.X34 Xenocrates, of Chalcedon, ca. 396-ca. 314 B.C. (Table B-BJ5)
626.Z18-.Z184 Zeno, of Tarsus (Table B-BJ5)
626.Z2-.Z24 Zeno, the Stoic (Table B-BJ5)

Alexandrian and early Christian philosophy
For the distinction in use between classes B and PA, see note at B165+
630 Collected works (nonserial)
631 General works
635 Apologists
638 Gnosticism
Hermetic philosophy see B667.H3+
641 Manicheism
645 Neo-Platonism
Class here only those works concerned with Patristic Neo-Platonism
For Greco-Roman philosophy see B517
647 Stoicism
Class here only those works concerned with Patristic Stoicism
For Greco-Roman philosophy see B528

Individual philosophers
Class here works that are not purely or mainly philosophical with their subjects in other classes, e..g., theology, literature, etc.
650 A - Athanasius
Subarrange each by Table B-BJ5
650.A2-.A24 Aeneas, of Gaza, 5th cent. (Table B-BJ5)
650.A4-.A44 Amelius, Neoplatonicus, 3rd cent. (Table B-BJ5)
650.A6-.A64 Ammonius Saccas, of Alexandria (Table B-BJ5)
650.A8-.A84 Arnobius, of Sicca (Table B-BJ5)

Ancient (600 B.C.-430 A.D.)
Occident
Alexandrian and early Christian philosophy
Individual philosophers -- Continued

653 Athanasius, Saint, Patriarch of Alexandria, d. 373 (Table B-BJ4)
653.5 Athanasius - Athenagoras
Subarrange each by Table B-BJ5
654 Athenagoras, 2nd cent. (Table B-BJ4)
654.5 Athenagoras - Augustine
Subarrange each by Table B-BJ5
655 Augustine, Saint, Bishop of Hippo (Table B-BJ4)
656 Augustine -Bardesanes
Subarrange each by Table B-BJ5
657 Bardesanes, 154-222 (Table B-BJ4)
657.5 Bardesanes - Basilides
Subarrange each by Table B-BJ5
658 Basilides, fl. 117-140 (Table B-BJ4)
658.5 Basilides - Boethius
Subarrange each by Table B-BJ5
659 Boethius, d. 524 (Table B-BJ4)
660 Boethius - Capella
Subarrange each by Table B-BJ5
661 Capella (Martianus Capella) (Table B-BJ4)
662 Capella - Carpocrates
663 Carpocrates (Table B-BJ4)
664 Carpocrates - Cassiodorus
Subarrange each by Table B-BJ5
665 Cassiodorus, Senator, ca. 487-ca. 580 (Table B-BJ4)
665.5 Cassiodorus - Clement
Subarrange each by Table B-BJ5
666 Clement of Alexandria, Saint, ca. 150-ca. 215 (Table B-BJ4)
667 Clement - Iamblichus
Subarrange each by Table B-BJ5
667.C6-.C64 Cyprian, Saint, Bishop of Carthage (Table B-BJ5)
667.D4-.D44 Dionysius Areopagita (Pseudo-Dionysius, the Areopagite) (Table B-BJ5)
667.G5-.G54 Gregory, of Nazianzus, Saint (Table B-BJ5)
667.G7-.G74 Gregory, of Nyssa, Saint, ca. 335-ca. 394 (Table B-BJ5)
667.H3-.H34 Hermes, Trismegistus (Table B-BJ5)
Cf. BF1598.H6 Occult sciences
Cf. PA3998.H5+ Literature
Cf. QB21 Astronomy
Cf. QD13 Chemistry
Cf. QD23.3+ Chemistry

Ancient (600 B.C.-430 A.D.)
Occident
Alexandrian and early Christian philosophy
Individual philosophers
Clement - Iamblichus -- Continued

667.H4-.H44 Hermogenes, the heretic, fl. ca. 200 (Table B-BJ5)
667.H5-.H54 Hippolytus, Antipope, ca. 170-235 or 6 (Table B-BJ5)
667.H8-.H84 Hypatia, d. 415 (Table B-BJ5)
669 Iamblichus, ca. 250-ca. 330 (Table B-BJ4)
670 Iamblichus - Irenaeus
Subarrange each by Table B-BJ5
671 Irenaeus, Saint, Bishop of Lyon (Table B-BJ4)
672 Irenaeus - Iz
Subarrange each by Table B-BJ5
672.I4-.I44 Isidore, of Alexandria, 5th cent. (Table B-BJ5)
672.I6-.64 Isidore, of Seville, Saint, d. 636 (Table B-BJ5)
672.I7-.I74 Isidore, the Gnostic, Son of Basilides (Table B-BJ5)
673 J - Julian
Subarrange each by Table B-BJ5
673.J6-.J64 Joannes Philoponus (Philoponus, John, 6th cent.) (Table B-BJ5)
674 Julian, Emperor of Rome, 331-363 (Julian, the Apostate) (Table B-BJ4)
674.5 Julian - Justin
Subarrange each by Table B-BJ5
675 Justin, Martyr, Saint (Table B-BJ4)
676 Justin - Lactantius
Subarrange each by Table B-BJ5
677 Lactantius, ca. 240-ca. 320 (Table B-BJ4)
678 Lactantius - Longinus
Subarrange each by Table B-BJ5
679 Longinus, Cassius, ca. 213-273 (Table B-BJ4)
680 Longinus - Marcion
Subarrange each by Table B-BJ5
680.M3-.M34 Macrobius, Ambrosius Aurelius Theodosius (Table B-BJ5)
681 Marcion, of Sinope, 2nd cent. (Table B-BJ4)
682 Marcion - Maxiumus
Subarrange each by Table B-BJ5
Martianus Capella see B661
683 Maximos, ho Ephesios, d. 372 (Table B-BJ4)
684 Maximos - Origen
Subarrange each by Table B-BJ5
684.M3-.M34 Methodius, of Olympus, Saint, d. 311 (Table B-BJ5)
684.M5-.M54 Minucius Felix, Marcus (Table B-BJ5)
684.N3-.N34 Nemesius, Bp. of Emesa (Table B-BJ5)

Ancient (600 B.C.-430 A.D.)
Occident
Alexandrian and early Christian philosophy
Individual philosophers
Maximos - Origen -- Continued

684.O6-.O64 Olympiodorus, the Younger, of Alexandria, 6th cent. (Table B-BJ5)
686 Origen - Pantaenus
Subarrange each by Table B-BJ5
686.O8-.O84 Origen (Table B-BJ5)
Origen. Works see BR65.O5+
Origen. Biography see BR1720.O7
687 Pantaenus, Saint, 2nd cent. (Table B-BJ4)
688 Pantaenus - Philo
Subarrange each by Table B-BJ5
689 Philo, of Alexandria (Table B-BJ4)
690 Philo - Philoponus
Subarrange each by Table B-BJ5
Philoponus, John, 6th cent. see B673.J6+
692 Philoponus - Plotinus
Subarrange each by Table B-BJ5
693 Plotinus (Table B-BJ4)
694 Plotinus - Plutarch
Subarrange each by Table B-BJ5
695 Plutarch, of Athens, d. ca. 431 (Table B-BJ4)
696 Plutarch - Porphyry
Subarrange each by Table B-BJ5
697 Porphyry, ca. 234-ca. 305 (Table B-BJ4)
698 Porphyry - Proclus
Subarrange each by Table B-BJ5
701 Proclus, ca. 410-485 (Table B-BJ4)
703 Proclus - Sz
Subarrange each by Table B-BJ5
703.S3-.S34 Sallustius (Table B-BJ5)
703.S5-.S54 Simplicius, of Cilicia (Table B-BJ5)
703.S7-.S74 Synesius, of Cyrene, Bishop of Ptolemais (Table B-BJ5)
703.S8-.S84 Syrianus (Table B-BJ5)
704 T - Tertullian
Subarrange each by Table B-BJ5
704.T3-.T34 Tatian, ca. 120-173 (Table B-BJ5)
705 Tertullian, ca. 160-ca. 230 (Table B-BJ4)
708 Tertullian - Z
Subarrange each by Table B-BJ5
708.T4-.T44 Themistius (Table B-BJ5)
708.V3-.V34 Valentinus, 2nd cent. (Table B-BJ5)

Medieval (430-1450)

	Medieval (430-1450) -- Continued
720	Collected works (nonserial)
721	General works
722.A-Z	By region or country, A-Z
	e.g.
722.B97	Byzantine Empire
722.K54	Kievan Rus
723	Influence of Arabic philosophy
725	Influence of Aristotle on Medieval thought
726	Influence of Northern Europe on Medieval thought
	Special topics
	Conceptualism see B731
728	Mysticism
	For modern and general mysticism see B828.A1+
731	Nominalism and realism
732	Platonism
	Cf. B645 Alexandrian and early Christian philosophy
734	Scholasticism
	Including Patristic and Scholastic philosophy
	For modern and general Scholasticism see B839.A1+
737	Summism
738.A-Z	Other special topics, A-Z
738.A37	Act
	Active intellect see B738.S68
738.A87	Authority
738.C65	Conscience
738.C657	Contingency
738.C66	Continuity
738.D5	Distinction
738.E46	Emotions
	Future contingents see BC21.F86
738.H3	Happiness
738.H8	Humanism
738.I33	Ideology
738.K56	Knowledge, Theory of
738.L33	Laity
738.L68	Love
738.M3	Materialism
738.M47	Metaphysics
	Mind see B738.S68
738.N3	Nature
738.O5	Ontology
738.R42	Reason
738.R44	Relation
738.S55	Science and philosophy
738.S57	Self
738.S59	Semiotics

B

Medieval (430-1450)
Special topics
Other special topics, A-Z -- Continued
738.S63 Skepticism
738.S68 Soul. Active intellect. Mind
738.T5 Time
738.T6 Totality
738.T73 Transcendentals
738.W55 Will
Arabian and Moorish philosophers. Islamic philosophers
740 Collected works (nonserial)
741 General works
743.A-Z By region, country, city, etc., A-Z
744.3 Influence of Greek philosophy
745.A-Z Special topics, A-Z
745.A34 Aesthetics
745.A7 Atomic theory
745.C6 Cosmology
745.D48 Dialectic
745.D5 Dicta philosophorum
745.E8 Evolution
745.F26 Faith
745.F3 Fatalism
745.G63 God
745.I34 Idealism
745.I5 Individualism
745.I54 Intellect
745.K53 Knowledge
745.L4 Learning and scholarship
745.M3 Man
745.M33 Matter
745.M4 Metaphysics
745.M57 Miracles
745.N38 Nature
745.N49 New and old
745.O3 Occasionalism
745.O56 Ontology
745.P64 Poetics
745.P66 Prophecy
745.P82 Psychology. ʻIlm al-nafs. Nafsānīyah
745.R4 Reason
745.S58 Soul
745.S63 Space and time
745.S93 Substance
745.W5 Will
746 Ikhwān al-Ṣafāʼ, (Brothers of Purity or Sincerity) إخوان الصفاء (Table B-BJ4)

Medieval (430-1450)
Arabian and Moorish philosophers. Islamic philosophers -- Continued
Individual philosophers
748 A - Averroes
Subarrange each by Table B-BJ5
748.A14-.A144 ʻAbd al-Razzāq al-Qāshānī, d. 1330? عبد الرزاق القاشاني (Table B-BJ5)
748.A2-.A24 Abū al-Barakāt Hibat Allāh ibn ʻAlī, fl. 1077-1164. ابو البركات هبة الله بن علي (Table B-BJ5)
748.A245-.A2454 Abū al-Faraj ʻAbd Allāh ibn al-Tayyib, d. 1043. ابو الفرج عبد الله بن الطيب (Table B-BJ5)
748.A25-.A254 Abū Ḥayyān al-Tawḥīdī, ʻAlī ibn Muḥammad, 10th cent. أبو حيان التوحيدي، علي بن محمد. (Table B-BJ5)
748.A36-.A364 Aḥmad ibn al-Ṭayyib, al-Sarakhsī, d. 899. سرخسي, أحمة بن الطيب (Table B-BJ5)
Alfarabi see B753.F3+
748.A39-.A394 Alhazen, 965-1039 (Table B-BJ5)
748.A44-.A444 ʻĀmirī, Abū al-Ḥasan Muḥammad ibn Yūsuf. عامري, ابو الحسن محمد بن يوسف (Table B-BJ5)
748.A56-.A564 Athīr al-Dīn al-Abharī, al-Mufaḍḍal ibn ʻUmar, d. 1265. اثير الدين الابهاري، المفضل بن عمر (Table B-BJ5)
748.A6-.A64 Avempace, d. 1138 or 9. ابن باجة (Table B-BJ5)
749 Averroës, 1126-1198. ابن رشد (Table B-BJ4)
751 Avicenna, 980-1037. ابن سينا (Table B-BJ4)
752 Avo-Az
752.A96-.A964 ʻAyn al-Quḍāh al-Hamadhānī, ʻAbd Allāh ibn Muḥammad, d. 1131. عين القضاه الهمذاني, عبد الله بن محمد (Table B-BJ5)
753 B - Z
Subarrange each by Table B-BJ5
753.B32-.B324 Bahmanyār ibn al-Marzubān, Abū al-Ḥasan, d. 1065 or 6. بهمنيار بن المرزبان,ابو الحسن (Table B-BJ5)
753.B34-.B344 Baṭalyawsī, ʻAbd Allāh ibn Muḥammad, 1052 or 3-1127. البطليوسي, عبد الله بن محمد (Table B-BJ5)
753.B82-.B824 Bulaydī, Muḥammad ibn Muḥammad, d. 1762 or 3. البليدي, محمد بن مجمد (Table B-BJ5)
753.D36-.D364 Dāmād, Muḥammad Bāqir ibn Muḥammad, d. 1631? داماد، محمد باقر بن محمد (Table B-BJ5)
753.D38-.D384 Dawwānī, Muḥammad ibn Asʻad, 1426 or 7-1512 or 13. دواني، محمد بن أسعد (Table B-BJ5)
753.F3-.F34 Fārābī. الفارابي (Table B-BJ5)
Findariskī, Abū al-Qāsim ibn Mīrzā Buzurg, d1640? see B753.M57+
753.G3-.G34 Ghazzālī, 1058-1111. الغزالي (Table B-BJ5)
753.I2-.I24 Ibn al-ʻArabī, 1165-1240. ابن العربي (Table B-BJ5)

Medieval (430-1450)
Arabian and Moorish philosophers. Islamic philosophers
Individual philosophers
B - Z -- Continued

753.I267-.I2674	Ibn al-Khammār, Abū al-Khayr al-Ḥasan ibn Suwār, b. 942. ابن الخمار, ابو الخير الحسن بن سوار (Table B-BJ5)
753.I27-.I274	Ibn ʻArafah al-Warghamī, Muḥammad ibn Muḥammad, 1316-1401. ابن عرفة الورغمي, محمد بن محمد (Table B-BJ5)
753.I3-.I34	Ibn Ḥazm, ʻAlī ibn Aḥmad, 994-1064. ابن حزم, علي بن احمد (Table B-BJ5)
753.I46-.I464	Ibn Masarrah, Muḥammad ibn ʻAbd Allāh, 882 or 3-931. ابن مسرة, محمد بن عبد الله (Table B-BJ5)
753.I474-.I4744	Ibn Miskawayh, Aḥmad ibn Muḥammad, d. 1030. ابن مسكويه, احمد بن محمد (Table B-BJ5)
753.I49-.I494	Ibn Sabʻīn, ʻAbd al-Ḥaqq ibn Ibrāhīm, 1216 or 17-1270. ابن سبعين, عبة الحق بن إبراهيم (Table B-BJ5)
753.I5-.I54	Ibn Ṭufayl, Muḥammad ibn ʻAbd al-Malik, d. 1185. ابن طفيل, محمد بن عبد الملك (Table B-BJ5)
753.K47-.K474	Khuwārizmī, Muḥammad ibn Aḥmad, d. 997 or 8. الخوارزمي, محمد بن احمد (Table B-BJ5)
753.K5-.K54	Kindī, d. ca. 873. الكندي (Table B-BJ5)
753.K6-.K64	Kirmānī, Ḥamīd al-Dīn Aḥmad ibn ʻAbd Allāh, fl. 1020. الكرماني (Table B-BJ5)
753.L34-.L344	Lāhījī, Ḥasan ibn ʻAbd al-Razzāq, ‡d 1635 or 6-1709 or 10. لاهيجي, حسن بن عبة الرزاق (Table B-BJ5)
753.L38-.L384	Lawkarī, Faḍl ibn Muḥammad, d. 1123 or 4. اللوكري, فضل بن محمد (Table B-BJ5)
753.M57-.M574	Mīr Findariskī, Abū al-Qāsim ibn Mīrzā Buzurg, d. 1640? فندرسکی، ابو القاسم بن میرزا بزرگ (Table B-BJ5)
	Mīr Dāmād, Muḥammad Bāqir ibn Muḥammad, d. 1631? see B753.D36+
753.M8-.M84	Mullā Ṣadrā, Muḥammad ibn Ibrāhīm, d. 1641. ملا صدرا, محمد بن إبراهيم (Table B-BJ5)
753.N37-.N374	Narāqī, Muḥammad Mahdī ibn Abī Ẕarr, d. 1794 or 5. النراقي، محمد مهدي بن ابي ذر (Table B-BJ5)
753.N39-.N394	Nayrīzī, Najm al-Dīn Maḥmūd, d. ca. 1526. النيريزي، نجم الدين محمود (Table B-BJ5)
753.O3-.O34	ʻObeyd Zākānī, Neẕām al-Dīn, d. ca. 1370. عبيد زاكاني، نظام الدين (Table B-BJ5)
753.R34-.R344	Rāghib al-Iṣfahānī, Abū al-Qāsim al-Ḥusayn ibn Muḥammad, d. 1108 or 9. راغب الإصفهاني, ابو القاسم الحسين بن محمد (Table B-BJ5)
753.R38-.R384	Rāzī, Abū Bakr Muḥammad ibn Zakarīyā, 865?-925? الرازي, ابو بكر محمد بن زكريا (Table B-BJ5)

Medieval (430-1450)
Arabian and Moorish philosophers. Islamic philosophers
Individual philosophers
B - Z -- Continued

753.R4-.R44 Rāzī, Fakhr al-Dīn Muḥammad ibn ʻUmar, 1149 or 50-1210. الرازي, فخر القين محمد بن عمر (Table B-BJ5)

753.S23-.S234 Sabzavārī, Hādī ibn Mahdī, b. 1797 or 8. سبزواري, هادي بن مهدي (Table B-BJ5)

Ṣadr al-Dīn Shīrāzī, Muḥammad ibn Ibrāhīm, d. 1641 see B753.M8+

753.S26-.S264 Sanūsī, Muḥammad ibn Yūsuf, ca. 1427-ca. 1490. سنوسي، محمد بن يوسف (Table B-BJ5)

753.S83-.834 Suhrawardī, Yaḥyá ibn Ḥabash, 1152 or 3-1191. السهروردي, يحيى بن حبش (Table B-BJ5)

753.T87-.T874 Ṭūsī, Naṣīr al-Dīn Muḥammad ibn Muḥammad, 1201-1274. الطوسي, نصير الدين محمد بن محمد (Table B-BJ5)

753.U8-.U84 ʻUmar ibn Sulaimān. عمر بن سليمان (Table B-BJ5)

753.Y3-.Y34 Yaḥyá ibn ʻAdī, ca. 893-974. يحيى بن عدي (Table B-BJ5)

Jewish philosophers
For Cabala (Occult sciences) see BF1585+
For the Cabala (Jewish religion) see BM525+
Cf. B154+ Ancient Jewish philosophy
Cf. B5800+ Modern Jewish philosophy

755 General works

757.A-Z Special topics, A-Z

757.E72 Eschatology

757.F7 Free will

757.G7 God

757.L38 Law

757.P45 Philosopher-kings

757.P7 Prophecies

757.P8 Psychology

757.S8 Space

Will see B757.F7

759.A-Z Individual philosophers, A-Z
Subarrange each by Table B-BJ5

759.A2-.A24 Abraham ben David, ha-Levi, ca. 1110-ca. 1180 (Table B-BJ5)

Aknin, Joseph ben Judah ben Jacob Ibn, ca. 1150-1220 see B759.I2+

759.A333-.A3334 Albelda, Moses ben Jacob, 15th/16th cent. (Table B-BJ5)

759.A5-.A54 Avicebron, 11th cent. (Table B-BJ5)

759.B53-.B534 Ben Shem Tov, Joseph, ca. 1400-ca. 1460 (Table B-BJ5)

Medieval (430-1450)
Jewish philosophers
Individual philosophers -- Continued

759.C4-.C44 Chasdai ben Abraham Crescas, 1340-ca. 1410 (Table B-BJ5)
Crescas, Ḥasdai, 1340-ca. 1410 see B759.C4+
Del-Medigo, Elijah, ca. 1460-1497 see B759.D44+
759.D44-.D444 Delmedigo, Elijah ben Moses Abba, ca. 1460-1497 (Table B-BJ5)
759.D53-.D534 Dhamārī, Manṣur Suleiman, 15th cent. (Table B-BJ5)
759.E56-.E564 Enoch ben Solomon al-Ḳusṭanṭini, fl. 1370 (Table B-BJ5)
759.F3-.F34 Falaquera, Shem Tov ben Joseph, ca. 1225-ca. 1295 (Table B-BJ5)
Gabirol, Ibn, 11th cent. see B759.A5+
Gersonides, 1288-1344 see B759.L4+
Gracian, Zerahiah ben Isaac ben Shealtiel, 13th cent. see B759.Z47+
759.H53-.H534 Hillel ben Samuel, ca. 1220-ca. 1295 (Table B-BJ5)
759.I2-.I24 Ibn Aknin, Joseph, ca. 1150-1220 (Table B-BJ5)
Ibn Daud, Abraham ben David, Halevi, ca. 1110-ca. 1180 see B759.A2+
759.I253-.I2534 Ibn Ezra, Abraham ben Meïr, 1092-1167 (Table B-BJ5)
759.I255-.I2554 Ibn Ezra, Moses, ca. 1060-ca. 1139 (Table B-BJ5)
759.I257-.I2574 Ibn Kammūnah, Saʻd ibn Manṣūr, 13th cent. (Table B-BJ5)
759.I26-.I264 Ibn Malkah, Judah ben Nissim, 14th cent. (Table B-BJ5)
759.I2697-.I26974 Ibn Shem Tov, Shem Tov ben Joseph ben Shem Tov, 15th cent. (Table B-BJ5)
759.I28-.I284 Ibn Zarza, Samuel, 14th cent. (Table B-BJ5)
Ibn Gabirol, 11th cent. see B759.A5+
759.I8-.I84 Israeli, Isaac, ca. 832-ca. 932 (Table B-BJ5)
759.J43-.J434 Jedaiah ben Abraham Bedersi, ca. 1270-ca. 1340 (Table B-BJ5)
759.J5-.J54 Joseph ben Jacob Ibn Ẓaddik, 1075-1149 (Table B-BJ5)
759.L4-.L44 Levi ben Gershom, 1288-1344 (Table B-BJ5)
759.M3-.M34 Maimonides, Moses, 1135-1204 (Table B-BJ5)
759.M64-.M644 Moses, of Narbonne, d. 1362 (Table B-BJ5)
759.S2-.S24 Saʻadia ben Joseph, 882-942 (Table B-BJ5)
Ẓaddik, Joseph ben Jacob Ibn, 1075-1149 see B759.J5+
759.Z47-.Z474 Zerahiah ben Isaac ben Shealtiel, 13th cent. (Table B-BJ5)

Oriental philosophers see B121+

	Medieval (430-1450) -- Continued
765.A-Z	European philosophers
	Subarrange each by Table B-BJ5
	Including Byzantine philosophers
	Class works that are not purely or mainly philosophical with their subject in other classes, e.g., Theology, literature, etc.
	For anonymous works see B765.Z9
	For letters of Abelard and Eloise see PA8201
765.A2-.A24	Abelard, Peter, 1079-1142 (Table B-BJ5)
765.A25-.A254	Adelard, of Bath, ca. 1116-1142 (Table B-BJ5)
765.A3-.A34	Ailly, Pierre d', 1350-1420? (Table B-BJ5)
765.A346-.A3464	Alanus, de Insulis, d. 1202 (Table B-BJ5)
765.A35-.A354	Alberti, Leon Battista, 1404-1472 (Table B-BJ5)
765.A39-.A394	Albertus, de Saxonia, d. 1390 (Table B-BJ5)
765.A4-.A44	Albertus, Magnus, Saint, 1193?-1280 (Table B-BJ5)
765.A6-.A64	Alcuin, 735-804 (Table B-BJ5)
	For biography see LB125.A4+
765.A7-.A74	Alexander, of Hales, ca. 1185-1245 (Table B-BJ5)
765.A75-.A754	Alfred, of Sareshel (Table B-BJ5)
765.A79-.A794	Anselm, of Laon, d. 1117 (Table B-BJ5)
765.A8-.A84	Anselm, Saint, Archbishop of Canterbury, 1033-1109 (Table B-BJ5)
765.A97-.A974	Aureolus, Petrus, ca. 1280-1322 (Table B-BJ5)
765.B2-.B24	Bacon, Roger, 1214?-1294 (Table B-BJ5)
765.B25-.B254	Barbo, Paolo, d. 1494 (Table B-BJ5)
765.B3-.B34	Bede, the Venerable, Saint, 673-735 (Table B-BJ5)
765.B4-.B44	Berengar, of Tours, ca. 1000-1088 (Table B-BJ5)
765.B5-.B54	Bernard, of Clairvaux, Saint, 1090 or 91-1153 (Table B-BJ5)
765.B543-.B5434	Bernard, de Trilia, 1240 (ca.)-1292 (Table B-BJ5)
765.B55-.B554	Bernard Silvestris, fl. 1136 (Table B-BJ5)
765.B56-.B564	Bēssariōn, Cardinal, 1403-1472 (Table B-BJ5)
765.B59-.B594	Billingham, Richard, 14th cent. (Table B-BJ5)
765.B68-.B684	Boethius, of Dacia, 13th cent. (Table B-BJ5)
765.B7-.B74	Bonaventure, Saint, Cardinal, ca. 1217-1274 (Table B-BJ5)
765.B77-.B774	Bradwardine, Thomas, 1290?-1349 (Table B-BJ5)
765.B78-.B784	Brinkley, Richard, 14th cent. (Table B-BJ5)
765.B84-.B844	Buridan, Jean, 1300-1358 (Table B-BJ5)
765.B848-.N8484	Burlaeus, Gualterus, 1275-1345? (Table B-BJ5)
765.C6-.C64	Colonna, Egidio, Archbishop of Bourges, ca. 1243-1316 (Table B-BJ5)
765.C7-.C74	Crathorn, 14th cent. (Table B-BJ5)
	Cusanus, Nicolaus, 1401-1464 see B765.N5+
765.D18-.D184	David, the Invincible (Table B-BJ5)
765.D2-.D24	David, of Dinant (Table B-BJ5)
765.D3-.D34	Dietrich, von Freiberg, ca. 1250-ca. 1310 (Table B-BJ5)
765.D47-.D474	Dominici, Giovanni, 1356?-1420? (Table B-BJ5)

	Medieval (430-1450)
	European philosophers, A-Z -- Continued
	Dominicus Gundissalinus, 12th cent. see B765.G98+
765.D7-.D74	Duns Scotus, John, ca. 1266-1308 (Table B-BJ5)
765.D9-.D94	Durandus, of Saint-Pourçain, Bishop of Meaux, ca. 1275-1334 (Table B-BJ5)
765.E3-.E34	Eckhart, Meister, d. 1327 (Table B-BJ5)
	Erigena, Johannes Scotus, ca. 810-ca. 877 see B765.J3+
765.F55-.F554	Francesco, da Prato, 14th cent. (Table B-BJ5)
765.F6-.F64	Francis, of Assisi, Saint, 1182-1226 (Table B-BJ5)
765.F65-.F654	Franciscus, de Marchia, 14th cent. (Table B-BJ5)
765.F66-.F664	Franciscus, de Mayronis, ca. 1285-ca. 1328 (Table B-BJ5)
765.F7-.F74	Fredegis, of Tours, d. 824 (Table B-BJ5)
765.G34-.G34	Garland, the Computist, 11th cent. (Table B-BJ5)
765.G39-.G394	Gennadius II, Patriarch of Constantinople, ca. 1405-ca. 1472 (Table B-BJ5)
765.G397-.G3974	Geraldus, Odonis, 1285-1349 (Table B-BJ5)
765.G4-.G44	Gerson, Jean, 1363-1429 (Table B-BJ5)
765.G45-.G454	Gilbert, de la Porrée, Bishop, ca. 1075-1154 (Table B-BJ5)
765.G5-.G54	Giles, of Lessines, ca. 1230-ca. 1304 (Table B-BJ5)
	Giles, of Rome, Archbishop of Bourges, ca. 1243-1316 see B765.C6+
765.G545-.G5454	Giovanni, da Ravenna, 1343-1408 (Table B-BJ5)
765.G59-.G594	Godfrey, of Fontaines, 13th/14th cent. (Table B-BJ5)
	Goethals, Henri, 1217-1293 see B765.H56+
765.G65-.G654	Gregory, of Rimini, d. 1358 (Table B-BJ5)
765.G7-.G74	Grosseteste, Robert, 1175?-1253 (Table B-BJ5)
765.G77-.G774	Guigo I, Prior of the Grande Chartreuse, 1083?-1136 (Table B-BJ5)
	Guigues, du Chastel, 1083?-1136 see B765.G77+
765.G8-.G84	Guilelmus, Arvernus, Bishop of Paris, d. 1249 (Table B-BJ5)
765.G86-.G864	Guilemus, de Rubione, fl. 1333 (Table B-BJ5)
765.G9-.G94	Guillaume, de Champeaux, Bishop, 1070?-1121 (Table B-BJ5)
765.G95-.G954	Guillaume, de Conches, 1080-ca. 1150 (Table B-BJ5)
765.G98-.G984	Gundissalinus, Dominicus, 12th cent. (Table B-BJ5)
765.H38-.H384	Heinrich von Gorkum, ca. 1386-1431 (Table B-BJ5)
765.H4-.H44	Heinrich von Oyta, 1397 (Table B-BJ5)
(765.H5-.H54)	Henricus Gandavensis, 1217-1293 see B765.H56+
765.H56-.H564	Henry, of Ghent, 1217-1293 (Table B-BJ5)
765.H57-.H574	Hervaeus Natalis, d. 1323 (Table B-BJ5)
765.H6-.H64	Hrabanus Maurus, Archbishop of Mainz, 784?-856 (Table B-BJ5)
765.H7-.H74	Hugh, of Saint-Victor, 1096?-1141 (Table B-BJ5)
765.J145-.J1454	Jan, z Kluczborka, ca. 1355-ca. 1436 (Table B-BJ5)

Medieval (430-1450)
European philosophers
Jan, van Ruusbroec, 1293-1381 see B765.R8+
765.J15-.J154 Jean, de Jandun (Table B-BJ5)
765.J3-.J34 Johannes, Scotus Erigena, ca. 810-ca. 877 (Table B-BJ5)
765.J36-.J364 Johannes de Siccavilla, ca 1215-1295 (Table B-BJ5)
765.J4-.J44 John, of Salisbury, Bishop of Chartres, d. 1180 (Table B-BJ5)
765.K5-.K54 Kilwardby, Robert, d. 1279 (Table B-BJ5)
765.L3-.L34 Lanfranc, Archbishop of Canterbury, 1005?-1089 (Table B-BJ5)
Lombard, Peter, Bishop of Paris, ca. 1100-1160 see B765.P3+
765.L8-.L84 Llull, Ramón, 1232?-1316 (Table B-BJ5)
765.M3-.M34 Marsilius, of Inghen, d. 1396 (Table B-BJ5)
765.M332-.M3324 Martin, of Alnwick (Table B-BJ5)
765.M36-.M364 Mattheus, Aurelianensis, 13th cent. (Table B-BJ5)
765.N5-.N54 Nicholas, of Cusa, Cardinal, 1401-1464 (Table B-BJ5)
765.N56-.N564 Nicolaus, de Autricuria, ca. 1300-ca. 1350 (Table B-BJ5)
765.O3-.O34 Ockham, William, ca. 1285-ca. 1349 (Table B-BJ5)
765.O36-.O364 Odonis, Gerald, ca. 1285-1348 (Table B-BJ5)
765.O5-.O54 Olivi, Pierre Jean, 1248 or 9-1298 (Table B-BJ5)
Oyta, Heinrich Totting von, d. 1397 see B765.H4+
765.P15-.P154 Pachymeres, George, 1242-ca. 1310 (Table B-BJ5)
765.P17-.P174 Paolo, Veneto, ca. 1370-1428 (Table B-BJ5)
765.P2-.P24 Peckham, John, d. 1292 (Table B-BJ5)
765.P3-.P34 Peter Lombard, Bishop of Paris, ca. 1100-1160 (Table B-BJ5)
765.P4-.P44 Petrus Thomae, ca. 1280-ca. 1340 (Table B-BJ5)
765.P75-.P754 Priscian, fl. ca. 500-530 (Table B-BJ5)
765.P8-.P84 Psellus, Michael (Table B-BJ5)
Rabanus Maurus, Archbishop of Mainz, 784?-856 see B765.H6+
765.R16-.R164 Ratramnus, monk of Corbie, d. ca. 868 (Table B-BJ5)
765.R2-.R24 Raymond, of Sabunde, d. 1436 (Table B-BJ5)
Rhabanus Maurus, Archbishop of Mainz, 784?-856 see B765.H6+
765.R4-.R44 Ricardus, de Mediavilla, ca. 1249-1308? (Table B-BJ5)
765.R5-.R54 Richard, of St. Victor, d. 1173 (Table B-BJ5)
765.R6-.R64 Robert of Melun, bp. of Hereford, d. 1167 (Table B-BJ5)
765.R66-.R664 Robertus, Anglicus, fl. 1272 (Table B-BJ5)
765.R7-.R74 Roscelin, of Compiègne, ca. 1050-ca. 1125? (Table B-BJ5)
765.R8-.R84 Ruusbroec, Jan van, 1293-1381 (Table B-BJ5)
Scotus, John Duns, ca. 1266-1308 see B765.D7+
Scotus Erigena, Johannes, ca. 810-ca. 877 see B765.J3+
Seuse, Heinrich, 1295-1366 see B765.S7+
765.S47-.S474 Sidrac, 13th cent. (Table B-BJ5)

	Medieval (430-1450)
	European philosophers, A-Z -- Continued
765.S5-.S54	Siger, of Brabant, ca. 1230-ca. 1283 (Table B-BJ5)
765.S6-.S64	Siger de Courtrai, 1341 (Table B-BJ5)
765.S65-.S654	Simone Fidati, da Cascia, d. 1348 (Table B-BJ5)
765.S67-.S674	Sneyth, Hugo, 13th cent. (Table B-BJ5)
765.S7-.S74	Suso, Heinrich, 1300?-1366 (Table B-BJ5)
765.T2-.T24	Tauler, Johannes, ca. 1300-1361 (Table B-BJ5)
	Thomae, Petrus, ca. 1280-ca. 1340 see B765.P4+
765.T4-.T44	Thomas, à Kempis, 1380-1471 (Table B-BJ5)
765.T5-.T54	Thomas, Aquinas, Saint, 1225?-1274 (Table B-BJ5)
765.T55-.T554	Thomas, de Argentina, d. 1357 (Table B-BJ5)
765.T56-.T564	Thomas, de Clivis, 14th cent. (Table B-BJ5)
765.V4-.V44	Vincent, of Beauvais, d. 1264 (Table B-BJ5)
765.W3-.W34	Walter, of Saint-Victor, fl. 1173 (Table B-BJ5)
	William, of Auvergne, Bishop of Paris, d. 1249 see B765.G8+
	William, of Champeaux, Bishop, 1070?-1121 see B765.G9+
	William, of Conches, 1080-ca. 1150 see B765.G95+
	William, of Ockham, ca. 1285-ca. 1349 see B765.O3+
765.W56-.W564	Witelo, 13th cent. (Table B-BJ5)
765.Z9	Anonymous works
	Renaissance
	Class works that are not purely or mainly philosophical with their subjects in other classes, e.g., Theology, literature, etc.
770	Collected works (nonserial)
775	General works
776.A-Z	By region or country, A-Z
	Special topics
778	Humanism
779	Skepticism
	Other special topics, A-Z
780.G74	Grief
	Including consolation
780.G76	Grotesque
780.L52	Liberty
780.M3	Man
780.N37	Nature
780.P44	Perplexity
780.P5	Platonism
780.S8	Stoicism
780.W5S8	Wisdom
	Individual philosophers
	For anonymous works see B785.Z9
781	A - Bruno
	Subarrange each by Table B-BJ5

	Renaissance
	Individual philosophers
	A - Bruno -- Continued
781.A3-.A34	Agrippa von Nettesheim, Heinrich Cornelius, 1486?-1535 (Table B-BJ5)
781.A52-.A524	Ambrogio, Teseo, 1469-1540 (Table B-BJ5)
781.B24-.B244	Bernardi, Antonio, 1502-1565 (Table B-BJ5)
781.B3-.B34	Bodin, Jean, 1530-1596 (Table B-BJ5)
781.B6-.B64	Böhme, Jakob, 1575-1624 (Table B-BJ5)
781.B7-.B74	Bovillus, Carolus, 1479-1567 (Table B-BJ5)
783	Bruno, Giordano, 1548-1600 (Table B-BJ4)
784	Bruno - Bz Subarrange each by Table B-BJ5
784.B5	Budé, Guillaume, 1468-1540
785	C - Z Subarrange each by Table B-BJ5
785.C15-.C154	Cajetan, Tommaso de Vio, 1469-1534 (Table B-BJ5)
	Calvin, Jean, 1509-1564 see BX9418
785.C2-.C24	Campanella, Tommaso, 1568-1639 (Table B-BJ5)
785.C3-.C34	Cardano, Girolamo, 1501-1576 (Table B-BJ5) Cf. Q155 Scientific works
785.C5-.C54	Charron, Pierre, 1541-1603 (Table B-BJ5)
785.C57-.C574	Clapis, Petrus Antonius, ca. 1440-1512 (Table B-BJ5)
785.C7-.C74	Córdoba, Fernando de, 1422-1486 (Table B-BJ5)
785.D3-.D34	Drohobych, Heorhii, ca. 1450-1494 (Table B-BJ5)
785.E6-.E64	Erasmus, Desiderius, d. 1536 (Table B-BJ5)
785.F3-.F34	Fernel, Jean, 1497-1558 (Table B-BJ5)
785.F43-.F434	Ficino, Marsilio, 1433-1499 (Table B-BJ5)
785.F73-.F734	Francke, Christian, b. 1549 (Table B-BJ5)
785.G2-.G24	Galilei, Galileo, 1564-1642 (Table B-BJ5) Cf. QB36.G2 Astronomy Cf. QB3 Astronomy Cf. QC123 Physics
	Gemistus Plethon, George, 15th cent. see B785.P56+
785.G38-.G384	Gemma, Cornelius, 1535-1579 (Table B-BJ5)
785.G4-.G44	Genua, Marco Antonio, 1491-1563 (Table B-BJ5)
785.G58-.G584	Giustiniani, Giovanni, ca. 1513-ca. 1556 (Table B-BJ5)
785.G7-.G74	Grotius, Hugo, 1583-1645 (Table B-BJ5)
785.H6-.H64	Hooker, Richard, 1553 or 4-1600 (Table B-BJ5)
785.L2-.L24	La Rameé, Pierre de, 1515-1572 (Table B-BJ5)
785.L3-.L34	León, Hebreo, b. ca. 1460 (Table B-BJ5)
785.L35-.L354	León, Luis de, 1527-1591 (Table B-BJ5)
785.L394-.L3944	Leonardo, da Vinci, 1452-1519 (Table B-BJ5)
785.L4-.L44	Lipsius, Justus, 1547-1606 (Table B-BJ5)
785.M2-.M24	Machiavelli, Niccolò, 1469-1527 (Table B-BJ5) Cf. DG738.14.M2 Biography
785.M23-.M234	Major, John, 1469-1550 (Table B-BJ5)

Renaissance
Individual philosophers
C - Z -- Continued

785.M244-.M2444 Manetti, Giannozzo, 1396-1459 (Table B-BJ5)
785.M298-.M2984 Maximus, the Greek, Saint, 1480-1556 (Table B-BJ5)
Cf. BX395.M37 Maximus as a theologian
785.M3-.M34 Mazzoni, Jacopo, 1548-1598 (Table B-BJ5)
785.M4-.M44 Melanchthon, Philipp, 1497-1560 (Table B-BJ5)
Mirandola, Giovanni Pico della, 1463-1494 see B785.P5+
785.M7-.M74 Montaigne, Michel de, 1533-1592 (Table B-BJ5)
Cf. PQ1641+ French literature
785.M8-.M84 More, Thomas, 1565-1625 (Table B-BJ5)
For biography and general works on More see DA334.M8
For More's Utopia see HX810.5
785.N3-.N34 Nifo, Agostino, ca. 1473-1545? (Table B-BJ5)
785.N4-.N44 Nizolio, Mario, 1498-1566 (Table B-BJ5)
785.O3-.O34 Ochino, Bernardino, 1487-1564 (Table B-BJ5)
785.P2-.P24 Paracelsus, 1493-1541 (Table B-BJ5)
Cf. BF1598.P2 Biography as a magician
Cf. QB26 Astrology
Cf. R147.P2 Biography as a physician
785.P4-.P44 Patrizi, Francesco, 1529-1597 (Table B-BJ5)
785.P46-.P464 Pereira, Gometius, b. 1500 (Table B-BJ5)
785.P5-.P54 Pico della Mirandola, Giovanni, 1463-1494 (Table B-BJ5)
785.P56-.P564 Plethon, George Gemistus, 15th cent. (Table B-BJ5)
785.P6-.P64 Poliziano, Angelo, 1454-1494 (Table B-BJ5)
Cf. PA8560+ Modern Latin literature
Cf. PQ4630.P5 Italian literature
785.P8-.P84 Pomponazzi, Pietro, 1462-1525 (Table B-BJ5)
785.P86-.P864 Porzio, Simone, 1496-1554 (Table B-BJ5)
Ramus, Petrus, 1515-1572 see B785.L2+
785.R6-.R64 Reuchlin, Johann, 1455-1522 (Table B-BJ5)
785.R73-.R734 Ricius, Paulus, fl. 1511-1532 (Table B-BJ5)
785.S13-.S134 Sabuco, Miguel (Table B-BJ5)
785.S136-.S1364 Sabuco de Nantes y Barrera, Oliva, b. 1562 (Table B-BJ5)
785.S15-.S154 Salutati, Coluccio, 1331-1406 (Table B-BJ5)
785.S2-.S24 Sánchez, Francisco, ca. 1550-ca. 1623 (Table B-BJ5)
785.S3-.S34 Savonarola, Girolamo, 1452-1498 (Table B-BJ5)
785.S4-.S44 Scaligero, Giulio Cesare, 1484-1558 (Table B-BJ5)
Cf. PA8575.S3 Modern Latin literature
785.S6-.S64 Servetus, Michael, 1511?-1553 (Table B-BJ5)
785.S65-.S654 Simoni, Simone, 1532-1602 (Table B-BJ5)
785.S7-.S74 Soto, Domingo de, 1494-1560 (Table B-BJ5)
785.S79-.S794 Steuco, Agostino, 1497?-1548 (Table B-BJ5)
785.S815-.S8154 Storella, Francesco Maria, 16th cent. (Table B-BJ5)

Renaissance
Individual philosophers
C - Z -- Continued

785.S82-.S824 Suárez, Francisco, 1548-1617 (Table B-BJ5)
785.T3-.T34 Telesio, Bernardino, 1509-1588 (Table B-BJ5)
785.V1138-.V11384 Valencia, Pedro de, 1555-1620 (Table B-BJ5)
785.V114-.V1144 Valla, Lorenzo, 1407-1457 (Table B-BJ5)
785.V28-.V284 Vázquez, Gabriel, 1551-1604 (Table B-BJ5)
785.V6-.V64 Vives, Juan Luis, 1492-1540 (Table B-BJ5)
785.V7-.V74 Volusenus, Florentius, 1504?-1546 or 7 (Table B-BJ5)
785.W3-.W34 Weigel, Erhard, 1625-1699 (Table B-BJ5)
785.Z9 Anonymous works, A-Z

Modern (1450/1600-)

790 Collected works (nonserial)

General works

790.5 Polyglot
791 English
792 French
793 German
794 Italian
795 Spanish and Portuguese
796 Russian and other Slavic
798.A-Z Other languages, A-Z
799 Comparative philosophy

By period

Renaissance see B770+

801 17th century
802 18th century. Philosophy of the enlightenment. Die Aufklärung

Cf. B833.A1+ Rationalism
Cf. B2621 Die Aufklärung (Germany)

803 19th century

Including works combining the 19th and early 20th centuries

20th century

804.A1 Collected works (nonserial)
804.A2-Z General works
805 21st century

Special topics and schools of philosophy

Topics are also classified under each country as a whole and under each country by period, e.g., B1571, 19th century English utilitarianism

Agnosticism

Cf. BL2700+ Rationalism in religion

808.A1 Periodicals, societies, etc.
808.A3-Z General works

Alienation

808.2.A1 Periodicals, societies, etc.

	Modern (1450/1600-)
	Special topics and schools of philosophy
	Alienation -- Continued
808.2.A3-Z	General works
	Analysis
808.5.A1	Periodicals, societies, etc.
808.5.A3-Z	General works
	Animism
	Cf. BD419+ The soul, immortality, etc.
	Cf. BF150+ Mind and body
808.6.A1	Periodicals, societies, etc.
808.6.A3-Z	General works
	Autonomy
808.67.A1	Periodicals, societies, etc.
808.67.A3-Z	General works
	Banality
808.7.A1	Periodicals, societies, etc.
808.7.A3-Z	General works
808.9	Consciousness
	Conservatism
809.A1	Periodicals, societies, etc.
809.A3-Z	General works
	Constructivism
809.13.A1	Periodicals, societies, etc.
809.13.A3-Z	General works
809.14	Contextualism
	Convention
809.15.A1	Periodicals, societies, etc.
809.15.A3-Z	General works
	Critical thinking
809.2.A1	Periodicals, societies, etc.
809.2.A3-Z	General works
	Criticism
	Cf. B814.A1+ Eclecticism
	Cf. B823.A1+ Idealism (Transcendentalism)
	Cf. B831.A1+ Positivism
	Cf. B837.A1+ Scepticism
	Cf. BD201 Limits of knowledge
809.3.A1	Periodicals, societies, etc.
809.3.A3-Z	General works
	Cynicism
809.5.A1	Periodicals, societies, etc.
809.5.A3-Z	General works
	Deconstruction
809.6.A1	Periodicals, societies, etc.
809.6.A3-Z	General works
	Dialectic

Modern (1450/1600-)
Special topics and schools of philosophy
Dialectic -- Continued
809.7.A1 Periodicals, societies, etc.
809.7.A3-Z General works
809.8 Dialectic materialism. Marxist philosophy
For works that discuss dialectical materialism in relation to a specific discipline, see that discipline, e.g., HM, Dialectical materialism and society
Cf. D16.9 Historical materialism
Cf. HX39.5.A2+ Socialism
809.82.A-Z By region or country, A-Z
809.83 Laws
809.832 Transformation of quantity to quality
809.833 Unity, or conflict of opposites
809.834 Negation of negation
809.84 Categories (General)
Difference
809.9.A1 Periodicals, societies, etc.
809.9.A3-Z General works
Dogmatism
810.A1 Periodicals, societies, etc.
810.A3-Z General works
Dualism
812.A1 Periodicals, societies, etc.
812.A3-Z General works
Eclecticism
814.A1 Periodicals, societies, etc.
814.A3-Z General works
Emotions
815.A1 Periodicals, societies, etc.
815.A3-Z General works
Empiricism (Associationalism)
Including the holism of Jan Christian Smuts
Cf. B1608.E6 Mill's empiricism
816.A1 Periodicals, societies, etc.
816.A3-Z General works
Epiphanism
817.A1 Periodicals, societies, etc.
817.A3-Z General works
Evolution. Holism
818.A1 Periodicals, societies, etc.
818.A3-Z General works
Existential phenomenology
818.5.A1 Periodicals, societies, etc.
818.5.A3-Z General works

Modern (1450/1600-)
Special topics and schools of philosophy -- Continued
Existentialism
Cf. B3279.J3+ Jaspers, Karl
819.A1 Periodicals, societies, etc.
819.A3-Z General works
Form
819.3 Periodicals, societies, etc.
819.32 General works
Freedom see B824.4.A+
Genealogy
819.5.A1 Periodicals, societies, etc.
819.5.A3-Z General works
General semantics
Class here works concerned with general semantics as set forth by Alfred Korzybski, founder of the Institute of General Semantics
Cf. B840.A1+ Semantics
820.A1 Periodicals, societies, etc.
820.A3-Z General works
Epistemics
820.3.A1 Periodicals, societies, etc.
820.3.A3-Z General works
Holism see B818.A+
Humanism. Neo-humanism
821.A1 Periodicals, societies, etc.
821.A3-Z General works
Idea
822.A1 Periodicals, societies, etc.
822.A3-Z General works
Idealism. Transcendentalism
Including works on the critical philosophy
For American transcendentalism see B905
823.A1 Periodicals, societies, etc.
823.A3-Z General works
Ideology
823.3.A1 Periodicals, societies, etc.
823.3.A3-Z General works
Imperialism see JC359
Individualism
Cf. BJ1474 Ethics
824.A1 Periodicals, societies, etc.
824.A3-Z General works
Instinct
824.14.A1 Periodicals, societies, etc.
824.14.A3-Z General works
Interaction

Modern (1450/1600-)
Special topics and schools of philosophy
Interaction -- Continued

824.15.A1	Periodicals, societies, etc.
824.15.A3-Z	General works
	Interpretation
824.17.A1	Periodicals, societies, etc.
824.17.A3-Z	General works
	Intersubjectivity
824.18.A1	Periodicals, societies, etc.
824.18.A3-Z	General works
	Irrationalism
824.2.A1	Periodicals, societies, etc.
824.2.A3-Z	General works
	Isolation
824.3.A1	Periodicals, societies, etc.
824.3.A3-Z	General works
	Liberty. Freedom Cf. JC585+ Political theory
824.4.A1	Periodicals, societies, etc.
824.4.A3-Z	General works
	Logical positivism
824.6.A1	Periodicals, societies, etc.
824.6.A3-Z	General works
	Materialism
825.A1	Periodicals, societies, etc.
825.A3-Z	General works
	Meaninglessness
825.2.A1	Periodicals, societies, etc.
825.2.A3-Z	General works
	Monadology
826.A1	Periodicals, societies, etc.
826.A3-Z	General works
	Monism
827.A1	Periodicals, societies, etc.
827.A3-Z	General works
	Mysticism
828.A1	Periodicals, societies, etc.
828.A3-Z	General works
	Naturalism
828.2.A1	Periodicals, societies, etc.
828.2.A3-Z	General works
828.25	Negativity
	Nihilism
828.3.A1	Periodicals, societies, etc.
828.3.A3-Z	General works
	Operationalism

Modern (1450/1600-)
Special topics and schools of philosophy
Operationalism -- Continued
828.35.A1 Periodicals, societies, etc.
828.35.A3-Z General works
Ordinary-language philosophy
828.36.A1 Periodicals, societies, etc.
828.36.A3-Z General works
Pansophy
828.4.A1 Periodicals, societies, etc.
828.4.A3-Z General works
Perception
828.45.A1 Periodicals, societies, etc.
828.45.A3-Z General works
Performative
828.47.A1 Periodicals, societies, etc.
828.47.A3-Z General works
Personalism
828.5.A1 Periodicals, societies, etc.
828.5.A3-Z General works
Pessimism and optimism
829.A1 Periodicals, societies, etc.
829.A3-Z General works
Phenomenology
Cf. B818.5.A1+ Existential phenomenology
Cf. B3279.H9+ Husserl, Edmund, 1859-1938
829.5.A1 Periodicals, societies, etc.
829.5.A3-Z General works
Pluralism
Cf. BD394 Unity and plurality
830.A1 Periodicals, societies, etc.
830.A3-Z General works
Polarity
830.5.A1 Periodicals, societies, etc.
830.5.A3-Z General works
Positivism
Class here general works only
For positivism in individual countries, see the numbers for that topic under each individual country, e.g. B1616.P6 Later 19th and 20th century England; B4515.P6 Spain and Portugal; etc.
831.A1 Periodicals, societies, etc.
831.A3-Z General works
Postmodernism
831.2.A1 Periodicals, societies, etc.
831.2.A3-Z General works
Practice

Modern (1450/1600-)
Special topics and schools of philosophy
Practice -- Continued
831.3.A1 Periodicals, societies, etc.
831.3.A3-Z General works
Pragmatics
Cf. P99.4.P72 Linguistics
831.5.A1 Periodicals, societies, etc.
831.5.A3-Z General works
Pragmatism
832.A1 Periodicals, societies, etc.
832.A3-Z General works
Praxeology
832.2.A1 Periodicals, societies, etc.
832.2.A3-Z General works
Private language problem
832.3.A1 Periodicals, societies, etc.
832.3.A3-Z General works
Rationalism
Cf. BL2700+ Rationalism in religion
833.A1 Periodicals, societies, etc.
833.A3-Z General works
Reaction
834.A1 Periodicals, societies, etc.
834.A3-Z General works
Realism
835.A1 Periodicals, societies, etc.
835.A3-Z General works
835.5 Reductionism
Relationism
836.A1 Periodicals, societies, etc.
836.A3-Z General works
Romanticism
836.5.A1 Periodicals, societies, etc.
836.5.A3-Z General works
Scepticism (Skepticism)
Cf. BL2700+ Rationalism in religion
837.A1 Periodicals, societies, etc.
837.A3-Z General works
Scholasticism. Neo-Scholasticism. Neo-Thomism
For medieval scholasticism see B734
839.A1 Periodicals, societies, etc.
839.A3-Z General works
Semantics. Meaning
Cf. B820+ General semantics
840.A1 Periodicals, societies, etc.
840.A3-Z General works

Modern (1450/1600-)
Special topics and schools of philosophy -- Continued
Spiritualism. The spiritual
Cf. B823.A1+ Idealism, transcendentalism
Cf. BL200 Theism
841.A1 Periodicals, societies, etc.
841.A3-Z General works
Structuralism
841.4.A1 Periodicals, societies, etc.
841.4.A3-Z General works
Subjectivity
841.6.A1 Periodicals, societies, etc.
841.6.A3-Z General works
Supervenience
841.8.A1 Periodicals. Societies, etc.
841.8.A3-Z General works
Theory
842.A1 Periodicals, societies, etc.
842.A3-Z General works
Utilitarianism
Cf. B1571 Nineteenth century English utilitarianism
843.A1 Periodicals, societies, etc.
843.A3-Z General works
Violence
844.A1 Periodicals, societies, etc.
844.A3-Z General works
846 Vision
849 Will
By region or country
United States
850 Collected works (nonserial)
General works. History
851 English
852 French
853 German
855.A-Z Other languages, A-Z
858 Elementary textbooks. Outlines, syllabi, etc.
861.A-Z Special topics, A-Z
Freedom see B861.L52
861.L52 Liberty. Freedom
By period
Colonial to 1750
Including works extending into next period
865 General works
868.A-Z Special topics, A-Z
Individual philosophers
Cf. BT-BX, Theology, theologians

Modern (1450/1600-)
By region or country
United States
By period
Colonial to 1750
Individual philosophers -- Continued

869 A - Edwards
Subarrange each by Table B-BJ5
869.C5-.C54 Cotton, John (Table B-BJ5)
870-874 Edwards, Jonathan (Table B-BJ3)
876 Edwards -Z
Subarrange each by Table B-BJ5
876.E3-.E34 Eliot, John (Table B-BJ5)
876.H7-.H74 Hopkins, Samuel (Table B-BJ5)
876.J5-.J54 Johnson, Samuel (Table B-BJ5)
876.M2-.M24 Mather, Cotton (Table B-BJ5)
876.W4-.W44 Williams, Roger (Table B-BJ5)

Revolutionary to 1800
878 General works
879.A-Z Special topics, A-Z
Individual philosophers
879.5 A - Franklin
Subarrange each by Table B-BJ5
879.5.C64-.C644 Colden, Cadwallader, 1688-1776 (Table B-BJ5)
Colden, Cadwallader, 1688-1776
880-884 Franklin, Benjamin, 1706-1790 (Table B-BJ3)
884.5 Franklin - Jefferson
Subarrange each by Table B-BJ5
885 Jefferson, Thomas, 1743-1826 (Table B-BJ4)
886 Jefferson - Paine
Subarrange each by Table B-BJ5
887 Paine, Thomas, 1737-1809 (Table B-BJ4)
888 Paine - Witherspoon
Subarrange each by Table B-BJ5
889 Witherspoon, John, 1723-1794 (Table B-BJ4)
890 Witherspoon - Z
Subarrange each by Table B-BJ5

19th and 20th centuries
893 General works
895 General special
Special aspects of the subject as a whole
Early 19th century to 1860
901 General works
Special topics
903 Scotch philosophy (Influence)

Modern (1450/1600-)
By region or country
United States
By period
19th and 20th centuries
Early 19th century to 1860
Special topics -- Continued

905 Transcendentalism. Brook Farm. Concord school of philosophy
Cf. B823.A1+ Idealism, transcendentalism (General)
906.A-Z Other special topics, A-Z
906.M35 Man
Individual philosophers
908 A - Emerson
Subarrange each by Table B-BJ5
908.A5-.A54 Alcott, Amos Bronson, 1799-1888 (Table B-BJ5)
908.B3-.B34 Beasley, Frederick, 1777-1845 (Table B-BJ5)
908.B6-.B64 Brownson, Orestes Augustus, 1803-1876 (Table B-BJ5)
908.B7-.B74 Burton, Asa, 1752-1836 (Table B-BJ5)
908.B79-.B794 Butchvarov, Panayot, 1933- (Table B-BJ5)
908.C4-.C44 Channing, William Ellery, 1780-1842 (Table B-BJ5)
908.C6-.C64 Clarke, James Freeman, 1810-1888 (Table B-BJ5)
Emerson, Ralph Waldo, 1803-1882 see PS1600+
921 Emerson - McCosh
Subarrange each by Table B-BJ5
921.F47-.F474 Ferré, Frederick (Table B-BJ5)
921.F6-.F64 Frothingham, Ephraim L. (Ephraim Langdon) (Table B-BJ5)
921.F7-.F74 Fuller, Margaret, 1810-1850 (Table B-BJ5)
921.H4-.H44 Hickok, Laurens P. (Laurens Perseus), ‡d 1798-1888 (Table B-BJ5)
921.H63-.H634 Hodge, Charles, 1797-1878 (Table B-BJ5)
921.J2-.J24 James, Henry, 1811-1882
921.K5-.K54 Knowlton, Charles, 1800-1850 (Table B-BJ5)
925-928 McCosh, James, 1811-1894 (Table B-BJ3a)
931 McCosh - Z
Subarrange each by Table B-BJ5
931.M3-.M34 Marsh, James, 1794-1842 (Table B-BJ5)
931.O4-.O44 Ogilvie, James, 1760-1820 (Table B-BJ5)
Ossoli, Sara Margarita, 1810-1850 see B921.F7+
931.P5-.P54 Porter, Noah, 1811-1892 (Table B-BJ5)

Modern (1450/1600-)
By region or country
United States
By period
19th and 20th centuries
Early 19th century to 1860
Individual philosophers
McCosh - Z -- Continued

931.R4-.R44 Ripley, George, 1802-1880 (Table B-BJ5)
931.S3-.S34 Seelye, Julius H. (Julius Hawley), 1824-1895 (Table B-BJ5)
931.T4-.T44 Thoreau, Henry David, 1817-1862 (Table B-BJ5)
931.U6-.U64 Upham, Thomas Cogswell, 1799-1872 (Table B-BJ5)
931.W25-.W254 Wasson, David Atwood, 1823-1887 (Table B-BJ5)
931.W3-.W34 Wayland, Francis, 1796-1865 (Table B-BJ5)
931.W5-.W54 Winslow, Hubbard, 1799-1864 (Table B-BJ5)

Later 19th and 20th centuries, 1860-2000

934 Collected works (nonserial)
935 General works
936 General special
Including special aspects of the subject as a whole

Special topics

938 Evolution
941 Idealism
Cf. B905 Transcendentalism
943 Monism
944.A-Z Other special topics, A-Z
944.A37 African American philosophy
944.A53 Analysis
944.D5 Dialectical materialism
944.E94 Existentialism
944.H3 Harvard school
944.H85 Humanism
944.M47 Metaphysics
944.N3 Naturalism
944.P4 Personalism
944.P48 Phenomenology
944.P5 Platonism
944.P67 Postmodernism
944.P72 Pragmatism
944.R4 Realism
944.S2 St. Louis movement
944.S4 Semantics
944.T54 Time

Modern (1450/1600-)
By region or country
United States
By period
19th and 20th centuries
Later 19th and 20th centuries, 1860-2000 -- Continued

945.A-Z	Individual philosophers, A-Z Subarrange each by Table B-BJ5
945.A26-.A264	Abbot, Francis Ellingwood, 1836-1903 (Table B-BJ5)
945.A27-.A274	Adams, E.M. (Elie Maynard), 1919-2003. (Table B-BJ5)
945.A286-.A2864	Adler, Mortimer Jerome, 1902-2001 (Table B-BJ5)
945.A3-.A34	Agushewitz, Reuben (Table B-BJ5)
945.A5-.A54	Alexander, Hartley Burr, 1873-1939 (Table B-BJ5)
945.A66-.A664	Appelbaum, David (Table B-BJ5)
945.A69-.A694	Arendt, Hannah, 1906-1975 (Table B-BJ5)
945.A94-.A944	Audi, Robert, 1941- (Table B-BJ5)
945.B12-.B124	Babbitt, Irving, 1865-1933 (Table B-BJ5)
945.B18-.B184	Baker, Lynne Rudder, 1944- (Table B-BJ5)
945.B2-.B24	Baldwin, James Mark, 1861-1934 (Table B-BJ5)
945.B3-.B34	Bascom, John, 1827-1911 (Table B-BJ5)
945.B376-.B3764	Beck, Lewis White (Table B-BJ5)
945.B4-.B44	Bellamy, Edward, 1850-1898 (Table B-BJ5)
945.B47-.B474	Bergmann, Gustav, 1906-1987 (Table B-BJ5)
945.B476-.B4764	Bernstein, Richard J. (Table B-BJ5)
945.B5-.B54	Blackwell, Antoinette Louisa Brown, 1825-1921 (Table B-BJ5)
945.B6-.B64	Bouwsma, O.K. (Table B-BJ5)
945.B7-.B74	Bowne, Borden Parker, 1847-1910 (Table B-BJ5)
945.B745-.B7454	Brockman, John, 1941- (Table B-BJ5)
945.B748-.B7484	Brown, Norman Oliver, 1913-2002 (Table B-BJ5)
945.B768-.B7684	Burge, Tyler (Table B-BJ5)
945.B77-.B774	Burke, Kenneth, 1897-1993 (Table B-BJ5)
945.B86-.B864	Burtt, Edwin A. (Edwin Arthur), 1892-1989 (Table B-BJ5)
945.B88-.B884	Butler, Judith, 1956- (Table B-BJ5)
945.C14-.C144	Caputo, John D. (Table B-BJ5)
945.C16-.C164	Carnap, Rudolf, 1891-1970 (Table B-BJ5)
945.C2-.C24	Carus, Paul, 1852-1919 (Table B-BJ5)
945.C27-.C274	Cavell, Stanley, 1926- (Table B-BJ5)
945.C37-.C374	Cerf, Walter, 1907-2001 (Table B-BJ5)
945.C46-.C464	Chisholm, Roderick M. (Table B-BJ5)
945.C47-.C474	Churchland, Paul M., 1942- (Table B-BJ5)

Modern (1450/1600-)
By region or country
United States
By period
19th and 20th centuries
Later 19th and 20th centuries, 1860-2000
Individual philosophers, A-Z -- Continued

945.C48-.C484 Clarke, W. Norris (William Norris), 1915- (Table B-BJ5)
945.C5-.C54 Cohen, Morris Raphael, 1880-1947 (Table B-BJ5)
945.C8-.C84 Creighton, James Edwin, 1861-1924 (Table B-BJ5)
945.C87-.C874 Cutrofello, Andrew, 1961- (Table B-BJ5)
945.D36-.D364 Danto, Arthur Coleman, 1924- (Table B-BJ5)
945.D38-.D384 Davidson, Donald, 1917-2003 (Table B-BJ5)
945.D385-.D3854 Deely, John N. (Table B-BJ5)
945.D39-.D394 Dennett, Daniel Clement (Table B-BJ5)
945.D397-.D3974 Deutsch, Eliot (Table B-BJ5)
945.D4-.D44 Dewey, John, 1859-1952 (Table B-BJ5)
For works in philosophy of education see LB875.D34+
945.D76-.D764 Dreyfus, Hubert L. (Table B-BJ5)
945.E3-.E34 Edman, Irwin, 1896-1954 (Table B-BJ5)
945.E4-.E44 Elgin, Catherine Z., 1948- (Table B-BJ5)
945.E8-.E84 Everett, Charles Carroll, 1829-1900 (Table B-BJ5)
945.F2-.F24 Feibleman, James Kern, 1904- (Table B-BJ5)
945.F3-.F34 Ferguson, James Henry (Table B-BJ5)
945.F35-.F354 Fergusson, Harvey, 1890-1971 (Table B-BJ5)
945.F39-.F394 Firth, Roderick, 1917-1987 (Table B-BJ5)
945.F4-.F44 Fiske, John, 1842-1901 (Table B-BJ5)
945.F63-.F634 Fodor, Jerry A. (Table B-BJ5)
945.F8-.F84 Fullerton, George Stuart, 1859-1925 (Table B-BJ5)
945.G59-.G594 Goldman, Alvin I., 1938- (Table B-BJ5)
945.G62-.G624 Goodman, Nelson (Table B-BJ5)
945.G73-.G734 Grene, Marjorie, 1910-2009 (Table B-BJ5)
945.H14-.H144 Haack, Susan (Table B-BJ5)
945.H2-.H24 Hall, G. Stanley (Granville Stanley), 1844-1924 (Table B-BJ5)
945.H26-.H264 Halle, Louis Joseph, 1910- (Table B-BJ5)
945.H28-.H284 Hammond, Albert L. (Albert Lanphier), 1892-1970 (Table B-BJ5)
945.H2846-.H28464 Hans, James S., 1950- (Table B-BJ5)
945.H285-.H2854 Harris, William Torrey, 1835-1909 (Table B-BJ5)
945.H35-.H354 Hartshorne, Charles, 1897-2000 (Table B-BJ5)
945.H38-.H384 Hearn, Lafcadio, 1850-1904 (Table B-BJ5)

Modern (1450/1600-)
By region or country
United States
By period
19th and 20th centuries
Later 19th and 20th centuries, 1860-2000
Individual philosophers, A-Z -- Continued

945.H4-.H44 Hebberd, S. S. (Stephen Southric), 1841-1922 (Table B-BJ5)
945.H45-.H454 Hempel, Carl G. (Carl Gustav), 1905-1997 (Table B-BJ5)
945.H5-.H54 Hibben, John Grier, 1861-1933 (Table B-BJ5)
945.H64-.H644 Hocking, William Ernest, 1873-1966 (Table B-BJ5)
945.H68-.H684 Hook, Sidney, 1902-1989 (Table B-BJ5)
945.H7-.H74 Howison, George Holmes, 1834-1917 (Table B-BJ5)
945.I35-.I354 Ihde, Don, 1934- (Table B-BJ5)
945.J2-.J24 James, William, 1842-1910 (Table B-BJ5)
For works in psychology, see subclass BF
945.K28-.K284 Kallen, Horace Meyer, 1882-1974 (Table B-BJ5)
945.K38-.K384 Kearney, Richard (Table B-BJ5)
945.K39-.K394 Kearns, John T., 1936- (Table B-BJ5)
945.K45-.K454 Kevelson, Roberta (Table B-BJ5)
945.K6-.K64 Klyce, Scudder, 1879-1933 (Table B-BJ5)
945.K79-.K794 Kripke, Saul A., 1940- (Table B-BJ5)
945.L2-.L24 Ladd, George Trumbull, 1842-1921 (Table B-BJ5)
945.L27-.L274 Langer, Susanne Katherina Knauth, 1895-1985 (Table B-BJ5)
945.L42-.L424 Lebowitz, Martin, 1921-1993 (Table B-BJ5)
945.L445-.L4454 Lehrer, Keith (Table B-BJ5)
945.L455-.L4554 Lewis, David K. (David Kellogg), 1941-2001 (Table B-BJ5)
945.L458-.L4584 Lingis, Alphonso, 1933- (Table B-BJ5)
945.L58-.L584 Lovejoy, Arthur O. (Arthur Oncken), 1873-1962 (Table B-BJ5)
945.L6-.L64 Lowber, James William, 1847-1930 (Table B-BJ5)
945.M24-.M244 Mackaye, James, 1872-1935 (Table B-BJ5)
945.M26-.M264 Machan, Tibor R. (Table B-BJ5)
945.M2945-.M29454 Mallin, Samuel B. (Table B-BJ5)
945.M298-.M2984 Marcuse, Herbert, 1898-1979 (Table B-BJ5)
945.M37-.M374 Marsh, James L. (Table B-BJ5)
945.M454-.M4544 McDermott, John J. (John Joseph), 1932- (Table B-BJ5)
945.M456-.M4564 McKeon, Richard (Richard Peter), 1900-1985 (Table B-BJ5)
945.M46-.M464 Mead, George Herbert, 1863-1931 (Table B-BJ5)

Modern (1450/1600-)
By region or country
United States
By period
19th and 20th centuries
Later 19th and 20th centuries, 1860-2000
Individual philosophers, A-Z -- Continued

945.M468-.M4684 Mensch, James R. (Table B-BJ5)
945.M476-.M4764 Miller, John William (Table B-BJ5)
945.M5-.M54 Morris, George Sylvester, 1840-1889 (Table B-BJ5)
945.M8-.M84 Münsterberg, Hugo, 1863-1916 (Table B-BJ5)
945.M96-.M964 Murphy, Arthur Edward, 1901-1962 (Table B-BJ5)
945.N33-.N334 Nagel, Thomas, 1937- (Table B-BJ5)
945.N35-.N354 Natanson, Maurice Alexander, 1924- (Table B-BJ5)
945.N484-.N4844 Neville, Robert C. (Table B-BJ5)
945.N53-.N534 Nielsen, Kai, 1926- (Table B-BJ5)
945.N6-.N64 Northrop, F.S.C. (Filmer Stuart Cuckow), 1893-1992 (Table B-BJ5)
945.N68-.N684 Nozick, Robert (Table B-BJ5)
945.O7-.O74 Otto, Max Carl, b. 1876 (Table B-BJ5)
945.P2-.P24 Palmer, George Herbert, 1842-1933 (Table B-BJ5)
945.P4-.P44 Peirce, Charles S. (Charles Sanders), 1839-1914 (Table B-BJ5)
945.P45-.P454 Perry, John, 1943- (Table B-BJ5)
945.P55-.P554 Plantinga, Alvin (Table B-BJ5)
945.P58-.P584 Polanyi, Michael, 1891-1976 (Table B-BJ5)
945.P69-.P694 Poteat, William H. (Table B-BJ5)
945.P87-.P874 Putnam, Hilary (Table B-BJ5)
945.Q5-.Q54 Quine, W. V. (Willard Van Orman) (Table B-BJ5)
945.R23-.R234 Rand, Ayn (Table B-BJ5)
945.R28-.R284 Rawls, John, 1921-2002 (Table B-BJ5)
945.R3-.R34 Raymond, George Lansing, 1839-1929 (Table B-BJ5)
945.R45-.P454 Rescher, Nicholas (Table B-BJ5)
945.R52-.R524 Rorty, Richard (Table B-BJ5)
945.R526-.R5264 Rosen, Stanley, 1929- (Table B-BJ5)
945.R527-.R5274 Rosenthal, Abigail L. (Table B-BJ5)
945.R53-.R534 Rothschild, Richard (Table B-BJ5)
945.R6-.R64 Royce, Josiah, 1855-1916 (Table B-BJ5)
945.R85-.R854 Ruprecht, Louis A. (Table B-BJ5)
945.S2-.S24 Santayana, George, 1863-1952 (Table B-BJ5)
945.S26-.S264 Schilpp, Paul Arthur, 1897-1993 (Table B-BJ5)
945.S326-.S3264 Schrag, Calvin O. (Table B-BJ5)
945.S33-.S334 Schroeder, Brian (Table B-BJ5)

Modern (1450/1600-)
By region or country
United States
By period
19th and 20th centuries
Later 19th and 20th centuries, 1860-2000
Individual philosophers, A-Z -- Continued

945.S34-.S344 Schurman, Jacob Gould, 1854-1942 (Table B-BJ5)
945.S354-.S3544 Schutz, Alfred, 1899-1959 (Table B-BJ5)
945.S44-.S444 Sellars, Wilfrid (Table B-BJ5)
945.S5-.S54 Shaw, Charles Gray, 1871-1949 (Table B-BJ5)
945.S6-.S64 Shields, Charles W. (Charles Woodruff), 1825-1904 (Table B-BJ5)
945.S65-.S654 Singer, Edgar A. (Edgar Arthur), 1873-1955 (Table B-BJ5)
945.S657-.S6574 Singer, Irving (Table B-BJ5)
945.S69-.S694 Smith, Henry Bradford, 1882-1938 (Table B-BJ5)
945.S714-.S7144 Smith, John E. (John Edwin), 1921-2009 (Table B-BJ5)
945.S727-.S7274 Sosa, Ernest (Table B-BJ5)
945.S73-.S734 Spaulding, Edward Gleason, 1873-1940 (Table B-BJ5)
945.S739-.S7394 Stallknecht, Newton Phelps, 1906- (Table B-BJ5)
945.S74-.S744 Stallo, J. B. (John Bernhard), 1823-1900 (Table B-BJ5)
945.S75-.S754 Stevens, Samuel Eugene, b. 1839 (Table B-BJ5)
945.S755-.S7554 Stich, Stephen P. (Table B-BJ5)
945.S8-.S84 Strauss, Leo (Table B-BJ5)
945.S87-.S874 Stroll, Avrum, 1921- (Table B-BJ5)
945.T39-.T394 Taylor, Mark C., 1945- (Table B-BJ5)
945.U54-.U544 Unger, Peter K. (Table B-BJ5)
945.V35-.V354 Van Inwagen, Peter (Table B-BJ5)
945.V47-.V474 Verene, Donald Phillip, 1937- (Table B-BJ5)
945.W396-.W3964 Weiss, Paul, 1901-2002 (Table B-BJ5)
945.W45-.W454 White, Morton Gabriel, 1917- (Table B-BJ5)
945.W483-.4834 Wild, John Daniel, 1902-1972 (Table B-BJ5)
945.W49-.W494 Will, Frederick L. (Table B-BJ5)
945.W7-.W74 Wright, Chauncey, 1830-1875 (Table B-BJ5)

21st century

946 General works
947.A-Z Special topics, A-Z
948.A-Z Individual philosophers, A-Z

Subarrange each by Table B-BJ5

948.C37-.C374 Card, Claudia (Table B-BJ)

Canada. British America

981 General works

Modern (1450/1600-)
By region or country
Canada. British America -- Continued
982 General special
Including special aspects of the subject as a whole
988.A-Z Special topics, A-Z
995.A-Z Individual philosophers, A-Z
Subarrange each by Table B-BJ5
995.B47-.B474 Bertrand, Pierre, 1946- (Table B-BJ5)
995.F33-.F334 Fackenheim, Emil L. (Table B-BJ5)
995.G72-.G724 Grant, George Parkin, 1918-1988 (Table B-BJ5)
995.H8-.H84 Huntsman, A. G. (Archibald Gowanlock), 1883- (Table B-BJ5)
995.L65-.L654 Lonergan, Bernard J.F. (Table B-BJ5)
995.T3-.T34 Taylor, Charles, 1931- (Table B-BJ5)
Latin America
1001 General works
1003 General special
Including special aspects of the subject as a whole
1008.A-Z Special topics, A-Z
1008.E5 Enlightenment
1008.H8 Humanism
1008.L53 Liberty
1008.M34 Man
1008.P6 Positivism
1008.P73 Pragmatism
1008.T5 Time
By region or country
1015-1019 Mexico (Table B-BJ9 modified)
1019.A-Z Individual philosophers, A-Z
Subarrange each by Table B-BJ5
1019.A45-.A454 Alonso de la Vera Cruz, fray, ca. 1507-1584 (Table B-BJ5)
1019.G28-.G284 Gaos, José, 1900-1969 (Table B-BJ5)
1019.N5-.N54 Nicol, Eduardo, 1907-1990 (Table B-BJ5)
1019.R35-.R354 Ramos, Samuel (Table B-BJ5)
1019.S28-.S284 Salmerón, Fernando, 1925- (Table B-BJ5)
1019.V3-.V34 Vasconcelos, José, 1881-1959 (Table B-BJ5)
1019.V45-.V454 Villegas, Abelardo (Table B-BJ5)
1019.V53-.V534 Villoro, Luis (Table B-BJ5)
Central America
1025 General works
1026.A-Z Individual philosophers, A-Z
Subarrange each by Table B-BJ5
Cuba and West Indies
1028 General works

	Modern (1450/1600-)
	By region or country
	Latin America
	By region or country
	Cuba and West Indies -- Continued
1029.A-Z	Individual philosophers, A-Z Subarrange each by Table B-BJ5
1029.A55-.A554	Alicea, Dennis (Table B-BJ5)
1029.C3-.C34	Caballero, José Agustín, 1762-1835 (Table B-BJ5)
1029.F35-.F354	Fanon, Frantz, 1925-1961 (Table B-BJ5)
1029.H67-.H674	Hostos, Eugenio María de, 1839-1903 (Table B-BJ5)
1029.L59-.L594	López de Medrano, Andrès, ca. 1780-1856 (Table B-BJ5)
1029.M3-.M34	Martí, José, 1853-1895 (Table B-BJ5)
1029.V29-.V294	Varela, Félix, 1788-1853 (Table B-BJ5)
	South America
1030-1034	Argentina (Table B-BJ9 modified)
1034.A-Z	Individual philosophers, A-Z Subarrange each by Table B-BJ5
1034.A8-.A84	Astrada, Carlos, 1894- (Table B-BJ5)
1034.B8-.B84	Bunge, Carlos O. (Carlos Octavio), 1875-1918 (Table B-BJ5)
1034.D87-.D874	Dussel, Enrique D. (Table B-BJ5)
1034.F46-.F464	Fernández de Agüero y Echave, Juan Manuel (Table B-BJ5)
1034.H47-.H474	Herrera Figueroa, Miguel, 1913- (Table B-BJ5)
1034.I6-.I64	Ingenieros, José, 1877-1925 (Table B-BJ5)
1034.K6-.K64	Korn, Alejandro, 1860-1936 (Table B-BJ5)
1034.M57-.M574	Mondolfo, Rodolfo, 1877-1976 (Table B-BJ5)
1034.Q54-.Q544	Quiles, Ismael (Table B-BJ5)
1034.R6-.R64	Romero, Francisco, 1891-1962 (Table B-BJ5)
1034.R67-.R674	Rougès, Alberto, 1880-1945 (Table B-BJ5)
1034.V5-.V54	Virasoro, Miguel Angel, 1900- (Table B-BJ5)
1035-1039	Bolivia (Table B-BJ9)
1040-1044	Brazil (Table B-BJ9 modified)
1044.A-Z	Individual philosophers, A-Z Subarrange each by Table B-BJ5
1044.A76-.A764	Arantes, Paulo Eduardo (Table B-BJ5)
1044.A8-.A84	Austregesilo, A. (Antonio), b. 1876 (Table B-BJ5)
1044.B28-.B284	Bandeira de Mello, Lydio Machado (Table B-BJ5)
1044.B29-.B294	Barbuy, Heraldo, 1913-1979 (Table B-BJ5)
1044.B4-.B44	Bevilaqua, Clovis, 1859-1944 (Table B-BJ5)
1044.B7-.B74	Brito, Raymundo de Farias, 1862-1917 (Table B-BJ5)
1044.C25-.C254	Cardoso, Vicente Licínio, 1889-1931 (Table B-BJ5)

Modern (1450/1600-)
By region or country
Latin America
By region or country
South America
Brazil
Individual philosophers, A-Z -- Continued
Farias Brito, Raymundo de, 1862-1917 see B1044.B7+
1044.F57-.F574 Flusser, Vilém, 1920-1991 (Table B-BJ5)
Mello, Lydio Machado Bandeira de see B1044.B28+
1044.M57-.M574 Miranda, Francisco Cavalcanti Pontes de, 1892- (Table B-BJ5)
1044.P55-.P554 Pinto, Alvaro Vieira (Table B-BJ5)
1044.R43-.R434 Reale, Miguel (Table B-BJ5)
1044.R68-.R684 Rouanet, Sérgio Paulo (Table B-BJ5)
1044.V29-.V294 Vaz, Henrique C. de Lima (Table B-BJ5)
1045-1049 Chile (Table B-BJ9 modified)
1049.A-Z Individual philosophers, A-Z
Subarrange each by Table B-BJ5
1049.M6-.M64 Molina, Enrique, 1871-1964 (Table B-BJ5)
1050-1054 Colombia (Table B-BJ9)
1055-1059 Ecuador (Table B-BJ9 modified)
1059.A-Z Individual philosophers, A-Z
Subarrange each by Table B-BJ5
1059.M68-.M684 Montalvo, Juan, 1832-1889 (Table B-BJ5)
1059.V3-.V34 Vasconez, Pablo Alfonso (Table B-BJ5)
1060-1064 Guianas (Table B-BJ9)
1065-1069 Paraguay (Table B-BJ9)
1070-1074 Peru (Table B-BJ9 modified)
1074.A-Z Individual philosophers, A-Z
Subarrange each by Table B-BJ5
1074.M57-.M574 Miró Quesada Cantuarias, Francisco, 1918- (Table B-BJ5)
1075-1079 Uruguay (Table B-BJ9 modified)
1079.A-Z Individual philosophers, A-Z
Subarrange each by Table B-BJ5
1079.A72-.A724 Ardao, Arturo (Table B-BJ5)
1079.N8-.N84 Núñez Regueiro, Manuel (Table B-BJ5)
1079.O7-.O74 Oribe, Emilio, 1893- (Table B-BJ5)
1080-1084 Venezuela (Table B-BJ9 modified)
1084.A-Z Individual philosophers, A-Z
Subarrange each by Table B-BJ5
1084.B45-.B454 Bello, Andrés, 1781-1865 (Table B-BJ5)
England. Ireland. Scotland. Wales
General works

Modern (1450/1600-)
By region or country
England. Ireland. Scotland. Wales
General works -- Continued
1111 English
1112 French
1113 German
1118.A-Z Other languages, A-Z
Special topics, A-Z
1121.P4 Platonism
1121.P7 Psychological elements
17th century
1131 General works
Special topics, A-Z
1133.C2 Cambridge Platonists
1133.K56 Knowledge, Theory of
1133.M38 Materialism
1133.P4 Pessimism
1133.S4 Scepticism
Individual philosophers
1148 A - Bacon
Subarrange each by Table B-BJ5
Bacon, Francis, 1561-1626
1150 Periodicals. Societies. Serials
1151 Dictionaries. Encyclopedias
Collected works
1153 Latin and English. By date
1154 English. By date
1155 Partial editions, extracts, selections, etc. By date
Translations
1156 Greek
1159 French
1160 German
1161 Italian
1162 Spanish and Portuguese
1163.A-Z Other. By language, A-Z, and date
Separate works
Latin works
1165-1169 Novum organu (Table B-BJ10)
1170-1174 De augmentis scientiarum (Table B-BJ10)
1180.A-Z Other, A-Z
Subarrange each by Table B-BJ13
1180.D6-.D63 De sapientia veterum (Table B-BJ13)
1180.H5-.H53 Historia vitae et mortis (Table B-BJ13)
English works
1190-1194 Advancement of learning (Table B-BJ10)
Essays see PR2206+

Modern (1450/1600-)
By region or country
England. Ireland. Scotland. Wales
17th century
Individual philosophers
Bacon, Francis, 1561-1626
Separate works
English works -- Continued
Sylva sylvarum see Q155
1195.A-Z Other, A-Z
Subarrange each by Table B-BJ13
1196 General special
1197 General works
Including biography, popular accounts, etc.
1197.5 Bacon, Alice Barnham (Bacon's wife)
1198 Criticism and interpretation
1199.A-Z Special topics, A-Z
1199.E8 Ethics
1199.H6 Homes
1199.L6 Logic
1199.M3 Man
1199.M4 Medicine
1199.M8 Mythology
1199.N38 Nature, Philosophy of
1199.O34 Objectivity
1199.P76 Progress
1199.S8 The state
1201 Bacon - Hobbes
Subarrange each by Table B-BJ5
1201.B43-.B434 Boyle, Robert, 1627-1691 (Table B-BJ5)
1201.B5-.B54 Brooke, Robert Greville, Baron, 1607-1643 (Table B-BJ5)
1201.B6-.B64 Browne, Thomas, Sir, 1605-1682 (Table B-BJ5)
1201.B7-.B74 Burthogge, Richard, 1638?-ca. 1700 (Table B-BJ5)
1201.C553-.C5534 Conway, Anne, 1631-1679 (Table B-BJ5)
1201.C6-.C64 Cudworth, Ralph, 1617-1688 (Table B-BJ5)
1201.C7-.C74 Culverwel, Nathanael, d. 1651? (Table B-BJ5)
1201.C8-.C84 Cumberland, Richard, 1631-1718 (Table B-BJ5)
1201.D2-.D24 Davies, John, Sir, 1569-1626 (Table B-BJ5)
1201.G2-.G24 Gale, Theophilus, 1628-1678 (Table B-BJ5)
1201.G5-.G54 Glanvill, Joseph, 1636-1680 (Table B-BJ5)
1201.H2-.H24 Harvey, Gideon, 1640?-1700? (Table B-BJ5)
1201.H3-.H34 Herbert of Cherbury, Edward Herbert, Baron, 1583-1648 (Table B-BJ5)
Hobbes, Thomas, 1588-1679
Collected works
1203 Latin and English

Modern (1450/1600-)
By region or country
England. Ireland. Scotland. Wales
17th century
Individual philosophers
Hobbes, Thomas, 1588-1679
Collected works
Latin and English -- Continued
1205 Partial editions, selections, etc.
Translations
1209 French
1210 German
1211 Italian
1212 Spanish and Portuguese
1214.A-Z Other languages, A-Z
Separate works
English works
Subarrange each by Table B-BJ12a
Elements of philosophy see B1239
Leviathan see JC153
Philosophical rudiments concerning government and society (his English translation of De cive) see JC153
1225 Questions concerning human liberty, necessity and chance (Table B-BJ12a)
1231 Tripos (Table B-BJ12a)
Elements of law, natural and politic see JC153
Human naturen see JC153
De corpore politico see JC153
1234 Of liberty and necessity (Table B-BJ12a)
1235.A-Z Other English works, A-Z
Latin works
Computatio see B1239
Elementa philosophica de cive see JC153
Elementorum philosophiae
Sectio I. Do corpore see QA33
1239 Part I. Computatio
1240 Sectio II. De homine
Sectio III. De cive see JC153
Examinatio et emendatio mathematicae hodiernae see QA33
1245 General special
1246 General works
Including biography, popular accounts, etc.
1247 Criticism and interpretation

Modern (1450/1600-)
By region or country
England. Ireland. Scotland. Wales
17th century
Individual philosophers
Hobbes, Thomas, 1588-1679 -- Continued
1248.A-Z Special topics, A-Z
e. g.
1248.E7 Ethics
1248.N3 Nature
1249 Hobbes - Locke
Subarrange each by Table B-BJ5
1249.L3-.L34 Le Grand, Antoine, d. 1699 (Table B-BJ5)
Locke, John, 1632-1704
Collected works
1253 English. By date
1254 Editions with commentary. By editor
1255 Partial editions, selections, etc.
Translations. By translator
1259 French
1260 German
1261 Italian
1262 Spanish and Portuguese
1263.A-Z Other languages, A-Z
Separate works
1270-1274 Conduct of the understanding (Table B-BJ10)
1280-1284 Elements of natural philosophy (Table B-BJ10)
Essay concerning human understanding
1289 Preliminary drafts. By editor
e. g.
1289.A2 Aaron
1290 Original texts. By date (Table B-BJ10)
1291 Editions with commentary. By editor (Table B-BJ10)
1292 Selections, paraphrases, etc. By date (Table B-BJ10)
1293 Translations (with or without notes). By language and translator or date (Table B-BJ10)
Assign two Cutter numbers, the first for language, the second for translator
1294 Commentaries, interpretation, and criticism (with or without translations)
1294.5.A-Z Other works, A-Z
1295 General special
1296 General works
Including biography, popular accounts, etc.

Modern (1450/1600-)
By region or country
England. Ireland. Scotland. Wales
17th century
Individual philosophers
Locke, John, 1632-1704 -- Continued
1297 Criticism and interpretation
1298.A-Z Special topics, A-Z
1298.E74 Ethics
1298.F73 Free will and determinism
1298.L36 Language and languages
1298.M4 Meaning
1298.R27 Reflection
1298.R4 Religion
1298.S64 Spirit
1298.S8 Substance
1298.U55 Universals
1299 Locke -Z
Subarrange each by Table B-BJ5
1299.L5-.L54 Lowde, James (Table B-BJ5)
1299.M6-.M64 More, Henry, 1614-1687 (Table B-BJ5)
1299.N27-.N274 Newcastle, Margaret Cavendish, Duchess of, 1624?-1674 (Table B-BJ5)
1299.N3-.N34 Newton, Isaac, Sir, 1642-1727 (Table B-BJ5)
1299.P2-.P24 Parker, Samuel, 1640-1688 (Table B-BJ5)
1299.R8-.R84 Rust, George, d. 1670 (Table B-BJ5)
1299.S6-.S64 Smith, John, 1618-1652 (Table B-BJ5)
1299.S8-.S84 Stillingfleet, Edward, 1635-1699 (Table B-BJ5)
1299.T3-.T34 Taylor, Jeremy, 1613-1667 (Table B-BJ5)
1299.W4-.W44 Whichcote, Benjamin, 1609-1683 (Table B-BJ5)
1299.W6-.W64 Worthington, John, 1618-1671 (Table B-BJ5)
18th century
1300 Collected works (nonserial)
1301 General works
1302.A-Z Special topics, A-Z
e. g.
1302.E65 Enlightenment
Individual philosophers
Class here individual English, Irish, and Welsh philosophers
For individual Scottish philosophers see B1403+
1302.5 A - Berkeley
Subarrange each by Table B-BJ5
Berkeley, George, 1685-1753
Collected works
1303 Original (vernacular) texts. By date
1304 Editions with commentary. By editor

Modern (1450/1600-)
By region or country
England. Ireland. Scotland. Wales
18th century
Individual philosophers
Berkeley, George, 1685-1753
Collected works -- Continued

1305 Partial editions, selections, etc. By editor or date

Translations
Subarrange by translator or date
Including translations with original texts

1306 Greek
1307 Latin
1308 English
1309 French
1310 German
1311 Italian
1312 Spanish and Portuguese
1313.A-Z Other languages, A-Z

Separate works

1315-1319 Alciphron (Table B-BJ10)

The querist see HC254.5

1320-1324 Siris (Table B-BJ10)
1325-1329 Three dialogues between Hylas and Philonous (Table B-BJ10)
1330-1334 Treatise on the principles of human knowledge (Table B-BJ10)
1335-1339 A new theory of vision (Table B-BJ10)
1340-1344 Commonplace book (Table B-BJ10)
1345 Spurious and apocryphal works
1346 Indexes, outlines, paraphrases, etc.
1347 Biography and memoirs (Table B-BJ14)
1348 Criticism and interpretation
1349.A-Z Special topics, A-Z
1349.A2 Abstraction
1349.C6 Concepts
1349.E8 Ethics
1349.G4 Geneticism
1349.I47 Immaterialism
1349.M35 Matter
1349.M47 Metaphysics
1349.O56 Ontology
1349.P4 Perception. Vision
1349.P45 Philosophical theology
1349.U6 Unity
1349.U8 Utilitarianism

Vision see B1349.P4

Modern (1450/1600-)
By region or country
England. Ireland. Scotland. Wales
18th century
Individual philosophers -- Continued

1352 Berkeley - Bolingbroke
Subarrange each by Table B-BJ5
1355-1358 Bolingbroke, Henry St. John, Viscount, 1678-1751 (Table B-BJ3a)
1359 Bolingbroke - Browne
Subarrange each by Table B-BJ5
1361 Browne, Peter, ca. 1666-1735 (Table B-BJ4)
1362 Browne - Butler
Subarrange each by Table B-BJ5
1363 Butler, Joseph, 1692-1752 (Table B-BJ4)
1364 Butler - Clarke
Subarrange each by Table B-BJ5
1365 Clarke, Samuel, 1675-1729 (Table B-BJ4)
1366 Clarke - Collins
Subarrange each by Table B-BJ5
1366.C6-.C64 Collier, Arthur, 1680-1732 (Table B-BJ5)
1367 Collins, Anthony, 1676-1729 (Table B-BJ4)
1368 Collins - Conybeare
Subarrange each by Table B-BJ5
1369 Conybeare, William Daniel, 1787-1857 (Table B-BJ4)
1370 Conybeare - Darwin
Subarrange each by Table B-BJ5
1371 Darwin, Erasmus, 1731-1802 (Table B-BJ4)
1373 Darwin - Hartley
Subarrange each by Table B-BJ5
1373.D7-.D74 Drummond, William, Sir, 1770?-1828 (Table B-BJ5)
1373.F67-.F674 Fordyce, David, 1711-1751 (Table B-BJ5)
1375-1378 Hartley, David, 1705-1757 (Table B-BJ3a)
1379 Hartley - Mandeville
Subarrange each by Table B-BJ5
1379.H8-.H84 Hutton, James, 1726-1797 (Table B-BJ5)
1381 Mandeville, Bernard, 1670-1733 (Table B-BJ4)
1382 Mandeville - Priestley
Subarrange each by Table B-BJ5
1382.P2-.P24 Paley, William, 1743-1805 (Table B-BJ5)
1383 Priestley, Joseph, 1733-1804 (Table B-BJ4)
1384 Priestley - Shaftesbury
Subarrange each by Table B-BJ5
1385-1388 Shaftesbury, Anthony Ashley Cooper, Earl of, 1671-1713 (Table B-BJ3a)
1390 Shaftesbury - Tindal
Subarrange each by Table B-BJ5

Modern (1450/1600-)
By region or country
England. Ireland. Scotland. Wales
18th century
Individual philosophers
Shaftesbury - Tindal -- Continued
1390.T4-.T4 Taylor, Brook, 1685-1731 (Table B-BJ5)
1391 Tindal, Matthew, 1653?-1733 (Table B-BJ4)
1392 Tindal - Toland
Subarrange each by Table B-BJ5
1393 Toland, John, 1670-1722 (Table B-BJ4)
1394 Toland - Wollaston
Subarrange each by Table B-BJ5
1394.T6-.T64 Tucker, Abraham, 1705-1774 (Table B-BJ5)
1394.W2-.W24 Watts, Isaac, 1674-1748 (Table B-BJ5)
1396 Wollaston - Woolston
Subarrange each by Table B-BJ5
1397 Woolston, Thomas, 1670-1733 (Table B-BJ4)
1398 Woolston - Z
Subarrange each by Table B-BJ5
Scottish philosophers, 18th and early 19th centuries
1401 General works
1402.A-Z Special topics, A-Z
1402.E55 Enlightenment
Social sciences
see class H
Individual philosophers
1403 A - Brown
Subarrange each by Table B-BJ5
1403.B3-.B34 Balfour, James, 1705-1795 (Table B-BJ5)
1403.B5-.B54 Beattie, James, 1735-1803 (Table B-BJ5)
1405-1408 Brown, Thomas, 1778-1820 (Table B-BJ3a)
1409 Brown - Ferguson
Subarrange each by Table B-BJ5
1410-1418 Ferguson, Adam, 1723-1816 (Table B-BJ2)
1419 Ferguson - Hamilton
Subarrange each by Table B-BJ5
1419.G47-.G474 Gerard, Alexander, 1728-1795 (Table B-BJ5)
1420-1428 Hamilton, William, Sir, 1788-1856 (Table B-BJ2 modified)
1428.A-Z Special topics, A-Z
1428.A25 Absolute, The
1430 Hamilton - Home
Subarrange each by Table B-BJ5
1435 Home, Henry, Lord Kames, 1696-1782 (Table B-BJ4)
1440 Home - Hume
Subarrange each by Table B-BJ5

Modern (1450/1600-)
By region or country
England. Ireland. Scotland. Wales
Scottish philosophers, 18th and early 19th centuries
Individual philosophers -- Continued
Hume, David, 1711-1776

1450 Periodicals. Societies. Serials
1451 Dictionaries
Collected works
1453 Original (vernacular) texts. By date
1454 Editions with commentary. By editor
1455 Partial editions, selections, etc. By editor or date
Translations
Subarrange by translator or date
Including translations with original texts
1456 Greek
1457 Latin
1458 English
1459 French
1460 German
1461 Italian
1462 Spanish and Portuguese
1463.A-Z Other languages, A-Z
Separate works
1465-1469 An enquiry concerning the principles of morals (Table B-BJ10)
1470-1474 Essays, moral and political (Table B-BJ10)
1475-1479 Essays, moral and political and literary (Table B-BJ10)
1480-1484 Philosophical essays concerning human understanding (Table B-BJ10)
1485-1489 A treatise of human nature (Table B-BJ10)
1493.A-Z Other works, A-Z
Subarrange each by Table B-BJ13
e. g.
1493.F64-.F643 Four dissertations (Table B-BJ13)
1495 Spurious and apocryphal works
1496 Indexes, outlines, paraphrases, etc.
1497 Biography and memoirs (Table B-BJ14)
1498 Criticism and interpretation
1499.A-Z Special topics, A-Z
1499.A4 Aesthetics
1499.B4 Belief and doubt
Body and mind see B1499.M47
1499.C38 Causation
1499.D4 Deism
1499.E45 Emotions

Modern (1450/1600-)
By region or country
England. Ireland. Scotland. Wales
Scottish philosophers, 18th and early 19th centuries
Individual philosophers
Hume, David, 1711-1776
Special topics, A-Z -- Continued

1499.E8 Ethics
1499.I6 Imagination
1499.I65 Inductive logic
1499.I67 Infinite
1499.J86 Justice
1499.K7 Knowledge, Theory of
1499.M47 Mind and body
1499.M5 The miraculous
1499.N37 Naturalism
1499.O57 Ontology
Passions see B1499.E45
1499.P7 Probabilities
1499.R4 Reason
1499.R45 Religion
1499.S4 Scepticism
1499.S45 Self
1499.S9 Sympathy
1499.5 Hume - Hutcheson
Subarrange each by Table B-BJ5
1500-1504 Hutcheson, Francis, 1694-1746 (Table B-BJ3 modified)
1504.A-Z Special topics, A-Z
1504.A33 Aesthetics
1507 Hutcheson - Mackintosh
Subarrange each by Table B-BJ5
Kames, Henry Home, Lord, 1696-1782 see B1435
1510-1518 Mackintosh, James, Sir, 1765-1832 (Table B-BJ2)
1519 Mackintosh - Monboddo
Subarrange each by Table B-BJ5
1520 Monboddo, James Burnett, Lord, 1714-1799 (Table B-BJ4)
1523 Monboddo - Oswald
Subarrange each by Table B-BJ5
1525 Oswald, James, d. 1793 (Table B-BJ4)
1527 Oswald - Reid
Subarrange each by Table B-BJ5
1530-1538 Reid, Thomas, 1710-1796 (Table B-BJ2)
1540 Reid - Smith
Subarrange each by Table B-BJ5
1545 Smith, Adam, 1723-1790 (Table B-BJ4)

Modern (1450/1600-)
By region or country
England. Ireland. Scotland. Wales
Scottish philosophers, 18th and early 19th centuries
Individual philosophers -- Continued

1547 Smith - Stewart
Subarrange each by Table B-BJ5

1550-1558 Stewart, Dugald, 1753-1828 (Table B-BJ2)

1559 Stewart - Z
Subarrange each by Table B-BJ5

19th and 20th centuries
General works

1561 English

1562 French

1563 German

1565.A-Z Other languages, A-Z

1567 General special
Including special aspects of the subject as a whole

Evolution see B818.A+

1568 Neo-Hegelianism
Class here 19th century English only

1568.5 Positivism

1569 Rationalism
Class here 19th century English only
Cf. B833.A1+ Rationalism (Modern)

1571 Utilitarianism

Earlier 19th century to 1860/1870

1573 General works

Individual philosophers
Class here individual English, Irish, and Welsh philosophers
For individual Scottish philosophers see B1403+

1574 A - Carlyle
Subarrange each by Table B-BJ5

1574.B3-.B34 Bentham, Jeremy, 1748-1832 (Table B-BJ5)

1574.B4-.B44 Blakey, Robert, 1795-1878 (Table B-BJ5)

1575-1578 Carlyle, Thomas, 1795-1881 (Table B-BJ3a)

1579 Carlyle - Coleridge
Subarrange each by Table B-BJ5

1583 Coleridge, Samuel Taylor, 1772-1834 (Table B-BJ4)

1584 Coleridge - Ferrier
Subarrange each by Table B-BJ5

1584.D5-.D54 Doherty, Hugh, d. 1891 (Table B-BJ5)

1585-1588 Ferrier, James Frederick, 1808-1864 (Table B-BJ3a)

Modern (1450/1600-)
By region or country
England. Ireland. Scotland. Wales
19th and 20th centuries
Earlier 19th century to 1860/1870
Individual philosophers -- Continued

1589 Ferrier - Lewes
Subarrange each by Table B-BJ5
1589.F4-.F44 Field, George, 1777?-1854 (Table B-BJ5)
1589.F7-.F74 Fraser, Alexander Campbell, 1819-1914 (Table B-BJ5)
1589.G75-.G754 Grote, George, 1794-1871 (Table B-BJ5)
1589.G8-.G84 Grote, John, d. 1866 (Table B-BJ5)
1589.H4-.H44 Hinton, James, 1822-1875 (Table B-BJ5)
1593 Lewes, George Henry, 1817-1878 (Table B-BJ4)
1594 Lewes - Mill
Subarrange each by Table B-BJ5
1594.M3-.M34 Mansel, Henry, 1820-1871 Longueville (Table B-BJ5)
1595-1598 Mill, James, 1773-1836 (Table B-BJ3a)
1599 Mill, James - Mill, John
Subarrange each by Table B-BJ5
1600-1608 Mill, John Stuart, 1806-1873 (Table B-BJ2 modified)
1608.A-Z Special topics, A-Z
1608.E6 Empiricism
1608.E8 Ethics
1608.L3 Language
1608.L5 Liberalism
1608.L6 Logic
1608.P7 Psychology
1608.R44 Religion
1608.S45 Semantics
1609 Mill - Smith
Subarrange each by Table B-BJ5
1609.S3-.S34 Saumarez, Richard, 1764-1835 (Table B-BJ5)
1611 Smith, Sydney, 1771-1845 (Table B-BJ4)
1612 Smith - Z
Subarrange each by Table B-BJ5
1612.W3-.W34 Wedgwood, Hensleigh, 1803-1891 (Table B-BJ5)
1612.W45-.W454 Whately, Richard, 1787-1863 (Table B-BJ5)
1612.W5-.W54 Whewell, William, 1794-1866 (Table B-BJ5)

Later 19th and 20th centuries
1614 Collected works (nonserial)
1615 General works
1616.A-Z Special topics, A-Z
1616.A53 Analysis

Modern (1450/1600-)
By region or country
England. Ireland. Scotland. Wales
19th and 20th centuries
Later 19th and 20th centuries
Special topics, A-Z -- Continued

1616.I5 Idealism
1616.P6 Positivism
1616.R3 Realism
1616.S87 Structuralism

Individual philosophers

1618 A - Darwin
Subarrange each by Table B-BJ5

1618.A4-.A44 Alexander, Samuel, 1859-1938 (Table B-BJ5)
1618.A57-.A574 Anscombe, G. E. M. (Gertrude Elizabeth Margaret) (Table B-BJ5)
1618.A7-.A74 Appleton, Charles Edward Cutts Birch, 1841-1879 (Table B-BJ5)
1618.A8-.A84 Austin, J. L. (John Langshaw), 1911-1960 (Table B-BJ5)
1618.A9-.A94 Ayer, A. J. (Alfred Jules), 1910-1989 (Table B-BJ5)
1618.B15-.B154 Baillie, J. B. (James Black), Sir, 1872-1940 (Table B-BJ5)
1618.B2-.B24 Bain, Alexander, 1810-1877 (Table B-BJ5)
1618.B28-.B284 Barfield, Owen, 1898-1997 (Table B-BJ5)
1618.B3-.B34 Bax, Ernest Belfort, 1854-1926 (Table B-BJ5)
Bennett, John G. (John Godolphin), 1897-1974 see BP610.B46+
1618.B45-.B454 Berlin, Isaiah, 1909-1997 (Table B-BJ5)
1618.B47-.B474 Bhaskar, Roy, 1944- (Table B-BJ5)
1618.B5-.B54 Bosanquet, Bernard, 1848-1923 (Table B-BJ5)
1618.B6-.B64 Bowman, Archibald Allan, 1883-1936 (Table B-BJ5)
1618.B7-.B74 Bradley, F. H. (Francis Herbert), 1846-1924 (Table B-BJ5)
1618.B743-.B7434 Branford, Benchara (Table B-BJ5)
1618.B77-.B774 Burke, John Benjamin Butler, 1873- (Table B-BJ5)
1618.B8-.B84 Burns, Cecil Delisle, 1879-1942 (Table B-BJ5)
1618.C2-.C24 Caird, Edward, 1835-1908 (Table B-BJ5)
1618.C3-.C34 Carr, Herbert Wildon, 1857-1931 (Table B-BJ5)
1618.C57-.C574 Clark, Stephen R. L. (Table B-BJ5)
1618.C6-.C64 Clifford, William Kingdon, 1845-1879 (Table B-BJ5)
1618.C65-.C654 Cohen, Jacques Judah, 1883- (Table B-BJ5)

Modern (1450/1600-)
By region or country
England. Ireland. Scotland. Wales
19th and 20th centuries
Later 19th and 20th centuries
Individual philosophers
A - Darwin -- Continued

1618.C7-.C74 Collingwood, R. G. (Robin George), 1889-1943 (Table B-BJ5)

1618.C8-.C84 Crozier, John Beattie, 1849-1921 (Table B-BJ5)

1620-1623 Darwin, Charles, 1809-1882 (Table B-BJ3a)

1626 Darwin - Green
Subarrange each by Table B-BJ5

1626.D47-.D474 Desmond, William, 1951- (Table B-BJ5)

1626.D5-.D54 Dixon, W. Macneile (William Macneile), 1866-1945 (Table B-BJ5)

1626.D85-.D854 Dummett, Michael A.E. (Table B-BJ5)

1626.E4-.E44 Ellis, Havelock, 1859-1939 (Table B-BJ5)

1626.E92-.E924 Evans, Gareth (Table B-BJ5)

1626.F56-.F564 Findlay, J. N. (John Niemeyer), 1903-1987 (Table B-BJ5)

1626.F567-.F5674 Finnis, John (Table B-BJ5)

1626.F573-.F5734 Flew, Antony, 1923-2010 (Table B-BJ5)

1626.G44-.G444 Gellner, Ernest (Table B-BJ5)

1626.G7-.G74 Graham, A. C. (Angus Charles) (Table B-BJ5)

1630-1638 Green, Thomas Hill, 1836-1882 (Table B-BJ2 modified)

1638.A-Z Special topics, A-Z

1638.E8 Ethics

1641 Green -Gz
Subarrange each by Table B-BJ5

1641.G48-.G484 Grice, H.P. (H. Paul) (Table B-BJ5)

1641.G5-.G54 Gurnhill, James, 1836-1928 (Table B-BJ5)

1645 H - Harrison
Subarrange each by Table B-BJ5

1645.H3-.H34 Haldane, J. S. (John Scott), 1860-1936 (Table B-BJ5)

1645.H4-.H44 Haldane, R. B. Haldane (Richard Burdon Haldane), Viscount, 1856-1928 (Table B-BJ5)

1646 Harrison - Lz
Subarrange each by Table B-BJ5

1646.H2-.H24 Harrison, Frederic, 1831-1923 (Table B-BJ5)

1646.H26-.H264 Harrison, Jonathan (Table B-BJ5)

1646.H65-.H654 Hobhouse, L. T. (Leonard Trelawny), 1864-1929 (Table B-BJ5)

1646.H7-.H74 Hodgson, Shadworth Hollway, 1832-1912 (Table B-BJ5)

	Modern (1450/1600-)
	By region or country
	England. Ireland. Scotland. Wales
	19th and 20th centuries
	Later 19th and 20th centuries
	Individual philosophers
	Harrison - Lz -- Continued
1646.H75-.H754	Hollis, Martin (Table B-BJ5)
1646.H76-.H764	Honderich, Ted (Table B-BJ5)
1646.H8-.H84	Hulme, T. E. (Thomas Ernest), 1883-1917 (Table B-BJ5)
1646.J7-.J74	Joad, C. E. M. (Cyril Edwin Mitchinson), 1891-1953 (Table B-BJ5)
1646.J8-.J84	Jones, Henry, Sir, 1852-1922 (Table B-BJ5)
1646.J862-.J8624	Jones, John Robert, 1911-1970 (Table B-BJ5)
1646.K46-.K464	Kenny, Anthony, 1931- (Table B-BJ5)
1646.K777-.K7774	Kolnai, Aurel (Table B-BJ5)
1646.L3-.L34	Laurie, Simon Somerville, 1829-1909 (Table B-BJ5)
1646.L48-.L484	Levy, H. (Hyman), 1889- (Table B-BJ5)
1646.L6-.L64	Lindsay, James, 1852-1923 (Table B-BJ5)
1646.L7-.L74	Lodge, Oliver, Sir, 1851-1940 (Table B-BJ5)
1647	M - Nettleship Subarrange each by Table B-BJ5
1647.M12-.M124	MacIntyre, Alasdair C. (Table B-BJ5)
1647.M13-.M134	Macmurray, John, 1891-1976 (Table B-BJ5)
1647.M14-.M144	McDowell, John Henry (Table B-BJ5)
1647.M15-.M154	McTaggart, John McTaggart Ellis, 1866-1925 (Table B-BJ5)
1647.M186-.M1864	Magee, Bryan (Table B-BJ5)
1647.M2-.M24	Martineau, James, 1805-1900 (Table B-BJ5)
1647.M4-.M44	Merz, John Theodore, 1840-1922 (Table B-BJ5)
1647.M47-.M474	Midgley, Mary, 1919- (Table B-BJ5)
1647.M5-.M54	Mitchell, William, Sir, 1861- (Table B-BJ5)
1647.M7-.M74	Moore, G. E. (George Edward), 1873-1958 (Table B-BJ5)
1647.M76-.M764	Morgan, Conway Lloyd (Table B-BJ5)
1647.M8-.M84	Muirhead, John H. (John Henry), 1855-1940 (Table B-BJ5)
1648	Nettleship, Richard Lewis, 1846-1892 (Table B-BJ4)
1649	Nettleship - Spencer Subarrange each by Table B-BJ5
1649.O34-.O344	Oakeshott, Michael, 1901-1990 (Table B-BJ5)
1649.P37-.P374	Parfit, Derek (Table B-BJ5)
1649.P6-.P64	Popper, Karl R. (Karl Raimund), 1902-1994 (Table B-BJ5)

Modern (1450/1600-)
By region or country
England. Ireland. Scotland. Wales
19th and 20th centuries
Later 19th and 20th centuries
Individual philosophers
Nettleship - Spencer -- Continued

1649.R25-.R254 Ramsey, Frank Plumpton, 1903-1930 (Table B-BJ5)
1649.R28-.R284 Ramsey, Ian T. (Table B-BJ5)
1649.R38-.R384 Ritchie, Arthur David, 1891-1967 (Table B-BJ5)
1649.R4-.R44 Ritchie, David George, 1853-1903 (Table B-BJ5)
1649.R5-.R54 Robertson, George Croom, 1842-1892 (Table B-BJ5)
1649.R6-.R64 Romanes, George John, 1848-1894 (Table B-BJ5)
1649.R7-.R74 Rose, Gillian (Table B-BJ5)
1649.R78-.R784 Roth, Leon, 1896-1963 (Table B-BJ5)
1649.R9-.R94 Russell, Bertrand, 1872-1970 (Table B-BJ5)
1649.R96-.R964 Ryle, Gilbert, 1900-1976 (Table B-BJ5)
1649.S15-.S154 Sainsbury, Geoffrey (Table B-BJ5)
1649.S21-.S214 Samuel, Herbert Louis Samuel, Viscount, 1870-1963 (Table B-BJ5)
1649.S23-.S234 Schiller, F. C. S. (Ferdinand Canning Scott), 1864-1937 (Table B-BJ5)
1649.S247-.S2474 Scruton, Roger (Table B-BJ5)
1649.S26-.S264 Searle, John R. (Table B-BJ5)
1649.S29-.S294 Seth, James, 1860-1924 (Table B-BJ5)
1649.S3-.S34 Seth Pringle-Pattison, A. (Andrew), 1856-1931 (Table B-BJ5)
1649.S375-.S3754 Sibley, Frank, 1923-1996 (Table B-BJ5)
1649.S4-.S44 Sidgwick, Henry, 1838-1900 (Table B-BJ5)
1649.S8-.S84 Spalding, Kenneth Jay, 1879- (Table B-BJ5)
1650-1658 Spencer, Herbert, 1820-1903 (Table B-BJ2)
1663 Spencer - Stirling
Subarrange each by Table B-BJ5
1665 Stirling, James Hutchison, 1820-1909 (Table B-BJ4)
1667 Stirling - Sz
Subarrange each by Table B-BJ5
1667.S25-.S254 Stocks, J. L. (John Leofric), 1882-1937 (Table B-BJ5)
1667.S3-.S34 Stokes, Adrian, 1902-1972 (Table B-BJ5)
1667.S37-.S374 Stout, George Frederick, 1860-1944 (Table B-BJ5)
1667.S38-.S384 Strawson, P.F. (Table B-BJ5)

Modern (1450/1600-)
By region or country
England. Ireland. Scotland. Wales
19th and 20th centuries
Later 19th and 20th centuries
Individual philosophers
Stirling - Sz -- Continued

1667.S4-.S44 Strong, Charles Augustus, 1862-1940 (Table B-BJ5)
1667.S5-.S54 Sully, James, 1842-1923 (Table B-BJ5)
1669 T - Wallace
Subarrange each by Table B-BJ5
1669.T2-.T24 Taylor, A. E. (Alfred Edward), 1869-1945 (Table B-BJ5)
1669.T3-.T34 Temple, William, 1881-1944 (Table B-BJ5)
1669.T5-.T54 Thomas, Elystan (Table B-BJ5)
1669.T57-.T574 Thomas, John, M.A. (Table B-BJ5)
1669.U8-.U84 Ussher, Arland (Table B-BJ5)
1669.V4-.V44 Veitch, John, 1829-1894 (Table B-BJ5)
1671 Wallace, William (Table B-BJ4)
1674 Wallace - Z
Subarrange each by Table B-BJ5
1674.W33-.W334 Ward, James, 1843-1925 (Table B-BJ5)
1674.W3348-.W33484 Warnock, G.J. (Geoffrey James), 1923- (Table B-BJ5)
1674.W335-.W3354 Warnock, Mary (Table B-BJ5)
1674.W337-.W3374 Wassermann, Gerhard D. (Table B-BJ5)
1674.W34-.W344 Watkin, E. I. (Edward Ingram), 1888-1981 (Table B-BJ5)
1674.W35-.W354 Whitehead, Alfred North, 1861-1947 (Table B-BJ5)
1674.W4-.W44 Whittaker, Thomas, 1856-1935 (Table B-BJ5)
1674.W49-.W494 Wiggins, David (Table B-BJ5)
1674.W495-.W4954 Williamson, Timothy (Table B-BJ5)
1674.W5-.W54 Wilson, John Cook, 1849-1915 (Table B-BJ5)
1674.W64-.W644 Wollheim, Richard, 1923-2003 (Table B-BJ5)
Scottish philosophers, 20th century
1681 General works
1682.A-Z Special topics, A-Z
France
General works
1801 English
1802 French
1803 German
1805.A-Z Other languages, A-Z
1809.A-Z Special topics, A-Z
1809.B62 Body, Human

Modern (1450/1600-)
By region or country
France
Special topics, A-Z -- Continued
1809.M3 Materialism
Cf. B1925.M25 18th century
1809.M7 Moralists
1809.S85 Subject
1809.T72 Travel
By period
17th century
1815 General works
1818.A-Z Special topics, A-Z
1818.C6 Court and courtiers
1818.L5 Libertines
Cf. PQ1130.L5 Libertinage
1818.M56 Mind and body
1818.O3 Occasionalism
1818.S3 Scepticism
Individual philosophers
1824 A - Bayle
Subarrange each by Table B-BJ5
1824.A86-.A864 Arnauld, Antoine, 1612-1694 (Table B-BJ5)
1825 Bayle, Pierre, 1647-1706 (Table B-BJ4)
1828 Bayle - Descartes
Subarrange each by Table B-BJ5
Descartes, René, 1596-1650
1830 Periodicals. Societies. Serials
1831 Dictionaries, lexicons, etc.
Collected works
1833 Original editions. By date
1835 Partial editions, selections, etc. By editor
Translations
1836.A-Z Latin. By translator, A-Z
1837.A-Z English. By translator, A-Z
1838.A-Z German. By translator, A-Z
1839.A-Z Italian. By translator, A-Z
Spanish and Portuguese. By translator, A-Z
1842.A-Z Other. By language and translator
Assign two cutters, the first for language, the second for translator
Separate works
1845-1849 Discours de la methode (Table B-BJ10)
1850-1854 Meditationes de prima philosophia (Table B-BJ10)
1855-1859 Les passions de l'ame (Table B-BJ10)
1860-1864 Principia philosophiae (Table B-BJ10)

Modern (1450/1600-)
By region or country
France
By period
17th century
Individual philosophers
Descartes, René, 1596-1650
Separate works -- Continued

1868.A-Z Other works, A-Z
e. g.
1868.R33 Recherche de la vérité par les lumières naturelles
1868.R4 Regulae ad directionem ingenii
1871 Indexes, outlines, paraphrases, etc.
1873 General works
Including biography, popular accounts, etc.
1875 Criticism and interpretation
1878.A-Z Special topics, A-Z
1878.A27 Act
1878.A4 Aesthetics
1878.A73 Architecture
1878.C3 Causation
1878.D82 Dualism
1878.E7 Ethics
1878.G7 God
1878.I5 Imagination
1878.I56 Inference
1878.K6 Knowledge, Theory of
1878.L34 Language
1878.M28 Material falsity
Mathematics
see class QA
1878.M43 Mechanism
1878.M5 Metaphysics
1878.M55 Mind and body
1878.M85 Music
1878.N3 Nature
1878.P47 Perception
1878.P49 Physiology
1878.R37 Reasoning
1878.R4 Religion
1878.R44 Representation
1878.R47 Rhetoric
1878.S55 Skepticism
1878.S67 Space and time
1878.S78 Subjectivity
1878.T44 Theodicy

Modern (1450/1600-)
By region or country
France
By period
17th century
Individual philosophers
Descartes, René, 1596-1650
Special topics, A-Z -- Continued

1878.T45 Theology
1878.T7 Transcendentalism
1878.W5 Will
1878.5 Descartes - Gassendi
Subarrange each by Table B-BJ5
1880-1888 Gassendi, Pierre, 1592-1655 (Table B-BJ2)
1889 Gassendi - Malebranche
Subarrange each by Table B-BJ5
1889.H7-.H74 Huet, Pierre-Daniel, 1630-1721 (Table B-BJ5)
1889.L15-.L154 La Grange, J. B. de (Jean Baptiste) (Table B-BJ5)
1889.L18-.L184 La Mothe Le Vayer, François de, 1583-1672 (Table B-BJ5)
1889.L3-.L34 Le Clerc, Jean, 1657-1736 (Table B-BJ5)
1890-1898 Malebranche, Nicolas, 1638-1715 (Table B-BJ2 modified)
1898.A-Z Special topics, A-Z
1898.E8 Ethics
1898.E95 Extension
1898.G6 God
1898.I39 Idea
1898.M4 Metaphysics
1898.S68 Soul
1899 Malebranche - Pascal
Subarrange each by Table B-BJ5
1899.M4-.M44 Mersenne, Marin, 1588-1648 (Table B-BJ5)
1900-1904 Pascal, Blaise, 1623-1662 (Table B-BJ3 modified)
1904.A-Z Special topics, A-Z
1904.E7 Ethics
1904.H86 Humanism
1904.M48 Methodology
1904.P52 Play
1904.R36 Reason
1904.S8 Suffering
1904.W58 Wit and humor
1907 Pascal - Z
Subarrange each by Table B-BJ5

18th century
1911 General works
1914-1925 Special topics

Modern (1450/1600-)
By region or country
France
By period
18th century
Special topics -- Continued

1914 Ideology
1917 Scepticism
1921 Traditionalism
1925.A-Z Other, A-Z
1925.E5 Enlightenment
1925.M25 Materialism
1925.M3 Matter
1925.P6 Positivism

Individual philosophers

1928 A - Alembert
Subarrange each by Table B-BJ5
1930-1938 Alembert, Jean Le Rond d', 1717-1783 (Table B-BJ2)
1939 Alembert - Bonnet
Subarrange each by Table B-BJ5
1939.A5-.A54 André, Yves Marie, 1675-1764 (Table B-BJ5)
1939.A6-.A64 Argens, Jean Baptiste de Boyer, marquis d', 1704-1771 (Table B-BJ5)
1939.A8-.A84 Azaïs, P. H. (Pierre Hyacinthe), 1766-1845 (Table B-BJ5)
1940-1948 Bonnet, Charles, 1720-1793 (Table B-BJ2)
1949 Bonnet - Bossuet
Subarrange each by Table B-BJ5
1950-1958 Bossuet, Jacques Bénigne, 1627-1704 (Table B-BJ2)
Cf. BX890 Roman Catholic Church
Cf. JC155 Political theory
Cf. PQ1725+ French literature
1959 Bossuet - Buffon
Subarrange each by Table B-BJ5
1959.B6-.B64 Boulanger, Nicolas Antoine (Table B-BJ5)
1959.B7-.B74 Buffier, Claude, 1661-1737 (Table B-BJ5)
1960-1968 Buffon, Georges Louis Leclerc, comte de, 1707-1788 (Table B-BJ2)
1969 Buffon - Cabanis
Subarrange each by Table B-BJ5
1970-1978 Cabanis, P. J. G. (Pierre Jean Georges), 1757-1808 (Table B-BJ2)
1979 Cabanis - Condillac
Subarrange each by Table B-BJ5

Modern (1450/1600-)
By region or country
France
By period
18th century
Individual philosophers
Cabanis - Condillac -- Continued

1979.C3-.C34 Cartaud de La Villate, François, 1700?-1737 (Table B-BJ5)

1980-1988 Condillac, Étienne Bonnot de, 1714-1780 (Table B-BJ2)

1989 Condillac - Condorcet
Subarrange each by Table B-BJ5

1990-1998 Condorcet, Jean-Antoine-Nicolas de Caritat, marquis de, 1743-1794 (Table B-BJ2)

1999 Condorcet - Destutt
Subarrange each by Table B-BJ5

2000-2008 Destutt de Tracy, Antoine Louis Claude, comte, 1754-1836 (Table B-BJ2)

2009 Destutt - Diderot
Subarrange each by Table B-BJ5

2010-2018 Diderot, Denis, 1713-1784 (Table B-BJ2 modified)
2018.A-Z Special topics, A-Z
2018.A4 Aesthetics
2018.E9 Ethics
2018.H64 Holism
Jews see B2018.J83
2018.J83 Judaism. Jews
2018.M3 Materialism

2019 Diderot - Fontenelle
Subarrange each by Table B-BJ5

2019.D8-.D84 Dupont de Nemours, Pierre Samuel, 1739-1817 (Table B-BJ5)

2020-2028 Fontenelle, M. de (Bernard Le Bovier), 1657-1757 (Table B-BJ2)

2029 Fontenelle - Fz
Subarrange each by Table B-BJ5

2029.F74-.F744 Fréret, Nicolas, 1688-1749 (Table B-BJ5)

2037 G - Gz
Subarrange each by Table B-BJ5

2037.G4-.G44 Gérard, Philippe Louis, 1737-1813 (Table B-BJ5)

2039 H - Helvetius
Subarrange each by Table B-BJ5

2040-2048 Helvétius, 1715-1771 (Table B-BJ2)

2049 Helvéticus - Holbach
Subarrange each by Table B-BJ5

Modern (1450/1600-)
By region or country
France
By period
18th century
Individual philosophers -- Continued

2050-2058 Holbach, Paul Henri Thiry, baron d', 1723-1789 (Table B-BJ2)

2059 Holbach - La Mettrie
Subarrange each by Table B-BJ5

2060-2068 La Mettrie, Julien Offray de, 1709-1751 (Table B-BJ2)

2069 La Mettrie - Lz
Subarrange each by Table B-BJ5

2075 M - Maupertuis
Subarrange each by Table B-BJ5

2080-2088 Maupertuis, 1698-1759 (Table B-BJ2)

2089 Maupertuis - Montesquieu
Subarrange each by Table B-BJ5

2090-2098 Montesquieu, Charles de Secondat, baron de, 1689-1755 (Table B-BJ2 modified)

2098.A-Z Special topics, A-Z

2098.E8 Ethics

2098.S6 Sociology of knowledge

2099 Montesquieu - Morelly
Subarrange each by Table B-BJ5

2100-2108 Morelly, M. (Table B-BJ2)

2109 Morelly - Quesnay
Subarrange each by Table B-BJ5

2109.N3-.N34 Naigeon, Jacques André, 1738-1810 (Table B-BJ5)

2110-2118 Quesnay, François, 1694-1774 (Table B-BJ2)

2119 Quesnay - Robinet
Subarrange each by Table B-BJ5

2120-2128 Robinet, J. B. (Jean Baptiste), 1735-1820 (Table B-BJ2)

2129 Robinet - Rousseau
Subarrange each by Table B-BJ5

2130-2138 Rousseau, Jean Jacques, 1712-1778 (Table B-BJ2 modified)
Cf. JC179 Political theory
Cf. LA121+ History of education
Cf. LB510+ Theory of education
Cf. PQ2030+ French literature

2138.A-Z Special topics, A-Z

2138.A37 Aesthetics

2138.A55 Alienation

Modern (1450/1600-)
By region or country
France
By period
18th century
Individual philosophers
Rousseau, Jean Jacques, 1712-1778
Special topics, A-Z -- Continued

2138.D47 Desire
2138.E8 Ethics
2138.H95 Humor
2138.I45 Imagination
2138.L67 Love
2138.M3 Man
2138.P45 Perception
2138.R4 Religion
2138.W37 War
2139 Rousseau - Saint-Martin
Subarrange each by Table B-BJ5
2145 Saint-Martin, Louis Claude de, 1743-1803 (Table B-BJ4)
2146 Saint-Martin - Sz
Subarrange each by Table B-BJ5
2147 T - Turgot
Subarrange each by Table B-BJ5
2147.T5-.T54 Tiphaigne de La Roche, Charles François, 1722-1774 (Table B-BJ5)
2150-2158 Turgot, Anne Robert Jacques, baron de l'Aulne, 1727-1781 (Table B-BJ2)
2159 Turgot - Volney
Subarrange each by Table B-BJ5
2160-2168 Volney, C.-F. (Constantin-François), 1757-1820 (Table B-BJ2)
2169 Volney - Voltaire
Subarrange each by Table B-BJ5
2170-2178 Voltaire, 1694-1778 (Table B-BJ2)
2178.A-Z Special topics, A-Z
2178.F9 Free will
2179 Voltaire - Z
Subarrange each by Table B-BJ5

19th century
2185 General works
2188.A-Z Special topics, A-Z
e. g.
2188.M9 Mysticism
2188.P7 Pragmatism
Individual philosophers

Modern (1450/1600-)
By region or country
France
By period
19th century
Individual philosophers -- Continued

2189 A - Alliot
Subarrange each by Table B-BJ5
2190 Alliot, François, b. l798 (Table B-BJ4)
2190.5 Alliot - Ampère
Subarrange each by Table B-BJ5
2191 Ampère, André Marie, 1775-1836 (Table B-BJ4)
2192 Ampère - Binet
Subarrange each by Table B-BJ5
2192.B3-.B34 Bautain, L. (Louis), 1796-1867 (Table B-BJ5)
2192.B4-.B44 Bernard, Claude, 1813-1878 (Table B-BJ5)
2193 Binet, Alfred, 1857-1911 (Table B-BJ4)
2194 Binet - Caro
Subarrange each by Table B-BJ5
2194.B4-.B44 Bonald, Louis-Gabriel-Ambroise, vicomte de, 1754-1840 (Table B-BJ5)
2194.B5-.B54 Boutroux, Émile, 1845-1921 (Table B-BJ5)
2195 Caro, E. (Elme-Marie), 1826-1887 (Table B-BJ4)
2197 Caro - Comte
Subarrange each by Table B-BJ5
Comte, Auguste, 1798-1857
2200 Periodicals. Societies. Serials
2201 Dictionaries
Collected works
2203 Original (vernacular) texts. By date
2204 Editions with commentary. By editor
2205 Partial editions, selections, etc. By editor or date
Translations
Subarrange by translator or date
Including translations with original texts
2206 Greek
2207 Latin
2208 English
2209 French
2210 German
2211 Italian
2212 Spanish and Portuguese
2212.A-Z Other, A-Z
Separate works
Letters
2214 French. By date

Modern (1450/1600-)
By region or country
France
By period
19th century
Individual philosophers
Comte, Auguste, 1798-1857
Separate works
Letters -- Continued

2215.A-Z Translations. By language, A-Z
2220-2224 Cours de philosophie positive (Table B-BJ10)
2225-2229 Discours sur l'ensemble du positivisme (Table B-BJ10)
2230-2234 Synthèse subjective (Table B-BJ10)
2240-2244 Système de politique positive (Table B-BJ10)
2245.A-Z Other works
Subarrange each by Table B-BJ13
e. g.
2245.A6-.A63 Appel aux conservateurs (Table B-BJ13)
2245.C27-.C273 Calendrier positiviste (Table B-BJ13)
2245.C3-.C33 Catéchisme positiviste (Table B-BJ13)
2245.C55-.C553 Circulaires annuelles (Table B-BJ13)
2245.D5-.D53 Discours sur l'esprit positif (Table B-BJ13)
2245.P6-.P63 Plan des travaux scientifiques (Table B-BJ13)
2246 Indexes, outlines, paraphrases, etc.
2247 Biography and memoirs (Table B-BJ14)
2248 Criticism and interpretation
2249.A-Z Special topics, A-Z
Anthropology see B2249.M36
2249.M36 Man
2249.P6 Positivism
2258 Comte - Cousin
Subarrange each by Table B-BJ5
2258.C6-.C64 Cournot, A. A. (Antoine Augustin), 1801-1877 (Table B-BJ5)
2260-2268 Cousin, Victor, 1792-1867 (Table B-BJ2)
2268.A-Z Special topics, A-Z
2268.R44 Religion
2270 Cousin - Hz
Subarrange each by Table B-BJ5
2270.D2-.D24 Damiron, Ph. (Philibert), 1794-1862 (Table B-BJ5)
2270.D7-.D74 Droz, Joseph, 1773-1850 (Table B-BJ5)
2270.D8-.D84 Dunan, Charles Stanislas, 1849- (Table B-BJ5)
2270.F6-.F64 Fouillée, Alfred, 1838-1912 (Table B-BJ5)
2270.F8-.F84 Franck, Adolphe, 1809-1893 (Table B-BJ5)
2270.F86-.F864 Frédault, Paul, 1850- (Table B-BJ5)

Modern (1450/1600-)
By region or country
France
By period
19th century
Individual philosophers
Cousin - Hz -- Continued

2270.G35-.G354 Gaultier, Jules de, 1858-1942 (Table B-BJ5)
2270.G45-.G454 Gérando, Joseph-Marie, baron de, 1772-1842 (Table B-BJ5)
2270.G5-.G54 Gobineau, Arthur, comte de, 1816-1882 (Table B-BJ5)
2270.G7-.G74 Guyau, Jean-Marie, 1854-1888 (Table B-BJ5)
2270.H3-.H34 Hamelin, Octave, 1856-1907 (Table B-BJ5)
2275 I - Jouffroy
Subarrange each by Table B-BJ5
2275.J6-.J64 Jobert, Antoine Claude Gabriel (Table B-BJ5)
2280-2288 Jouffroy, Théodore, 1796-1842 (Table B-BJ2)
2289 Jouffroy - Lamennais
Subarrange each by Table B-BJ5
2289.L16-.L164 Lachelier, Jules, 1832-1918 (Table B-BJ5)
2289.L18-.L184 Lagneau, Jules, 1851-1894 (Table B-BJ5)
2289.L2-.L24 Lamarck, Jean Baptiste Pierre Antoine de Monet de, 1744-1829 (Table B-BJ5)
2290-2298 Lamennais, Félicité Robert de, 1782-1854 (Table B-BJ2)
2299 Lamennais - Laromiguière
Subarrange each by Table B-BJ5
2300-2308 Laromiguière, Pierre, 1756-1837 (Table B-BJ2)
2312 Laromiguière - Leroux
Subarrange each by Table B-BJ5
2312.L4-.L44 Lequier, Jules, 1814-1862 (Table B-BJ5)
2315 Leroux, Pierre, 1797-1871 (Table B-BJ4)
2317 Leroux - Maine
Subarrange each by Table B-BJ5
2320-2328 Maine de Biran, Pierre, 1766-1824 (Table B-BJ2)
2328.A-Z Special topics, A-Z
2328.O5 Ontology
2328.P7 Psychology
2331 Maine - Mz
Subarrange each by Table B-BJ5
2331.M27-.M274 Maistre, Joseph Marie, comte de, 1753-1821 (Table B-BJ5)
2331.M3-.M34 Mallet, Charles Auguste, 1807-1875 (Table B-BJ5)
2331.M5-.M54 Michelet, Jules, 1798-1874 (Table B-BJ5)

Modern (1450/1600-)
By region or country
France
By period
19th century
Individual philosophers -- Continued

2332 N - Nz
Subarrange each by Table B-BJ5
2332.N7 Nourrisson, Jean Felix, 1825-1899
2333 O - Oz
Subarrange each by Table B-BJ5
2335 P - Ravaisson-Mollien
Subarrange each by Table B-BJ5
2335.P3-.P34 Perron, François (Table B-BJ5)
2337 Ravaisson, Félix, 1813-1900 (Table B-BJ4)
2339 Ravaisson - Renan
Subarrange each by Table B-BJ5
2339.R3-.R34 Rémusat, Charles de, 1797-1875 (Table B-BJ5)
2340-2348 Renan, Ernest, 1823-1892 (Table B-BJ2)
2349 Renan - Renouvier
Subarrange each by Table B-BJ5
2350-2358 Renouvier, Charles, 1815-1903 (Table B-BJ2)
2363 Renouvier - Reynaud
Subarrange each by Table B-BJ5
2363.R4-.R44 Rey, Abel, 1873-1940 (Table B-BJ5)
2365 Reynaud, J. (Jean), 1806-1863 (Table B-BJ4)
2369 Reynaud - Royer
Subarrange each by Table B-BJ5
2369.R5-.R54 Ribert, Léonce (Table B-BJ5)
2369.R6-.R64 Rosny, Léon de, 1837-1914 (Table B-BJ5)
2370-2378 Royer-Collard, Pierre Paul, 1763-1845 (Table B-BJ2)
2379 Royer - Saint-Simon
Subarrange each by Table B-BJ5
2380-2388 Saint-Simon, Henri, comte de, 1760-1825 (Table B-BJ2)
2389 Saint-Simon - Saisset
Subarrange each by Table B-BJ5
2390 Saisset, Emile, 1814-1863 (Table B-BJ4)
2391 Saisset - Secrétan
Subarrange each by Table B-BJ5
2391.S4-.S44 Schoebel, C. (Charles), 1813-1888 (Table B-BJ5)
2392 Secrétan, Charles, 1815-1895 (Table B-BJ4)
2395 Secrétan - Simon
Subarrange each by Table B-BJ5
2400 Simon, Jules, 1814-1896 (Table B-BJ4)

Modern (1450/1600-)
By region or country
France
By period
19th century
Individual philosophers -- Continued

2401 Simon - Sully
Subarrange each by Table B-BJ5
2403 Sully Prudhomme, 1839-1907 (Table B-BJ4)
2404 Sully-Prudhomme - Taine
Subarrange each by Table B-BJ5
2405-2408 Taine, Hippolyte, 1828-1893 (Table B-BJ3a)
2409 Taine - Tarde
Subarrange each by Table B-BJ5
2411 Tarde, Gabriel de, 1843-1904 (Table B-BJ4)
2413 Tarde - Vacherot
Subarrange each by Table B-BJ5
2415 Vacherot, E. (Etienne), 1809-1897 (Table B-BJ4)
2417 Vacherot - Z
Subarrange each by Table B-BJ5

20th century
2421 General works
2424.A-Z Special topics, A-Z
2424.A5 Analogy
2424.D5 Dialectical materialism. Marxist philosophy
2424.E95 Existentialism
2424.F45 Feminism
2424.H43 Hegelianism
2424.I3 Idealism
Marxist philosophy see B2424.D5
2424.P45 Perception. Vision
2424.P47 Personalism
2424.P55 Phenomenology
2424.P7 Pragmatism
2424.R4 Realism
2424.S75 Structuralism
Vision see B2424.P45
2430.A-Z Individual philosophers, A-Z
Subarrange each by Table B-BJ5
Alain, 1868-1951 see B2430.C49+
2430.A47-.A474 Althusser, Louis, 1918-1990 (Table B-BJ5)
2430.A5-.A54 Andler, Charles, 1866-1933 (Table B-BJ5)
2430.B25-.B254 Bachelard, Gaston, 1884-1962 (Table B-BJ5)
2430.B27-.B274 Badiou, Alain (Table B-BJ5)
2430.B338-.B3384 Barthel, Ernst, 1890-1953 (Table B-BJ5)
2430.B3395-.B33954 Bataille, Georges, 1897-1962 (Table B-BJ5)
2430.B3397-.B33974 Baudrillard, Jean, 1929-2007 (Table B-BJ5)

Modern (1450/1600-)
By region or country
France
By period
20th century
Individual philosophers, A-Z -- Continued

2430.B34-.B344 Beauvoir, Simone de, 1908-1986 (Table B-BJ5)
2430.B345-.B3454 Bégout, Bruce (Table B-BJ5)
2430.B35-.B354 Benda, Julien, 1867-1956 (Table B-BJ5)
2430.B36-.B364 Berger, Gaston (Table B-BJ5)
Bergson, Henri, 1859-1941
Collected works
2430.B37 French. By date
2430.B38 Translations
2430.B4A-.B4Z Separate works, A-Z
e. g.
2430.B4D4 Deux sources de la morale et de la religion
2430.B4E47 Énergie spirituelle
2430.B4E7 Évolution créatrice
2430.B4I4 Introduction à la métaphysique
2430.B4M3 Matière et mémoire
2430.B4P36 La pensée et le mouvant
2430.B4P4 Perception du changement
2430.B43 Biography and criticism
2430.B5-.B54 Bertrand-Barraud, Daniel (Table B-BJ5)
2430.B57-.B574 Blanchot, Maurice (Table B-BJ5)
2430.B58-.B584 Blondel, Maurice, 1861-1949 (Table B-BJ5)
2430.B5876-.B58764 Borella, Jean (Table B-BJ5)
2430.B75-.B754 Brunschvicg, Léon, 1869-1944 (Table B-BJ5)
2430.C3-.C34 Calvet, Adolphe (Table B-BJ5)
2430.C35-.C354 Camus, Albert, 1913-1960 (Table B-BJ5)
2430.C355-.C3554 Canguilhem, Georges, 1904-1995 (Table B-BJ5)
2430.C357-.C3574 Caraco, Albert (Table B-BJ5)
2430.C358-.C3584 Castoriadis, Cornelius, 1922-1997 (Table B-BJ5)
2430.C36-.C364 Cavaillés, Jean, 1903-1944 (Table B-BJ5)
2430.C365-.C3654 Certeau, Michel de (Table B-BJ5)
2430.C49-.C494 Chartier, Émile, 1868-1951 (Table B-BJ5)
2430.C5-.C514 Chevalier, Jacques, 1882-1962 (Table B-BJ5a)
2430.C52-.C524 Chicoteau, M. H. (Marcel Henri), 1915- (Table B-BJ5)
2430.C525-.C5254 Cioran, E. M. (Emile M.), 1911-1995 (Table B-BJ5)
2430.C63-.C634 Clément, Catherine, 1939- (Table B-BJ5)
2430.C635-.C6354 Comte-Sponville, André (Table B-BJ5)
2430.C65-.C654 Corbin, Henry (Table B-BJ5)
2430.C66-.C664 Cotti, Claude (Table B-BJ5)
2430.C67-.C674 Coutrot, Jean, 1895-1941 (Table B-BJ5)
2430.C68-.C684 Couturat, Louis, 1868-1914 (Table B-BJ5)

Modern (1450/1600-)
By region or country
France
By period
20th century
Individual philosophers, A-Z -- Continued

2430.C7-.C74 Cresson, André, 1869-1950 (Table B-BJ5)
2430.D29-.D294 Dagognet, François (Table B-BJ5)
2430.D45-.D454 Deleuze, Gilles, 1925-1995 (Table B-BJ5)
2430.D48-.D484 Derrida, Jacques (Table B-BJ5)
2430.D485-.D4854 Desanti, Jean Toussaint (Table B-BJ5)
2430.D89-.D894 Durand, Gilbert, 1921- (Table B-BJ5)
2430.E75-.E754 Eribon, Didier (Table B-BJ5)
2430.F66-.F664 Fontenay, Elisabeth de (Table B-BJ5)
2430.F72-.F724 Foucault, Michel, 1926-1984 (Table B-BJ5)
2430.G35-.G354 Garaudy, Roger (Table B-BJ5)
2430.G4-.G44 Geiger, Louis Bertrand, 1906-1983 (Table B-BJ5)
2430.G471-.G4714 Gilson, Etienne, 1884-1978 (Table B-BJ5)
2430.G49-.G494 Girard, René, 1923- (Table B-BJ5)
2430.G5-.G54 Giry, Martial (Table B-BJ5)
2430.G6-.G64 Gouhier, Henri Gaston, 1898-1994 (Table B-BJ5)
2430.G75-.G754 Grimaldi, Nicolas (Table B-BJ5)
2430.G78-.G784 Guattari, Félix, 1930-1992 (Table B-BJ5)
2430.G8-.G84 Guénon, René (Table B-BJ5)
2430.G85-.G854 Guitton, Jean (Table B-BJ5)
2430.H33-.H334 Hadot, Pierre (Table B-BJ5)
2430.H4-.H44 Hébert, Marcel, 1851-1916 (Table B-BJ5)
2430.H45-.H454 Henry, Michel, 1922-2002 (Table B-BJ5)
2430.H8-.H84 Huisman, Denis (Table B-BJ5)
2430.I7-.I74 Irigaray, Luce (Table B-BJ5)
2430.I9-.I94 Izoulet, Jean Bernard Joachim, 1854-1929 (Table B-BJ5)
2430.J28-.J284 Janicaud, Dominique, 1937- (Table B-BJ5)
2430.J3-.J34 Jankélévitch, Vladimir (Table B-BJ5)
2430.J43-.J434 Jeanson, Francis, 1922-2009 (Table B-BJ5)
2430.J85-.J854 Jullien, François, 1951- (Table B-BJ5)
2430.K64-.K644 Kofman, Sarah (Table B-BJ5)
2430.K65-.K654 Kojève, Alexandre, 1902-1968 (Table B-BJ5)
2430.K754-.K7544 Kristeva, Julia, 1941- (Table B-BJ5)
2430.L14-.L144 Laberthonnière, Lucien, 1860-1932 (Table B-BJ5)
2430.L1466-.L14664 Lacoue-Labarthe, Philippe (Table B-BJ5)
2430.L15-.L154 Lacroix, Jean, 1900-1986 (Table B-BJ5)
2430.L357-.L3574 Largeault, Jean (Table B-BJ5)
2430.L36-.L364 Lautman, Albert, 1908-1944 (Table B-BJ5)
2430.L37-.L374 Lavelle, Louis, 1883-1951 (Table B-BJ5)
2430.L39-.L394 Le Dœuff, Michèle (Table B-BJ5)
2430.L398-.L3984 Legendre, Pierre, 1930- (Table B-BJ5)

Modern (1450/1600-)
By region or country
France
By period
20th century
Individual philosophers, A-Z -- Continued

2430.L4-.L44 Legris, Joachim (Table B-BJ5)
2430.L48-.L484 Lévinas, Emmanuel (Table B-BJ5)
2430.L52-.L524 Lévy, Benny (Table B-BJ5)
2430.L53-.L534 Lévy, Bernard Henri (Table B-BJ5)
2430.L67-.L674 Loreau, Max (Table B-BJ5)
2430.L8-.L84 Lupasco, Stéphane, 1900-1988 (Table B-BJ5)
2430.L96-.L964 Lyotard, Jean François, 1924-1998 (Table B-BJ5)
2430.M22-.M224 Macherey, Pierre (Table B-BJ5)
2430.M25-.M254 Marcel, Gabriel, 1889-1973 (Table B-BJ5)
2430.M28-.M284 Marion, Jean-Luc, 1946- (Table B-BJ5)
2430.M3-.M34 Maritain, Jacques, 1882-1973 (Table B-BJ5)
2430.M36-.M364 Maugé, Francis (Table B-BJ5)
2430.M376-.M3764 Merleau-Ponty, Maurice, 1908-1961 (Table B-BJ5)
2430.M4-.M44 Meyerson, Émile, 1859-1933 (Table B-BJ5)
Mochi, Alberto see B3636.M6+
2430.M66-.M664 Molinié, Jean-A. (Table B-BJ5)
2430.M67-.M674 Monthaye, Gaston, 1871- (Table B-BJ5)
2430.M676-.M6764 Morin, Edgar (Table B-BJ5)
2430.M69-.M694 Mounier, Emmanuel, 1905-1950 (Table B-BJ5)
2430.M8-.M84 Muller, Maurice (Table B-BJ5)
2430.N36-.N364 Nancy, Jean-Luc (Table B-BJ5)
2430.O54-.O544 Onfray, Michel, 1959- (Table B-BJ5)
2430.P3-.P34 Paliard, Jacques, 1887-1953 (Table B-BJ5)
2430.P35-.P354 Papaïōannou, Kōstas, 1925- (Table B-BJ5)
2430.P37-.P374 Parain, Brice, 1897-1971 (Table B-BJ5)
2430.R27-.R274 Rancière, Jacques (Table B-BJ5)
2430.R5-.R54 Richet, Charles Robert, 1850-1935 (Table B-BJ5)
2430.R55-.R554 Ricoeur, Paul (Table B-BJ5)
2430.R58-.R584 Rosset, Clément (Table B-BJ5)
2430.R59-.R594 Rougier, Louis Auguste Paul, 1889- (Table B-BJ5)
2430.R6-.R64 Roupnel, Gaston, 1871-1946 (Table B-BJ5)
2430.R7-.R74 Roussel-Despierres, Francois, 1864- (Table B-BJ5)
2430.S3-.S34 Sartre, Jean Paul, 1905-1980 (Table B-BJ5)
2430.S345-.S3454 Schérer, René (Table B-BJ5)
2430.S37-.S374 Schweitzer, Albert, 1875-1965 (Table B-BJ5)
Cf. BX4827.S35 Schweitzer as theologian
Cf. CT1018.S45 Schweitzer, Albert (General biography)
Cf. ML416.S33 Schweitzer as musician
Cf. R722.32.S35 Schweitzer as medical missionary

Modern (1450/1600-)
By region or country
France
By period
20th century
Individual philosophers, A-Z -- Continued
2430.S4-.S44 Seillière, Ernest Antoine Aimé Léon, Baron, 1866- (Table B-BJ5)
2430.S46-.S464 Serres, Michel (Table B-BJ5)
2430.S5-.S54 Simart, Maurice (Table B-BJ5)
2430.S546-.S5464 Simon, Yves René Marie, 1903-1961 (Table B-BJ5)
2430.S55-.S554 Simondon, Gilbert (Table B-BJ5)
2430.S752-.S7524 Stiegler, Bernard (Table B-BJ5)
2430.T3-.T34 Tassy, Edme, 1876- (Table B-BJ5)
2430.T37-.T374 Teilhard de Chardin, Pierre (Table B-BJ5)
2430.T4-.T44 Thibon, Gustave, 1904- (Table B-BJ5)
2430.T74-.T744 Tresmontant, Claude (Table B-BJ5)
2430.V33-.V334 Vallin, Georges (Table B-BJ5)
2430.V36-.V364 Van Heijenoort, Jean, 1912-1986 (Table B-BJ5)
2430.W4-.W44 Weber, Louis (Table B-BJ5)
2430.W461-.W4614 Weil, Eric (Table B-BJ5)
2430.W47-.W474 Weil, Simone, 1909-1943 (Table B-BJ5)
21st century
2431 General works
2432.A-Z Special topics, A-Z
2433.A-Z Individual philosophers, A-Z
2433.C46-.C464 Chouraqui, Bernard (Table B-BJ5)
2433.E58-.E584 Enthoven, Raphaël (Table B-BJ5)
2433.L37-.L374 Laruelle, Francois (Table B-BJ5)
2433.M45-.M454 Meillassoux, Quentin, 1967- (Table B-BJ5)
2433.R54-.R544 Riffard, Pierre A. (Table B-BJ5)
2433.R66-.R664 Romano, Claude, 1967- (Table B-BJ5)
Germany. Austria (German)
General works
2521 English
2522 French
2523 German
2525.A-Z Other languages, A-Z
2528.A-Z Special topics, A-Z
2528.C66 Consolation
2528.G73 Greek influences
2528.I85 Islam
2528.L7 Loyalty. "Treue"
2528.N38 Nature
2528.S83 Subjectivity
2528.T56 Time
By period

Modern (1450/1600-)
By region or country
Germany. Austria (German)
By period -- Continued
17th century
2535 General works
2538.A-Z Special topics, A-Z
Individual philosophers
2543 A - Bekker
Subarrange each by Table B-BJ5
2545 Bekker, Balthasar, 1634-1698 (Table B-BJ4)
2547 Bekker - Leibniz
Subarrange each by Table B-BJ5
2547.C5-.C54 Clauberg, Johann, 1622-1665 (Table B-BJ5)
Leibniz, Gottfried Wilhelm, Freiherr von, 1646-1716
2550 Periodicals. Societies. Serials
2551 Dictionaries
Collected works
2553 Original (vernacular) texts. By date
2554 Editions with commentary. By editor
2555 Partial editions, selections, etc. By editor or date
Translations
Subarrange by translator or date
Including translations with original texts
2556 Greek
2557 Latin
2558 English
2559 French
2560 German
2561 Italian
2562 Spanish and Portuguese
2563.A-Z Other languages, A-Z
Separate works
2565 Animadversiones ad Cartesii principia philosophiae (Table B-BJ12)
2566 Considerations sur le principe de vie et sur les natures plastiques (Table B-BJ12)
2567 De arte combinatoria (Table B-BJ12)
2568 De primae philosophiae emendatione et de notione substantiae (Table B-BJ12)
2569 De principio individui (Table B-BJ12)
2570 De vero methodo philosophiae et theologiae (Table B-BJ12)
2571 De vita beata (Table B-BJ12)
2572 Discours de métaphysique (Table B-BJ12)

Modern (1450/1600-)
By region or country
Germany. Austria (German)
By period
17th century
Individual philosophers
Leibniz, Gottfried Wilhelm, Freiherr von, 1646-1716
Separate works -- Continued

2575-2579 Meditationes de cognitione, veritate, et ideis (Table B-BJ10)
2580 Monadologie (Table B-BJ12)
2581 Nouveaux essais sur l'entendement humain (Table B-BJ12)
2582 Principes de la nature et de la grâce (Table B-BJ12)
2583 Refutation inédite de Spinoza (Table B-BJ12)
2584 Sur Dieu, l'âme, l'espace, la durée (Table B-BJ12)
2585-2589 Système nouveau de la nature de la communication des substances (Table B-BJ10)
2590 Théodicée (Table B-BJ12)
2591.A-Z Other, A-Z
Subarrange each by Table B-BJ13
2595 Spurious and apocryphal works
2596 Indexes, outlines, paraphrases, etc.
2597 Biography and memoirs (Table B-BJ14)
2598 Criticism and interpretation
2599.A-Z Special topics, A-Z
2599.A37 Aesthetics
2599.A54 Angels
2599.C33 Cabala
2599.C5 China
2599.C57 Consciousness
2599.E85 Ethics
2599.F69 France
2599.F7 Free will
2599.G46 Geometry
2599.G63 God
2599.H5 History
2599.I5 Individuation
2599.I53 Infinite
2599.J8 Justice
2599.K7 Knowledge
2599.L35 Language
2599.L8 Logic
2599.M6 Metaphor

Modern (1450/1600-)
By region or country
Germany. Austria (German)
By period
17th century
Individual philosophers
Leibniz, Gottfried Wilhelm, Freiherr von, 1646-1716
Special topics, A-Z -- Continued

2599.M7 Metaphysics
2599.M8 Monadology
2599.O7 Optimism
2599.R38 Relations
2599.R4 Religion
2599.S7 Space and time
2599.S87 Subjectivity
2599.S9 Substance
2599.S94 Sufficient reason
2599.T38 Theodicy
2599.T78 Truth
2599.W5 Wisdom
2602 Leibniz - Pufendorf
Subarrange each by Table B-BJ5
2603 Pufendorf, Samuel, Freiherr von, 1632-1694 (Table B-BJ4)
Cf. JC156 Political theory
2604 Pufendorf - Thomasius
Subarrange each by Table B-BJ5
2604.R5-.R54 Ritschel, George, 1616-1683 (Table B-BJ5)
2605 Thomasius, Christian, 1655-1728 (Table B-BJ4)
2607 Thomasius - Tschirnhaus
Subarrange each by Table B-BJ5
2609 Tschirnhaus, Ehrenfried Walther von, 1651-1708 (Table B-BJ4)
2611 Tschirnhaus - Z
Subarrange each by Table B-BJ5

18th century
2615 General works
Special topics
2621 Die Aufklärung
2628.A-Z Other, A-Z
2628.A52 Analysis
2628.E5 English philosophy (Influence)
2628.M3 Materialism
2628.S34 Self
Individual philosophers
2631 A - Abbt
Subarrange each by Table B-BJ5

Modern (1450/1600-)
By region or country
Germany. Austria (German)
By period
18th century
Individual philosophers -- Continued

2632 Abbt, Thomas, 1738-1766 (Table B-BJ4)

2633 Abbt - Baumeister
Subarrange each by Table B-BJ5

2634 Baumeister, Friedrich Christian, 1709-1785 (Table B-BJ4)

2635 Baumeister - Baumgarten
Subarrange each by Table B-BJ5

2637 Baumgarten, Alexander Gottlieb, 1714-1762 (Table B-BJ4)

2639 Baumgarten - Bilfinger
Subarrange each by Table B-BJ5

2640-2643 Bilfinger, Georg Bernhard, 1693-1750 (Table B-BJ3a)

2644 Bilfinger - Buddeus
Subarrange each by Table B-BJ5

2645-2648 Buddeus, Joannes Franciscus, 1667-1729 (Table B-BJ3a)

2650 Buddeus - Creuz
Subarrange each by Table B-BJ5

2651 Creuz, Friedrich Karl Casimir, Freiherr von, 1724-1770 (Table B-BJ4)

2653 Creuz - Crusius
Subarrange each by Table B-BJ5

2654 Crusius, Christian August, 1715-1775 (Table B-BJ4)

2655 Crusius - Engel
Subarrange each by Table B-BJ5

2657 Engel, Johann Jacob, 1741-1802 (Table B-BJ4)

2659 Engel - Garve
Subarrange each by Table B-BJ5

2660-2663 Garve, Christian, 1742-1798 (Table B-BJ3a)

2664 Garve - Hz
Subarrange each by Table B-BJ5

2670 I - Lambert
Subarrange each by Table B-BJ5

2673 Lambert, Johann Heinrich, 1728-1777 (Table B-BJ4)

2674 Lambert - Lez
Subarrange each by Table B-BJ5

Lessing, Gotthold Ephraim, 1729-1781 see PT2415

Modern (1450/1600-)
By region or country
Germany. Austria (German)
By period
18th century
Individual philosophers -- Continued

2681 Li - Lossius
Subarrange each by Table B-BJ5
2681.L4-.L44 Lichtenberg, Georg Christoph, 1742-1799 (Table B-BJ5)
2682 Lossius, Johann Christian, 1743-1813 (Table B-BJ4)
2683 Lossius - Meier
Subarrange each by Table B-BJ5
2685 Meier, Georg Friedrich, 1718-1777
2687 Meier - Mendelssohn
Subarrange each by Table B-BJ5
2690-2693 Mendelssohn, Moses, 1729-1786 (Table B-BJ3a)
2694 Mendelssohn - Nicolai
Subarrange each by Table B-BJ5
2695-2698 Nicolai, Friedrich, 1733-1811 (Table B-BJ3a)
2699 Nicolai - Steinbart
Subarrange each by Table B-BJ5
2699.O4-.O44 Oetinger, Friedrich Christoph, 1702-1782 (Table B-BJ5)
2699.P3-.P34 Platner, Ernst, 1744-1818 (Table B-BJ5)
2699.P5-.P54 Ploucquet, Gottfried, 1716-1790 (Table B-BJ5)
2699.R4-.R44 Reimarus, Hermann Samuel, 1694-1768 (Table B-BJ5)
2705-2708 Steinbart, Gotthilf Samuel, 1738-1809 (Table B-BJ3a)
2709 Steinbart - Tetens
Subarrange each by Table B-BJ5
2709.S6-.S64 Sulzer, Johann Georg, 1720-1779 (Table B-BJ5)
2710-2713 Tetens, Johann Nicolas, 1736-1807 (Table B-BJ3a)
2714 Tetens - Tiedemann
Subarrange each by Table B-BJ5
2715 Tiedemann, Dietrich, 1748-1803 (Table B-BJ4)
2717 Tiedemann - Wolff
Subarrange each by Table B-BJ5
2720-2728 Wolff, Christian, Freiherr von, 1679-1754 (Table B-BJ2)
2728.A-Z Special topics, A-Z
2728.E84 Ethics
2728.L54 Linguistics
2728.L57 Logic
2728.L6 Love

Modern (1450/1600-)
By region or country
Germany. Austria (German)
By period
18th century
Individual philosophers
Wolff, Christian, Freiherr von, 1679-1754
Special topics, A-Z -- Continued
2728.M4 Metaphysics
2728.O5 Ontology
2728.P79 Psychology
2728.S36 Science
2729 Wolf - Z
Subarrange each by Table B-BJ5
Later 18th and early 19th centuries
Including 19th century (General)
2741 General works
2743 General special
Including special aspects of the subject as a whole
Special topics
2745 German transcendental idealism
2748.A-Z Other, A-Z
2748.B43 Bhagavadgītā
2748.D53 Dialectic
2748.I5 Internationalism
2748.M23 Man
2748.N35 Nature
2748.R37 Reason
2748.R64 Romanticism
2748.S44 Self
2748.S83 Sublime, The
2748.T73 Tradition
2748.U55 Unity
Individual philosophers
2750-2799 Kant, Immanuel, 1724-1804
2750 Periodicals. Societies. Serials
2751 Dictionaries
Collected works
2753 Original (vernacular) texts. By date
2754 Editions with commentary. By editor
2755 Partial editions, selections, etc. By editor or date
Translations
Subarrange by translator or date
Including translations with original texts
2756 Greek
2757 Latin

Modern (1450/1600-)
By region or country
Germany. Austria (German)
By period
Later 18th and early 19th centuries
Individual philosophers
Kant, Immanuel, 1724-1804
Collected works
Translations -- Continued

2758 English
2759 French
2760 German
2761 Italian
2762 Spanish and Portuguese
2763.A-Z Other languages, A-Z

Separate works

2765 Gedanken von der wahren Schatzung der lebendigen Krafte (Table B-BJ12)
2766 Grundlegung zur Metaphysik der Sitten (Table B-BJ12)
Cf. B2785 Metaphysik der Sitten
2770-2774 Kritik der praktischen Vernunft (Table B-BJ10)
2775-2779 Kritik der reinen Vernunft (Table B-BJ10)
2780-2784 Kritik der Urteilskraft (Table B-BJ10)
Cf. B2794.E7+ Erste Einleitung in die Kritik der Urteilskraft
2785 Metaphysik der Sitten (Table B-BJ12)
Cf. B2766 Grundlegung zur Metaphysik der Sitten
Part 1. Metaphysische Anfangsgründe der Rechtslehre
see class K
2785.5 Part 2. Metaphysische Anfangsgründe der tugendlehre (Table B-BJ12)
2786 Metaphysische Anfangsgründe der Naturwissenschaft (Table B-BJ12)
2787 Prolegomena (Table B-BJ12)
2788-2792 Religion innerhalb der Grenzen der blossen Vernunft (Table B-BJ10)
2793 Traume eines Geistersehers (Table B-BJ12)
2794.A-Z Other works, A-Z
Subarrange each by Table B-BJ13
e. g.
2794.A5-.A53 Analogien der Erfahrung (Table B-BJ13)
2794.A6-.A63 Anthropologie in pragmatischer Hinsicht (Table B-BJ13)

Modern (1450/1600-)
By region or country
Germany. Austria (German)
By period
Later 18th and early 19th centuries
Individual philosophers
Kant, Immanuel, 1724-1804
Separate works
Other works, A-Z -- Continued
Beobachtungen über das Gefühl des Schönen und Erhabenen see BH181+

2794.D4-.D43 De mundi sensibilis forma (Table B-BJ13)

2794.E7-.E73 Erste Einleitung in die Kritik der Urteilskraft (Table B-BJ13)

2794.O6-.O63 Opus postumum (Table B-BJ13)

Philosophia practica universalis una cum ethica see B2794.V6+

2794.P55-.P553 Physische Geographie (Table B-BJ13)

2794.S8-.S83 Streit der Facultäten (Table B-BJ13)

2794.V6-.V63 Eine Vorlesung Kants über Ethik, im Auftrage der Kant-gesellschaft (Table B-BJ13)

2794.W6-.W63 Worin besteht der Fortschritt zum Besseren im Menschengeschlecht? (Table B-BJ13)

2795 Spurious and apocryphal works

2796 Indexes, outlines, paraphrases, etc.

2797 Biography and memoirs (Table B-BJ14)

2798 Criticism and interpretation

2799.A-Z Special topics, A-Z

2799.A28 Act

2799.A4 Aesthetics

2799.A53 Analogy

2799.A6 Antinomy

2799.A7 Apperception

2799.B4 Belief

2799.B63 Body, Human

2799.C3 Causality

2799.C66 Communities

2799.C78 Comprehension (Theory of knowledge). Understanding

2799.C8 Cosmology

2799.C82 Cosmopolitanism

2799.C84 Creativity. Creative ability

2799.D33 Deception

2799.D47 Dialectic

2799.D5 "Ding an sich" (Thing in itself)

Education
see class L

Modern (1450/1600-)
By region or country
Germany. Austria (German)
By period
Later 18th and early 19th centuries
Individual philosophers
Kant, Immanuel, 1724-1804
Special topics, A-Z -- Continued

2799.E5	Emotions
	Epistemology see B2799.K7
2799.E8	Ethics
2799.E85	Eudaemonism
2799.E9	Experience
2799.F8	Free will
2799.G6	God
2799.G65	Good and evil
2799.H36	Happiness
2799.H47	Hermeneutics
	History see D16.8
2799.H67	Hope
	Human body see B2799.B63
2799.H9	Hypothesis
2799.I4	Idea
2799.I42	Idealism
2799.I48	Illusion
2799.I55	Imagination
2799.J8	Judgment
2799.J87	Justice
2799.K54	Kingdom of God
2799.K7	Knowledge, Theory of. Epistemology
2799.L26	Language
(2799.L3)	Law see class K
2799.L49	Liberty
2799.L5	Life
2799.L8	Logic Cf. B2799.T7 Transcendental logic
2799.M25	Man
	Marriage law see class K
	Mathematics see subclass QA
2799.M43	Matter
2799.M5	Metaphysics
2799.M514	Methodology
2799.M52	Mind. Philosophy of mind
2799.M55	Modality

Modern (1450/1600-)
By region or country
Germany. Austria (German)
By period
Later 18th and early 19th centuries
Individual philosophers
Kant, Immanuel, 1724-1804
Special topics, A-Z -- Continued

2799.M6 Monadology
2799.M68 Movement
2799.M9 Mysticism
2799.N37 Nature
2799.N43 Necessity
2799.O2 Objectivity
2799.O5 Ontology
2799.P3 Pantheism
2799.P4 Personality
Philosophy of mind see B2799.M52
Political science see D16.8
2799.P67 Promises
Psychology see BF1+
2799.R35 Reality
2799.R4 Religion
2799.R45 Representation
2799.S29 Schematism
Science
see class Q
2799.S37 Self
2799.S4 Semantics
2799.S43 Semiotics
2799.S47 Sex differences
2799.S54 Skepticism
Socialism
see subclass HX
Sociology
see subclass HM
2799.S7 Space and time
2799.S88 Subjectivity
2799.S9 Substance
2799.S94 Symbolism
2799.T3 Teleology
2799.T45 Theodicy
2799.T5 Time
2799.T7 Transcendental logic. Transcendentalism
2799.T8 Truth
Understanding see B2799.C78
2799.V5 Virtue

	Modern (1450/1600-)
	By region or country
	Germany. Austria (German)
	By period
	Later 18th and early 19th centuries
	Individual philosophers
	Kant, Immanuel, 1724-1804
	Special topics, A-Z -- Continued
2799.W37	War
	Fichte, Johann Gottlieb, 1762-1814
2800	Periodicals. Societies. Serials
2801	Dictionaries
	Collected works
2803	Original (vernacular) texts. By date
2804	Editions with commentary. By editor
2805	Partial editions, selections, etc. By editor or date
	Translations
	Subarrange by translator or date
	Including translations with original texts
2806	Greek
2807	Latin
2808	English
2809	French
2810	German
2811	Italian
2812	Spanish and Portuguese
2813.A-Z	Other languages, A-Z
	Separate works
2814	Bericht an das Publikum über das Wesen der neuesten Philosophie (Table B-BJ12)
2820-2824	Grundlage der gesamten Wissenschaftslehre (Table B-BJ10)
	Grundlage des Naturrechts see JC181
2825-2829	Grundriss des Eigentümlichen der Wissenschaftslehre (Table B-BJ10)
2830-2834	Kritik aller Offenbarung (Table B-BJ10)
	Reden an die deutsche Nation see DD199
2838	System der Sittenlehre (Table B-BJ12)
2841	Über den Grund unseres Glaubens (Table B-BJ12)
2844.A-Z	Other works, A-Z
	Subarrange each by Table B-BJ13
	e. g.
2844.A6-.A63	Anweisung zum seligen Leben (Table B-BJ13)
2844.B5-.B53	Bestimmung des Menschen (Table B-BJ13)

Modern (1450/1600-)
By region or country
Germany. Austria (German)
By period
Later 18th and early 19th centuries
Individual philosophers
Fichte, Johann Gottlieb, 1762-1814
Separate works
Other works, A-Z -- Continued

2844.E5-.E53 Einige Vorlesungen über die Bestimmung des Gelehrten (Table B-BJ13)

2844.L6-.L63 Fichtes und Schellings philosophischer Briefwechsel (Table B-BJ13)

Letters

2844.S8-.S83 Staatslehre (Table B-BJ13)

2844.U4-.U43 Über das Wesen des Gelehrten und seine Erscheinungen im Gebiete der Freiheit (Table B-BJ13)

Über die Bestimmung des Gelehrten see B2844.E5+

2845 Spurious and apocryphal works

2846 Indexes, outlines, paraphrases, etc.

2847 Biography and memoirs (Table B-BJ14)

2848 Criticism and interpretation

2849.A-Z Special topics, A-Z

2849.A2 The absolute

2849.A8 Atheism, Charge of

2849.C5 Christianity

2849.D5 Dialectic

Education
see class L

2849.E8 Ethics

2849.E9 Evil

2849.F7 Free will

2849.G5 God

2849.H57 History

2849.I3 Idealism

2849.I37 Image

2849.I4 Imagination

2849.I5 Individuality

2849.I58 Intersubjectivity

2849.K7 Knowledge

2849.L35 Language

2849.L48 Liberty

2849.L5 Life

2849.L6 Logic

2849.M9 Mysticism

Modern (1450/1600-)
By region or country
Germany. Austria (German)
By period
Later 18th and early 19th centuries
Individual philosophers
Fichte, Johann Gottlieb, 1762-1814
Special topics, A-Z -- Continued

2849.N37 Nature
2849.R44 Religion
Socialism
see subclass HX
2849.S65 Space and time
Sociology
see subclass HM
2849.S92 Subject
Will see B2849.F7

Schelling, Friedrich Wilhelm Joseph von, 1775-1854

2850 Periodicals. Societies. Serials
2851 Dictionaries
Collected works
2853 Original (vernacular) texts. By date
2854 Editions with commentary. By editor
2855 Partial editions, selections, etc. By editor or date
Translations
2856 Greek
2857 Latin
2858 English
2859 French
2860 German
2861 Italian
2862 Spanish and Portuguese
2863.A-Z Other languages, A-Z
Separate works
2864 Bruno; oder, Über das natürliche und göttliche Princip der Dinge (Table B-BJ12)
2865 Darlegung des wahren Verhältnis der Naturphilosophie zur verbesserten Fichteschen Lehre (Table B-BJ12)
2866 Darstellung meines Systems der Philosophie (Table B-BJ12)
2867 Denkmal der Schrift Jakobis von den göttlichen Dingen (Table B-BJ12)
Einleitung in die Philosophie der Mythologie see BL310

Modern (1450/1600-)
By region or country
Germany. Austria (German)
By period
Later 18th and early 19th centuries
Individual philosophers
Schelling, Friedrich Wilhelm Joseph von, 1775-1854
Separate works -- Continued

2868 Einleitung zu dem Entwurf eines Systems der Naturphilosophie (Table B-BJ12)

2868.5 Erster Entwurf eines Systems der Naturphilosophie (Table B-BJ12)

2869 Fernere Darstellungen aus dem Systems der Philosophie (Table B-BJ12)

2870 Ideen zu einer Philosophie der Natur (Table B-BJ12)

Philosophie der Kunst see N64

2872 Philosophie und Religion (Table B-BJ12)

2874 Philosophische Briefe über Dogmatis-mus und Kriticismus (Table B-BJ12)

Philosophische Untersuchungen über das Wesen der menschlichen Freiheit see BJ1460+

2878 System der gesamten Philosophie und der Naturphilosophie insbesondere (Table B-BJ12)

2880-2884 System des transscendentalen Idealismus (Table B-BJ10)

Über das Wesen der menschlichen Freiheit see BJ1460+

2888 Über die Möglichkeit einer Form der Philosophie überhaupt (Table B-BJ12)

Verhältniss der Naturphilosophie zur verbesserten Fichteschen Lehre see B2865

2891 Vom ich als Princip der Philosophie (Table B-BJ12)

2892 Von der Weltseele (Table B-BJ12)

2893 Vorlesungen über die Methode des akademischen Studimus (Table B-BJ12)

2894.A-Z Other works, A-Z

Subarrange each by Table B-BJ13

e. g.

2894.C4-.C43 Clara; oder, Über den Zusammenhang der Natur mit der Geisterwelt (Table B-BJ13)

2894.W4-.W43 Weltalter (Table B-BJ13)

2895 Spurious and apocryphal works

Modern (1450/1600-)
By region or country
Germany. Austria (German)
By period
Later 18th and early 19th centuries
Individual philosophers
Schelling, Friedrich Wilhelm Joseph von, 1775-1854 -- Continued

2896 Indexes, outlines, paraphrases, etc.
2897 Biography and memoirs (Table B-BJ14)
2898 Criticism and interpretation
2899.A-Z Special topics, A-Z
2899.A23 The absolute
2899.C74 Creation
2899.D5 Dialectic
2899.E84 Ethics
2899.G6 God
2899.H5 History
2899.I53 India
2899.L5 Liberty
2899.M45 Melancholy
2899.M48 Metaphysics
2899.M88 Mysticism
2899.M9 Mythology
2899.N3 Nature
2899.P47 Personality
2899.P58 Polarity
Political science see JC233
2899.R38 Reason
2899.R4 Religion

Hegel, Georg Wilhelm Friedrich, 1770-1831
2900 Periodicals. Societies. Serials
2901 Dictionaries
Collected works
2903 Original (vernacular) texts. By date
2904 Editions with commentary. By editor
2905 Partial editions, selections, etc. By editor or date
Translations
Subarrange by translator or date
Including translations with original texts
2906 Greek
2907 Latin
2908 English
2909 French
2910 Italian
2911 Italian

Modern (1450/1600-)
By region or country
Germany. Austria (German)
By period
Later 18th and early 19th centuries
Individual philosophers
Hegel, Georg Wilhelm Friedrich, 1770-1831
Collected works
Translations -- Continued
2912 Spanish and Portuguese
2913.A-Z Other languages, A-Z
Separate works
2914 Abhandlungen (Table B-BJ12)
2915-2919 Encyklopädie der philosophischen Wissenschaften im Grundrisse (Table B-BJ10)
2921 Glauben und Wissen (Table B-BJ12)
(2923) Grundlinien der Philosophie des Rechts
see class K
Naturrecht und Staatswissenschaft
see class K
2925-2929 Phänomenologie des Geistes (Table B-BJ10)
2931 Philosophische Propadeutik (Table B-BJ12)
System der Philosophie see B2915+
2933 Über das Verhältnis der Naturphilosophie zur Philosophie überhaupt (Table B-BJ12)
Vorlesungen über die Ästhetik see N64
2936 Vorlesungen über die Geschichte der Philosophie (Table B-BJ12)
Vorlesungen über die Philosophie der Geschichte see D16.8
2938-2940 Vorlesungen über die Philosophie der Religion (Table B-BJ11)
2941 Wer denkt Abstrakt? (Table B-BJ12)
2942 Wissenschaft der Logik (Table B-BJ12)
2944.A-Z Other works, A-Z
Subarrange each by Table B-BJ13
2945 Spurious and apocryphal works
2946 Indexes, outlines, paraphrases, etc.
2947 Biography and memoirs (Table B-BJ14)
2948 Criticism and interpretation
2949.A-Z Special topics, A-Z
2949.A28 The absolute
2949.A3 Act
2949.A4 Aesthetics
2949.A44 Africa
2949.A5 Alienation

Modern (1450/1600-)
By region or country
Germany. Austria (German)
By period
Later 18th and early 19th centuries
Individual philosophers
Hegel, Georg Wilhelm Friedrich, 1770-1831
Special topics, A-Z -- Continued

2949.B44 Beginning
2949.C45 China
2949.C49 Concept
2949.C5 The concrete
2949.C6 Consciousness
2949.C63 Contingency
2949.C64 Contradiction
2949.C8 Cosmology
2949.D43 Death
2949.D44 Death of God
2949.D47 Desire
2949.D5 Dialectic
2949.E17 East, Knowledge of
2949.E7 Eschatology
2949.E75 Essence
2949.E8 Ethics
2949.E87 Experience
2949.F7 Free will
2949.G63 God
Cf. B2949.D44 Death of God
2949.G73 Greece, Knowledge of
2949.H35 Hermeneutics
2949.H37 Hermetism
2949.H45 Hinduism
History see D16.8
2949.H9 Hypothesis
2949.I53 Indic philosophy
2949.J47 Jesus Christ
2949.J84 Judaism
2949.K5 Knowledge
2949.L25 Language
Law
see class K
2949.L5 Liberty
2949.L8 Logic
2949.L84 Love
2949.M3 Man
2949.M32 Many
2949.M36 Memory

Modern (1450/1600-)
By region or country
Germany. Austria (German)
By period
Later 18th and early 19th centuries
Individual philosophers
Hegel, Georg Wilhelm Friedrich, 1770-1831
Special topics, A-Z -- Continued

2949.M4 Metaphysics
2949.M43 Methodology
2949.M55 Mind, Philosophy of
2949.M9 Myth
2949.N3 Nature
2949.N4 Negativity
2949.N46 Neoplatonism
2949.O5 Ontology
2949.O75 Original sin
2949.P4 Personality
Political science see JC233
Psychology see BF1+
2949.R25 Reason
2949.R255 Recognition
2949.R26 Reflection
2949.R28 Relation
2949.R3 Religion
2949.R4 Revelation
2949.S54 Skepticism
2949.S6 Social philosophy
2949.S75 Spirit
The state
see subclass JC
2949.S83 Subjectivity
2949.S9 Substance
2949.T48 Thought and thinking
2949.T54 Time
2949.T64 Tragic, The
2949.T7 Trinity
2949.T78 Truth
2949.W4 Whole and parts
2949.W67 Work

Other philosophers
2949.5 A - Baader
Subarrange each by Table B-BJ5
2950-2954 Baader, Franz von, 1765-1841 (Table B-BJ3)
2955 Baader - Bardili
Subarrange each by Table B-BJ5
2955.B2-.B24 Baggesen, Jens, 1764-1826 (Table B-BJ5)

Modern (1450/1600-)
By region or country
Germany. Austria (German)
By period
Later 18th and early 19th centuries
Individual philosophers
Other philosophers
Baader - Bardili -- Continued
Cf. PT8122 German literature

2956 Bardili, Christoph Gottfried, 1761-1808 (Table B-BJ4)

2957 Bardili - Beck
Subarrange each by Table B-BJ5

2958 Beck, Jakob Sigismund, 1761-1840 (Table B-BJ4)

2959 Beck - Beneke
Subarrange each by Table B-BJ5

2960-2964 Beneke, Friedrich Eduard, 1798-1854 (Table B-BJ3)

2967 Beneke - Feuerbach, L.
Subarrange each by Table B-BJ5

Bolzano, Bernard, 1781-1848 see B4805.B65+

2967.C2-.C24 Carové, Friedrich Wilhelm, 1789-1852 (Table B-BJ5)

2967.C3-.C34 Carus, Carl Gustav, 1789-1869 (Table B-BJ5)

2967.C52-.C524 Chalybäus, Heinrich Moritz, 1796-1862 (Table B-BJ5)

2967.E46-.E464 Eichhorn, Johann Gottfried, 1752-1827 (Table B-BJ5)

2967.E5-.E54 Einsiedel, August von, 1754-1837 (Table B-BJ5)

2970-2973 Feuerbach, Ludwig, 1804-1872 (Table B-BJ3a)

2974 Feuerbach, L. - Fries
Subarrange each by Table B-BJ5

2974.F2-.F24 Feuerbach, Paul Johann Anselm, Ritter von, 1775-1833 (Table B-BJ5)

2974.F3-.F34 Fichte, Immanuel Hermann, 1796-1879 (Table B-BJ5)

2974.F4-.F44 Fischer, Karl Phil. (Karl Philipp), 1807-1885 (Table B-BJ5)

2975-2979 Fries, Jakob Friedrich, 1773-1843 (Table B-BJ3)

2979.A-Z Special topics, A-Z

2979.E8 Ethics

2979.S9 Subjectivity

2986 Fries - Goethe
Subarrange each by Table B-BJ5

2986.F6-.F64 Fröbel, Friedrich, 1782-1852 (Table B-BJ5)

Modern (1450/1600-)
By region or country
Germany. Austria (German)
By period
Later 18th and early 19th centuries
Individual philosophers
Other philosophers
Fries - Goethe -- Continued
Cf. LB631+ Theory of education
2987 Goethe, Johann Wolfgang von, 1749-1832 (Table B-BJ4)
Cf. PT2193 German literature
2988 Goethe - Hamann
Subarrange each by Table B-BJ5
2988.G8-.G84 Günther, Anton, 1783-1863 (Table B-BJ5)
2990-2993 Hamann, Johann Georg, 1730-1788 (Table B-BJ3a)
Cf. PT2287.H9 German literature
2995 Hamann - Herbart
Subarrange each by Table B-BJ5
Hardenberg, Friedrich, Freiherr von, 1772-1801 see B3071
Herbart, Johann Friedrich, 1776-1841
Cf. LB641+ Theory of education
3000 Periodicals. Societies. Serials
3001 Dictionaries
Collected works
3003 Original (vernacular) texts. By date
3004 Editions with commentary. By editor
3005 Partial editions, selections, etc. By editor or date
Translations
Subarrange by translator or date
Including translations with original texts
3006 Greek
3007 Latin
3008 English
3009 French
3010 German
3011 Italian
3012 Spanish and Portuguese
3013.A-Z Other languages, A-Z
Separate works
3015-3019 Allgemeine Metaphysik (Table B-BJ10)
3020-3024 Allgemeine praktische Philosophie (Table B-BJ10)
3025-3029 Hauptpunkte der Logik (Table B-BJ10)

Modern (1450/1600-)
By region or country
Germany. Austria (German)
By period
Later 18th and early 19th centuries
Individual philosophers
Other philosophers
Herbart, Johann Friedrich, 1776-1841
Separate works -- Continued

3030-3034 Hauptpunkte der Metaphysik (Table B-BJ10)
3035-3039 Kurze Encyklopädie der Philosophie (Table B-BJ10)
3041 Lehrbuch zur Einleitung in die Philosophie (Table B-BJ12)
Lehrbuch zur Psychologie see BF131+
3042 Psychologie als Wissenschaft neu gegründet auf Erfahrung, Metaphysik und Mathematik (Table B-BJ12)
3043 Psychologische Untersuchungen
3044.A-Z Other works, A-Z
Subarrange each by Table B-BJ13
3045 Spurious and apocryphal works
3046 Indexes, outlines, paraphrases, etc.
3047 Biography and memoirs (Table B-BJ14)
3048 Criticism and interpretation
3049.A-Z Special topics, A-Z
3049.E8 Ethics
3050 Herbart - Herder
Subarrange each by Table B-BJ5
3051 Herder, Johann Gottfried, 1744-1803 (Table B-BJ4)
Cf. PT2351+ German literature
3053 Herder - Jacobi
Subarrange each by Table B-BJ5
3053.H55-.H554 Hülsen, August Ludewig (Table B-BJ5)
3053.H6-.H64 Humboldt, Alexander von, 1769-1859 (Table B-BJ5)
3053.H7-.H74 Humboldt, Wilhelm, freiherr von, 1767-1835 (Table B-BJ5)
3055-3059 Jacobi, Friedrich Heinrich, 1743-1819 (Table B-BJ3)
3060 Jacobi - Krause
Subarrange each by Table B-BJ5
3060.J3-.J34 Jerusalem, Karl Wilhelm, 1747-1772 (Table B-BJ5)
3061 Krause, Karl Christian Friedrich, 1781-1832 (Table B-BJ4)

Modern (1450/1600-)
By region or country
Germany. Austria (German)
By period
Later 18th and early 19th centuries
Individual philosophers
Other philosophers -- Continued

3062 Krause - Krug
Subarrange each by Table B-BJ5

3063 Krug, Wilhelm Traugott, 1770-1842 (Table B-BJ4)

3064 Krug - Maimon
Subarrange each by Table B-BJ5

3065-3069 Maimon, Salomon, 1754-1800 (Table B-BJ3)

3070 Maimon - Novalis
Subarrange each by Table B-BJ5

3070.M6-.M64 Molitor, Franz Joseph, 1779-1860 (Table B-BJ5)

3070.M8-.M84 Müller, Adam Heinrich, Ritter von Nitterdorf, 1779-1829 (Table B-BJ5)

3070.M9-.M94 Müller, J. Georg (Johann Georg), 1759-1819 (Table B-BJ5)

3071 Novalis, 1772-1801 (Table B-BJ4)
Pseudonym of Friedrich Hardenberg

3072 Novalis - Oken
Subarrange each by Table B-BJ5

3073 Oken, Lorenz, 1779-1851 (Table B-BJ4)

3075 Oken - Reinhold, E.
Subarrange each by Table B-BJ5

3077 Reinhold, Ernst (Ernst Christian Gottlieb), 1793-1855 (Table B-BJ4)

3078 Reinhold, E. - Reinhold, K.
Subarrange each by Table B-BJ5

3080-3084 Reinhold, Karl Leonhard, 1758-1823 (Table B-BJ3)

3086 Reinhold, K. - Schleiermacher
Subarrange each by Table B-BJ5

3086.S3-.S34 Schiller, Friedrich, 1759-1805 (Table B-BJ5)
Cf. PT2496.E8 Esthetics (Schiller in German literature)
Cf. PT2496.P4 Philosophy (Schiller in German literature)

3086.S4-.S44 Schlegel, August Wilhelm von, 1767-1845 (Table B-BJ5)

3086.S5-.S54 Schlegel, Friedrich von, 1772-1829 (Table B-BJ5)

3090-3098 Schleiermacher, Friedrich, 1768-1834 (Table B-BJ2 modified)

Modern (1450/1600-)
By region or country
Germany. Austria (German)
By period
Later 18th and early 19th centuries
Individual philosophers
Other philosophers
Schleiermacher, Friedrich, 1768-1834 -- Continued
3098.A-Z Special topics, A-Z
3098.A38 Aesthetics
3098.D5 Dialectic
3098.E7 Ethics
3098.H35 Happiness
3098.H45 Hermeneutics
3098.R3 Religion
3098.S34 Self
3099 Schleiermacher - Schopenhauer
Subarrange each by Table B-BJ5
Schopenhauer, Arthur, 1788-1860
3100 Periodicals. Societies. Serials
3101 Dictionaries
Collected works
3103 Original (vernacular) texts. By date
3104 Editions with commentary. By editor
3105 Partial editions, selections, etc. By editor or date
Translations
Subarrange by translator or date
Including translations with original texts
3106 Greek
3107 Latin
3108 English
3109 French
3110 German
3111 Italian
3112 Spanish and Portuguese
3113.A-Z Other languages, A-Z
Separate works
3114 Die beiden Grundprobleme der Ethik (Table B-BJ12)
3115-3119 Parerga und Paralipomena (Table B-BJ10)
3120-3124 Über die vierfache Wurzel des Satzes vom zureichenden Grunde (Table B-BJ10)
3135-3139 Die welt als Wille und Vorstellung (Table B-BJ10)

Modern (1450/1600-)
By region or country
Germany. Austria (German)
By period
Later 18th and early 19th centuries
Individual philosophers
Other philosophers
Schopenhauer, Arthur, 1788-1860
Separate works -- Continued

3144.A-Z Other works, A-Z
Subarrange each by Table B-BJ13
e. g.
3144.U3-.U33 Über den Willen in der Natur (Table B-BJ13)
3145 Spurious and apocryphal works
3146 Indexes, outlines, paraphrases, etc.
3147 Biography and memoirs (Table B-BJ14)
3148 Criticism and interpretation
3149.A-Z Special topics, A-Z
3149.A4 Aesthetics
Education
see class L
3149.F7 Free will
3149.K7 Knowledge
3149.L6 Love
3149.M3 Man
3149.N38 Nature
3149.R42 Religion
3149.W74 Woman
3151 Schopenhauer - Sd
Subarrange each by Table B-BJ5
3151.S4-.S44 Schulze, Gottlob Ernst, 1761-1833 (Table B-BJ5)
3151.S6-.S64 Schwegler, Albert, 1819-1857 (Table B-BJ5)
3152 Se - Ste
Subarrange each by Table B-BJ5
3152.S5-.S54 Solger, Karl Wilhelm Ferdinand, 1780-1819 (Table B-BJ5)
3152.S8-.S84 Steffens, Henrich, 1773-1845 (Table B-BJ5)
3152.S9-.S94 Steinheim, Salomon Ludwig (Table B-BJ5)
3153 Sth - Sz
Subarrange each by Table B-BJ5
3153.S75-.S754 Stirner, Max, 1806-1856 (Table B-BJ5)
3154 T - Trendelenburg
Subarrange each by Table B-BJ5
3154.T48-.T484 Tetens, Johann Nicolas, 1736-1807 (Table B-BJ5)

Modern (1450/1600-)
By region or country
Germany. Austria (German)
By period
Later 18th and early 19th centuries
Individual philosophers
Other philosophers -- Continued

3155-3158 Trendelenburg, Friedrich Adolf, 1802-1872 (Table B-BJ3a)

3159 Trendelenburg - Ulrici
Subarrange each by Table B-BJ5

3159.T6-.T64 Troxler, Ignaz Paul Vitalis, 1780-1866 (Table B-BJ5)

3160-3168 Ulrici, Hermann, 1806-1884 (Table B-BJ2)

3170 Ulrici - Wagner
Subarrange each by Table B-BJ5

3171 Wagner, Johann Jakob, 1775-1841 (Table B-BJ4)

3173 Wagner - Weisse
Subarrange each by Table B-BJ5

3175 Weisse, Christian Hermann, 1801-1866 (Table B-BJ4)

3177 Weisse - Z
Subarrange each by Table B-BJ5

Later 19th and 20th centuries
Including works after about 1850

3180 Collected works (nonserial)

3181 General works

3183 Constructivism

3183.5 Critical theory. Frankfurt school of philosophy

3184 Genius

3184.5 Historicism

3185 Idealism

3185.7 Immanence

3186 Individuation

3187 Language

3188 Materialism

3190 Monism

3191 Naturalism

3192 Neo-Kantianism

3192.5 Origin

3194 Pessimism and optimism

3197 Positivism

3197.5 Primitivism

3197.6.A-Z Other topics, A-Z

3197.6.S63 Space and time

Individual philosophers

3198 Anonymous

Modern (1450/1600-)
By region or country
Germany. Austria (German)
By period
Later 19th and 20th centuries
Individual philosophers -- Continued

3199 A - Avenarius
Subarrange each by Table B-BJ5
3199.A3-.A34 Adorno, Theodor W., 1903-1969 (Table B-BJ5)
3199.A39-.A394 Albert, Hans, 1921- (Table B-BJ5)
3199.A53-.A534 Anders, Günther, 1902-1992 (Table B-BJ5)
3199.A6-.A64 Apel, Karl-Otto (Table B-BJ5)
3199.A7-.A74 Arnoldt, Emil, 1828-1905 (Table B-BJ5)
3200-3208 Avenarius, Richard, 1843-1896 (Table B-BJ2)
3209 Avenarius - Brauer
Subarrange each by Table B-BJ5
3209.B16-.B164 Baeumker, Clemens, 1853-1924 (Table B-BJ5)
3209.B2-.B24 Bahnsen, Julius, 1830-1881 (Table B-BJ5)
3209.B25-.B254 Barthel, Ernst, 1890-1953 (Table B-BJ5)
3209.B3-.B34 Bauch, Bruno, 1877-1942 (Table B-BJ5)
3209.B36-.B364 Baumgarten, Arthur, 1884-1966 (Table B-BJ5)
3209.B5-.B54 Beck, Friedrich Alfred, 1899- (Table B-BJ5)
3209.B56-.B564 Becker, Oskar, 1889-1964 (Table B-BJ5)
3209.B58-.B584 Benjamin, Walter, 1892-1940 (Table B-BJ5)
3209.B6-.B64 Bense, Max, 1910-1990 (Table B-BJ5)
3209.B7-.B74 Biedermann, Gustav, 1815-1890 (Table B-BJ5)
3209.B75-.B754 Bloch, Ernst, 1885-1977 (Table B-BJ5)
3209.B83-.B834 Blumenberg, Hans (Table B-BJ5)
3209.B87-.B874 Boltzmann, Ludwig, 1844-1906 (Table B-BJ5)
3210 Bräuer, Ernst Wasa, 1889- (Table B-BJ4)
3211 Bräuer - Brentano
Subarrange each by Table B-BJ5
3212 Brentano, Franz Clemens, 1838-1917 (Table B-BJ4)
3213 Brentano - Büchner
Subarrange each by Table B-BJ5
3213.B2-.B24 Brentano, Margherita von, 1922-1995 (Table B-BJ5)
3213.B4-.B44 Brod, Max, 1884-1968 (Table B-BJ5)
3213.B6-.B64 Brühlmann, Otto, 1883- (Table B-BJ5)
3213.B7-.B74 Brünner, Constantin, 1862-1937 (Table B-BJ5)
3213.B8-.B84 Buber, Martin, 1878-1965 (Table B-BJ5)
3215 Büchner, Ludwig, 1824-1899 (Table B-BJ4)
3216 Büchner - Dilz
Subarrange each by Table B-BJ5
Carnap, Rudolf, 1891-1970 see B945.C16+
3216.C27-.C274 Carneri, B.

Modern (1450/1600-)
By region or country
Germany. Austria (German)
By period
Later 19th and 20th centuries
Individual philosophers
Büchner - Dilz -- Continued

3216.C3-.C34 Cassirer, Ernst, 1874-1945 (Table B-BJ5)
3216.C45-.C454 Chlebik, Franz (Table B-BJ5)
3216.C5-.C54 Class, Gustav (Table B-BJ5)
3216.C7-.C74 Cohen, Hermann, 1842-1918 (Table B-BJ5)
3216.C76-.C764 Cohn, Jonas, 1869-1947 (Table B-BJ5)
3216.C77-.C774 Conrad-Martius, Hedwig, 1888-1966 (Table B-BJ5)
3216.C78-.C784 Cornelius, Hans, 1935- (Table B-BJ5)
3216.D2-.D24 Delius, Rudolf von, 1878-1946 (Table B-BJ5)
3216.D25-.D254 Dessoir, Max, 1867-1947 (Table B-BJ5)
3216.D295-.D2954 Deubler, Konrad, 1814-1884 (Table B-BJ5)
3216.D3-.D34 Deussen, Paul, 1845-1919 (Table B-BJ5)
3216.D4-.D44 Deutinger, Martin, 1815-1864 (Table B-BJ5)
3216.D6-.D64 Dietzgen, Joseph, 1828-1888 (Table B-BJ5)
3216.D8-.D84 Dilthey, Wilhelm, 1833-1911 (Table B-BJ5)
3217 Din - Driesch
Subarrange each by Table B-BJ5
3217.D3-.D34 Dingler, Hugo, 1881-1954 (Table B-BJ5)
3217.D5-.D54 Döblin, Alfred, 1878-1957 (Table B-BJ5)
3217.D72-.D724 Drews, Arthur, 1865-1935 (Table B-BJ5)
3218 Driesch, Hans, 1867-1941 (Table B-BJ4)
3219 Driesch - Dühring
Subarrange each by Table B-BJ5
3219.D7-.D74 Drobisch, Moritz Wilhelm, 1802-1896 (Table B-BJ5)
3220-3223 Dühring, E. (Eugen), 1833-1921 (Table B-BJ3a)
3224 Dühring - Erdmann
Subarrange each by Table B-BJ5
3224.D7-.D74 Dyroff, Adolf, 1866-1943 (Table B-BJ5)
3224.E2-.E24 Ebner, Ferdinand, 1882-1931 (Table B-BJ5)
3224.E37-.E374 Ehrenberg, Hans, 1883-1958 (Table B-BJ5)
3224.E6-.E64 Engels, Friedrich, 1820-1895 (Table B-BJ5)
3225 Erdmann, Johann Eduard, 1805-1892 (Table B-BJ4)
3227 Erdmann - Ez
Subarrange each by Table B-BJ5
3227.E7-.E74 Eucken, Rudolf, 1846-1926 (Table B-BJ5)
3229 F - Fechner
Subarrange each by Table B-BJ5
3229.F2-.F24 Falckenberg, Richard, 1851-1920 (Table B-BJ5)

	Modern (1450/1600-)
	By region or country
	Germany. Austria (German)
	By period
	Later 19th and 20th centuries
	Individual philosophers -- Continued
3230-3238	Fechner, Gustav Theodor, 1801-1887 (Table B-BJ2)
3240	Fechner - Fischer, K.
	Subarrange each by Table B-BJ5
3240.F48-.F484	Feyerabend, Paul, 1924-1994 (Table B-BJ5)
3240.F49-.F494	Figal, Günter, 1949- (Table B-BJ5)
3240.F52-.F524	Fink, Eugen (Table B-BJ5)
3240.F53-.F534	Fischer, Engelbert Lorenz, 1845-1923 (Table B-BJ5)
3240.F58-.F584	Fischer, Franz, 1929-1970 (Table B-BJ5)
3241	Fischer, Kuno, 1824-1907 (Table B-BJ4)
3244	Fischer, K. - Fra
	Subarrange each by Table B-BJ5
3244.F18-.F184	Flach, Werner, 1930- (Table B-BJ5)
3244.F2-.F24	Flake, Otto, 1880-1963 (Table B-BJ5)
3244.F27-.F274	Frank, Adolf (Table B-BJ5)
3244.F28-.F284	Frank, Erich, 1883-1949 (Table B-BJ5)
3244.F3-.F34	Franze, Paul Christian (Table B-BJ5)
3245	Fre - Fz
	Subarrange each by Table B-BJ5
3245.F2-.F24	Frege, Gottlob, 1848-1925 (Table B-BJ5)
3245.F3-.F34	Freyer, Hans, 1887-1969 (Table B-BJ5)
3245.F38-.F384	Friedlaender, Salomo, 1871-1946 (Table B-BJ5)
3245.F5-.F54	Frimmel, Theodor von, 1853-1928 (Table B-BJ5)
3245.F7-.F74	Frohschammer, Jakob, 1821-1893 (Table B-BJ5)
3248	G - Görland
	Subarrange each by Table B-BJ5
3248.G3-.G34	Gadamer, Hans-Georg, 1900-2002 (Table B-BJ5)
3248.G38-.G384	Gehlen, Arnold, 1904-1976 (Table B-BJ5)
3248.G4-.G44	Geyser, Joseph, 1869-1948 (Table B-BJ5)
3248.G48-.G484	Glockner, Hermann, 1896- (Table B-BJ5)
3248.G5-.G54	Glogau, Gustav, 1844-1895 (Table B-BJ5)
3249	Görland, Albert, 1869-1952 (Table B-BJ4)
3250	Görland - Göschel
	Subarrange each by Table B-BJ5
3251	Göschel, Karl Friedrich, 1784-1861 (Table B-BJ4)
3252	Göschel - Gro
	Subarrange each by Table B-BJ5
3252.G6-.G64	Goldschmidt, Kurt Walter, 1877- (Table B-BJ5)
3252.G642-.G6424	Goldschmidt, Ludwig, 1853-1931 (Table B-BJ5)
3252.G6425-.G64254	Goldstein, Julius, 1873-1929 (Table B-BJ5)

Modern (1450/1600-)
By region or country
Germany. Austria (German)
By period
Later 19th and 20th centuries
Individual philosophers
Göschel - Gro -- Continued

3252.G65-.G654 Grave, Friedrich, 1881- (Table B-BJ5)
3252.G68-.G684 Grebe, Wilhelm, 1897- (Table B-BJ5)
3252.G7-.G74 Greinert, Willy (Table B-BJ5)
3252.G8-.G84 Groethuysen, Bernhard, 1880-1946 (Table B-BJ5)
3254 Gru - Gz
Subarrange each by Table B-BJ5
3254.G7-.G74 Gruppe, O. F. (Otto Friedrich), 1804-1876 (Table B-BJ5)
3254.G85-.G854 Günther, Gotthard (Table B-BJ5)
3254.G86-.G864 Gurwitsch, Aron (Table B-BJ5)
3258 H - Haeckel
Subarrange each by Table B-BJ5
3258.H32-.H324 Habermas, Jürgen (Table B-BJ5)
3260-3268 Haeckel, Ernst, 1834-1919 (Table B-BJ2)
3269 Haeckel - Hartmann, Ed
Subarrange each by Table B-BJ5
3269.H3 Haecker, Theodor, 1879-1945
3270-3278 Hartmann, Eduard von, 1842-1906 (Table B-BJ2)
3279 Hartmann, Ed - Koz
Subarrange each by Table B-BJ5 unless otherwise indicated
3279.H2-.H24 Hartmann, Nicolai, 1882-1950 (Table B-BJ5)
3279.H3-.H34 Haym, R. (Rudolf), 1821-1901 (Table B-BJ5)
Heidegger, Martin, 1889-1976
3279.H45 Collected works. By date
3279.H46 Selected works. By date
3279.H47A-.H47Z Translations. By language, A-Z, and date
For translations of individual works see B3279.H48A+
3279.H48A-.H48Z Separate works. By title, A-Z
3279.H485 Letters. By date
3279.H49A-.H49Z Biography, criticism, etc., A-Z
3279.H497-.H4974 Heinrichs, Johannes, 1942- (Table B-BJ5)
3279.H5-.H54 Helmholtz, Hermann von, 1821-1894 (Table B-BJ5)
3279.H546-.H5464 Henrich, Dieter, 1927- (Table B-BJ5)
3279.H55-.H554 Hensel, Paul, 1860-1930 (Table B-BJ5)
3279.H6-.H64 Herbertz, Richard, b. 1878 (Table B-BJ5)
3279.H7-.H74 Hessen, Robert (Table B-BJ5)

Modern (1450/1600-)
By region or country
Germany. Austria (German)
By period
Later 19th and 20th centuries
Individual philosophers
Hartmann, Ed - - Koz

	Heymans, Gerard, 1857-1930 see B4075.H55+
3279.H84-.H844	Heyse, Hans, 1891- (Table B-BJ5)
3279.H8448-.H84484	Höffe, Otfried (Table B-BJ5)
3279.H8453-.H84534	Honecker, Martin, 1888-1941 (Table B-BJ5)
3279.H8454-.H84544	Hönigswald, Richard, 1875-1947 (Table B-BJ5)
3279.H847-.H8474	Horkheimer, Max, 1895-1973 (Table B-BJ5)
3279.H87-.H874	Hueck, Walter, b. 1898 (Table B-BJ5)
3279.H9-.H94	Husserl, Edmund, 1859-1938 (Table B-BJ5)
3279.J15-.J154	Jacoby, Günther, 1881-1969 (Table B-BJ5)
3279.J17-.J174	Jahn, Aegidius (Table B-BJ5)
3279.J2-.J24	Janke, Hans (Table B-BJ5)
3279.J27-.J274	Jansen, Bernhard, 1877-1942 (Table B-BJ5)
3279.J3-.J34	Jaspers, Karl, 1883-1969 (Table B-BJ5)
3279.J6-.J64	Jodl, Friedrich, 1849-1914 (Table B-BJ5)
3279.J66-.J664	Jonas, Hans, 1903-1993 (Table B-BJ5)
3279.J8-.J84	Junge, Reinhard (Table B-BJ5)
3279.K15-.K154	Kaibel, Franz, 1880-1935 (Table B-BJ5)
3279.K155-.K1554	Kambartel, Friedrich (Table B-BJ5)
3279.K2-.K24	Kann, Albert (Table B-BJ5)
3279.K25-.K254	Kassner, Rudolf, 1873-1959 (Table B-BJ5)
3279.K29-.K294	Kaufmann, Felix, 1895-1949 (Table B-BJ5)
3279.K3-.K34	Kemmerich, Max (Table B-BJ5)
3279.K4-.K44	Keyserling, Hermann, Graf von, 1880-1946 (Table B-BJ5)
3279.K5-.K54	Kirchmann, J. H. von (Julius Hermann), 1802-1884 (Table B-BJ5)
3279.K6-.K64	Klages, Ludwig, 1872-1956 (Table B-BJ5)
3279.K68-.K684	Klein, Hans-Dieter (Table B-BJ5)
3279.K7-.K74	Kleinpeter, Hans (Table B-BJ5)
3279.K79-.K794	Koeber, R. (Raphael), 1848-1923 (Table B-BJ5)
3279.K8-.K84	Kolbenheyer, E. G. (Erwin Guido), 1878-1962 (Table B-BJ5)
3279.K86-.K864	König, Josef, 1893-1974 (Table B-BJ5)
3280	Kr - Lange Subarrange each by Table B-BJ5
3280.K5-.K54	Krieck, Ernst, 1882-1947 (Table B-BJ5)
3280.K8-.K84	Krueger, Felix, 1874-1948 (Table B-BJ5)
3280.K9-.K94	Kühnemann, Eugen, 1868-1946 (Table B-BJ5)
3280.L3-.L34	Laas, Ernst, 1837-1885 (Table B-BJ5)
3280.L36-.L364	Landsberg, Paul-Louis, 1901-1944 (Table B-BJ5)

	Modern (1450/1600-)
	By region or country
	Germany. Austria (German)
	By period
	Later 19th and 20th centuries
	Individual philosophers -- Continued
3281	Lange, Friedrich Albert, 1828-1875 (Table B-BJ4)
3283	Lange - Lazarus
	Subarrange each by Table B-BJ5
3283.L3-.L34	Lask, Emil, 1875-1915 (Table B-BJ5)
3283.L5-.L54	Lasker, Emanuel, 1868-1941 (Table B-BJ5)
3285	Lazarus, Moritz, 1824-1903 (Table B-BJ4)
3286	Lazarus - Lipps, T.
	Subarrange each by Table B-BJ5
3286.L4-.L44	Lessing, Theodor, 1872-1933 (Table B-BJ5)
3286.L5-.L54	Liebmann, Otto, 1840-1912 (Table B-BJ5)
3286.L6-.L64	Lindemann, Hans Adalbert (Table B-BJ5)
3286.L7-.L74	Lipps, G. F. (Gottlob Friedrich), 1865-1931 (Table B-BJ5)
3287	Lipps, Theodor, 1851-1914 (Table B-BJ4)
3288	Lipps, T. - Lotze
	Subarrange each by Table B-BJ5
3288.L54-.L544	Litt, Theodor, 1880-1962 (Table B-BJ5)
3288.L66-.L664	Lorenz, Kuno, 1932- (Table B-BJ5)
3288.L67-.L674	Lotz, Johannes Baptist, 1903- (Table B-BJ5)
3290-3298	Lotze, Hermann, 1817-1881 (Table B-BJ2)
3298.A-Z	Special topics, A-Z
3298.F7	Free will
3299	Lotze - Mach
	Subarrange each by Table B-BJ5
3299.L68-.L684	Löwith, Karl, 1897-1973 (Table B-BJ5)
3299.L8-.L84	Ludowici, August (Table B-BJ5)
3299.L85-.L854	Lugmayer, Karl, 1892-1972 (Table B-BJ5)
3300-3303	Mach, Ernst, 1838-1916 (Table B-BJ3a)
3305	Mach - Mayer
	Subarrange each by Table B-BJ5
3305.M7-.M74	Marx, Karl, 1818-1883 (Table B-BJ5)
	For biography see HX39.5.A53+
3308	Mayer, Julius Robert von, 1814-1878 (Table B-BJ4)
3309	Mayer - Nietzsche
	Subarrange each by Table B-BJ5
3309.M2-.M24	Meinong, A. (Alexius), 1853-1920 (Table B-BJ5)
3309.M38-.M384	Menzer, Paul, 1873-1960 (Table B-BJ5)
3309.M4-.M44	Messer, August, 1867-1937 (Table B-BJ5)
3309.M443-.M4434	Messer, Max (Table B-BJ5)
3309.M45-.M454	Meyer, Hans (Table B-BJ5)
3309.M5-.M54	Michelet, Karl Ludwig, 1801-1893 (Table B-BJ5)

Modern (1450/1600-)
By region or country
Germany. Austria (German)
By period
Later 19th and 20th centuries
Individual philosophers
Mayer - Nietzsche -- Continued

3309.M56-.M564 Misch, Georg, 1878-1965 (Table B-BJ5)
3309.M6-.M64 Möbius, P. J. (Paul Julius), 1853-1907 (Table B-BJ5)
3309.M7-.M74 Müller, Johannes, 1864-1949 (Table B-BJ5)
3309.M746-.M7464 Müller, Max, 1906-1994 (Table B-BJ5)
3309.M8-.M84 Mutius, Gerhard von, 1872-1934 (Table B-BJ5)
3309.N2-.N24 Natorp, Paul, 1854-1924 (Table B-BJ5)
3309.N3-.N34 Nelson, Leonard, 1882-1927 (Table B-BJ5)
3309.N39-.N394 Neurath, Otto, 1882-1945 (Table B-BJ5)
3309.N4-.N44 Neustadt, Maximilian, 1863- (Table B-BJ5)
3310-3318 Nietzsche, Friedrich Wilhelm, 1844-1900 (Table B-BJ2 modified)
3313.A-Z Separate works. By title, A-Z

Subarrange each by Table B-BJ13 unless otherwise specified

Also sprach Zarathustra
3313.A4 Original text. By date
3313.A42 Selections, paraphrases, etc. By date
3313.A43A-.A43Z Translations. By language, A-Z, and date
3313.A44 Commentaries, interpretation, and criticism (with or without translations)
3318.A-Z Special subjects, A-Z
3318.A4 Aesthetics
3318.A54 Animals
3318.A87 Authority
Body, Human see B3318.H85
3318.B73 Brahmanism
3318.B83 Buddhism
3318.C35 Christianity
3318.C56 Classicism
3318.C64 The comic
3318.C8 Culture
3318.D35 Decadence
3318.D5 Dialectic
3318.E36 Economics
3318.E37 Ecstasy
3318.E46 Emotions
3318.E88 Eternal return
3318.E9 Ethics
Evil see B3318.G66

Modern (1450/1600-)
By region or country
Germany. Austria (German)
By period
Later 19th and 20th centuries
Individual philosophers
Nietzsche, Friedrich Wilhelm, 1844-1900
Special subjects, A-Z

3318.F45	Femininity
3318.F54	Finalism
3318.G45	Genealogy
3318.G46	Genius
3318.G66	Good and evil
3318.H44	Hermeneutics
3318.H47	Heroes
3318.H6	Homes
3318.H85	Human body
3318.H87	Humanities
3318.I3	Ideology
3318.J83	Judaism
3318.J87	Justice
3318.K7	Knowledge, Theory of
3318.L25	Language
3318.L43	Liberty
3318.L5	Literature
3318.M27	Man
3318.M4	Metaphor
3318.M5	Metaphysics
3318.M54	Methodology
3318.N3	Nature, Philosophy of
3318.N54	Nihilism
3318.O5	Ontology
3318.O75	Oriental philosophy
3318.P47	Perspective
3318.P53	Platonism
3318.P68	Power
	Psychology see BF1+
3318.R4	Religion
3318.R7	Romanticism
3318.S45	Self
3318.S8	Superman
3318.T44	Theater
3318.T5	Time
3318.T78	Truth
3318.V25	Values
3318.W37	War

Modern (1450/1600-)
By region or country
Germany. Austria (German)
By period
Later 19th and 20th centuries
Individual philosophers -- Continued

3319 Nietzsche - Paulsen
Subarrange each by Table B-BJ5
3319.N55-.N554 Nink, Caspar, 1885-1975 (Table B-BJ5)
3319.N65-.N654 Nohl, Herman, 1879-1960 (Table B-BJ5)
3319.O25-.O254 Odefey, Martin Richard (Table B-BJ5)
3319.O27-.O274 Oehler, Klaus (Table B-BJ5)
3319.O3-.O34 Oesterreich, Traugott Konstantin, 1880-1949 (Table B-BJ5)
3319.O8-.O84 Ostwald, Wilhelm, 1853-1932 (Table B-BJ5)
3321 Paulsen, Friedrich, 1846-1908 (Table B-BJ4)
3323 Paulsen - Rosenkranz
Subarrange each by Table B-BJ5
3323.P3-.P34 Petzoldt, Joseph, 1862-1929 (Table B-BJ5)
3323.P43-.P434 Pieper, Josef, 1904-1997 (Table B-BJ5)
3323.P5-.P54 Planck, Karl Christian, 1819-1880 (Table B-BJ5)
3323.P56-.P564 Plessner, Helmuth, 1892-1985 (Table B-BJ5)
3323.P59-.P594 Port, Kurt, 1896-1979 (Table B-BJ5)
3323.P6-.P64 Prantl, Karl (Table B-BJ5)
3323.P8-.P84 Przywara, Erich, 1889-1972 (Table B-BJ5)
3323.R2-.R24 Raab, Friedrich, 1890-1936 (Table B-BJ5)
3323.R33-.R334 Radenhausen, Christian, b. 1813 (Table B-BJ5)
3323.R336-.R3364 Rahner, Karl, 1904-1984 (Table B-BJ5)
3323.R34-.R344 Rée, Paul, 1849-1901 (Table B-BJ5)
3323.R35-.R354 Rehmke, Johannes, 1848-1930 (Table B-BJ5)
3323.R37-.R374 Reichenau, Irmgard, 1886- (Table B-BJ5)
3323.R39-.R394 Reinach, Adolf, 1883-1918? (Table B-BJ5)
3323.R442-.R4424 Reininger, Robert, 1869-1955 (Table B-BJ5)
3323.R445-.R4454 Reinke, J. (Johannes), 1849-1931 (Table B-BJ5)
3323.R447-.R4474 Rensch, Bernhard, 1900-1990 (Table B-BJ5)
3323.R45-.R454 Rettig, Heinrich, 1900- (Table B-BJ5)
3323.R495-.R4954 Rickert, Heinrich, 1863-1936 (Table B-BJ5)
3323.R5-.R54 Riehl, Alois, 1844-1924 (Table B-BJ5)
3323.R6-.R64 Riezler, Kurt, 1882-1955 (Table B-BJ5)
3323.R66-.R664 Rohde, Erwin, 1845-1898 (Table B-BJ5)
3323.R665-.R6654 Rohs, Peter (Table B-BJ5)
3323.R67-.R674 Rombach, Heinrich, 1923- (Table B-BJ5)
3323.R68-.R684 Roniger, Emil, 1883- (Table B-BJ5)
3325 Rosenkranz, Karl, 1805-1879 (Table B-BJ4)
3327 Rosenkranz - Rz
Subarrange each by Table B-BJ5
3327.R6-.R64 Rosenzweig, Franz, 1886-1929 (Table B-BJ5)

Modern (1450/1600-)
By region or country
Germany. Austria (German)
By period
Later 19th and 20th centuries
Individual philosophers -- Continued

3329 S - Si
Subarrange each by Table B-BJ5
3329.S2-.S24 Saitschick, Robert, 1868-1965 (Table B-BJ5)
3329.S3-.S34 Sapper, Karl (Table B-BJ5)
3329.S43-.S434 Schaeffler, Richard (Table B-BJ5)
3329.S44-.S444 Schafheitlin, Adolf (Table B-BJ5)
3329.S45-.S454 Schapp, Wilhelm, 1884- (Table B-BJ5)
3329.S48-.S484 Scheler, Max, 1874-1928 (Table B-BJ5)
3329.S492-.S4924 Schmalenbach, Herman, 1885-1950 (Table B-BJ5)
3329.S4957-.S49574 Schmitz, Hermann (Table B-BJ5)
3329.S4967-.S49674 Schrödinger, Erwin, 1887-1961 (Table B-BJ5)
3329.S497-.S4974 Schuppe, Wilhelm, 1836-1913 (Table B-BJ5)
3329.S55-.S554 Siegel, Carl, 1872- (Table B-BJ5)
3329.S56-.S564 Sigwart, Christoph, 1830-1904 (Table B-BJ5)
3329.S6-.S64 Simmel, Georg, 1858-1918 (Table B-BJ5)
3332 Sk - Steiner
Subarrange each by Table B-BJ5
3332.S25-.S254 Sloterdijk, Peter, 1947- (Table B-BJ5)
3332.S28-.S284 Sonnemann, Ulrich (Table B-BJ5)
3332.S29-.S294 Spaemann, Robert (Table B-BJ5)
3332.S3-.S34 Spann, Othmar, 1878-1950 (Table B-BJ5)
3332.S4-.S44 Spengler, Oswald, 1880-1936 (Table B-BJ5)
3332.S47-.S474 Spicker, Gideon, 1840-1912 (Table B-BJ5)
3332.S5-.S54 Spir, African, 1837-1890 (Table B-BJ5)
3332.S6-.S64 Steffen, Albert, 1884-1963 (Table B-BJ5)
3332.S67-.S674 Stein, Edith, Saint, 1891-1942 (Table B-BJ5)
Cf. BX4705.S814 Life as a Catholic nun
3332.S7-.S74 Stein, Heinrich, Freiherr von, 1857-1887 (Table B-BJ5)
3333 Steiner, Rudolf, 1861-1925 (Table B-BJ4)
For anthroposophy see BP595.S894+
For biography and criticism see BP595.S895
3334 Steiner - Steinthal
Subarrange each by Table B-BJ5
3335 Steinthal, Heymann, 1823-1899 (Table B-BJ4)
3336 Steinthal - Stern
Subarrange each by Table B-BJ5
3337 Stern, William, 1871-1938 (Table B-BJ4)
3338 Stern - Strauss
Subarrange each by Table B-BJ5

Modern (1450/1600-)
By region or country
Germany. Austria (German)
By period
Later 19th and 20th centuries
Individual philosophers
Stern - Strauss -- Continued

3338.S82-.S824 Stockhausen, Alma von (Table B-BJ5)
3340-3343 Strauss, David Friedrich, 1808-1874 (Table B-BJ3a)
3344 Strauss - Stumpf
Subarrange each by Table B-BJ5
3344.S6-.S64 Strümpell, Ludwig, 1812-1899 (Table B-BJ5)
3345 Stumpf, Carl, 1848-1936 (Table B-BJ4)
3346 Stumpf - Tönnies
Subarrange each by Table B-BJ5
3346.T3-.T34 Teichmuller, Gustav, 1832-1888 (Table B-BJ5)
3346.T35-.T354 Teller, Jürgen (Table B-BJ5)
3346.T6-.T64 Thöne, Franz, 1884- (Table B-BJ5)
3348 Tönnies, Ferdinand, 1855-1936 (Table B-BJ4)
3349 Tönnies - Ueberweg
Subarrange each by Table B-BJ5
3349.T83-.T834 Tugendhat, Ernst (Table B-BJ5)
3351 Ueberweg, Friedrich, 1826-1871 (Table B-BJ4)
3354 Ueberweg - Vogt
Subarrange each by Table B-BJ5
3354.U47-.U474 Ulrici, Hermann, 1806-1884 (Table B-BJ5)
3354.V48-.V484 Vaihinger, Hans, 1852-1933 (Table B-BJ5)
3354.V64-.V644 Vetter, August, 1887-1976 (Table B-BJ5)
3354.V8-.V84 Vischer, Friedrich Theodor, 1807-1887 (Table B-BJ5)
3354.V88-.V884 Voegelin, Eric, 1901-1985 (Table B-BJ5)
3355 Vogt, Karl Christoph, 1817-1895 (Table B-BJ4)
3356 Vogt - Volkelt
Subarrange each by Table B-BJ5
3357 Volkelt, Johannes, 1848-1930 (Table B-BJ4)
3359 Volkelt - Weber
Subarrange each by Table B-BJ5
3359.V6-.V64 Von Hildebrand, Dietrich, 1889-1977 (Table B-BJ5)
3359.W5-.W54 Wachsmuth, Guenther, 1893- (Table B-BJ5)
3359.W6-.W64 Wahle, Richard, 1857-1935 (Table B-BJ5)
3359.W7-.W74 Waldenfels, Bernhard, 1934- (Table B-BJ5)
3361 Weber, Max, 1864-1920 (Table B-BJ4)
3363 Weber - Willmann
Subarrange each by Table B-BJ5
3363.W4-.W44 Wechssler, Eduard, 1869-1949 (Table B-BJ5)

Modern (1450/1600-)
By region or country
Germany. Austria (German)
By period
Later 19th and 20th centuries
Individual philosophers
Weber - Willmann -- Continued

3363.W5-.W54 Weininger, Otto, 1880-1903 (Table B-BJ5)
3363.W63-.W634 Weinstein, Max B. (Max Bernhard), b. 1852 (Table B-BJ5)
3363.W64-.W644 Weischedel, Wilhelm, 1905-1975 (Table B-BJ5)
3363.W75-.W754 Welte, Bernhard (Table B-BJ5)
3365 Willmann, Otto, 1839-1920 (Table B-BJ4)
3368 Willmann - Windelband
Subarrange each by Table B-BJ5
3371 Windelband, W. (Wilhelm), 1848-1915 (Table B-BJ4)
3376 Windelband - Wundt
Subarrange each by Table B-BJ5
3376.W56-.W564 Wittgenstein, Ludwig, 1889-1951 (Table B-BJ5 modified)
3376.W563A-.W563Z7 Separate works, A-Z
Philosophische Untersuchungen
3376.W563P529 Original work. By date
3376.W563P53 English translations. By date
3376.W563P5312-.W563P5319 Other translations. By language (alphabetically) and date
3376.W563P532-.W563P5329 Criticism
Tractatus logico-philosophicus
3376.W563T73 Original work. By date
3376.W563T7312-.W563T7319 Translations. By language (alphabetically) and date
3376.W563T73195 Selections. By date
3376.W563T732-.W563T739 Criticism
3376.W6-.W64 Wolff, Hermann Heinrich Rudolf, 1842-1896 (Table B-BJ5)
3380-3388 Wundt, Wilhelm Max, 1832-1920 (Table B-BJ2)
3390 Wundt - Zeller
Subarrange each by Table B-BJ5
3391 Zeller, Eduard, 1814-1908 (Table B-BJ4)
3393 Zeller - Ziegler, T.
Subarrange each by Table B-BJ5
3393.Z7-.Z74 Ziegler, Leopold, 1881-1958 (Table B-BJ5)
3395 Ziegler, Theobald, 1846-1918 (Table B-BJ4)

	Modern (1450/1600-)
	By region or country
	Germany. Austria (German)
	By period
	Later 19th and 20th centuries
	Individual philosophers -- Continued
3396	Ziegler, T. - Zz
	Subarrange each by Table B-BJ5
3396.Z76-.Z764	Zirm, Eduard Konrad (Table B-BJ5)
	21st century
3397	General works
3398.A-Z	Special topics, A-Z
3399.A-Z	Individual philosophers, A-Z
	Subarrange each by Table B-BJ5
3399.N53-.N534	Nida-Rümelin, Julian, 1954- (Table B-BJ5)
	Greece (Modern)
3500	Collected works (nonserial)
3501	General works
3511.A-Z	Special topics, A-Z
3511.E54	Enlightenment
3511.M3	Man
3511.S6	Soul
3515.A-Z	Individual philosophers, A-Z
	Subarrange each by Table B-BJ5
3515.A75-.A754	Arnellos, Iōannēs G., 1870-1948 (Table B-BJ5)
3515.A94-.A944	Axelos, Kōstas (Table B-BJ5)
3515.B5-.B54	Blēsidēs, Thrasyboulos St. (Table B-BJ5)
3515.B6-.B64	Boreas, Theophilos, 1870- (Table B-BJ5)
3515.D4-.D44	Demopoulos, P.N. (Table B-BJ5)
3515.K3-.K34	Kairēs, Theophilos, 1784-1853 (Table B-BJ5)
3515.K4-.K44	Kanellopoulos, Panagiōtēs, 1902- (Table B-BJ5)
3515.M3-.M34	Makrakēs, Apostolos, 1831-1905 (Table B-BJ5)
3515.M43-.M434	Menagias, Iōannēs, 1811-1870 (Table B-BJ5)
3515.P34-.P344	Papagiōrgēs, Kōstēs (Table B-BJ5)
3515.R35-.R354	Ramphos, Stelios (Table B-BJ5)
3515.R65-.R654	Rōmanos, Odysseas (Table B-BJ5)
3515.T45-.T454	Theodōrakopoulos, Iōannēs Nikolaou, 1900- (Table B-BJ5)
3515.V73-.V734	Vrailas-Armenēs, Petros, 1812 or 13-1884 (Table B-BJ5)
	Italy
3551	General works
3561.A-Z	Special topics, A-Z
3561.C3	Cartesianism
3561.E95	Experience
	By period
	17th century

Modern (1450/1600-)
By region or country
Italy
By period
17th century -- Continued
3571 General works
3575.A-Z Special topics, A-Z
Individual philosophers
3578 A - Vico
Subarrange each by Table B-BJ5
3578.B34-.B344 Baldelli, Nicolas, 1573-1655 (Table B-BJ5)
3578.C35-.C354 Caloprese, Gregorio, 1650-1715 (Table B-BJ5)
3578.G74-.G744 Gravina, Gianvincenzo, 1664-1718 (Table B-BJ5)
3578.L5-.L54 Liceti, Fortunio, 1577-1657 (Table B-BJ5)
3578.M36-.M364 Mastri, Bartolomeo, 1602-1673 (Table B-BJ5)
3578.R8-.R84 Rucellai, Orazio Ricasoli (Table B-BJ5)
3578.V3-.V34 Vanini, Giulio Cesare, 1585-1619 (Table B-BJ5)
3580-3583 Vico, Giambattista, 1668-1744 (Table B-BJ3a)
3585 Vico - Z
Subarrange each by Table B-BJ5
18th century
3591 General works
3595.A-Z Special topics, A-Z
3595.E54 Enlightenment
3598.A-Z Individual philosophers, A-Z
Subarrange each by Table B-BJ5
3598.G3-.G34 Genovesi, Antonio, 1712-1769 (Table B-BJ5)
3598.R3-.R34 Radicati, Alberto, conte di Passerano, 1698-1737 (Table B-BJ5)
3598.V3-.V34 Valperga di Caluso, Tommaso, 1737-1815 (Table B-BJ5)
3598.V6-.V64 Volpi, Gio. Antonio, 1686-1766 (Table B-BJ5)
3598.Z3-.Z34 Zanotti, Francesco Maria, 1692-1777 (Table B-BJ5)
19th and 20th centuries
3601 General works
Special topics
3605 Positivism
3608 Scholasticism
3609.A-Z Other topics, A-Z
3609.A8 Atheism
3609.C45 Christianity
3609.I3 Idealism
3609.N44 Negativity
3609.N46 Neopaganism
3609.P7 Pragmatism
Individual philosophers
Subarrange each by Table B-BJ5

	Modern (1450/1600-)
	By region or country
	Italy
	By period
	19th and 20th centuries
	Individual philosophers -- Continued
3611	A - Ardigò
3611.A23-.A234	Abbagnano, Nicola, 1901-1990 (Table B-BJ5)
3611.A3-.A34	Acri, Francesco, 1834-1913 (Table B-BJ5)
3611.A4-.A44	Agamben, Giorgio, 1942- (Table B-BJ5)
3611.A445-.A4454	Agazzi, Evandro (Table B-BJ5)
3611.A5-.A54	Albergamo, F. (Francesco), 1896- (Table B-BJ5)
3611.A59-.A594	Aliotta, Antonio, 1881-1964 (Table B-BJ5)
3611.A64-.A644	Antiseri, Dario (Table B-BJ5)
3611.A73-.A734	Arata, Carlo (Table B-BJ5)
3612	Ardigò, Roberto, 1828-1920 (Table B-BJ4)
3613	Ardigò - Bz Subarrange each by Table B-BJ5
3613.B3-.B34	Banfi, Antonio, 1886-1957 (Table B-BJ5)
3613.B346-.B3464	Barié, Giovanni Emanuele, 1894-1956 (Table B-BJ5)
3613.B35-.B354	Battaglia, Felice, 1902-1977 (Table B-BJ5)
3613.B385-.B3854	Bencivenga, Ermanno, 1950- (Table B-BJ5)
3613.B4-.B44	Bertini, Giovanni Maria, 1818-1876 (Table B-BJ5)
3613.B53-.B534	Bonatelli, Francesco, 1830-1911 (Table B-BJ5)
3613.B56-.B564	Bontadini, Gustavo (Table B-BJ5)
	Bonavino, Cristoforo see B3618
3613.B57-.B574	Bori, Pier Cesare (Table B-BJ5)
3613.B6-.B64	Botti, Luigi, 1879- (Table B-BJ5)
3613.B76-.B764	Brescia, Giuseppe (Table B-BJ5)
3614	C - Ferrari Subarrange each by Table B-BJ5
3614.C14-.C144	Cacciari, Massimo (Table B-BJ5)
3614.C21-.C214	Calderoni, Mario, 1879-1914 (Table B-BJ5)
3614.C222-.C2224	Calogero, Guido, 1904- (Table B-BJ5)
3614.C26-.C264	Camera, Ugo (Table B-BJ5)
3614.C2738-.C27384	Cantoni, Carlo, 1840-1906 (Table B-BJ5)
3614.C275-.C2754	Cantoni, Remo, 1914-1978 (Table B-BJ5)
3614.C276-.C2764	Capitini, Aldo (Table B-BJ5)
3614.C277-.C2774	Caracciolo, Alberto, 1918- (Table B-BJ5)
3614.C2784324-.C27843244	Caramella, Santino (Table B-BJ5)
3614.C2784335-.C27843354	Carchia, Gianni (Table B-BJ5)
3614.C28-.C284	Carlini, Armando (Table B-BJ5)
3614.C2845-.C28454	Castelli, Enrico, 1900-1977 (Table B-BJ5)
3614.C285-.C2854	Cattaneo, Carlo, 1801-1869 (Table B-BJ5)

	Modern (1450/1600-)
	By region or country
	Italy
	By period
	19th and 20th centuries
	Individual philosophers
	C - Ferrari -- Continued
3614.C3-.C34	Ceretti, Pietro, 1823-1884 (Table B-BJ5)
3614.C52-.C524	Ciancio, Claudio (Table B-BJ5)
3614.C56-.C564	Colli, Giorgio (Table B-BJ5)
3614.C58-.C584	Colorni, Eugenio (Table B-BJ5)
3614.C6-.C64	Comparetti, Piero Milani (Table B-BJ5)
3614.C7-.C74	Croce, Benedetto, 1866-1952 (Table B-BJ5)
3614.D36-.D364	De Feo, Nicola Massimo (Table B-BJ5)
3614.D37-.D374	De Michelis, Enrico, 1877-1938 (Table B-BJ5)
	De Ruggiero, Guido, 1888-1948 see B3649.R8+
3614.D445-.D4454	Del Noce, Augusto, 1910- (Table B-BJ5)
	Della Volpe, Galvano, 1895-1968 see B3656.V65+
	Di Marzio, Cornelio see B3636.M36+
3614.D8-.D84	Durante, Emilio (Table B-BJ5)
3614.E92-.E924	Evola, Julius, 1898-1974 (Table B-BJ5)
3614.F136-.F1364	Fabro, Cornelio (Table B-BJ5)
3614.F1367-.F13674	Faggin, Giuseppe, 1906-1995 (Table B-BJ5)
3615	Ferrari, Giuseppe, 1811-1876 (Table B-BJ4)
3616	Ferrari - Franchi Subarrange each by Table B-BJ5
3616.F17-.F174	Ferretti, Giuseppe Luigi, 1880- (Table B-BJ5)
3616.F2-.F24	Ferro, Andrea Alberto, 1877- (Table B-BJ5)
3616.F5-.F54	Filippi, Liutprando (Table B-BJ5)
3616.F56-.F564	Fiorentino, Francesco, 1834-1884 (Table B-BJ5)
3616.F6-.F64	Fioruzzi, Vittorio (Table B-BJ5)
3618	Franchi, Ausonio (Table B-BJ4) Pseudonym of Cristoforo Bonavino
3619	Franchi - Galluppi Subarrange each by Table B-BJ5
3619.G29-.G294	Galimberti, Umberto (Table B-BJ5)
3619.G3-.G34	Galli, Gallo, 1889- (Table B-BJ5)
3620-3623	Galluppi, Pasquale, 1770-1846 (Table B-BJ3a)
3624	Galluppi - Gioberti Subarrange each by Table B-BJ5
3624.G4-.G44	Gemelli, Agostino, 1878-1959 (Table B-BJ5)
3624.G5-.G54	Gentile, Giovanni, 1875-1944 (Table B-BJ5)
3624.G542-.G5424	Gerratana, Valentino (Table B-BJ5)
3624.G545-.G5454	Geymonat, Ludovico (Table B-BJ5)
3624.G55-.G554	Giannotti, Alfredo (Table B-BJ5)
3625-3628	Gioberti, Vincenzo, 1801-1852 (Table B-BJ3a)

Modern (1450/1600-)
By region or country
Italy
By period
19th and 20th centuries
Individual philosophers -- Continued

3629 Gioberti - Gnz
Subarrange each by Table B-BJ5
3629.G55-.G554 Giusso, Lorenzo, 1899- (Table B-BJ5)
3629.G56-.G564 Givone, Sergio, 1944- (Table B-BJ5)
3630 Go - Kz
Subarrange each by Table B-BJ5
3630.G6-.G64 Goffredo, Donato (Table B-BJ5)
3630.G7-.G74 Grassi, Ernesto (Table B-BJ5)
3630.G8-.G84 Guzzo, Augusto, 1894-1986 (Table B-BJ5)
3631 L - Ld
Subarrange each by Table B-BJ5
3631.L23-.L234 Labanca, Baldassare, 1829-1913 (Table B-BJ5)
3631.L3-.L34 Labriola, Antonio, 1843-1904 (Table B-BJ5)
3631.L55-.L554 Lanza del Vasto, Joseph Jean, 1901-1981 (Table B-BJ5)
3632 Le - Liberatore
Subarrange each by Table B-BJ5
3633 Liberatore, Matteo, 1810-1892 (Table B-BJ4)
3634 Liberatore - Mamiani
Subarrange each by Table B-BJ5
3634.L3-.L34 Limentani, Ludovico, 1884-1940 (Table B-BJ5)
3634.L4-.L44 Lombardi, Franco, 1906- (Table B-BJ5)
3634.L7-.L74 Luporini, Cesare, 1909-1993 (Table B-BJ5)
3635 Mamiani della Rovere, Terenzio, conte, 1799-1885 (Table B-BJ4)
3636 Mamiani - Romagnosi
Subarrange each by Table B-BJ5
3636.M26-.M264 Marciani, Armando (Table B-BJ5)
3636.M3-.M34 Martinetti, Piero, 1872-1943 (Table B-BJ5)
3636.M36-.M364 Marzio, Cornelio di (Table B-BJ5)
3636.M3642-.M36424 Masnovo, Amato, 1876-1955 (Table B-BJ5)
3636.M3644-.M36444 Mathieu, Vittorio (Table B-BJ5)
3636.M367-.M3674 Maturi, Sebastiano, 1843-1917 (Table B-BJ5)
3636.M4-.M44 Mele, Angelo (Table B-BJ5)
3636.M49-.M494 Michelstaedter, Carlo, 1887-1910 (Table B-BJ5)
3636.M6-.M64 Mochi, Alberto (Table B-BJ5)
3636.M655-.M6554 Moiso, Francesco, 1944- (Table B-BJ5)
3636.M7-.M74 Moretti-Costanzi, Teodorico (Table B-BJ5)
3636.M87-.M874 Mura, Gaspare (Table B-BJ5)
3636.N36-.N364 Nardi, Bruno (Table B-BJ5)
3636.N38-.N384 Natoli, Salvatore (Table B-BJ5)

Modern (1450/1600-)
By region or country
Italy
By period
19th and 20th centuries
Individual philosophers
Mamiani - Romagnosi -- Continued

3636.N48-.N484	Neri, Guido D. (Table B-BJ5)
3636.N53-.N534	Nicolini, Fausto, 1879-1965 (Table B-BJ5)
3636.O7-.O74	Orestano, Francesco, 1873-1945 (Table B-BJ5)
3636.O8-.O84	Ottonello, Pier Paolo (Table B-BJ5)
3636.P15-.P154	Paci, Enzo, 1911- (Table B-BJ5)
3636.P17-.P174	Padovani, Umberto Antonio, 1894- (Table B-BJ5)
3636.P2-.P24	Papàsogli, Giorgio (Table B-BJ5)
3636.P28-.P284	Papi, Fulvio (Table B-BJ5)
3636.P3-.P34	Papini, Giovanni, 1881-1956 (Table B-BJ5)
3636.P36-.P364	Pareyson, Luigi (Table B-BJ5)
3636.P365-.P3654	Parinetto, Luciano (Table B-BJ5)
3636.P368-.P3684	Parrini, Paolo (Table B-BJ5)
3636.P56-.P564	Piovani, Pietro (Table B-BJ5)
3636.P67-.P674	Preti, Giulio (Table B-BJ5)
3636.P7-.P74	Prini, Pietro (Table B-BJ5)
3636.Q34-.Q344	Quarto di Palo, Angelo (Table B-BJ5)
3636.R27-.R274	Raschini, Maria Adelaide (Table B-BJ5)
3636.R3-.R34	Ravasi, Elio (Table B-BJ5)
3636.R4-.R44	Rensi, Giuseppe, 1871-1941 (Table B-BJ5)
3636.R5-.R54	Rignano, Eugenio, 1870-1930 (Table B-BJ5)
3638	Romagnosi, Giandomenico, 1761-1835 (Table B-BJ4)
3639	Romagnosi - Rosmini Serbati Subarrange each by Table B-BJ5
3640-3648	Rosmini, Antonio, 1797-1855 (Table B-BJ2)
3648.A-Z	Special topics, A-Z
3648.C7	Creation
3648.E54	Enlightenment
3648.E7	Ethics
3648.G63	God
3648.L35	Language
3648.L5	Liberty
3648.O5	Ontology
3648.P74	Progress
3648.R38	Religion
3648.R4	Religious experience
3648.S65	Spirituality
3648.T78	Truth
3649	Rosmini Serbati - Rz Subarrange each by Table B-BJ5

Modern (1450/1600-)
By region or country
Italy
By period
19th and 20th centuries
Individual philosophers
Rosmini Serbati - Rz -- Continued
3649.R8-.R84 Ruggiero, Guido de, 1888-1948 (Table B-BJ5)
3650 S - Sanseverino
Subarrange each by Table B-BJ5
3650.S3-.S34 Saitta, Giuseppe (Table B-BJ5)
3651 Sanseverino, Gaetano, 1811-1865 (Table B-BJ4)
3652 Sanseverino - Varisco
Subarrange each by Table B-BJ5
3652.S26-.S264 Santucci, Antonio (Table B-BJ5)
3652.S35-.S354 Scaravelli, Luigi (Table B-BJ5)
3652.S45-.S454 Sciacca, Michele Federico, 1908-1975 (Table B-BJ5)
3652.S48-.S484 Semerari, Giuseppe (Table B-BJ5)
3652.S49-.S494 Severino, Emanuele (Table B-BJ5)
3652.S55-.S554 Solmi, Edmondo, 1874-1912 (Table B-BJ5)
3652.S64-.S644 Spaventa, Bertrando, 1817-1883 (Table B-BJ5)
3652.S69-.S694 Spirito, Ugo, 1896- (Table B-BJ5)
3652.S76-.S764 Stefanini, Luigi, 1891-1956 (Table B-BJ5)
3652.T55-.T554 Tilgher, Adriano, 1887-1941 (Table B-BJ5)
3652.U2-.U24 Ubaldi, Pietro (Table B-BJ5)
3652.V33-.V334 Vailati, Giovanni, 1863-1909 (Table B-BJ5)
3653 Varisco, Bernardino, 1850-1933 (Table B-BJ4)
3654 Varisco - Ventura
Subarrange each by Table B-BJ5
3654.V38-.V384 Vattimo, Gianni, 1936- (Table B-BJ5)
3655 Ventura, Gioacchino, 1792-1861 (Table B-BJ4)
3656 Ventura - Z
Subarrange each by Table B-BJ5
3656.V49-.V494 Vidari, Giovanni, 1871-1934 (Table B-BJ5)
3656.V65-.V654 Volpe, Galvano della, 1895-1968 (Table B-BJ5)
Netherlands (Low Countries)
3801 General works
3821.A-Z Special topics, A-Z
By period
17th century
3871 General works
3875.A-Z Special topics, A-Z
Individual philosophers
3899 A - Geulincx
Subarrange each by Table B-BJ5
3899.A3-.A34 Acosta, Uriel, ca. 1585-1640 (Table B-BJ5)

Modern (1450/1600-)
By region or country
Netherlands (Low Countries)
By period
17th century
Individual philosophers
A - Geulincx -- Continued

3899.C8-.C84	Cuper, Françiscus, fl. 1676 (Table B-BJ5)
	Geulincx, Arnold, 1624-1669
3900	Periodicals. Societies. Serials
3901	Dictionaries
	Collected works
3903	Original (vernacular) texts. By date
3904	Editions with commentary. By editor
3905	Partial editions, selections, etc. By editor or date
	Translations
	Subarrange by translator or date
	Including translations with original texts
3906	Greek
3907	Latin
3908	English
3909	French
3910	German
3911	Italian
3912	Spanish and Portuguese
3913.A.-3913.Z	Other languages, A-Z
	Separate works
3915-3919	Ethica (Table B-BJ10)
3920-3924	Logica fundamentis suis restituta (Table B-BJ10)
3925-3929	Metaphysica vera et ad mentem peripateticam (Table B-BJ10)
3931	Methodus inveniendi argumenta (Table B-BJ12)
3933	Physica vera (Table B-BJ12)
3935-3939	Quaestiones quodlibeticae (Table B-BJ10)
3944.A-Z	Other, A-Z
	Subarrange each by Table B-BJ13
3945	Spurious and apocryphal works
3946	Indexes, outlines, paraphrases, etc.
3947	Biography and memoirs (Table B-BJ14)
3947.2	Criticism and interpretation
3947.5.A-Z	Special topics, A-Z
3948	Geulincx - Spinoza
	Subarrange each by Table B-BJ5
3948.H4-.H44	Heidanus, Abraham, 1597-1678 (Table B-BJ5)

Modern (1450/1600-)
By region or country
Netherlands (Low Countries)
By period
17th century
Individual philosophers
Geulincx - Spinoza -- Continued

3948.H5-.H54 Helmont, Franciscus Mercurius van, 1614-1699 (Table B-BJ5)
3948.N53-.N534 Nieuwentyt, Bernard, 1654-1718 (Table B-BJ5)

Spinoza, Benedictus de, 1632-1677
3950 Periodicals. Societies. Serials
3951 Dictionaries

Collected works
3953 Original (vernacular) texts. By date
3954 Editions with commentary. By editor
3955 Partial editions, selections, etc. By editor or date

Translations
Subarrange by translator or date
Including translations with original texts
3956 Greek
3957 Latin
3958 English
3959 French
3960 German
3961 Italian
3962 Spanish and Portuguese
3963.A-Z Other languages, A-Z

Separate works
3964 Epistolae (Table B-BJ12)
3970-3974 Ethica (Table B-BJ10)
3975-3979 Tractatus de Deo et homine eiusque felicitate (Table B-BJ10)
3980-3984 Tractatus de intellectus- emendatione (Table B-BJ10)
3985 Tractatus theologico-politicus (Table B-BJ12)
3994.A-Z Other, A-Z
Subarrange each by Table B-BJ13
3995 Spurious and apocryphal works
3996 Indexes, outlines, paraphrases, etc.
3997 Biography and memoirs (Table B-BJ14)
3998 Criticism and interpretation
3999.A-Z Special topics, A-Z
3999.A35 Aesthetics
3999.A7 Art
3999.C38 Causation

Modern (1450/1600-)
By region or country
Netherlands (Low Countries)
By period
17th century
Individual philosophers
Spinoza, Benedictus de, 1632-1677
Special topics, A-Z -- Continued

3999.C66 Contemporary, The
3999.D4 Desire
3999.E5 Emotions
3999.E8 Ethics
3999.E9 Expression
3999.F8 Free will
3999.H45 Hermeneutics
3999.I3 Imagination. Imaginary
3999.I4 Immortality
3999.I57 Intuition
3999.J8 Judaism
3999.K7 Knowledge, Theory of
3999.M33 Man
3999.M43 Medicine
3999.M45 Metaphysics
3999.M5 Mind and body
3999.M66 Monism
3999.N34 Nature
3999.O6 Ontology
3999.P38 Perception
3999.P68 Power
3999.R4 Religion
3999.S34 Scholasticism
3999.T4 Time
3999.T6 Toleration
3999.T7 Truth
4000 Spinoza - Z
Subarrange each by Table B-BJ5
4000.V64-.V644 Voet, Gijsbert, 1589-1676 (Table B-BJ5)
4000.V83-.V834 Vries, Gerard de, 1648-1705 (Table B-BJ5)

18th century
4005 General works
4011.A-Z Special topics, A-Z
Individual philosophers
4015 A - Hemsterhuis
Subarrange each by Table B-BJ5
4020-4028 Hemsterhuis, François, 1721-1790 (Table B-BJ2)
4030 Hemsterhuis - Z
Subarrange each by Table B-BJ5

	Modern (1450/1600-)
	By region or country -- Continued
	Netherlands (Holland)
4041	General works
4045.A-Z	Special topics, A-Z
	19th and 20th centuries
	Individual philosophers
4051	A - Heusde Subarrange each by Table B-BJ5
4051.B5-.B54	Bierens de Haan, J. D. (Johannes Diderik), 1866-1943 (Table B-BJ5)
4051.B62-.B624	Boer, Theodorus de, 1932- (Table B-BJ5)
4051.D6-.D64	Dooyeweerd, H. (Herman), 1894-1977 (Table B-BJ5)
4051.H4-.H44	Hartsen, F. A. (Frederik Anthony), 1838-1877 (Table B-BJ5)
4051.H47-.H474	Hessing, Jacob, 1874-1944 (Table B-BJ5)
4060-4068	Heusde, Philip Willem van, 1778-1839 (Table B-BJ2)
4075	Heusde - Opzoomer Subarrange each by Table B-BJ5
4075.H55-.H554	Heymans, Gerard, 1857-1930 (Table B-BJ5)
4075.H64-.H644	Hoeven, Johan van der (Table B-BJ5)
4075.H66-.H664	Hollak, J. H. A. (Table B-BJ5)
4075.M3-.M34	Mannoury, Gerrit, 1867- (Table B-BJ5)
4080-4088	Opzoomer, Cornelis, 1821-1892 (Table B-BJ2)
4095	Opzoomer - Z Subarrange each by Table B-BJ5
4095.P45-.P454	Peursen, Cornelis Anthonie van, 1920- (Table B-BJ5)
4095.P55-.P554	Polak, Leo, 1880-1941 (Table B-BJ5)
4095.P67-.P674	Pos, Hendrik Josephus, 1898-1955 (Table B-BJ5)
4095.S3-.S34	Sandberg, Kees (Table B-BJ5)
4095.S4-.S44	Schelven, Theodore van (Table B-BJ5)
4095.V47-.V474	Verhaar, John W.M. (Table B-BJ5)
4095.V48-.V484	Verhoeven, Corn (Table B-BJ5)
4095.V64-.V644	Vollenhoven, D. H. Theodoor (Dirk Hendrik Theodoor), 1892-1978 (Table B-BJ5)
	Belgium
4151	General works
4155.A-Z	Special topics, A-Z
4155.P66	Positivism
	19th and 20th centuries
	Individual philosophers
4157	A - Decoster Subarrange each by Table B-BJ5
4158	Decoster, Paul, 1886-1939 (Table B-BJ4)

Modern (1450/1600-)
By region or country
Belgium
19th and 20th centuries
Individual philosophers -- Continued
4159 Decoster - Gruyer
Subarrange each by Table B-BJ5
Delarue, Gabriel Jules see B4170+
4159.F55-.F554 Flam, Léopold (Table B-BJ5)
4161 Gruyer, L. A. (Louis Auguste), 1778-1866 (Table B-BJ4)
4165 Gruyer - Strada
Subarrange each by Table B-BJ5
4165.L33-.L334 Ladrière, Jean (Table B-BJ5)
4165.M49-M494 Meyer, Michel, 1950- (Table B-BJ5)
4165.P75-.P754 Prigogine, I. (Ilya) (Table B-BJ5)
4165.R44-.R444 Regt, Herman C. D. G. de, 1963- (Table B-BJ5)
4170-4173 Strada, J. (Table B-BJ3a)
Pseudonym of Gabriel Jules Delarue
4175 Strada - Z
Subarrange each by Table B-BJ5
Russia
4201 General works
4208.A-Z Special topics, A-Z
By period
17th and 18th centuries
4211 General works
4215.A-Z Special topics, A-Z
4215.E5 Enlightenment
4218.A-Z Individual philosophers, A-Z
Subarrange each by Table B-BJ5
4218.K6-.K64 Kozel'skii, I͡Akov Pavlovich, ca. 1728-ca. 1794 (Table B-BJ5)
4218.S47-.S474 Skovoroda, Hryhoriĭ Savych, 1722-1794 (Table B-BJ5)
For Skovoroda's literary works (Russian) see PG3317.S56
For Skovoroda's literary works (Ukrainian) see PG3948.S532
19th and 20th centuries
4231 General works
4235.A-Z Special topics, A-Z
4235.C7 Criticism
4235.E5 Enlightenment
4235.H4 Hegelianism
4235.H57 History
4235.H85 Humanism

Modern (1450/1600-)
By region or country
Russia
By period
19th and 20th centuries
Special topics, A-Z -- Continued

4235.I3 Idealism
4235.L69 Love
4235.M3 Materialism
4235.N36 Names
4235.P47 Personality. Personalism
4235.P67 Positivism
4235.S25 Salvation

Individual philosophers

4238 A - Grot
Subarrange each by Table B-BJ5

4238.A5-.A54 Antonovich, M. (Maksim), 1835-1918 (Table B-BJ5)
4238.A87-.A874 Avakov, Aleksandr V. (Aleksandr Vladimirovich), 1954- (Table B-BJ5)
4238.B3-.B34 Belinsky, Vissarion Grigoryevich, 1811-1848 (Table B-BJ5)
4238.B4-.B44 Berdi͡aev, Nikolaĭ, 1874-1948 (Table B-BJ5)
4238.B8-.B84 Bulgakov, Sergeĭ Nikolaevich, 1871-1944 (Table B-BJ5)

Chaadaev, P. I͡A. (Petr I͡Akovlevich), 1794-1856
Collected works (nonserial)
Original texts. By date

4238.C47A1 General works
4238.C47A2 Partial editions, selections, etc. By date
4238.C48A-.C48Z Translations. By language, A-Z, and date
4238.C49A-.C49Z7 Separate works, A-Z

Biography, criticism, etc.

4238.C49Z8-.C49Z99 Dictionaries, indexes, concordances, etc.
4238.C5A1-.C5A19 Periodicals. Societies. Serials
4238.C5A2-.C5Z General works
4238.C55-.C554 Chelpanov, Georgiĭ Ivanovich, 1862-1936 (Table B-BJ5)
4238.C6-.C64 Chernyshevsky, Nikolay Gavrilovich, 1828-1889 (Table B-BJ5)
4238.D33-.D334 Dandaron, B.D. (Bidii͡a Dandarovich) (Table B-BJ5)
4238.D35-.D354 Danilevskiĭ, N. I͡A. (Nikolaĭ I͡Akovlevich), 1822-1885 (Table B-BJ5)
4238.D6-.D64 Dobroli͡ubov, N. A. (Nikolaĭ Aleksandrovich), 1836-1861 (Table B-BJ5)
4238.D77-.D774 Druskin, I͡Akov, 1902-1980 (Table B-BJ5)

Modern (1450/1600-)
By region or country
Russia
By period
19th and 20th centuries
Individual philosophers
A - Grot -- Continued

4238.E7-.E74 Ėrn, V. F. (Vladimir Frant͡sevich), 1882-1917 (Table B-BJ5)

4238.F4-.F44 Fedorov, Nikolaĭ Fedorovich, 1828-1903 (Table B-BJ5)

4238.F5-.F54 Fialko, Nathan, 1881- (Table B-BJ5)

4238.F73-.F734 Frank, S. L. (Semen Li͡udvigovich), 1877-1950 (Table B-BJ5)

4238.F76-.F764 Frolov, Ivan Timofeevich (Table B-BJ5)

4238.G5-.G54 Gershenzon, M. O. (Mikhail Osipovich), 1869-1925 (Table B-BJ5)

4238.G56-.G564 Gessen, Sergeĭ Iosifovich, 1887-1950 (Table B-BJ5)

4238.G64-.G644 Gorskiĭ, Aleksandr Konstantinovich, 1886-1943 (Table B-BJ5)

4238.G67-.G674 Gri͡aznov, B.S. (Boris Semenovich), 1929-1978 (Table B-BJ5)

4238.G72-.G724 Groĭs, Boris (Table B-BJ5)

4240-4248 Grot, N. I͡A. (Nikolaĭ I͡Akovlevich), 1852-1899 (Table B-BJ2)

4249 Grot - Preobrazhenskii

Subarrange each by Table B-BJ5

(4249.G8-.G84) Gurdjieff, Georges Ivanovitch, 1872-1949

see BP605.G8+

4249.I4-.I44 Il'in, I. A. (Ivan Aleksandrovich), 1883-1954 (Table B-BJ5)

4249.J34-.J344 Jakovenko, Boris V. (Boris Valentinovich), 1884-1949 (Table B-BJ5)

4249.K29-.K294 Kagan, M. S. (Moiseĭ Samoĭlovich) (Table B-BJ5)

4249.K35-.K354 Karinskii, Mikhail Ivanovich, 1840-1917 (Table B-BJ5)

4249.K37-.K374 Karsavin, L.P. (Lev Platonovich), 1882-1952 (Table B-BJ5)

4249.K5-.K54 Khomi͡akov, A. S. (Alekseĭ Stepanovich), 1804-1860 (Table B-BJ5)

4249.K56-.K564 Kireevskiĭ, Ivan Vasil'evich, 1806-1856 (Table B-BJ5)

4249.K57-.K574 Korol'kov, A.A. (Aleksandr Arkad'evich) (Table B-BJ5)

4249.L36-.L364 Lavrov, P. L. (Petr Lavrovich), 1823-1900 (Table B-BJ5)

Modern (1450/1600-)
By region or country
Russia
By period
19th and 20th centuries
Individual philosophers
Grot - Preobrazhenskii -- Continued

4249.L38-.L384 Lenin, Vladimir Il'ich, 1870-1924 (Table B-BJ5)
4249.L4-.L44 Leont'ev, Konstantin, 1831-1891 (Table B-BJ5)
4249.L55-.L554 Lopatin, Lev Mikhaĭlovich, 1855-1920 (Table B-BJ5)
4249.L58-.L584 Losev, Alekseĭ Fedorovich (Table B-BJ5)
4249.L6-.L64 Losskiĭ, N. O. (Nikolaĭ Onufrievich), 1870-1965 (Table B-BJ5)
4249.M374-.M3744 Mărjani, Shihabetdin, 1818-1889 (Table B-BJ5)
4249.M52-.M524 Mikhaĭlov, F.T. (Feliks Trofimovich) (Table B-BJ5)
4249.M64-.M644 Molotkov, Egor, 1855-1926 (Table B-BJ5)
4249.M66-.M664 Mordinov, A. E. (Avksentiĭ Egorovich) (Table B-BJ5)
4249.P4-.P44 Petrov, Grigoriĭ Spiridonovich, 1868-1927 (Table B-BJ5)
4249.P52-.P524 Pisarev, D. I. (Dmitriĭ Ivanovich), 1840-1868 (Table B-BJ5)
4249.P55-.P554 Plekhanov, Georgiĭ Valentinovich, 1856-1918 (Table B-BJ5)
4250-4258 Preobrazhenskiĭ, Vasiliĭ Petrovich (Table B-BJ2)
4259 Preobrazhenskiĭ - Solov'ev
Subarrange each by Table B-BJ5
4259.R55-.R554 Roberty, E. de (Eugène), 1843-1915 (Table B-BJ5)
4259.R6-.R64 Roerich, Nicholas, 1874-1947 (Table B-BJ5)
4259.R69-.R694 Rozanov, V. V. (Vasiliĭ Vasil'evich), 1856-1919 (Table B-BJ5)
4259.S36-.S364 Semak, Oleg, 1951-1995 (Table B-BJ5)
4259.S4337-.S43374 Shcherbatskoĭ, F. I. (Fedor Ippolitovich), 1866-1942 (Table B-BJ5)
4259.S5-.S54 Shestov, Lev, 1866-1938 (Table B-BJ5)
4259.S546-.S5464 Shiffers, Evgeniĭ, 1934-1997 (Table B-BJ5)
4259.S55-.S554 Shinkaruk, V. I. (Vladimir Illarionovich), 1928- (Table B-BJ5)
4259.S56-.S564 Shpakovskiĭ, Anatoliĭ Ignat'evich, 1895- (Table B-BJ5)
4259.S566-.S5664 Shpet, Gustav, 1879-1937 (Table B-BJ5)
4260-4268 Solov'ev, V. S. (Vladimir Sergeevich) (Table B-BJ2)
4269 Solov'ev - Troit͡skiĭ
Subarrange each by Table B-BJ5
4269.S65 Spir, African, 1837-1890 (Table B-BJ5)

Modern (1450/1600-)
By region or country
Russia
By period
19th and 20th centuries
Individual philosophers
Solov'ev - Troit͡skiĭ -- Continued
4269.S9 Strakhov, N. (Nikolaĭ), 1828-1896
4270-4278 Troit͡skiĭ, Matveĭ Mikhaĭlovich (Table B-BJ2)
4279 Troit͡skiĭ - Z
Subarrange each by Table B-BJ5
4279.T83 Tugarinov, V. P. (Vasiliĭ Petrovich), 1898-1978 (Table B-BJ5)
(4279.U7) Uspenskiĭ, P. D. (Petr Demʹi͡anovich), 1878-1947
see BP605.G9A+ ; BP605.G94U75
Scandinavia
4301 General works
By period
4305 17th century
4308 18th century
4311 19th century
4315.A-Z Special topics, A-Z
Denmark
4325 General works
4328.A-Z Special topics, A-Z
By period
17th and 18th centuries
4335 General works
4338.A-Z Special topics, A-Z
4341.A-Z Individual philosophers, A-Z
Subarrange each by Table B-BJ5
4341.E5-.E54 Eilschov, Frederik Christian, 1725-1750 (Table B-BJ5)
19th century
4345 General works
4348.A-Z Special topics, A-Z
Individual philosophers
4351 A - Brøchner
Subarrange each by Table B-BJ5
4353 Bröchner, H. (Hans), 1820-1875 (Table B-BJ4)
4355 Brøchner - Høffding
Subarrange each by Table B-BJ5
4360-4368 Høffding, Harald, 1843-1931 (Table B-BJ2)
4369 Høffding - Kierkegaard
Subarrange each by Table B-BJ5
4370-4378 Kierkegaard, Søren, 1813-1855 (Table B-BJ2 modified)

Modern (1450/1600-)
By region or country
Scandinavia
Denmark
By period
19th century
Individual philosophers
Kierkegaard, Søren, 1813-1855 -- Continued

4378.A-Z Special topics, A-Z
4378.A4 Aesthetics
4378.A52 Antisemitism
4378.A53 Anxiety
Authorship see B4378.P74
4378.B43 Becoming
4378.B52 Bible
4378.B66 Book collecting. Books and reading
4378.C5 Christianity
4378.C6 Consciousness
4378.D43 Death
4378.D47 Despair
4378.D5 Dialectic
4378.E8 Ethics
4378.F68 Free will
Freedom see B4378.L53
4378.F7 French literature, Knowledge of
4378.H34 Happiness
4378.I57 Interest
4378.I76 Irony
4378.K56 Knowledge, Theory of
4378.L35 Language
4378.L53 Liberty
4378.L6 Love
4378.M35 Man
4378.M48 Metaphor
4378.M66 Mood
4378.M68 Movement
4378.N3 Nature
4378.O5 Ontology
4378.P44 Phenomenology
4378.P74 Pseudonymous writings. Authorship
4378.R43 Recognition
4378.R44 Religion
4378.R46 Repetition
4378.R48 Revelation
4378.R6 Romanticism
4378.S4 Self
4378.S52 Simplicity

Modern (1450/1600-)
By region or country
Scandinavia
Denmark
By period
19th century
Individual philosophers
Kierkegaard, Søren, 1813-1855
Special topics, A-Z -- Continued

4378.S76 Style
4378.S8 Subjectivity
4378.S84 Suffering
4378.T5 Time
4378.T7 Truth
4378.V56 Violence
4378.W65 Women
4380 Kierkegaard - Kroman
Subarrange each by Table B-BJ5
4381 Kroman, K. (Kristian), 1846-1925 (Table B-BJ4)
4382 Kroman - Martensen
Subarrange each by Table B-BJ5
4383 Martensen, H. (Hans), 1808-1884 (Table B-BJ4)
4384 Martensen - Nielsen
Subarrange each by Table B-BJ5
4385 Nielsen, Rasmus, 1809-1884 (Table B-BJ4)
4386 Nielsen - Ørsted
Subarrange each by Table B-BJ5
4387 Ørsted, Hans Christian, 1777-1851 (Table B-BJ4)
4388 Ørsted - Sibbern
Subarrange each by Table B-BJ5
4389 Sibbern, Frederik Christian, 1785-1872 (Table B-BJ4)
4390 Sibbern - Z
Subarrange each by Table B-BJ5

20th century

4392 General works
4394.A-Z Special topics, A-Z
4395.A-Z Individual philosophers, A-Z
Subarrange each by Table B-BJ5
4395.I77-.I774 Iversen, Herbert, 1890-1920 (Table B-BJ5)
4395.L3-.L34 Lambek, C. (Christian), 1870-1947 (Table B-BJ5)

Iceland

4402 General works
4404.A-Z Special topics, A-Z
4406.A-Z Individual philosophers, A-Z
Subarrange each by Table B-BJ5

Norway

Modern (1450/1600-)
By region or country
Scandinavia
Norway -- Continued
4411 General works
4415.A-Z Special topics, A-Z
By period
17th and 18th centuries
4421 General works
4425.A-Z Special topics, A-Z
4428.A-Z Individual philosophers, A-Z
Subarrange each by Table B-BJ5
19th century
4431 General works
4435.A-Z Special topics, A-Z
4438.A-Z Individual philosophers, A-Z
Subarrange each by Table B-BJ5
20th century
4441 General works
4443.A-Z Special topics, A-Z
4445.A-Z Individual philosophers, A-Z
Subarrange each by Table B-BJ5
4445.E47-.E474 Elster, Jon, 1940- (Table B-BJ5)
4445.H43-.H434 Hegge, Hjalmar (Table B-BJ5)
Sweden
4455 General works
4458.A-Z Special topics, A-Z
By period
17th and 18th centuries
4461 General works
4465.A-Z Special topics, A-Z
4468.A-Z Individual philosophers, A-Z
Subarrange each by Table B-BJ5
4468.R9-.R94 Rydelius, Andreas, 1671-1738 (Table B-BJ5)
4468.S7-.S74 Stiernhielm, Georg, 1598-1672 (Table B-BJ5)
4468.S8-.S84 Swedenborg, Emanuel, 1688-1772 (Table B-BJ5)
19th century
4471 General works
4475.A-Z Special topics, A-Z
Individual philosophers
4478 A - Boström
Subarrange each by Table B-BJ5
4478.B6-.B64 Biberg, Nils Fredrik, 1776-1827 (Table B-BJ5)
4480-4488 Boström, Christopher Jacob, 1797-1866 (Table B-BJ2 modified)
4488.A-Z Special topics, A-Z
4488.F7 Free will

Modern (1450/1600-)
By region or country
Scandinavia
Sweden
By period
19th century
Individual philosophers -- Continued
4489 Boström - Z
Subarrange each by Table B-BJ5
4489.G4-.G44 Geijer, Erik Gustaf, 1783-1847 (Table B-BJ5)
4489.G7-.G74 Grubbe, Samuel, 1786-1853 (Table B-BJ5)
4489.H6-.H64 Höijer, Benjamin Carl Henrik, 1767-1812 (Table B-BJ5)
4489.H8-.H84 Hvalgren, Emanuel (Table B-BJ5)
4489.L3-.L34 Landquist, John, 1881-1974 (Table B-BJ5)
4489.N6-.N64 Norström, Vitalis, 1856-1916 (Table B-BJ5)
20th century
4491 General works
4493.A-Z Special topics, A-Z
4493.E95 Existentialism
4495.A-Z Individual philosophers, A-Z
Subarrange each by Table B-BJ5
4495.K35-.K354 Kanger, Stig (Table B-BJ5)
4495.L5-.L54 Ljungström, Oscar, 1868- (Table B-BJ5)
4495.V3-.V34 Vannérus, Allen (Table B-BJ5)
Spain and Portugal
4511 General works
4515.A-Z Special topics, A-Z
4515.H85 Humanism
4515.P6 Positivism
4515.S3 Scholasticism
By period
4521 17th century
4525 18th century
4528 19th century
4530 20th century
Spain
4561 General works
4565.A-Z Special topics, A-Z
4565.K7 Krausism
4565.P65 Positivism
4565.R4 Reason
4565.T5 Time
4568.A-Z Individual philosophers, A-Z
Subarrange each by Table B-BJ5
4568.A4-.A44 Alvarado, Francisco, 1756-1814 (Table B-BJ5)
4568.A443-.A4434 Alvarez Guerra, Jose, 1778-1860 (Table B-BJ5)

Modern (1450/1600-)
By region or country
Spain and Portugal
Spain
Individual philosophers, A-Z -- Continued

4568.A46-.A464 Amor Ruibal, Angel María, 1869-1930 (Table B-BJ5)
4568.A7-.A74 Aranguren, José Luis L., 1909-1996 (Table B-BJ5)
4568.B2-.B24 Balmes, Jaime Luciano, 1810-1848 (Table B-BJ5)
4568.B63-.B634 Bofill, Jaime, 1910-1965 (Table B-BJ5)
4568.C36-.C364 Caramuel Lobkowitz, Juan, 1606-1682 (Table B-BJ5)
4568.C367-.C3674 Cardona, Carlos (Table B-BJ5)
4568.D6-.D64 Dorado y Montero, Pedro, 1861-1919 (Table B-BJ5)
4568.F4-.F44 Feijoo, Benito Jerónimo, 1676-1764 (Table B-BJ5)
4568.G28-.G284 Ganivet, Angel, 1865-1898 (Table B-BJ5)
Cf. PQ6613.A5 Ganivet as an author
4568.G29-.G294 García Bacca, Juan David, 1901-1992 (Table B-BJ5)
4568.G3-.G34 García Morente, Manuel, 1886-1942 (Table B-BJ5)
4568.G5-.G54 Giner de los Ríos, Francisco, 1839-1915 (Table B-BJ5)
4568.G8-.G84 Gutiérrez, Marcelino, 1858-1893 (Table B-BJ5)
4568.H83-.H834 Huarte Osacar, Juan, 1941- (Table B-BJ5)
4568.I4-.I44 Imaz, Eugenio, 1900-1951 (Table B-BJ5)
4568.J64-.J644 John of St. Thomas, 1589-1644 (Table B-BJ5)
4568.L3-.L34 Larrea, Juan (Table B-BJ5)
4568.L4-.L44 Ledesma Ramos, Ramiro, 1905-1936 (Table B-BJ5)
4568.L54-.L544 Lledó Iñigo, Emilio (Table B-BJ5)
4568.M37-.M374 Marías, Julián, 1914-2005 (Table B-BJ5)
4568.M386-.M3864 Mate, Reyes (Table B-BJ5)
4568.O7-.O74 Ortega y Gasset, José, 1883-1955 (Table B-BJ5)
4568.P37-.P374 París, Carlos (Table B-BJ5)
4568.P4-.P44 Pérez Gonzáles, Francisco (Table B-BJ5)
4568.P65-.P654 Polo, Leonardo (Table B-BJ5)
4568.R6-.R64 Roig Gironella, Juan (Table B-BJ5)
4568.S24-.S244 Sádaba, Javier (Table B-BJ5)
4568.S3-.S34 Sanz del Rio, Julián, 1814-1869 (Table B-BJ5)
4568.T5-.T54 Tierno Galván, Enrique (Table B-BJ5)
4568.T75-.T754 Trias, Eugenio, 1942- (Table B-BJ5)
4568.U5-.U54 Unamuno y Jugo, Miguel, 1864-1936 (Table B-BJ5)
4568.V58-.V584 Viqueira, Xoán Vicente, 1886-1924 (Table B-BJ5)
4568.X5-.X54 Xirau, Joaquín, 1895- (Table B-BJ5)
4568.Z34-.Z344 Zambrano, María (Table B-BJ5)
4568.Z75-.Z754 Zubeldia y de Inda, Néstor de (Table B-BJ5)
4568.Z8-.Z84 Zubiri, Xavier (Table B-BJ5)

Portugal

4591 General works
4595.A-Z Special topics, A-Z
4595.S4 Scholasticism

	Modern (1450/1600-)
	By region or country
	Spain and Portugal
	Portugal -- Continued
4598.A-Z	Individual philosophers, A-Z
	Subarrange each by Table B-BJ5
4598.C33-.C334	Caeiro, Francisco da Gama, 1928- (Table B-BJ5)
4598.C34-.C344	Caramuel Lobkowitz, Juan, 1606-1682 (Table B-BJ5)
4598.C6-.C64	Coimbra, Leonardo, 1883-1936 (Table B-BJ5)
4598.C8-.C84	Cunha Seixas, José Maria da, 1836-1895 (Table B-BJ5)
	Melo, Martinho Nobre de, 1891-1985 see B4598.N6+
4598.N6-.N64	Nobre de Mello, Martinho, 1891-1985 (Table B-BJ5)
4598.P7-.P74	Proença, Raul (Table B-BJ5)
4598.R5-.R54	Ribeiro, Álvaro, 1905-1981 (Table B-BJ5)
	Seixas, J. M. da Cunha (José Maria da Cunha), 1836-1895 see B4598.C8+
4598.V4-.V44	Verney, Luis Antonio, 1713-1792 (Table B-BJ5)
	Switzerland
	Cf. B1801+ France
4625	General works
4628.A-Z	Special topics, A-Z
	By period
4635	17th century
4638	18th century
4641	19th century
4643	20th century
4651.A-Z	Individual philosophers, A-Z
	Subarrange each by Table B-BJ5
4651.B25-.B254	Bachofen, Johann Jakob, 1815-1887 (Table B-BJ5)
4651.B37-.B374	Barth, Heinrich, 1890-1965 (Table B-BJ5)
4651.B5-.B54	Biedermann, Aloys Emanuel, 1819-1885 (Table B-BJ5)
4651.C47-.C474	Chouet, Jean-Robert (Table B-BJ5)
4651.H2-.H24	Haller, Albrecht von, 1708-1777 (Table B-BJ5)
4651.H3-.H34	Hebler, C. (Carl), 1821-1898 (Table B-BJ5)
4651.H4-.H44	Hersch, Jeanne (Table B-BJ5)
4651.J65-.J654	Jollien, Alexandre, 1975- (Table B-BJ5)
4651.M3-.M34	Marty, Anton, 1847-1914 (Table B-BJ5)
4651.P3-.P34	Pestalozzi, Johann Heinrich, 1746-1827 (Table B-BJ5)
4651.P53-.P534	Picard, Max, 1888-1965 (Table B-BJ5)
4651.R8-.R84	Ruefenacht, Eduard (Table B-BJ5)
4651.V5-.V54	Vinet, Alexandre Rodolphe, 1797-1847 (Table B-BJ5)
	Eastern Europe
4670	Periodicals. Societies. Serials
4670.5	Congresses
4671	Collected works (nonserial)
4672	General works

	Modern (1450/1600-)
	By region or country
	Eastern Europe -- Continued
4673	General special
	Including special aspects of the subject as a whole
4674.A-Z	Special topics, A-Z
	By period
4677	17th century
4678	18th century
4679	19th century
4680	20th century
	By region or country
4687-4691	Poland (Table B-BJ16 modified)
4691.A-Z	Individual philosophers, A-Z
	Subarrange each by Table B-BJ5
4691.A2-.A24	Abramowski, Edward, 1868-1918 (Table B-BJ5)
4691.A4-.A44	Ajdukiewicz, Kazimierz (Table B-BJ5)
4691.B76-.B764	Bruliński, Władysław, 1915- (Table B-BJ5)
4691.B87-.B874	Burski, Adam, 1560-1611 (Table B-BJ5)
4691.C93-.C934	Czeżowski, Tadeusz (Table B-BJ5)
4691.E58-.E584	Elzenberg, Henryk, 1887-1967 (Table B-BJ5)
4691.G35-.G354	Garfein-Garski, Stanisław, 1867-1928 (Table B-BJ5)
4691.H5-.H54	Hoene-Wroński, Józef Maria, 1776-1853 (Table B-BJ5)
4691.I53-.I534	Ingarden, Roman, 1893- (Table B-BJ5)
4691.K5857-.K58574	Kochanowski, J. K. (Jan Korwin), 1869-1949 (Table B-BJ5)
4691.K586-.K5864	Kołakowski, Leszek (Table B-BJ5)
4691.K588-.K5884	Koniński, Karol Ludwik, 1891-1943 (Table B-BJ5)
4691.K59-.K594	Kotarbiński, Tadeusz (Table B-BJ5)
4691.K6-.K64	Kozłowski, W. M. (Władysław Mieczysław), 1859-1935 (Table B-BJ5)
4691.K72-.K724	Krąpiec, Mieczysław Albert (Table B-BJ5)
4691.L37-.L374	Legowicz, Jan (Table B-BJ5)
4691.L83-.L834	Lutosławski, Wincenty (Table B-BJ5)
4691.M54-.M544	Michalski, Konstanty (Table B-BJ5)
4691.S37-.S374	Schaff, Adam (Table B-BJ5)
4691.S52-.S524	Skorulski, Antoni Adam, 1715-1777 (Table B-BJ5)
4691.S525-.S5254	Ślęczka, Kazimierz (Table B-BJ5)
4691.S66-.S664	Stachniuk, Jan (Table B-BJ5)
4691.S94-.S944	Swieżawski, Stefan (Table B-BJ5)
4691.T56-.T564	Tischner, Józef (Table B-BJ5)
4691.T9-.T94	Twardowski, Kazimierz, 1866-1938 (Table B-BJ5)
4691.W65-.W654	Wolniewicz, Bogusław (Table B-BJ5)
4691.Z38-.Z384	Zdziechowski, Marjan, 1861-1938 (Table B-BJ5)
4711-4715	Finland (Table B-BJ16 modified)

	Modern (1450/1600-)
	By region or country
	Eastern Europe
	By region or country
	Finland -- Continued
4715.A-Z	Individual philosophers, A-Z Subarrange each by Table B-BJ5
4715.H5-.H54	Hintikka, Jaakko, 1929- (Table B-BJ5)
4715.P54-.P544	Pilhstrom, Sami (Table B-BJ5)
	Constituent republics of the former Soviet Union
4721-4725	Estonia (Table B-BJ16)
4731-4735	Latvia (Table B-BJ16 modified)
4735	Individual philosophers, A-Z Subarrange each by Table B-BJ5
4735.C44-.C444	Celms, Teodors, 1893-1989 (Table B-BJ5)
4741-4745	Lithuania (Table B-BJ16 modified)
4745	Individual philosophers, A-Z Subarrange each by Table B-BJ5
4745.G57-.G574	Girnius, Juozas, 1915- (Table B-BJ5)
4751-4755	Ukraine (Table B-BJ16)
4756-4760	Belarus (Table B-BJ16)
(4761-4765)	Georgia (Republic) see B5099.A+
4765.2-.6	Kazakhstan (Table B-BJ16)
4766-4770	Kyrgyzstan (Table B-BJ16)
(4771-4775)	Azerbaijan see B5099.A+
4776-4780	Turkmenistan (Table B-BJ16)
(4781-4785)	Armenia (Republic) see B5099.A+
4786-4790	Uzbekistan (Table B-BJ16)
4791-4795	Moldova (Table B-BJ16)
4796-4800	Tajikistan (Table B-BJ16)
4801-4805	Czechoslovakia. Czech Republic (Table B-BJ16 modified)
4805.A-Z	Individual philosophers, A-Z Subarrange each by Table B-BJ5
4805.B65-.B654	Bolzano, Bernard, 1781-1848 (Table B-BJ5)
4805.D73-.D734	Dratvová, Albína, 1892-1969 (Table B-BJ5)
4805.F58-.F584	Fischer, J.L. (Josef Ludvik), 1894-1973 (Table B-BJ5)
4805.H78-.H784	Hrušovský, Igor (Table B-BJ5)
4805.K58-.K584	Klíma, Ladislav, 1878-1928 (Table B-BJ5)
4805.K636-.K6364	Komárková, Božena, 1903- (Table B-BJ5)
4805.N68-.N684	Novak, Mirko (Table B-BJ5)
4805.P38-.P384	Patočka, Jan, 1907-1977 (Table B-BJ5)
4805.S24-.S244	Šafařik, Josef, 1907-1992 (Table B-BJ5)

Modern (1450/1600-)
By region or country
Eastern Europe
By region or country
Czechoslovakia. Czech Republic
Individual philosophers, A-Z -- Continued

4805.S53-.S534 Smetana, Augustin, 1814-1851 (Table B-BJ5)
4805.S7-.S74 Štitný, Tomáš, 1325-1404 or 5 (Table B-BJ5)
4805.S8-.S84 Svoboda, Emil, 1878-1948 (Table B-BJ5)
Tomáš ze Štítného, 1325-1404 or 5 see B4805.S7+
4805.W45-.W454 Weltsch, Felix, 1884-1964 (Table B-BJ5)
4811-4815 Hungary (Table B-BJ16)
4821-4825 Romania (Table B-BJ16 modified)
4825.A-Z Individual philosophers, A-Z
Subarrange each by Table B-BJ5
4825.B33-.B334 Bagdasar, N. (Nicolae), 1896-1971 (Table B-BJ5)
4825.B55-.B554 Blaga, Lucian, 1895-1961 (Table B-BJ5)
4825.C56-.C564 Cioran, E. M. (Emile M.), 1911-1995 (Table B-BJ5)
4825.F46-.F464 Flonta, Mircea (Table B-BJ5)
4825.I65-.I654 Ionescu, Nae, 1890-1940 (Table B-BJ5)
4825.L55-.L554 Liiceanu, Gabriel, 1942- (Table B-BJ5)
4825.N65-.N654 Noica, Constantin (Table B-BJ5)
4825.P36-.P364 Patapievici, H.-R., 1957- (Table B-BJ5)
4825.R3-.R34 Ralea, Mihai, 1896-1964 (Table B-BJ5)
4825.R67-.R674 Roșca, Dumitru D., 1895-1980 (Table B-BJ5)
4825.T87-.T874 Țuțea, Petre (Table B-BJ5)
4831-4835 Bulgaria (Table B-BJ16)
4841-4845 Yugoslavia (Table B-BJ16)
4846.31-.35 Croatia (Table B-BJ16)
4851-4855 Albania (Table B-BJ16)
Greece (Modern) see B3500+
4861-4865 Macedonia (Republic) (Table B-BJ16)
4866-4870 Slovenia (Table B-BJ16 modified)
4871-4875 Turkey (Table B-BJ16)
Asia
5000 Periodicals. Societies. Serials
5000.5 Congresses
5003 Collected works (nonserial)
5005 General works
5010 General special
5015.A-Z Special topics, A-Z
5015.E45 Emotions
5015.H36 Hermeneutics
5015.L68 Love
5015.M35 Man
5015.S34 Self
5015.S67 Spirituality

Modern (1450/1600-)
By region or country
Asia -- Continued
By period
5017 17th century
5018 18th century
5019 19th century
5020 20th century
Middle East
For Arab countries see B5295
5025 General works
5027 General special
5028.A-Z Special topics, A-Z
5040-5044 Iraq (Table B-BJ17)
5045-5049 Lebanon (Table B-BJ17)
5050-5054 Syria (Table B-BJ17)
Turkey see B4871+
5055-5059 Israel (Table B-BJ17)
5060-5064 Jordan (Table B-BJ17)
5065-5069 Saudi Arabia (Table B-BJ17)
5070-5074 Iran (Table B-BJ17)
5099.A-Z Other countries, A-Z
Subarrange each by Table B-BJ18
Southern Asia. Indian Ocean region
5105 General works
5107 General special
5108.A-Z Special topics, A-Z
By country
5120-5124 Afghanistan (Table B-BJ17)
5125-5129 Pakistan (Table B-BJ17 modified)
5129.A-Z Individual philosophers, A-Z
Subarrange each by Table B-BJ5 except where otherwised specified
Class here individual Pakistani philosophers from the period 1600-present
Iqbal, Muhammad, Sir, 1877-1938
Collected works
5129.I57 Original texts. By date
5129.I571 Partial editions, selections, etc. By editor or date
5129.I58A-.I58Z Translations. By language, A-Z, and date
5129.I59A-.I59Z7 Separate works, A-Z
Biography, autobiography, criticism, etc.
5129.I59Z8-.I59Z99 Dictionaries, indexes, concordances, etc.
5129.I6A1-.I6A19 Periodicals. Societies. Serials
5129.I6A3 Autobiography, diaries, etc. By date
5129.I6A4 Letters. By date

Modern (1450/1600-)
By region or country
Asia
Southern Asia. Indian Ocean region
By country
Pakistan
Individual philosophers, A-Z
Iqbal, Muhammad, Sir, 1877-1938
Biography, autobiography, criticism, etc. -- Continued

5129.I6A5	Speeches. By date
5129.I6A6-.I6Z	General works
5130-5134	India (Table B-BJ17 modified)
5134.A-Z	Individual philosophers, A-Z Subarrange each by Table B-BJ5 Class here individual Indian philosophers from the period 1600-present
5134.A22-.A224	Abhedānanda, Swami, 1866-1939 (Table B-BJ5)
5134.B384-.B3844	Barlingay, Surendra Sheodas, 1919-1997 (Table B-BJ5)
5134.B47-.B474	Bhabha, Homi K., 1949- (Table B-BJ5)
5134.C47-.C474	Chattopadhyaya, Debiprasad (Table B-BJ5)
5134.D35-.D354	D'Andrade, Joseph Casimiro Patrocinio, 1888-1949 (Table B-BJ5)
5134.D57-.D574	Diwan Chand, 1888- (Table B-BJ5)
5134.D87-.D874	Dutt, Mohenda Nath (Table B-BJ5)
	Gandhi, Mahatma, 1869-1948 see DS481.G3
5134.G42-.G424	Ghose, Aurobindo, 1872-1950 (Table B-BJ5)
5134.K73-.K734	Krishna, Daya (Table B-BJ5)
5134.K75-.K754	Krishnamurti, J. (Jiddu), 1895-1986 (Table B-BJ5)
5134.M58-.M584	Misra, Ganeswar, 1917-1985 (Table B-BJ5)
5134.M64-.M644	Mohanty, J. N. (Jitendra Nath), 1928- (Table B-BJ5)
5134.P74-.P744	Prasad, Rajendra, 1926- (Table B-BJ5)
5134.R33-.R334	Radhakrishnan, S (Sarvepalli), 1888-1975 (Table B-BJ5)
5134.R3493-.R34934	Raju, P.T. (Poolla Tirupati), 1904- (Table B-BJ5)
5134.S23-.S234	Sadāśiva Śivācārya, 1901- (Table B-BJ5)
5134.S332-.S3324	Sanghavi, Sukhalji (Table B-BJ5)
5134.T27-.T274	Tagore, Rabindranath, 1861-1941 (Table B-BJ5)
5134.V58-.V584	Vivekananda, Swami, 1863-1902 (Table B-BJ5)
5135-5139	Sri Lanka (Table B-BJ17)
5140-5144	Burma. Myanmar (Table B-BJ17)
5145-5149	Bangladesh (Table B-BJ17)
	Eastern Asia. Southeast Asia. The Far East
5165	General works
5167	General special

	Modern (1450/1600-)
	By region or country
	Asia
	Eastern Asia. Southeast Asia. The Far East -- Continued
5168.A-Z	Special topics, A-Z
5168.C6	Confucian philosophy
5168.N38	Nature
	By country
5180-5184	Thailand (Table B-BJ17)
5185-5189	Laos (Table B-BJ17)
5190-5194	Cambodia (Table B-BJ17)
5195-5199	Vietnam (Table B-BJ17)
5200-5204	Malaysia (Table B-BJ17)
	Including Malaya, Singapore, Brunei, North Borneo and Sarawak
5210-5214	Indonesia (Table B-BJ17)
5220-5224	Philippines (Table B-BJ17)
5230-5234	China (Table B-BJ17 modified)
5234.A-Z	Individual philosophers, A-Z
	Subarrange each by Table B-BJ5
	Class here individual Chinese philosophers from the period 1600-present
5234.A35-.A354	Ai, Siqi, 1910-1966. 艾思奇 (Table B-BJ5)
5234.C4492-.C44924	Chang, Tai-nien. 張岱年; 张岱年 (Table B-BJ5)
5234.C4496-.C44964	Chang, Tung-sun, 1886- . 張東蓀; 张东荪 (Table B-BJ5)
5234.C45-.C454	Chang, Yüan-fu. 張元夫; 张元夫 (Table B-BJ5)
5234.C495-.C4954	Ch‘eng, Chung-ying, 1935- . 成中英 (Table B-BJ5)
5234.C52-.C524	Cheng, Kuan-ying, 1842-1922. 鄭觀應; 郑观应 (Table B-BJ5)
	Cheng, Zhongying, 1935- 成中英 see B5234.C495+
5234.C528-.C5284	Chin, Yüeh-lin, 1895- . 金岳霖 (Table B-BJ5)
5234.C53-.C534	Ch‘ing Sheng-tsu, Emperor of China, 1654-1722. 清聖祖; 清圣祖 (Table B-BJ5)
5234.C66-.C664	Chou, Kuo-p‘ing, 1945- . 周國平; 周国平 (Table B-BJ5)
5234.C68-.C684	Chou, T‘ai-ku, d. 1832. 周太谷 (Table B-BJ5)
5234.C75-.C754	Chu, Shun-shui, 1600-1682. 朱舜水 (Table B-BJ5)
	Dai, Zhen, 1724-1777. 戴震 see B5234.T32+
	Fang, Dongmei. 方東美; 方东美 see B5234.F34+
5234.F32-.F324	Fang, I-chih, 1611-1671. 方以智 (Table B-BJ5)
5234.F34-.F344	Fang, Tung-mei. 方東美; 方东美 (Table B-BJ5)
	Fang, Yizhi, 1611-1671. 方以智 see B5234.F32+

Modern (1450/1600-)
By region or country
Asia
Eastern Asia. Southeast Asia. The Far East
By country
China
Individual philosophers, A-Z -- Continued

5234.F4-.F44 Feng, Youlan, 1895-1990. 馮友蘭; 冯友兰 (Table B-BJ5)
5234.G8-.G84 Gu, Yanwu, 1613-1682. 顧炎武; 顾炎武 (Table B-BJ5)
5234.H68-.H684 Hsiung, Shih-li, 1885-1968. 熊十力 (Table B-BJ5)
5234.H75-.H754 Huang, Daozhou, 1585-1646. 黄道周 (Table B-BJ5)
5234.H792-.H7924 Huang, Zongxi, 1610-1695. 黄宗羲 (Table B-BJ5)
5234.J536-.J5364 Jiao, Xun, 1763-1820. 焦 循 (Table B-BJ5)
Jin, Yuelin, 1895- . 金岳霖 see B5234.C528+
5234.K36-.K364 Kang, Youwei, 1858-1927. 康有為; 康有为 (Table B-BJ5)
Kangxi, Emperor of China, 1654-1722. 康熙 see B5234.C53+
5234.L36-.L364 Lao, Siguang. 勞思光 (Table B-BJ5)
Li, Deshun. 李德順; 李德顺 see B5234.L457+
(5234.L45-.L454) Li, Erh-ch'ü, 1627-1705. 李顒;李颙
see B5234.L483+
5234.L455-.L4554 Li, Fu, 1673-1750. 李紱; 李绂 (Table B-BJ5)
5234.L457-.L4574 Li, Te-shun. 李德順; 李德顺 (Table B-BJ5)
5234.L47-.L474 Li, Tsung-wu, 1879-1943. 李宗吾 (Table B-BJ5)
5234.L483-.L4834 Li, Yong, 1627-1705. 李顒;李颙 (Table B-BJ5)
5234.L49-.L494 Liang, Qichao, 1873-1929. 梁啟超; 梁启超 (Table B-BJ5)
5234.L524-.L5244 Liang, Shuming, 1893- 梁漱溟 (Table B-BJ5)
5234.L56-.L564 Liu, Xiaobo. 劉曉波; 刘晓波 (Table B-BJ5)
5234.L87-.L874 Lu, Shiyi, 1611-1672. 陸世儀; 陆世仪 (Table B-BJ5)
5234.M32-.M324 Ma, Yifu, 1883-1967. 馬一孚; 马一孚 (Table B-BJ5)
5234.M67-.M674 Mou, Zongsan. 牟宗三 (Table B-BJ5)
5234.P35-.P354 Pan, Baishi. 潘栢世 (Table B-BJ5)
5234.S99-.S994 Sun, Wanpeng. 孫萬鵬; 孙万鹏 (Table B-BJ5)
5234.T32-.T324 Tai, Chen, 1724-1777. 戴震 (Table B-BJ5)
5234.T33-.T334 T'ang, Chen, 1630-1704. 唐甄 (Table B-BJ5)
5234.T34-.T344 Tang, Junyi, 1909-1978. 唐君毅 (Table B-BJ5)
Tang, Zhen, 1630-1704. 唐甄 see B5234.T33+
(5234.W327-.W3274) Wang, Chi, 1498-1583. 王畿
see B128.W28+
Wang, Dao, 1487-1547. 王道 see B128.W265+

Modern (1450/1600-)
By region or country
Asia
Eastern Asia. Southeast Asia. The Far East
By country
China
Individual philosophers, A-Z -- Continued

5234.W33-.W334 Wang, Fuzhi, 1619-1692. 王夫之 (Table B-BJ5)
(5234.W337-.W3374) Wang, Gen, 1483-1541. 王艮
see B128.W277+
Wang, Ji, 1498-1583. 王畿 see B128.W28+
(5234.W357-.W3574) Wang, Tao, 1487-1547. 王道
see B128.W265+
(5234.W78-.W784) Wu, Cheng, 1249-1333. 吳澄; 吴澄
see B128.W73+
(5234.W82-.W824) Wu, Tinghan, 1490?-1559. 吳廷翰; 吴廷翰
see B128.W82+
Xiong, Shili, 1885-1968. 熊十力 see B5234.H68+
Yan, Fu, 1853-1921. 嚴復; 严复 see B5234.Y39+
Yan, Yuan, 1635-1704. 顏元; 颜元 see B5234.Y46+
5234.Y29-.Y294 Yang, Xianzhen. 陽獻珍; 陽猷珍 (Table B-BJ5)
5234.Y39-.Y394 Yen, Fu, 1853-1921. 嚴復; 严复 (Table B-BJ5)
5234.Y46-.Y464 Yen, Yüan, 1635-1704. 顏元; 颜元 (Table B-BJ5)
5234.Y5-.Y54 Yin, Haiguang. 殷海光 (Table B-BJ5)
Zhang, Dainian. 張岱年; 张岱年 see B5234.C4492+
Zhang, Dongsun, 1886- . 張東蓀; 张东荪 see B5234.C4496+
Zhang, Yuanfu. 張元夫; 张元夫 see B5234.C45+
Zheng, Guanying, 1842-1922. 鄭觀應; 郑观应 see B5234.C52+
Zhou, Guoping, 1945- . 周國平; 周国平 see B5234.C66+
Zhou, Taigu, d. 1832. 周太谷 see B5234.C68+
Zhu, Shunshui, 1600-1682. 朱舜水 see B5234.C75+

5240-5244 Japan (Table B-BJ17 modified)
5243.A-Z Special topics, A-Z
5243.H84 Human body
5243.K6 Kokugaku
5243.M5 Mitogaku
(5243.N4) Neo-Confucianism
see B5243.N45
Oyomei philosophy see B5243.Y6
5243.P48 Phenomenology
5243.S83 Subjectivity

Modern (1450/1600-)
By region or country
Asia
Eastern Asia. Southeast Asia. The Far East
By country
Japan
Special topics, A-Z -- Continued

5243.Y6 Yōmeigaiku

5244.A-Z Individual philosophers, A-Z

Subarrange each by Table B-BJ5 unless otherwise indicated

Class here individual Japanese philosophers from the period 1600-present

5244.A63-.A634 Andō, Shōeki, fl. 1744-1763 (Table B-BJ5)
5244.A79-.A794 Asaka, Gonsai, 1791-1860 (Table B-BJ5)
5244.A85-.A854 Ashino, Tokurin, 1696-1776 (Table B-BJ5)
5244.B38-.B384 Bitō, Jishū, 1747-1814 (Table B-BJ5)
5244.D39-.D394 Dazai, Shundai, 1680-1747 (Table B-BJ5)
5244.H37-.H374 Hayashi, Ryōsai, 1807-1849 (Table B-BJ5)
5244.H47-.H474 Hirata, Atsutane, 1776-1843 (Table B-BJ5)
5244.H4835-.H48354 Hiromatsu, Wataru (Table B-BJ5)
5244.H484-.H4844 Hirose, Tansō, 1782-1856 (Table B-BJ5)
5244.I36-.I364 Ikai, Keish, 1761-1845 (Table B-BJ5)
5244.I43-.I434 Imamichi,Tomonobu, 1922- (Table B-BJ5)
5244.I76-.I764 Itō, Jinsai, 1627-1705 (Table B-BJ5)
5244.I86-.I864 Itō, Tōgai, 1670-1736 (Table B-BJ5)
5244.K23-.K234 Kada, Azumamaro, 1669-1736 (Table B-BJ5)
5244.K25-.K254 Kaibara, Ekiken, 1630-1714 (Table B-BJ5)
5244.K556-.K5564 Koga, Seiri, 1750-1817 (Table B-BJ5)
5244.K6-.K64 Kōsaka, Masaaki, 1900-1969 (Table B-BJ5)
5244.K67-.K674 Kozai, Yoshishige, 1901- (Table B-BJ5)
5244.K844-.K8444 Kuki, Shūzō, 1888-1941 (Table B-BJ5)
5244.K85-.K854 Kumazawa, Banzan, 1619-1691 (Table B-BJ5)
5244.K8756-.K87564 Kusaba, Senzan, 1819-1887 (Table B-BJ5)
5244.M38-.M384 Matsuzaki, Kōdō, 1771-1844 (Table B-BJ5)
5244.M54-.M544 Miki, Kiyoshi, 1897-1945 (Table B-BJ5)
5244.M57-.M574 Mishima, Chūshū, 1830-1919 (Table B-BJ5)
5244.M58-.M584 Miura, Baien, 1723-1789 (Table B-BJ5)
5244.M59-.M594 Miyake, Setsurei, 1860-1945 (Table B-BJ5)
5244.M5946-.M59464 Miyake, Shōsai, 1662-1741 (Table B-BJ5)
5244.M65-.M654 Motoda, Eifu, 1818-1891 (Table B-BJ5)
5244.M67-.M674 Motoori, Noringa, 1730-1801 (Table B-BJ5)
5244.M88-.M884 Mutai, Risaku, 1890-1974 (Table B-BJ5)
5244.N28-.N284 Nakae, Toju, 1608-1648 (Table B-BJ5)
5244.N29-.N294 Nakakōji, Akira (Table B-BJ5)
5244.N295-.N2954 Nakamura, Yūjirō, 1925- (Table B-BJ5)
5244.N52-.N524 Nishi, Amane, 1829-1897 (Table B-BJ5)

Modern (1450/1600-)
By region or country
Asia
Eastern Asia. Southeast Asia. The Far East
By country
Japan
Individual philosophers, A-Z -- Continued

5244.N54-.N544 Nishibe, Susumu, 1939- (Table B-BJ5)
5244.N55-.N554 Nishida, Kitarō, 1870-1945 (Table B-BJ5)
5244.N57-.N574 Nishimura, Shigeki, 1828-1902 (Table B-BJ5)
5244.N58-.N584 Nishitani, Keiji, 1900- (Table B-BJ5)
5244.O35-.O354 Ogyū, Sorai, 1666-1728 (Table B-BJ5)
Ohsawa, Georges, 1893-1966 see B5244.S35+
5244.O385-.O3854 Ōkuni, Takamasa, 1793-1871 (Table B-BJ5)
5244.O54-.O544 Ōnishi, Hajime, 1864-1900 (Table B-BJ5)
5244.O57-.O574 Ono, Kakuzan, 1701-1770 (Table B-BJ5)
5244.O83-.O834 Ōta, Kinjō, 1765-1825 (Table B-BJ5)
5244.S336-.S3364 Saitō, Norimasa (Table B-BJ5)
5244.S35-.S354 Sakurazawa, Yukikazu, 1893-1966 (Table B-BJ5)
5244.S37-.S374 Satō, Issai, 1772-1859 (Table B-BJ5)
5244.S39-.S394 Satō, Naokata, 1650-1719 (Table B-BJ5)
5244.T26-.T264 Takahashi, Fumi, 1901-1945 (Table B-BJ5)
5244.T28-.T284 Takahashi, Sekisui, 1769-1848 (Table B-BJ5)
Tanabe, Hajime, 1885-1962
Collected works (nonserial)
5244.T336 Original texts. By date
5244.T337 Partial editions, selections, etc. By date
5244.T338A-.T338Z Translations. By language, A-Z, and date
5244.T339A-.T339Z Separate works, A-Z
Biography, autobiography, criticism, etc.
5244.T339Z8-.T339Z99 Dictionaries, indexes, concordances, etc.
5244.T34A1-.T34A19 Periodicals. Societies. Serials
5244.T34A3 Autobiography, diaries, etc. By date
5244.T34A4 Letters. By date
5244.T34A5 Speeches. By date
5244.T34A6-.T34Z General works
5244.T65-.T654 Tominaga, Nakamoto, 1715-1746 (Table B-BJ5)
5244.U29-.U294 Ueda, Shizuteru, 1926- (Table B-BJ5)
5244.U45-.U454 Umemoto, Katsumi, 1912-1974 (Table B-BJ5)
5244.W294-.W2944 Wakabayashi, Kyōsai, 1679-1732 (Table B-BJ5)
5244.W35-.W354 Watsuji, Tetsuro, 1889-1960 (Table B-BJ5)
5244.Y26-.Y264 Yamaga, Soko, 1622-1685 (Table B-BJ5)
5244.Y279-.Y2794 Yamazaki, Ansai, 1618-1682 (Table B-BJ5)
5250-5254 Korea (Table B-BJ17 modified)
5253.A-Z Special topics, A-Z
5253.C66 Cosmology

Modern (1450/1600-)
By region or country
Asia
Eastern Asia. Southeast Asia. The Far East
By country
Korea
Special topics, A-Z -- Continued
5253.F68 Four beginnings and seven feelings thesis
5253.H83 Hun'gu school
5253.K53 Kiho school
5253.N36 Nammyŏng school
5253.S57 Sirhak school
5254.A-Z Individual philosophers, A-Z
Subarrange each by Table B-BJ5 unless otherwise indicated
Class here individual Korean philosophers from the period 1600-present.
Kim, Hyong-sok, 1920-
5254.K498 Collected works
5254.K4981 Partial editions, selections, etc.
5254.K499A-.K499Z Translations. By language, A-Z
For translations of individual works see B5254.K5A+
5254.K5A-.K5Z Separate works. By title, A-Z
5254.K512 Biography
5289.A-Z Other countries, A-Z
Subarrange each by Table B-BJ18
5295 Arab countries
Africa
5300 Periodicals. Societies. Serials
5300.5 Congresses
5303 Collected works (nonserial)
5305 General works
5310 General special
5315.A-Z Special topics, A-Z
5315.E45 Emotions
5315.H36 Hermeneutics
5315.K56 Knowledge, Theory of
5315.L68 Love
5315.M35 Man
5315.S34 Self
By period
5317 17th century
5318 18th century
5319 19th century
5320 20th century
Northern Africa

Modern (1450/1600-)
By region or country
Africa
Northern Africa -- Continued
5335 General works
5337 General special
5338.A-Z Special topics, A-Z
5338.R38 Rationalism
By country
5340-5344 Egypt (Table B-BJ17 modified)
5344.A-Z Individual philosophers, A-Z
Subarrange each by Table B-BJ5
5344.I9-.I94 'Izzat, 'Abd al-'Aziz, 1907- (Table B-BJ5)
5345-5349 Libya (Table B-BJ17)
5350-5354 Tunisia (Table B-BJ17)
5355-5359 Algeria (Table B-BJ17)
5360-5364 Morocco (Table B-BJ17)
Sub-Saharan Africa
5375 General works
5377 General special
5378.A-Z Special topics, A-Z
5378.P45 Philosophical anthropology
East Africa
5385 General works
5387 General special
5388.A-Z Special topics, A-Z
By country
5400-5404 Sudan (Table B-BJ17)
5405-5409 Ethiopia (Table B-BJ17)
5410-5414 Somali Republic (Table B-BJ17)
5415-5419 Kenya (Table B-BJ17)
5420-5424 Uganda (Table B-BJ17)
5425-5429 Tanzania (Table B-BJ17)
5430-5434 Mozambique (Table B-BJ17)
5449.A-Z Other countries, A-Z
Subarrange each by Table B-BJ18
Islands (East African Coast)
5460-5464 Madagascar (Table B-BJ17)
5489.A-Z Other islands, A-Z
Subarrange each by Table B-BJ18
West Africa (Spanish Sahara to Zaire)
5495 General works
5497 General special
5498.A-Z Special topics, A-Z
5619.A-Z Special countries, A-Z
Subarrange each by Table B-BJ18
5619.N6-.N63 Nigeria (Table B-BJ18)

Modern (1450/1600-)
By region or country
Africa -- Continued
Southern Africa
5625 General works
5627 General special
5628.A-Z Special topics, A-Z
By country
5640-5644 South Africa (Table B-BJ17)
5679.A-Z Other countries, A-Z
Subarrange each by Table B-BJ18
Oceania
5685-5689 General works (Table B-BJ17)
By country, island group, or island
5700-5704 Australia (Table B-BJ17 modified)
5704.A-Z Individual philosophers, A-Z
Subarrange each by Table B-BJ5
5704.A75-.A754 Armstrong, David Malet (Table B-BJ5)
5704.G35-.G354 Gaita, Raimond, 1946- (Table B-BJ5)
5704.G37-.G374 Gasking, D. A. T. (Douglas Aidan Trist), 1911-1994 (Table B-BJ5)
5704.J33-.J334 Jackson, Frank, 1943- (Table B-BJ5)
5704.M33-.M334 Mackie, J. L. (John Leslie) (Table B-BJ5)
5704.P37-.P374 Passmore, John Arthur (Table B-BJ5)
5704.S55-.S554 Singer, Peter, 1946- (Table B-BJ5)
5710-5714 New Zealand (Table B-BJ17 modified)
5714.A-Z Individual philosophers, A-Z
Subarrange each by Table B-BJ5
5714.P74 Prior, A. N. (Arthur N.), 1914-1969 (Table B-BJ5)
5739.A-Z Other, A-Z
Subarrange each by Table B-BJ18
By religion
Cf. BJ1188+ Religious ethics
Cf. BJ1188 Religious ethics
Judaism
For specific regions or countries, see B851+
Cf. B154+ Ancient Jewish philosophy
Cf. B755+ Medieval Jewish philosophy
5800 History
5802.A-Z Special topics, A-Z
5802.A89 Autonomy
5802.G46 Genocide
5802.M48 Metaphysics
5802.N65 Nonbeing
5802.P67 Postmodernism
5802.P78 Psychoanalysis

Logic

1 Periodicals. Serials
4 Societies
5 Congresses
6 Collected works (nonserial)
9 Dictionaries. Encyclopedias
History
General works
11 Early through 1800
15 1801-
Special topics, A-Z
21.A6 Augmentation
21.E64 Epistemics
21.F86 Future contingents
21.I6 Inference
21.I64 Insolubilia
Cf. B2799.A6 Antinomy (Kant)
Qua propositions see BC21.R43
21.R43 Reduplication. Qua propositions
21.S6 Sophisms
21.S9 Syllogisms
21.T5 Thesis
By period
Ancient
Oriental (Buddhist, Hindu, etc.)
25 General works
Individual logicians
see subclass B
26.A-Z Special topics, A-Z
26.A6 Argumentation
26.C38 Categories
26.C65 Consequentia
26.E64 Epistemics
26.F86 Future contingents
26.I6 Inference
26.I64 Insolubilia
Cf. B2799.A6 Antinomy (Kant)
26.M63 Modality
26.S6 Sophisms
26.S9 Syllogisms
26.T5 Thesis
Grecian
28 General works
Individual logicians
see subclass B
29.A-Z Special topics, A-Z
For list of topics see BC26.A+

History
By period
Ancient -- Continued
Roman
31 General works
Individual logicians
see subclass B
32.A-Z Special topics, A-Z
For list of topics see BC26.A+
Medieval
Including Islamic and Arabic
34 General works
Individual logicians
see subclass B
35.A-Z Special topics, A-Z
For list of topics see BC26.A+
Modern
38 General works
Individual logicians
see subclass B
39.A-Z Special topics, A-Z
For list of topics see BC26.A+
39.5.A-Z By region or country, A-Z
Biography
see subclass B
40-48 Special systems and theories (Table B-BJ6)
50 Philosophy. Methodology. Relation to other topics
51 Relation to speculative philosophy
53 Relation to psychology
55 Relation to ethics
57 Other
59 Study and teaching. Research
General works, treatises, and advanced textbooks
Deductive logic
Including deductive and inductive combined
Early works through 1800
60 Latin
61 English
62 French
63 German
66.A-Z Other. By language, A-Z
1801-
71 English
72 French
73 German
74 Italian
75 Spanish and Portuguese

General works, treatises, and advanced textbooks
Deductive logic
1801- -- Continued
76 Russian and other Slavic
78.A-Z Other. By language, A-Z
Inductive and empirical logic
80 Early works through 1800
1801-
91 English
92 French
93 German
94 Italian
95 Spanish and Portuguese
99.A-Z Other. By language, A-Z
Elementary textbooks. Outlines, syllabi, etc.
Early works through 1800
101 English
105.A-Z Other. By language, A-Z
1801-
108 English
111 French
114 German
116 Russian and other Slavic
117.A-Z Other. By language, A-Z
121 Genetic and evolutionary logic
122 Transcendental logic
126 Many-valued logic
128 First-order logic
129 Free logic
Symbolic and mathematical logic
Cf. BC199.T9 Type theory
131 Early works through 1800
135 1801-
136 Logic diagrams
Mechanical logical methods and systems. "Logic machines"
137 Early works through 1800
138 1801-
141 Logic of chance. Probability
Cf. HA29+ Statistics
Cf. QA273.A1+ Mathematics
Cf. QH323.5 Biology
143 Plausibility
145 Deontic logic
Logic for professional classes
151 Lawyers
156 Legislators

Logic for professional classes -- Continued

161.A-Z Other. By class, A-Z

e. g.

161.B8 Businessmen

161.P5 Physicians

161.T4 Teachers

Special topics

171 Truth and error. Certitude

Cf. BD181 Origin and sources of knowledge (Epistemology)

Cf. BJ1420+ Truth and falsehood (Ethics)

172 Categories

173 Proof

175 Fallacies

177 Reasoning, argumentation, etc.

181 Propositions. Prediction. Judgment

183 Hypothesis

185 Syllogisms. Enthymeme. Sorites. Dilemma, etc.

199.A-Z Other special topics, A-Z

199.A26 Abduction

199.A28 Act

Cf. B105.A35 Act (Philosophy)

199.B4 Belief and doubt

Cf. BD215 Epistemology

199.C38 Causation

199.C47 Change

199.C5 Commands

199.C55 Concepts

199.C56 Conditionals

199.C6 Contradiction

199.C66 Counterfactuals

199.D38 Defeasible reasoning

199.D4 Definition

199.D56 Disjunction

Doubt see BC199.B4

199.D8 Duality

199.E58 Entailment

199.E7 Equilibrium

199.E9 Experience

199.E93 Extension

199.F5 Fictions

199.F53 First principles

199.F6 Form

199.I4 Identity

199.I43 Implication

199.I45 Inconsistency

199.I47 Inference

Special topics

Other special topics, A-Z -- Continued

199.I5 Intention

199.L54 Limit

199.L6 Logical atomism

199.M6 Modality

Cf. QA9.46 Mathematical logic

199.N3 Names

199.N4 Negation

199.O6 Opposition

199.P2 Paradox

199.P7 Possibility

199.P73 Presupposition

199.Q4 Question

199.R44 Relevance

199.S5 Signification

199.T4 Tense. Time

Time see BC199.T4

199.T9 Type theory

199.V34 Vagueness

199.V4 Verification

199.V5 Vicious circle principle

Speculative philosophy
General philosophical works
Introduction to philosophy
Early works through 1800
10 Latin
11 English and American
12 French and Belgian
13 German
15 Other (not A-Z)
1801-
21 English and American
22 French and Belgian
23 German
24 Italian
25 Spanish and Portuguese
26 Russian and other Slavic
28 Other (not A-Z)
30-38 Elementary textbooks. Outlines, syllabi, etc. (Table B-BJ6)
41 Addresses, essays, lectures
Metaphysics
Cf. B532.M48 Greco-Roman philosophy
Cf. B738.M47 Medieval philosophy
95 Collected works (nonserial)
General works, treatises, and advanced textbooks
100-108 Early through 1800 (Table B-BJ6)
111-118 1801- (Table B-BJ6a)
125 Metaphysics of the school. Scholastic philosophy
Cf. B734 Scholasticism
Cf. B839.A1+ Scholasticism
131 Elementary textbooks. Outlines, syllabi, etc.
Epistemology. Theory of knowledge
Class here general works only
Cf. B132.K6 Hindu philosophy
Cf. B398.K7 Plato
Cf. B2799.K7 Kant
143 Collected works (nonserial)
General works
150-158 Early through 1800 (Table B-BJ6)
161-168 1801- (Table B-BJ6a)
171 Truth. Error. Certitude, etc.
Cf. BC171 Truth and error. Certitude (Logic)
Cf. BJ1420+ Truth and falsehood (Ethics)
Epistemology and sociology. Sociology of knowledge
175 General works
175.5.A-Z Special topics, A-Z
175.5.M84 Multiculturalism
175.5.P65 Political correctness

Epistemology. Theory of knowledge -- Continued
176 Epistemology and ethics. Intellectual virtues
177 Epistemology and evolution
Epistemology and science see Q174+
181 Origins and sources of knowledge
Cf. B808+ Topics in modern philosophy (Rationalism, empiricism, etc.)
181.3 A priori
181.5 Comprehension of knowledge
Cf. BF325 Psychology of comprehension
181.7 Memory
Cf. BF370+ Psychology
Cf. LB1063+ Education
182 Criterion
183 Inquiry
184 Decision-making
185 Encounter
190 Analogy
201 Limits of knowledge
Cf. B808+ Topics in modern philosophy (Agnosticism, scepticism, nihilism, positivism, etc.)
209 Authority
211 The unknowable. "Ding an sich"
212 Justification
212.5 Verification. Empirical verification. Verifiability
Epistemics see B820.3.A1+
213 Other minds
214 Senses and sensation
Cf. BF231+ Psychology
Cf. QP431+ Physiology
214.5 Body. Somatic aspects
215 Belief. Faith
Cf. BC199.B4 Logic
216 Hope
217 Double truth
218 Integration
218.5 Modality
219 Nonexistent objects
220 Objectivity
221 Relativity of knowledge
222 Subjectivity
223 Subject
225 Paradigm
232 Value. Worth
Cf. BF778 Psychology of values, meaning
233 Perfection
234 Infallibility

Epistemology. Theory of knowledge -- Continued
235 Abstraction. Generalization
236 Comparison. Resemblance. Identity
237 Explanation
238.A-Z Other special topics, A-Z
238.F68 Foundationalism
238.I58 Internalism
238.T47 Testimony
Methodology
Including classification of the sciences
Cf. Q177 Science
History of theory (of method) see BD240+
Theory of method, criticism, history see BD240+
General works
240 Early through 1800
241 1801-
255 Interdisciplinary approach to knowledge
258 Formalization of knowledge
260 Heuristic
265 Thought experiments
Ontology
General works
300-308 Early through 1800 (Table B-BJ6)
311-318 1801- (Table B-BJ6a)
331 Being. Nature of reality. Substance. First philosophy
Cf. B808+ Topics in modern philosophy (Dualism, materialism, personality, spiritualism, subjective idealism, etc.)
332 The concrete
336 Entity
340 Situation
348 Perspective
352 Phenomenalism. Attributes of being
Cf. B829.5.A+ Phenomenology
357 Ontologism
360 Silence
362 Transcendence
372 Becoming. Process
373 Change
374 Disposition
375 The catastrophical
390 Division
394 Unity and plurality
395 The one
395.5 Haecceity

Ontology -- Continued
396 Whole and parts (Philosophy). "Ganzheit"
Cf. B818.A+ Holism
Cf. BF202 Psychology
397 All (Philosophy)
398 Nothing (Philosophy)
399 Holes
401 Secret (Philosophy)
411 Finite and infinite
Including the conditioned and unconditioned
Cf. BD620+ Space, time, matter and motion
416 The absolute
417 Necessity
Mind
418 Early works through 1800
1801-
418.3 English
418.5.A-Z Other languages, A-Z
418.8 Artificial life
The soul. Spirit. Immortality, etc.
Cf. BL-BP, Special religions
Cf. BL-BX, Religion
Cf. BF1001+ Psychic research
Cf. BL530 Comparative religion
Cf. BT740+ The soul (Theology)
Cf. BT919+ Immortality (Theology)
419 Collected works (nonserial)
General works
420 Early through 1800
1801-
421 English
422.A-Z Other languages, A-Z
423 General special
Including special aspects of the subject as a whole
426 Preexistence of the soul. Metempsychosis
427 Angels
Cf. BL477 Angels in comparative religion
Cf. BT960+ Angels in theology
428 Soul of animals
Cf. BF660+ Animal psychology
429 Institutions
Life
Including general works on the philosophy of life
Cf. BD418.8 Artificial life
Cf. BJ1+ Ethics
430 Early works through 1800
431 1801-

	Ontology
	Life -- Continued
435	General special
	Including special aspects of the subject as a whole
436	Love
437	Struggle
438	Power
438.5	Self
439	Self-deception
440	Fear
443	Birth
	Death
443.8	Study and teaching. Research
443.9.A-Z	By region or country, A-Z
444	General works
445	Suicide
450	Philosophical anthropology
460.A-Z	Other special topics, A-Z
460.O74	Other as a philosophical concept
460.P67	Possessiveness
460.T76	Tropes
	Cosmology
493	Collected works (nonserial)
494	History
	By period
495	Ancient
495.5	Medieval
496	Modern
497	History of the theories of microcosms and macrocosms
	General works
500-508	Early through 1800 (Table B-BJ6)
511-518	1801- (Table B-BJ6a modified)
518.A-Z	Other languages, A-Z
	e. g.
518.L3	Latin (Modern)
523	Addresses, essays, lectures
	Cf. BD701 Curiosa, etc.
	Teleology. Causation. Final cause. Design and purpose
	Cf. BD411 Finite and infinite
	General works
530-538	Early through 1800 (Table B-BJ6)
541-548	1801- (Table B-BJ6a)
553	Mechanism. Mechanical theories of the universe
	Including mechanism and theism
555	Theism
	Cf. BL200 Natural theology

Cosmology
Teleology. Causation. Final cause. Design and purpose -- Continued
558 Pantheism
Cf. BL220 Natural theology
560 Panpsychism
573 Philosophy of religion
581 Philosophy of nature
Cause and effect
591 General works
595 Chance
Evolution see B818.A+; QH359+
Space, time, matter and motion
620 General works
621 Space
Cf. HM654 Sociology
626 Space and matter
632 Space and time
638 Time. Beginning
639 Eternal return
640 The contemporary
642 Presentism
643 Number and quantity
645 Cosmic harmony
646 Structure of matter. Atomism, etc.
Cf. BD331 Being, nature of reality, etc.
Cf. QC170+ Structure of matter and ether, including molecular, atomic and nuclear physics
648 Matter and form. Hylomorphism
652 Matter and motion. Force
655 Plurality of worlds. Life on other planets
Cf. QB54 Astronomy
701 Miscellaneous speculations. Curiosa, etc.
Cf. Q173 Miscellaneous speculations on the universe

	Psychology
	Periodicals. Serials
	Cf. B1+ Philosophy
	Cf. BF1001+ Psychic research
	Cf. QP351 Neurophysiology and neuropsychology
1.A1-.A3	Polyglot
1.A4-Z	English
2	French and Belgian
3	German
4	Italian
5	Spanish and Portuguese
8.A-Z	Other. By language, A-Z
11-18	Societies (Table B-BJ6a)
20	Congresses
	Collected works (nonserial)
21.A1	Polyglot
21.A2-Z	English
22	French
23	German
24	Italian
25	Spanish and Portuguese
26	Russian and other Slavic
28.A-Z	Other, A-Z
30	Directories
31	Dictionaries. Encyclopedias
32	Terminology. Nomenclature
38	Philosophy. Relation to other topics
38.5	Methodology
	Cf. BF76.5 Psychological research
	Cf. BF176 Psychological tests and testing
	Mathematical and statistical methods. Psychometrics
39	General works
39.2.A-Z	Special methods, A-Z
39.2.A52	Analysis of variance
39.2.F32	Factor analysis
39.2.F88	Fuzzy sets
39.2.I84	Item response theory
39.2.M85	Multidimensional scaling
39.2.R44	Regression analysis
39.2.S34	Set analysis
39.2.S7	Statistical hypothesis testing
39.3	Human behavior models
39.4	Biographical methods
39.5	Electronic data processing. Computer models and simulation
39.8	Descriptive psychology
39.9	Critical psychology

Philosophy. Relation to other topics -- Continued
40 Content psychology
Relation to other topics
41 Relation to critical and speculative philosophy
Including psychologism
44 Relation to logic
47 Relation to ethics and conduct
51 Relation to theology and religion
Cf. BF204.7 Transpersonal psychology
Cf. BL53+ Religious psychology
54 Relation to teaching
56 Relation to economics, business, etc.
Cf. HF5548.7+ Industrial psychology
57 Relation to sociology
Relation to population and demography see HB849.44
Relation to history see D16+
Relation to political science see JA74.5
61 Relation to law
64 Relation to natural sciences
Relation to medicine
see R726.5+ General; RC49+ Psychosomatic medicine; RC435+ Psychiatry
Relation to physiology see QP360+
Relation to self-improvement see BF636+
75 Practice of psychology. Economics of psychology practice
Including business methods and employment surveys
76 Vocational guidance
76.3 Psychologists in government
76.4 Ethics in psychology and in psychological research
76.45 Racism in psychology
76.5 Research
Cf. BF180+ Experimental psychology
76.6.A-Z Special topics, A-Z
76.6.A83 Audiovisual aids
76.6.E94 Experiential research
76.6.H47 Hermeneutics
76.6.I57 Internet (Computer network)
Cf. BF76.78 Computer network resources
76.6.L65 Longitudinal studies
76.6.O27 Observation
76.6.S56 Single subject research
Communication in psychology
76.7 General works
76.72 Information centers
76.75 Information services

Communication in psychology -- Continued

76.78 Computer network resources

Including the Internet

Cf. BF76.6.I57 The Internet as a research tool

76.8 Psychological literature

Study and teaching

77 General works

78 Problems, exercises, examinations

79 Laboratory manuals

79.5 Electronic data processing

80 Equipment and supplies

Cf. BF198.5 Experimental psychology apparatus

80.3 Audiovisual aids

80.7.A-Z By region or country, A-Z

Under each country:

.x	*General works*
.x2	*Individual institutions. By place, A-Z*

80.8 Licensure. Certification

80.9 Pictorial works. Atlases

History

Including the history of educational psychology

81-88 General works (Table B-BJ6a)

By period

91 Ancient

93 Medieval

95 Modern

98 Renaissance

101 18th century

103 19th century

105 20th century

(107) Special topics

see the topic

(107.A8) Association of ideas

see BF365+

(107.C6) Comparative psychology

see BF660+

(107.L4) Learning

see BF318+

108.A-Z By region or country, A-Z

Biography

Including biography of psychoanalysts

109.A1 Collective

109.A2-Z Individual, A-Z

Early works through 1850

110 Latin

111-118 Other (Table B-BJ6a)

1851-

1851- -- Continued
121-128 General works, treatises and advanced textbooks (Table B-BJ6a)
131-138 Handbooks, manuals, etc. (Table B-BJ6a)
139 Elementary textbooks
141 Outlines, syllabi, etc.
145 Popular works
Cf. BF638+ New thought
149 Addresses, essays, lectures
149.5 Juvenile works
149.8 Facetiae, satire, etc.
150-172 Mind and body
General works
150-158 Early works through 1850 (Table B-BJ6)
161-168 1851- (Table B-BJ6a)
171 Addresses, essays, lectures
172 Alexander technique
Cf. RA781.5 Health
Psychoanalysis
For psychoanalytic studies of individual persons, see the biography of the person concerned
For biography of psychoanalysts see BF109.A1+
For psychoanalysis applied to childhood see BF721+
Cf. B5802.P78 Jewish philosophy and psychoanalysis
Cf. BF315 Subconsciousness
Cf. RC500+ Psychiatry
Cf. RJ504.2 Child analysis
173.A2 Periodicals. Societies. Serials
173.A25-Z General works
175 General special
175.3 Juvenile works
175.4.A-Z Relation to other topics, A-Z
Art see N72.P74
Arts see NX180.P7
175.4.C68 Counseling. Psychoanalytic counseling
175.4.C84 Culture
Education see LB1092
175.4.E86 Evolution
175.4.F45 Feminism
175.4.H57 History
175.4.H84 Human geography
175.4.H85 Humanities
175.4.P45 Philosophy
Psychoanalytic counseling see BF175.4.C68
175.4.R34 Racism
175.4.R44 Religion
175.4.S65 Social sciences

Psychoanalysis -- Continued

175.45 Psychoanalytic theories of development

175.5.A-Z Special topics, A-Z

175.5.A33 Adlerian psychology
175.5.A35 Affect
175.5.A36 Aggressiveness
175.5.A52 Anima
175.5.A53 Animus
175.5.A55 Anus. Anality
175.5.A72 Archetype
175.5.B64 Body image
175.5.C37 Castration complex
175.5.C65 Coincidence. Synchronicity
175.5.D4 Death instinct
175.5.D44 Defense mechanisms
175.5.D74 Dreams
175.5.E35 Ego
175.5.E45 Electra complex
175.5.F36 Fantasy
175.5.F45 Femininity
175.5.I4 Id
175.5.I43 Identification
175.5.I53 Individuation
175.5.J69 Joy
175.5.L55 Liminality
175.5.L68 Love
Cf. BF575.L8 Emotion
175.5.M37 Masculinity
175.5.M95 Myth
175.5.O22 Object constancy
175.5.O24 Object relations
175.5.O33 Oedipus complex
175.5.O7 Orality
175.5.P35 Parapraxis
175.5.P37 Passivity
175.5.P47 Persona
175.5.P54 Pleasure principle
175.5.P68 Projection
175.5.P72 Psychic energy
175.5.P75 Psychic trauma
175.5.R4 Reality
175.5.R43 Representation
175.5.R44 Repression
175.5.S25 Scapegoat
175.5.S44 Self
175.5.S48 Sex
175.5.S49 Sex differences

Psychoanalysis
Special topics, A-Z -- Continued
175.5.S52 Sexism
175.5.S55 Shadow
175.5.S92 Sublimation
175.5.S93 Superego
175.5.S95 Symbolism
Synchronicity see BF175.5.C65
175.5.T73 Transitional objects
175.5.W67 Work
175.5.W75 Writing
176 Psychological tests and testing
For works on testing a particular aspect of behavior, or group of people, see the aspect or group in classes A - Z
Cf. BF431+ Intelligence testing
Cf. BF698.5+ Personality testing
Cf. BF719.6+ Psychological testing of infants
Cf. BF722.3+ Psychological testing of children
Cf. BF724.25 Psychological testing of teenagers
Cf. LB1131+ Education
176.2 Computer applications. Electronic data processing
176.5 Behavioral assessment
Experimental psychology
Cf. QP351+ Physiology
180 Periodicals. Societies. Serials
181-188 General works (Table B-BJ6a)
191-198 Elementary textbooks. Outlines, syllabi, etc. (Table B-BJ6a)
198.5 Instruments and apparatus
198.7 Psychological experiments, etc.
Laboratory manuals see BF79
Adlerian psychology see BF175.5.A33
199 Behaviorism. Neobehaviorism. Behavioral psychology
Cf. BF319+ Conditioned response
200 Interbehavioral psychology
201 Cognitive psychology
Cf. BF309+ Cognition
201.3 Discursive psychology
201.4 Feminist psychology
201.5 Functionalism
202 Whole and parts (Psychology). "Ganzheit"
Cf. BD396 Philosophy
203 Gestalt psychology. Gestalt perception
Cf. BF698.8.A+ Personality tests
Human potential movement see BF637.H85
204 Humanistic psychology
204.5 Phenomenological psychology. Existential psychology
Cf. BF41 Psychologism

204.6 Positive psychology
204.7 Transpersonal psychology
207 Psychotropic drugs and other substances
Cf. QP801.A+ Physiological effects
Cf. RC483+ Psychiatric psychopharmacology
Cf. RC566.A+ Narcotic addiction. Drug abuse
Cf. RM315+ Medical psychopharmacology
209.A-Z Special drugs and other substances, A-Z
209.A43 Alcohol
209.A93 Ayahuasca
209.C3 Cannabis. Marijuana. Hashish
209.H34 Hallucinogenic drugs
209.H36 Hallucinogenic mushrooms
Hashish see BF209.C3
209.L9 Lysergic acid diethylamide
Marihuana see BF209.C3
209.M4 Mescaline
209.N52 Nicotine
209.T5 Thiazinamium
Tobacco see BF209.N52
210 Electronic behavior control
Anatomy and physiology of the nervous system see QP361+; RC360+
Sensation
For physiological discussions see QP431+
General works
231 Early works through 1800
233 1801-
237 Psychophysics
Including Weber's and Fechner's law, etc.
Cf. QP360+ Physiology
Special senses
Vision. Visual perception
Cf. BF203 Gestalt perception
Cf. QP474+ Physiology
241 General works
Visual perception testing
241.4 General works
241.5.A-Z Individual tests of visual perception, A-Z
241.5.D48 Developmental Test of Visual Perception
241.7 Brightness perception
242 Face perception
243 Picture perception
245 Motion perception
Hearing. Auditory perception
Cf. QP460+ Physiology
251 General works

Sensation
Special senses
Hearing. Auditory perception -- Continued
Auditory perception testing
251.4 General works
251.5.A-Z Special tests of auditory perception, A-Z
251.5.M85 Multiple Auditory Processing Assessment
251.5.T44 Test of Auditory-Perceptual Skills-Revised
251.5.T46 Test of Auditory-Perceptual Skills-Upper Level
261 Taste
Cf. QP456 Physiology
271 Smell
Cf. QP458 Physiology
275 Touch and other cutaneous senses
Cf. QP450+ Physiology
281 Temperature sense
285 Muscle sense
291 Static sense
Cf. QP471+ Position, equilibrium, etc.
292 Sense perceptions (General)
Space perception and behavior see BF469
Form perception
For Gestalt psychology see BF203
293 General works
294 Pattern perception
Movement. Motor ability. Motor learning. Perceptual-motor learning
Cf. BF433.M68 Motor ability and intelligence
Cf. GV452 Movement education
295 General works
Motor ability testing
295.4 General works
295.5.A-Z Special tests of motor ability or perceptual-motor processes, A-Z
295.5.T46 Test of Visual Motor Integration
295.5.T47 Test of Visual-Motor Skills (Upper Level)
Other senses, A-Z
299.G6 Glassy sensation
299.O7 Orientation
Size judgment see BF299.S5
299.S5 Size perception. Size judgment
299.S9 Synthetic sense

Consciousness. Cognition
Cf. BD143+ Epistemology
Cf. BD300+ Ontology
Cf. BF201 Cognitive psychology
Cf. BF203 Gestalt perception
Cf. BF698.9.C63 Cognition and personality
Cf. BF720.C63 Cognition in infants
Cf. BF723.C5 Cognition in children
Cf. BF724.55.C63 Cognition and age in adulthood
Cf. BF724.85.C64 Cognition in old age

309 Periodicals. Societies. Serials
311 General works
313 Schemas
314 Cognitive maps
315 The unconscious mind, etc. Subconsciousness
Cf. BF173+ Psychoanalysis
Cf. RC489.S827 Subconsciousness
315.2 Context effects
315.5 Intuition
316 Introspection
316.6 Mental representation
317 Reactions. Reaction time, etc.
317.5 Tacit knowledge
318 Learning
Cf. BF370+ Memory
Cf. BF724.85.C64 Learning in old age
Cf. LB1060+ Learning in education
318.5 Experiential learning
Conditioned response
Cf. BF199 Behaviorism
Cf. QP416 Neurophysiology
319 General works
319.5.A-Z Special topics, A-Z
319.5.A79 Autoshaping
319.5.A8 Aversive stimuli
319.5.A9 Avoidance conditioning
319.5.B5 Biofeedback training
Cf. RC489.B53 Psychotherapy
Biological rhythms see BF637.B55
319.5.E4 Emotional conditioning
319.5.E9 Extinction
319.5.F4 Feedback
319.5.I45 Implicit learning
319.5.O6 Operant conditioning. Operant behavior
319.5.P34 Paired-association learning
319.5.P8 Punishment
319.5.R4 Reinforcement

Consciousness. Cognition
Learning
Conditioned response
Special topics, A-Z -- Continued
319.5.R48 Reward
Cf. BF505.G6 Goal
Cf. BF505.R48 Motivation
319.5.S7 Stimulus generalization
319.5.S73 Stimulus intensity
319.5.S75 Stimulus satiation
319.5.V4 Verbal conditioning
321 Apperception. Attention
Cf. BF433.A6 Apperception (Mental tests)
323.A-Z Special topics, A-Z
323.A27 Absent-mindedness
(323.C5) Concious attitudes
see BF327
323.C8 Curiosity
323.D36 Danger perception
323.D5 Distraction
Dogmatism see BF698.35.D64
323.E2 Efficiency
323.E7 Errors
323.E8 Expectation
323.F45 Field dependence
323.F5 First impressions
323.I48 Inhibition
323.I5 Interest
323.I52 Interference
323.J63 Joint attention
323.L5 Listening
323.O2 Observation
323.P66 Pötzl phenomenon
323.S4 Secondary function
323.S55 Similarity
323.S63 Social perception
Including stereotype formation
323.S8 Subliminal perception
323.V5 Vigilance
325 Comprehension. Understanding
327 Attitude. Conscious attitudes
Cf. BF378.A75 Attitudinal influences on memory
Habit. Adjustment
335 General works
Testing
335.4 General works
335.5.A-Z Individual tests of habit or adjustment, A-Z

Consciousness. Cognition
Habit. Adjustment
Testing
Individual tests of habit or adjustment, A-Z -- Continued
335.5.C66 Coping Response Inventory
Special topics, A-Z
337.A92 Avoidance
Cf. BF319.5.A9 Avoidance conditioning
337.B74 Breaking habits
337.C62 Cognitive balance
337.C63 Cognitive dissonance
337.C65 Compensation
Dissonance, Cognitive see BF337.C63
337.E9 Exercise
337.I6 Interference
337.R28 Rationalization
(337.R35) Repression
see BF175.5.R44
337.R4 Retroactive interference
Nature and nurture
Cf. B818.A+ Evolution
Cf. QH438.5 Physiology
Cf. QH457 Behavior genetics
341 General works
343 General special
e.g. Heredity in royalty
346.A-Z Special topics, A-Z
346.M8 Musicians
346.S5 Siamese twins
353 Environmental psychology
Cf. GT165.5 Psychological aspects of dwellings
Cf. NA2542.4 Human factors in architecture
353.5.A-Z Special topics, A-Z
353.5.A45 Altitude
353.5.C53 City and town life
353.5.C55 Climate
353.5.C74 Crowding
353.5.H84 Humidity
353.5.N37 Nature
353.5.N65 Noise
Space see BF469
353.5.S87 Sustainable development
353.5.W4 Weather
355 Posture

Consciousness. Cognition -- Continued
357 Imitation. Mimicry
Cf. B818.A+ Evolution
Cf. BF699+ Genetic psychology
Cf. QH546 Ecology
Association and reproduction of ideas
365 General works
Special
367 Mental imagery
Cf. BF408+ Creative processes
Cf. RC489.F35 Psychotherapy
Memory
Cf. BD181.7 Philosophy
Cf. LB1063+ Education
Cf. QP406 Physiology
370 Early works through 1850
371 1851-
Including theory of memory, memory curve, etc.
Memory testing
375 General works
375.5.A-Z Special tests, A-Z
375.5.M45 Memory Assessment Scales
375.5.W43 Wechsler Memory Scale
375.5.W53 Wide Range Assessment of Memory and Learning
376 Disorders of the memory
Cf. RC394.M46 Organic memory disorders
378.A-Z Special topics, A-Z
378.A3 Advertising
378.A33 Age factors
378.A75 Attitudinal influences
378.A87 Autobiographical memory
378.C7 Color
378.C72 Context effects
378.D45 Déjà vu
378.E17 Early memories
378.E94 Expertise
378.F55 Flashbulb memory
378.F7 Forgetting
378.H54 Hindsight bias
378.I55 Implicit memory
378.I6 Inhibition
378.I65 Interruption. Zeigarnik effect
378.I68 Involuntary memory
378.L65 Long-term memory
378.M65 Mood
378.N47 News broadcasts
378.N8 Numbers

Consciousness. Cognition
Association and reproduction of ideas
Special
Memory
Special topics, A-Z -- Continued

378.P76 Prospective memory
378.R4 Recognition
378.R44 Reminiscing
378.S45 Selectivity
378.S46 Sentences
378.S54 Short-term memory
378.S65 Social aspects
378.S7 Sounds
Zeignarnik effect see BF378.I65
Mnemonics. Memory training
380 Collected works (nonserial)
381 History of mnemonic systems
General works
383 Early works through 1850
385 1851-
387.A-Z Special topics, A-Z
387.N34 Names
390 Perseveration
395.A-Z Other special, A-Z
Creative processes. Imagination. Invention
Cf. B105.C74 Philosophy
Cf. BF433.O7 Intelligence and creative ability
Cf. HX522 Communism and creative ability
Cf. Q172.5.C74 Creative ability in science
408 General works
General special
410 Psychology of inspiration
411 Other
412 Genius. Gifted
Cf. BF724.3.G53 Gifted teenagers
416.A-Z Studies of men and women of genius. By name, A-Z
e. g.
416.A1 Collective
416.B7 Brontë, Charlotte
416.Z8 Zola, Émile
418 Genius and heredity
Cf. BF341+ Heredity
423 Genius and mental illness
426 Genius and mental retardation

Consciousness. Cognition -- Continued
Intelligence. Mental ability. Intelligence testing. Ability testing
For works on testing particular abilities (Musical, mathematical, etc.), see the subject in classes M, Q, etc.
Cf. HF5381.7 Occupational aptitude tests
Cf. QP398 Physiology

431 General works
431.3 Problems, exercises, examinations
431.5.A-Z By region or country, A-Z
432.A-Z By specific group of people, A-Z
432.A1 General works
African Americans see BF432.N5
432.A84 Asian Americans
Blacks see BF432.N5
432.B7 Brain-damaged persons
432.C48 Children
432.C5 Chinese. Chinese Americans
432.C54 Cleft palate children
432.D4 Deaf
432.D45 Dementia patients
432.I5 Indians
432.J4 Jews
432.M37 Mental disabilities, People with
432.M4 Mexicans
432.N5 Negroes. Blacks. African Americans
432.S63 Social disabilities, People with
432.3 Multiple intelligences
432.5.A-Z Special tests of mental ability, intelligence or cognition, A-Z
432.5.B55 Binet-Simon test
432.5.C35 Canadian intelligence test
432.5.C64 Cognitive Abilities Test
432.5.C65 Cognitive Control Battery
432.5.C66 Cognitive Levels Test
432.5.C67 Comprehensive Test of Nonverbal Intelligence
432.5.D37 Das-Naglieri Cognitive Assessment System
432.5.D49 Differential Ability Scales
432.5.D53 Differential Aptitude Test
432.5.G64 Goodenough draw-a-man test
432.5.H35 Hammill Multiability Intelligence Test
432.5.I53 Infant Mullen Scales of Early Learning
432.5.I55 Intelligence tests for preliterates
432.5.K38 Kaufman Assessment Battery for Children
432.5.K39 Kaufman Brief Intelligence Test
432.5.L4 Learning Potential Assessment Device
432.5.L44 Leiter International Performance Scale
432.5.M36 Matrix Analogies Test
432.5.M83 Mullen Scales of Early Learning

Consciousness. Cognition
Intelligence. Mental ability. Intelligence testing. Ability testing
Special tests of mental ability, intelligence or cognition, A-Z -- Continued

432.5.M85 Multidimensional Aptitude Battery
432.5.N64 Non-Verbal Ability Tests
432.5.N65 Nonverbal intelligence tests
432.5.O84 Otis quick-scoring mental ability tests
432.5.P42 Peabody picture vocabulary test
432.5.Q53 Quick Cognitive Inventory
432.5.R38 Raven's Progressive Matrices
432.5.R48 Reynolds Intellectual Assessment Scales
432.5.S35 Schaie-Thurstone Adult Mental Abilities Test
432.5.S55 Slosson Intelligence Test
432.5.S8 Stanford-Binet test
432.5.S83 Stanford-Ohwaki-Kohs tactile block design for intelligence test for the blind
432.5.S85 Stoelting Brief Nonverbal Intelligence test
432.5.W4 Wechsler Adult Intelligence Scale
432.5.W42 Wechsler Intelligence Scale for Children
432.5.W423 Wechsler Nonverbal Scale of Ability
432.5.W424 Wechsler Preschool and Primary Scale of Intelligence
432.5.W54 Wide Range Intelligence Test
432.5.W66 Woodcock-Johnson Tests of Cognitive Abilities
433.A-Z Special topics, A-Z
433.A3 Age and intelligence
433.A6 Apperception
Cf. BF698.8.C4 Children's Apperception Test
Cf. BF698.8.T5 Thematic apperception test
433.B6 Body size and intelligence
Creativity and intelligence see BF433.O7
Economic status see BF433.S63
G factor see BF433.G45
433.G45 General factor. G factor
Intelligence and creativity see BF433.O7
Intelligence and motor ability see BF433.M68
Intelligence and personality see BF698.9.I6
Intelligence and socioeconomic status see BF433.S63
Maze learning see BF433.M3
433.M3 Mazes. Maze learning
433.M4 Mechanical aptitude
433.M5 Mirror drawing
433.M68 Motor ability and intelligence
433.O7 Originality. Creativity and intelligence
433.P6 Planning ability
Puzzle learning see BF433.P8
433.P8 Puzzles. Puzzle learning

Consciousness. Cognition
Intelligence. Mental ability. Intelligence testing. Ability testing
Special topics, A-Z -- Continued
433.S48 Sex differences
433.S63 Socioeconomic status and intelligence
Mental deficiency see RC569.7+
Thought and thinking
441 General works
442 Reasoning
Abstraction. Conceptualization
443 General works
Testing of abstraction or conceptualization
443.4 General works
443.5.A-Z Special tests of abstraction or conceptualization, A-Z
443.5.W55 Wisconsin Card Sorting Test
444 Information processing
444.5 Domain specificity
445 Categorization. Seriation
446 Comparison
447 Judgment
448 Decision making
Including decision making tests
449 Problem solving
449.5 Insight
Psycholinguistics. Psychology of meaning
Cf. B832.3.A+ Private language problem
Cf. BF582 Language and emotions
Cf. LB1139.L3 Language (Child study)
Cf. P37 Psycholinguistics (General), and from the linguistic viewpoint
455.A1 Periodicals. Societies. Serials
455.A3-Z General works
456.A-Z Psychology of reading, spelling, etc., A-Z
e. g.
456.D7 Drawing
Cf. BF723.D7 Child psychology
Mathematics see BF456.N7
Mirror writing see BF456.W8
456.N7 Numbers. Mathematics
456.R2 Reading
456.S8 Spelling
456.W8 Writing. Mirror writing
For psychological aspects of rhetoric see P301.5.P75
Cf. P211.6 Psychological aspects of written communication (General and linguistic)

Consciousness. Cognition
Psycholinguistics. Psychology of meaning -- Continued
458 Symbolism
Cf. BC131+ Symbolic and mathematical logic
Cf. BF175.5.S95 Psychoanalysis
Cf. BF698.8.T8 Tua test
461 Popular works
463.A-Z Special topics, A-Z
463.D47 Description
463.I58 Invective
463.M4 Meaning (Thought, language)
463.O2 Obscenity
463.Q47 Questioning
463.S64 Speech perception
Cf. P37.5.S68 Speech perception (General and from the linguistic viewpoint)
463.U5 Uncertainty
463.V45 Verbal ability
467 Time, space, causality, etc.
Cf. BD620+ Cosmology
468 Time
469 Space
471 Change
475 Rhythm in movement, music, speech, etc.
Cf. BF637.B55 Biological rythms
481 Work
For influence on posture see BF355
Cf. BJ1498 Leisure
Cf. HD4904+ Philosophy of labor
Cf. HD4904.5 Fatigue
482 Fatigue. Mental fatigue
Cf. LB1075 Educational psychology
Cf. QP421 Physiology
Cf. RC552.N5 Neurasthenia
485 Laziness
491 Normal illusions
Cf. BF1001+ Psychology of the subconscious, psychic research, occult sciences
Cf. QP495 Optical illusions
493.A-Z Special illusions, A-Z
e. g.
493.C7 Conjuring deceptions
Synesthesia
Cf. RC394.S93 Neurology
495 General works

Consciousness. Cognition
Synesthesia -- Continued
497 Colored audition
Including pseudochromesthesia, photism, phonism, color hearing, color music
498 Number forms
499.A-Z Other topics, A-Z
Motivation
Cf. BF723.M56 Child psychology
Cf. QP409 Physiology
501 Periodicals. Serials
501.3 Societies
501.5 Congresses
501.7 Collected works (nonserial)
503 General works
504 Addresses, essays, lectures
504.3 Juvenile works
505.A-Z Special topics, A-Z
505.G6 Goal
Including goal attainment tests
505.R48 Reward
Cf. BF319.5.R48 Conditioned response
511 Affection. Feeling. Emotion
Cf. BF698.9.E45 Emotions and personality
Cf. QP401 Physiology
515 Pleasure and pain
Cf. BJ1480+ Ethics
521 The feelings. Sensibility. Mood
Emotion
Cf. BF723.A+ Emotions of children
Cf. BF724.3.A+ Emotions of adolescents
531-538 General works (Table B-BJ6a)
Popular works. The "passions," etc.
550-558 Early through 1850 (Table B-BJ6)
560-568 1851- (Table B-BJ6)
575.A-Z Special forms of emotion, etc., A-Z
575.A3 Aggressiveness. Violence
Cf. RC569.5.A34 Aggressiveness (Psychopathology)
575.A35 Agitation
575.A45 Ambivalence
575.A5 Anger
Cf. RC569.5.A53 Psychopathology
575.A6 Anxiety
575.A75 Apologizing
575.A85 Assertiveness
Cf. RC489.A77 Psychopathology
575.A86 Attachment

BF

Affection. Feeling. Emotion
Emotion
Special forms of emotion, etc., A-Z -- Continued

575.A88 Autonomy. Freedom
575.A886 Aversion
(575.A89) Avoidance
see BF337.A92
575.A9 Awe
575.B3 Bashfulness
Bereavement see BF575.G7
575.B67 Boredom
575.C35 Calmness
575.C8 Courage
Criticism see BF637.C74
575.C88 Crying
575.D34 Dependency
575.D35 Deprivation (General)
575.D4 Desire
575.D45 Despair
575.D57 Disappointment
(575.D63) Dogmatism
575.E4 Ecstasy
575.E45 Egoism
575.E5 Elation
575.E53 Embarrassment
575.E55 Empathy
575.E6 Enthusiasm
575.E65 Envy
575.E83 Escape
575.F14 Failure. Losing
575.F16 Fanaticism
575.F2 Fear
575.F5 Fighting
575.F62 Fragility
Freedom see BF575.A88
575.F66 Friendship
575.F7 Frustration
575.G44 Generosity. Giving
Cf. BF637.H4 Helping behavior
Cf. BF789.G5 Gifts
Giving see BF575.G44
575.G68 Gratitude
575.G7 Grief. Bereavement. Separation
575.G8 Guilt
575.H26 Han
575.H27 Happiness. Joy
575.H3 Hate

Affection. Feeling. Emotion
Emotion
Special forms of emotion, etc., A-Z -- Continued

575.H4 Helplessness
575.H56 Hope
575.H6 Hostility
Humor see BF575.L3
575.H85 Humiliation
575.I46 Impulse
Cf. RC569.5.I46 Impulsive personality
575.I48 Innocence
575.I5 Intimacy
575.J4 Jealousy
Joy see BF575.H27
575.L3 Laughter. Humor
575.L7 Loneliness
Losing see BF575.F14
Loss see BF575.D35
575.L8 Love
Cf. BF175.5.L68 Psychoanalysis
Cf. BF575.U57 Unrequited love
575.M44 Melancholy
575.N35 Narcissism
Cf. RC553.N36 Psychopathology
575.N6 Nostalgia
(575.O67) Optimism
see BF698.35.O57
(575.P4) Pessimism
see BF698.35.P49
575.P9 Prejudice
Privacy see BF637.P74
Procrastination see BF637.P76
575.R33 Regret
575.R35 Rejection
575.R36 Relatedness
575.R37 Repentance
575.S23 Sadness
575.S35 Security
575.S37 Self-acceptance
575.S39 Self-confidence
575.S4 Self-consciousness (Sensitivity)
Self-respect see BF697.5.S46
575.S42 Sensuality
Separation see BF575.G7
575.S45 Shame
575.S48 Sharing

BF

Affection. Feeling. Emotion
Emotion
Special forms of emotion, etc., A-Z -- Continued
575.S75 Stress
Cf. HF5548.85 Job stress
Cf. RC455.4.S87 Psychiatry
Cf. RG580.S73 Obstetrics
575.S8 Surprise
575.S9 Sympathy
575.T43 Tenderness
575.T45 Threat
575.T5 Timidity
575.T7 Trust
575.U57 Unrequited love
Violence see BF575.A3
575.W8 Worry
Emotional intelligence. Emotional intelligence testing
576 General works
576.3 Problems, exercises, examinations
576.8.A-Z Special tests of emotional ability and intelligence, A-Z
576.8.E56 Emotional Judgment Inventory
576.8.S45 Simmons Personal Survey
578 Emotional contagion
582 Language and emotions
Expression of the emotions
585 Early works through 1850
588 1851-
591 Expression of the emotions in humans
Cf. QP401 Physiology
Expression of the emotions in children see BF723.E6
592.A-Z Special forms of expression, A-Z
592.F33 Face
592.V64 Voice
593 Expression of the emotions in animals
Will. Volition. Choice. Control
Cf. BF724.55.C66 Control and age in adulthood
General works
608 Early through 1850
611-618 1851- (Table B-BJ6a)
619 Commitment
Cf. RC569.5.C65 Lack of commitment (Psychiatry)
619.5 Intentionalism
620-628 Freedom of the will (Table B-BJ6)
Class here psychological works only
For ethics see BJ1460+
Cf. BV741 Religious liberty
Cf. JC571 Political liberty

Will. Volition. Choice. Control -- Continued
632 Self-control. Willpower. Self-help techniques
Cf. BJ1+ Ethics
632.5 Manipulation or control by others
633 Brainwashing
634 Confession
635 Diseases and disorders of the will. Errors and abnormalities
Applied psychology
For application to a special field, see subject in classes B - Z
Cf. HF5548.7+ Industrial psychology
Cf. LB1027.55 School psychology
Cf. RC466.8+ Clinical psychology
636.A1 Periodicals. Societies. Serials
636.A2-Z General works
636.3 Operational psychology
Counseling psychology. Counseling
For counseling of specific groups of people or specific problems, see the group or the problem
Cf. BF175.4.C68 Psychoanalytic counseling
Cf. BF637.M45 Mentoring
Cf. BV4012.2 Pastoral counseling
Cf. HD7255.5 Rehabilitation counseling
Cf. HF5381+ Vocational guidance
Cf. HF5549.5.C8 Employee counseling
Cf. LB1027.5+ Educational counseling
Cf. R727.4 Health counseling
636.5 Periodicals. Serials
636.52 Congresses
636.54 Dictionaries. Encyclopedias
636.6 General works
636.64 Vocational guidance
636.65 Study and teaching
636.67 Moral and ethical aspects. Professional ethics
636.68 Religious aspects. Spirituality
636.7.A-Z Special topics, A-Z
636.7.C76 Cross-cultural counseling
636.7.G76 Group counseling
636.7.H86 Humanistic counseling
636.7.P44 Peer counseling
636.7.R44 Re-evaluation counseling
636.7.S57 Short-term counseling
637.A-Z Special topics (not otherwise provided for), A-Z
Altruism see BF637.H4
637.A77 Attention-seeking
637.A84 Audiovisual aids

Applied psychology
Special topics (not otherwise provided for), A-Z -- Continued
637.A87 Authority
Cf. BF723.A78 Child psychology
637.B4 Behavior modification
Cf. LB1060.2 Behavior modification in learning
Cf. RC489.B4 Behavior therapy in clinical application
Biofeedback training see BF319.5.B5
637.B55 Biological rhythms. Biorhythm charting
For special applications, see the field
Biorhythm charting see BF637.B55
Body language see BF637.N66
637.B85 Bullying
637.C4 Change
Coaching, Personal see BF637.P36
637.C45 Communication. Interpersonal communication
Class here works on the psychological aspects of communication in general and of interpersonal communication
For works on general and linguistic aspects of interpersonal communication see P94.7
Cf. BF637.V64 Voice
Cf. HM1166+ Social psychology
Cf. P96.P75+ Psychological aspects of mass media
Communication, Nonverbal see BF637.N66
637.C47 Competition
637.C5 Conduct of life
Conflict management see BF637.I48
637.C54 Consolation
637.C56 Consultation
(637.C6) Counseling. Group counseling
see BF636.5+
637.C74 Criticism
637.D42 Deception
Cf. BF697.5.S426 Self-deception
Discussion leadership see LC6519
637.D65 Doppelgängers
637.E53 Encouragement
637.E95 Excuses
Eye contact see BF637.N66
Falsehood see BF637.T77
637.F67 Forgiveness
Gesture see BF637.N66
Group counseling see BF636.7.G76
637.H4 Helping behavior. Altruism
637.H46 Hesitation
637.H83 Hugging

Applied psychology
Special topics (not otherwise provided for), A-Z -- Continued

637.H85 Human potential movement
637.I46 Impostor phenomenon
Interpersonal communication see BF637.C45
637.I48 Interpersonal conflict
Including interpersonal conflict tests and confict management
637.I5 Interviewing
637.L36 Laterality
637.L4 Leadership
637.L53 Life change events
Lying see BF637.T77
637.M4 Meditation
Cf. BF637.T68 Transcendental meditation
Cf. BL627 Religious meditation
637.M45 Mentoring
637.N4 Negotiation
637.N46 Neurolinguistic programming
637.N66 Nonverbal communication. Body language
Including eye contact, gesture, etc.
637.O72 Oral behavior. Oral habits
637.O94 Overachievement
637.P3 Peace of mind
637.P36 Personal coaching
637.P4 Persuasion
Cf. BF774 Psychology of influence, pattern and example
637.P7 Praise
637.P74 Privacy. Secrecy
637.P76 Procrastination
637.P84 Punishment
637.R4 Reconciliation
637.R45 Relaxation
Cf. RA785 Personal health
637.R48 Revenge
637.R57 Risk-taking
Cf. RC569.5.R58 Behavior problems
Secrecy see BF637.P74
637.S36 Seduction
Self-actualization see BF637.S4
637.S37 Self-defeating behavior
Self-defense, Verbal see BF637.V47
637.S38 Self-efficacy
637.S4 Self-realization. Self-actualization
Cf. BF710 Maturation
637.S42 Self-sacrifice
637.S46 Separation-individuation

Applied psychology
Special topics (not otherwise provided for), A-Z -- Continued
637.S64 Solitude
637.S8 Success
Cf. BF724.3.S9 Adolescence. Youth
Cf. HF5386 Success in business
637.T43 Teasing
637.T5 Time, Use of
637.T68 Transcendental meditation
Cf. BF637.M4 Meditation
Cf. RC489.M43 Meditation as psychotherapy
637.T77 Truthfulness and falsehood
Cf. BF637.D42 Deception
637.U53 Underachievement
637.V47 Verbal self-defense
637.V64 Voice-defense
Cf. BF592.V64 Expression of the emotions
Work see BF481
New Thought. Menticulture, etc.
638 Periodicals. Societies. Serials
General works
639 English
641 Other languages (not A-Z)
645 General special
Including special aspects of the subject as a whole
Biography
648.A1 Collective
648.A2-Z Individual, A-Z
Comparative psychology. Animal and human psychology
For animal behavior see QL750+
For animal psychology see QL785+
660 Early works through 1870
671-678 1871- (Table B-BJ6a)
Special topics
see the particular topic in BF, e.g., Special forms of emotion BF575.A-Z
(683) Motivation
see BF501+
685 Instinct
Psychology of sex. Sexual behavior
Cf. BF175.5.S48 Psychoanalysis
Cf. GN484.3+ Ethnology
Cf. HQ12+ Sociology
Cf. QL761 Sexual behavior in animals
692 General works
692.15 Sexual animosity

Psychology of sex. Sexual behavior -- Continued
Sex role. Sex differences
Cf. BF433.S48 Intelligence
Cf. HQ1075+ Sociology
692.2 General works
Testing of sex role or sex differences
692.3 General works
692.35.A-Z Special tests, A-Z
692.35.B44 Bem Sex-Role Inventory
692.5 Psychology of men. Masculinity
Cf. BF175.5.M37 Psychoanalysis
Psychology of women see HQ1206+
Differential psychology. Individuality. Self
Including psychology of individual differences
697 General works
697.5.A-697.Z Special aspects, A-Z
697.5.B63 Body image
Self-acceptance see BF575.S37
697.5.S426 Self-deception
697.5.S427 Self-disclosure
697.5.S428 Self-doubt
Self-esteem see BF697.5.S46
697.5.S429 Self-hate
697.5.S43 Self-perception
697.5.S44 Self-presentation
697.5.S45 Self-preservation. Self-protective behavior
Self-protective behavior see BF697.5.S45
697.5.S46 Self-respect. Self-esteem
697.5.S47 Self-talk
697.5.S65 Social aspects
Personality
Cf. BF1156.P44 Personality and hypnotism
698.A1 Periodicals. Societies. Serials
698.A2-Z General works
698.2 Personality change
Personality types. Typology
698.3 General works
Cf. BF818 Character
698.35.A-Z Special personality traits or aspects, A-Z
698.35.A36 Acquisitiveness
698.35.A87 Authoritarianism
698.35.C45 Charisma
698.35.C67 Constancy
698.35.D48 Determination
698.35.D64 Dogmatism
698.35.E54 Enneagram
698.35.E98 Extraversion

Personality
Personality types
Special personality traits or aspects, A-Z -- Continued

698.35.I55 Inner child
698.35.I58 Intercorrelation of traits
698.35.I59 Introversion
698.35.L62 Locus of control
698.35.M34 Machiavellianism
698.35.N44 Negativism
698.35.O57 Optimism
698.35.P36 Passivity
698.35.P43 Pedantry
698.35.P47 Perfectionism
698.35.P49 Pessimism
698.35.P67 Possessiveness
698.35.R47 Resilience
698.35.S45 Sensation seeking
698.35.S47 Sensitivity
698.35.S83 Submissiveness
698.4 Personality assessment. Research
Cf. RC469+ Psychiatric examination
Personality testing
698.5 General works
698.7 Projective techniques
698.75 Q technique
698.8.A-Z Special tests, A-Z
Including individual personality tests for children
698.8.A32 Adjective Check List
698.8.A34 Adjective generation technique
698.8.A36 Adult Personality Inventory
698.8.A4 Allport-Vernon study of values test
698.8.A8 Association tests
698.8.A88 Attentional and Interpersonal Style Inventory
698.8.B37 Basic Personality Inventory
698.8.B4 Bender gestalt test
698.8.B42 Berkeley Personality Profile
698.8.B47 Birkman Method of Personality Testing
698.8.B5 Blacky pictures test
698.8.C25 California Psychological Inventory
698.8.C4 Children's apperception test
698.8.C45 Children's Personality Questionnaire
698.8.C6 Color pyramid test
698.8.C64 Columbus test
698.8.C66 Comrey Personality Scales
698.8.D43 Defense Mechanisms Inventory
698.8.D49 Dewey Color System
698.8.D68 Draw-a-Family Test

Personality
Personality assessment. Research
Personality testing
Special tests, A-Z -- Continued

698.8.D7 Draw-a-Person Test
698.8.D9 Dynamic personality inventory
698.8.E3 Edwards personal preference schedule
698.8.E47 Eidetic parents test
698.8.E5 Eight card redrawing test
698.8.E9 Experiential world inventory
698.8.F35 Fairy Tale Test
698.8.F53 FIRO-B
698.8.F56 Five-Factor Nonverbal Personality Questionnaire
698.8.F6 Four picture Test
698.8.F7 Frieling test
698.8.F8 Fungus test
698.8.G5 Giessen test
698.8.G67 Gordon Personal Profile-Inventory
698.8.G74 Group Environment Scale
698.8.G8 Guilford-Zimmerman temperament survey
698.8.H3 Hand test
698.8.H35 Harrower inkblot test
698.8.H5 High school personality questionnaire
698.8.H53 Hoffer-Osmond diagnostic test
698.8.H54 Hogan Personality Inventory
698.8.H55 Holtzman inkblot technique
698.8.H6 House-Tree-Person Technique
Cf. BF698.8.K55 Kinetic-House-Tree-Person Technique
Cf. RJ503.7.H68 Child psychiatry
698.8.H86 Hutchins Behavior Inventory
698.8.I53 Index of Personality Characteristics
698.8.I58 Inventory for Counseling and Development
698.8.J33 Jackson Personality Inventory
698.8.K3 Kahn test of symbol arrangement
698.8.K5 Kinder-Angst-Test
698.8.K53 Kinetic family drawing test
698.8.K55 Kinetic-House-Tree-Person Technique
Cf. BF698.8.H6 House-Tree-Person Technique
698.8.K83 Kvebæk family sculpture technique
698.8.L54 LIFO Survey
698.8.L6 Lowenfeld Mosaics
698.8.L8 Luescher test
698.8.M24 Machover Draw-a-Person Test
698.8.M28 Mannheimer biographical inventory
698.8.M3 Maudsley personality inventory
698.8.M35 Measures of Psychosocial Development

Personality
Personality assessment. Research
Personality testing
Special tests, A-Z -- Continued

698.8.M38 Meyer-Kendall Assessment Survey
698.8.M44 Michigan picture test
698.8.M5 Minnesota Multiphasic Personality Inventory
698.8.M8 Multidimensional symbol test
698.8.M87 Murphy-Meisgeier Type Indicator for Children
698.8.M94 Myers-Briggs Type Indicator
698.8.N39 Navy Computer Adaptive Personality Scales
698.8.N46 NEO Personality Inventory
698.8.N66 Nonverbal Personality Questionnaire
698.8.O23 Object Relations Technique
698.8.O24 Objective-analytic test
698.8.O45 OMNI Personality Inventory
698.8.P16 PONS test
698.8.P3 Pattenoire test
698.8.P34 Pavlovian Temperament Survey
698.8.P37 Pearson-Marr Archetype Indicator
698.8.P43 Personal orientation inventory
698.8.P44 Personal Style Inventory
698.8.P45 Personality-interest test
698.8.P47 Personality Inventory for Children
698.8.P48 Personality questionnaire
698.8.P5 Picture arrangement test
698.8.P53 Picture interpretation tests
698.8.P55 Picture story test
698.8.P57 Pikunas Graphoscopic Scale
698.8.P74 Preferential Shapes Test
698.8.P76 Projective assessment of aging method
Questionnaires, Personality see BF698.8.P48
698.8.R28 Rayid method
698.8.R38 Repertory grid technique
698.8.R45 Riso Enneagram Type Indicator
698.8.R5 Rorschach Test
698.8.R6 Rosenzweig picture-frustration test
698.8.R65 Rotter Incomplete Sentences Blank
698.8.S2 SRA youth inventory
698.8.S27 Scenotest
698.8.S33 Senior Apperception Technique
698.8.S35 Sentence completion test
698.8.S36 Separation Anxiety Test
698.8.S37 Serial mirror technique
698.8.S4 Seven-squares test
698.8.S5 Sixteen Personality Factor Questionnaire
698.8.S64 Social intelligence and personality

Personality
Personality assessment. Research
Personality testing
Special tests, A-Z -- Continued

698.8.S74 State-Trait Anger Expression Inventory
698.8.S75 Street gestalt completion test
698.8.S79 Symbolic profile test
698.8.S8 Symonds Picture Story Test
698.8.S85 Szondi test
698.8.T3 Tasks of emotional development test
698.8.T35 Taylor-Johnson Temperament Analysis
698.8.T39 Temperament Assessment Battery for Children
698.8.T4 Tennessee self-concept scale
698.8.T5 Thematic apperception test
698.8.T53 Three-dimensional personality test
698.8.T55 Three person test
698.8.T7 Tree test
698.8.T8 Tua test
698.8.V5 Village test
698.8.W3 Wartegg-Biedma test
698.8.W33 Wartegg test
698.8.W34 Wartegg-Vetter test
698.8.W6 World test
698.8.Y3 Yatabe-Guilford personality test
698.8.Z8 Zulliger test
698.9.A-Z Special topics, A-Z
698.9.A3 Academic achievement and personality
698.9.A4 Age factors
Behavior genetics see QH457
698.9.B5 Biological aspects of personality
698.9.C63 Cognition and personality
698.9.C74 Creative ability and personality
698.9.C8 Culture and personality. Culture conflict
Culture and conflict see BF698.9.C8
698.9.E45 Emotions and personality
698.9.E95 Explanatory style
698.9.I34 Idiodynamics
698.9.I6 Intelligence and personality
698.9.O3 Occupation and personality
698.9.P47 Personal construct theory
698.9.P6 Politics and personality
698.9.S55 Situation and personality
698.9.S63 Social aspects of personality
698.9.S64 Social intelligence and personality
698.95 Evolutionary psychology
Cf. GN281+ Human evolution

BF

Genetic psychology
Cf. QH457 Behavior genetics
699 Periodicals. Societies. Serials
General works
700 Early through 1880
701-708 1881- (Table B-BJ6a)
710 Maturation. Maturity
Cf. BF637.S4 Self-realization
711 General special
Including special aspects of the subject as a whole
Developmental psychology
Cf. BF175.45 Psychoanalytic theories of development
712 Periodicals. Societies. Serials
712.5 Congresses
712.7 Dictionaries
713 General works
713.5 Addresses, essays, lectures
714 Context effects. Person-context relations
717 Psychology of play
Cf. BF720.P56 Infant play
Cf. GV1202.92+ Children's games
Cf. HQ782 Play in child life
Cf. LB1137 Play in education
719 Infant psychology. Newborn infant psychology
719.5 Philosophy. Methodology. Relation to other subjects
Assessment. Testing
719.6 General works
719.65.A-Z Individual tests, A-Z
For individual intelligence tests see BF432.5.A+
(719.65.C65) Communication and Symbolic Behavior Scales Developmental Profile
see BF722.35.C63
720.A-Z Special topics, A-Z
720.A24 Ability
720.A58 Anxiety
Cf. BF720.S85 Stranger anxiety
720.A83 Attachment behavior
720.A85 Attention
720.A92 Auditory perception
Birth, Premature see BF720.P7
720.C63 Cognition
720.C65 Communication
Including nonverbal communication
720.C78 Crying
720.D58 Distress
720.E35 Ego
720.E45 Emotion (General)

Developmental psychology
Infant psychology. Newborn infant psychology
Special topics, A-Z -- Continued

720.F32 Face perception
720.F38 Father and infant
720.F4 Fear
720.I45 Imagination
720.I55 Individuality. Individual differences
720.I57 Institutional care
Language see P118
Learning see BF318
Locomotion see BF720.M69
720.M38 Maternal deprivation
720.M45 Memory
720.M68 Mother and infant
720.M69 Motor ability
Nonverbal communication see BF720.C65
720.P37 Parent and infant
Cf. BF720.F38 Father and infant
Cf. BF720.M68 Mother and infant
720.P47 Perception
Cf. BF720.V57 Visual perception
720.P56 Play. Symbolic play
720.P7 Premature birth
720.P73 Prenatal influences
720.R43 Regression
720.S44 Self. Self-perception
720.S443 Self-respect
720.S45 Senses and sensation. Stimulation
720.S48 Sex. Sex role
Sex role see BF720.S48
720.S53 Sleep
720.S63 Social interaction. Socialization
Social perception. Social cognition see BF720.S63
Socialization see BF720.S63
720.S67 Speech perception
Stimulation see BF720.S45
720.S85 Stranger anxiety
720.S86 Stress
Symbolic play see BF720.P56
720.V57 Vision. Visual perception
Visual perception see BF720.V57

Child psychology
Cf. D16.16 Psychohistory
Cf. HQ771+ Child psychology for parents
Cf. LB1050.9+ Educational psychology

721 General works

Developmental psychology
Child psychology -- Continued
Philosophy. Methodology. Relation to other subjects
722 General works
Assessment. Testing
For testing of special topics, including tests see BF723.A+
Cf. BF432.C48 Intelligence testing of children
Cf. RJ503.3 Child psychiatry
722.3 General works
722.35.A-Z Individual tests, A-Z
For individual intelligence tests see BF432.5.A+
For individual personality tests see BF698.8.A+
722.35.B44 Behavior Assessment System for Children
722.35.B46 Behavioral and Emotional Rating Scale
722.35.C63 Communication and Symbolic Behavior Scales. Communication and Symbolic Behavior Scales Developmental Profile
722.35.C65 Control, Agency, and Means-Ends Interview
723.A-Z Special topics, A-Z
723.A25 Ability
723.A26 Abstraction
Achievement see BF723.P365
Achievement motivation see BF723.M56
723.A28 Adaptability
723.A3 Adopted children
Cf. BF723.F6 Foster children
723.A33 Adult-child relations
Cf. BF723.P25 Parent-child relations
723.A35 Aggressiveness
723.A37 Altruism
723.A4 Anger
723.A45 Animals
Cf. SF411.47 Psychology of pet owners
Antipathy see BF723.P75
723.A5 Anxiety
723.A74 Assertiveness
723.A75 Attachment behavior
723.A755 Attention
723.A76 Attitude change
723.A77 Auditory perception
723.A78 Authority
723.A8 Authorship. Children as authors
723.A87 Autonomy. Freedom
723.B3 Bashfulness. Shyness
723.B37 Beauty, Personal
Bereavement see BF723.G75

Developmental psychology
Child psychology
Special topics, A-Z -- Continued

723.B5 Birth order
Body and mind see BF723.M48
723.B6 Body image
Cf. BF723.B63 Body schema
Body language see BF723.C57
723.B63 Body schema
Cf. BF723.B6 Body image
Brothers and sisters see BF723.S43
723.C25 Caring
723.C27 Categorization
723.C3 Cause and effect, Concept of
723.C4 Chance
Cf. BF723.R57 Risk-taking
723.C43 Character
Child-adult relations see BF723.A33
Child-grandparent relations see BF723.G68
Children as authors see BF723.A8
723.C47 Choice
723.C5 Cognition. Cognitive styles. Genetic epistemology
Including special kinds of thinking, e.g., critical thinking
Cognitive styles see BF723.C5
723.C55 Color vision
723.C57 Communication
Including nonverbal communication and body language
723.C58 Comparison
Competence see BF723.P365
723.C6 Competition
723.C64 Comprehension
723.C645 Concrete operations
723.C647 Conflict
Cf. BF723.I645 Interpersonal conflict
723.C65 Conscience
723.C68 Conservation
723.C69 Cooperativeness
723.C694 Courage
723.C7 Creative ability
Cf. LB1062 Imagination (Educational psychology)
Critical thinking see BF723.C5
723.C8 Curiosity
723.D3 Death
Cf. RJ249 Terminally ill children
723.D34 Decision making
723.D37 Defense mechanisms
723.D4 Deprivation (General)

Developmental psychology
Child psychology
Special topics, A-Z -- Continued

723.D47 Disappointment
723.D5 Disasters (Reaction to)
723.D54 Discipline
Cf. HQ770.4 Child rearing
723.D7 Drawing
Cf. LB1139.D7 Child study
Cf. N351 Children as artists
Dreaming see BF1099.C55
723.E37 Egoism
723.E4 Eidetic imagery
723.E44 Embarrassment
723.E598 Emotional problems
723.E6 Emotions (General)
723.E67 Empathy
Environmental psychology see BF353
723.E8 Ethics
723.E9 Exceptional children
723.E93 Executive ability
723.E95 Experience
723.F27 Failure
Falsehood see BF723.T8
723.F28 Fantasy
723.F35 Father and child
Father-separated children see BF723.P33
723.F4 Fear
723.F5 Fighting
Finger-sucking see HQ784.F5
723.F6 Foster children
Freedom see BF723.A87
723.F68 Friendship
723.F7 Frustration
Genetic epistemology see BF723.C5
723.G48 Gifted boys
723.G5 Gifted children
Cf. BF723.G48 Gifted boys
Cf. BF723.G52 Gifted girls
723.G52 Gifted girls
723.G63 God
723.G68 Grandparent-child relations
Graphology see BF905.C5
723.G7 Gratitude
723.G75 Grief. Bereavement
723.G83 Guilt
723.H32 Habit breaking

Developmental psychology
Child psychology
Special topics, A-Z -- Continued

723.H37 Happiness
723.H38 Hate
723.H45 Helping behavior
723.H67 Homophobia
723.H7 Honesty
723.H85 Humor
723.I4 Identification
Identity see BF723.I56
723.I47 Imagery
723.I49 Imaginary conversation
723.I5 Imagination
723.I53 Imitation
723.I56 Individuality. Identity
Infant psychology see BF719
723.I63 Information processing in children
Intellect. Intelligence see BF432.C48
723.I64 Interest. Interests
723.I645 Interpersonal conflict
723.I646 Interpersonal relations
723.I65 Interviewing
723.I68 Introversion
723.J4 Jealousy
723.J6 Joy
723.J8 Judgment
Language see LB1139.L3
723.L25 Laterality
723.L3 Laughter
723.L4 Leadership
Learning see BF318
723.L64 Loneliness
723.L68 Loss
723.M3 Magnitude
723.M35 Maternal deprivation
723.M37 Meditation
723.M4 Memory
Including long-term memory and short-term memory
Mental ability see BF432.C48
723.M43 Mental representation
723.M48 Mind and body
Mind, Philosophy of see BF723.P48
723.M54 Moral development
723.M55 Mother and child
723.M56 Motivation
Motor ability see BF723.M6

Developmental psychology
Child psychology
Special topics, A-Z -- Continued

723.M6	Movement. Motor ability
723.N44	Need
	Nonverbal communication see BF723.C57
723.N8	Number concept
723.N84	Nurturing behavior
723.O3	Obstinacy
723.O5	Only child
723.O67	Optimism
723.P25	Parent-child relations
723.P255	Parental deprivation
	Cf. BF723.M35 Maternal deprivation
	Cf. BF723.P33 Paternal deprivation
723.P26	Parental rejection
723.P3	Passivity
723.P33	Paternal deprivation
723.P36	Perception
	Cf. BF723.V5 Visual perception
723.P365	Performance. Competence. Achievement
723.P37	Periodicity
723.P39	Perseveration
723.P4	Personality. Personality development
	Cf. BF698.5+ Personality testing
723.P48	Philosophy of mind
723.P5	Physical concepts
	Play see BF717
723.P67	Possibility
	Precocity see BF723.G5
723.P75	Prejudice. Antipathy
723.P8	Problem solving
	Problems, Emotional see BF723.E598
	Psychosexual development see BF723.S4
723.Q4	Questions
723.Q5	Quintuplets
723.R3	Race awareness
723.R4	Reasoning
723.R44	Rejection
	Cf. BF723.P26 Parental rejection
723.R46	Resilience
723.R48	Reward
723.R53	Rights
723.R57	Risk-taking
	Cf. BF723.C4 Chance
723.S15	Sadness
723.S17	Schemas

Developmental psychology
Child psychology
Special topics, A-Z -- Continued

723.S2 Searching behavior
723.S22 Security
723.S24 Self
723.S25 Self-control
723.S26 Self-disclosure
723.S28 Self-perception
723.S29 Self-reliance
723.S3 Self-respect
723.S35 Sensation
723.S4 Sex
723.S42 Sex role
723.S425 Shadow (Psychoanalysis)
723.S428 Sharing
Shyness see BF723.B3
723.S43 Sibling relations
Sisters and brothers see BF723.S43
723.S45 Sleep
Social consciousness see HQ783
723.S6 Social perception
723.S62 Social skills. Socialization
Including social skills development tests
723.S624 Solitude
723.S63 Space perception
Speech see LB1139.L3
723.S65 Speech perception
723.S7 Stealing
723.S74 Stories
723.S75 Stress
723.S77 Success
723.S78 Suffering
723.S8 Suggestibility
Suicide see HV6546
723.S87 Surprise
723.S94 Symbolism
723.T3 Talebearing. Tattling
Tattling see BF723.T3
Television watching see HQ784.T4
723.T53 Temperament
723.T55 Tenacity
723.T6 Time
723.T64 Timidity
723.T72 Touch
723.T78 Trust
723.T8 Truthfulness and falsehood

Developmental psychology
Child psychology
Special topics, A-Z -- Continued
723.T9 Twins
723.V5 Vision. Visual perception
Cf. BF241.5.A+ Individual tests of visual perception
Visual perception see BF723.V5
723.W3 War (Reactions to)
Cf. HQ784.W3 Social aspects
723.W65 Wonder
723.W67 Worry
Writing see BF456.W8
724 Adolescence. Youth
Cf. HQ35 Sex relations
Cf. LB1135 Child study (Education)
724.2 Philosophy. Methodology. Relation to other subjects
724.25 Assessment. Testing
For testing of special topics, including individual tests see BF724.3.A+
724.3.A-Z Special topics, A-Z
724.3.A32 Adjustment
724.3.A34 Aggressiveness
724.3.A55 Anger
724.3.A57 Anxiety
724.3.A77 Assertiveness
724.3.A84 Attachment behavior
724.3.A88 Autonomy
724.3.B36 Bashfulness
Bereavement see BF724.3.G73
724.3.B55 Body image
724.3.B6 Boredom
724.3.C5 Choice
724.3.C58 Cognition
724.3.C6 Communication
724.3.C63 Competition
724.3.C65 Conflict
Cf. BF724.3.I56 Interpersonal conflict
724.3.C73 Creative ability
724.3.D43 Death
724.3.D47 Decision-making
724.3.D7 Drawing
724.3.E45 Embarrassment
724.3.E5 Emotion
Environmental psychology see BF353
724.3.E8 Ethics
Ethnic attitudes see BF724.3.R3
Falsehood and truthfulness see BF724.3.T78

Developmental psychology
Adolescence. Youth
Special topics, A-Z -- Continued

724.3.F34 Fear
724.3.F64 Friendship
724.3.F7 Frustration
724.3.G53 Gifted
724.3.G73 Grief. Bereavement. Separation
Cf. BF724.3.S38 Separation anxiety
724.3.H35 Happiness
724.3.H38 Hate
724.3.I28 Identification
724.3.I3 Identity
724.3.I5 Imagination
724.3.I55 Interpersonal communication
724.3.I56 Interpersonal conflict
Cf. BF724.3.C65 Conflict
724.3.I58 Interpersonal relations
724.3.J4 Jealousy
724.3.J8 Judgment
724.3.J87 Justice
724.3.L4 Leadership
Learning see BF318
724.3.L64 Loneliness
724.3.L66 Loss
724.3.L68 Love
724.3.M46 Memory
Including long-term memory and short-term memory
724.3.M64 Mood
724.3.M65 Motivation
724.3.N35 Narcissism
724.3.P4 Personality
Cf. BF698.5+ Personality testing
724.3.R3 Race awareness. Ethnic attitudes
724.3.R4 Reasoning
724.3.R44 Rejection
724.3.R47 Resilience
724.3.S25 Self-actualization
724.3.S3 Self-disclosure
724.3.S35 Self-perception
724.3.S36 Self-respect
Separation see BF724.3.G73
724.3.S38 Separation anxiety
724.3.S4 Sex. Sex role. Sex difference
Sex differences see BF724.3.S4
Sex role see BF724.3.S4
Social development see HQ793+; LB1135

Developmental psychology
Adolescence. Youth
Special topics, A-Z -- Continued
724.3.S86 Stress
724.3.S9 Success
724.3.T56 Time
Including time perception, time perspective
724.3.T78 Truthfulness and falsehood
724.3.V3 Values
724.3.W67 Worry
Adulthood
724.5 General works
724.55.A-Z Special topics, A-Z
724.55.A35 Aging
724.55.C63 Cognition and age. Thought and thinking and age
724.55.C66 Control and age
724.6 Middle age
Cf. HQ1059.4+ Sociology
724.65.A-Z Special topics, A-Z
724.65.L66 Loss
724.65.M53 Midlife crisis
724.65.S44 Self-actualization
Old age
724.8 General works
724.85.A-Z Special topics, A-Z
724.85.A47 Altruism
Bereavement see BF724.85.G73
724.85.C64 Cognition. Thought and thinking. Learning
724.85.C66 Control
724.85.C73 Creative ability
724.85.D43 Death
724.85.D44 Decision making
724.85.E56 Emotions
724.85.G54 Gifted older people
724.85.G73 Grief. Bereavement. Separation
724.85.H35 Happiness
724.85.H6 Humor
724.85.H65 Home
724.85.I57 Interpersonal communication
724.85.L42 Leadership
724.85.L64 Loneliness
724.85.L67 Loss
724.85.M45 Memory
724.85.M67 Motivation
724.85.P47 Personality
724.85.R45 Reminiscing
724.85.S39 Self-esteem

Developmental psychology
Adulthood
Old age
Special topics, A-Z -- Continued
Self-actualization see BF724.85.S45
724.85.S43 Self-perception
724.85.S45 Self-realization. Self-actualization
Separation see BF724.85.G73
724.85.S48 Sex
724.85.S64 Social perception
724.85.S92 Suffering
725 Class psychology
Cf. BF408+ Creative processes, genius
Cf. BF692+ Sex psychology
727.A-Z By class, A-Z
Agriculturists see S494.5.P76
Artists see N71+
Blind see HV1571+
Criminals see HV6080+
Deaf see HV2350+
Farmers see S494.5.P76
727.H3 Handicapped. People with disabilities
Cf. BF727.P57 People with physical disabilities
Musicians see ML3838
People with disabilities see BF727.H3
People with physical disabilities see BF727.P57
Pet owners see SF411.47
727.P5 Pharmacists
727.P57 Physical disabilities, People with
Police see HV7936.P75
Prisoners see HV6089
727.P7 Prisoners of war
Undertakers see RA622+
Race and ethnic psychology see GN270+
Culture conflict see BF698.9.C8
751 Psychology of nations
753 General special
Including special aspects of the subject as a whole, e.g. National characteristics, etc.
(755) By nation
see classes D, E, F
761-768 Psychology of evidence (Table B-BJ6a)
Cf. BF365+ Association of ideas, creative processes, comparison, judgment, reasoning, etc.
773 Psychology of belief, faith, etc.
Cf. BL53+ Psychology of religion
774 Psychology of influence, pattern, and example

BF

775 Psychology of the marvelous
778 Psychology of values, meaning
Cf. BD232 Theory of value, worth
Cf. BF723.M54 Moral development (Child psychology)
789.A-Z Psychology of other special subjects, A-Z
Advertising see HF5822
789.A6 Ambition
Art
see classes BH and N
Business see HF5386
Chess see GV1448
Clothing see GT524
Clubs see HS2521
789.C7 Color
Cf. BF698.8.C6 Color pyramid test
Cf. BF698.8.L8 Luescher test
789.D4 Death
Cf. BF723.D3 Child study
Cf. BF724.85.D43 Death in old age
Cf. R726.8 Terminal care
Cf. RC552.F42 Psychopathological fear of death
789.D5 Disasters
Dreams see BF1074+
789.D7 Drowning
789.E94 Evil
789.F29 False alarms
789.F5 Fire
789.F8 Funerals
789.G5 Gifts and giving
Giving see BF789.G5
789.J8 Justice
789.L53 Light
789.M6 Motion pictures
789.M65 Mountains
Music see ML3830
Police work see HV7936.P75
Pregnancy see RG560
Recreation see GV14.4
Self-mutilation see RC552.S4
Sleep see BF1068+
789.S6 Smoking
Sports see GV706.4
Success see BF637.S8; BF724.3.S9
789.S8 Suffering
Suicide (Crime) see HV6543+
Suicide (Personality disorder) see RC569
War see U22.3

Psychology of other special subjects, A-Z -- Continued
789.W3 Water
Temperament
General works
795 Early through 1850
798 1851-
800-808 Popular works (Table B-BJ6)
811 Addresses, essays, lectures
818 Character
For characters and characteristics in literature, see class P
For personality traits or types see BF698.3+
Cf. BJ1518+ Ethics
Cf. PR1309.C47 Literary collections of character sketches or criticism in English
Popular works
821-828 Early through 1850 (Table B-BJ6a)
831-838 1851- (Table B-BJ6a)
839 Addresses, essays, lectures
Physiognomy
839.8 Dictionaries. Encyclopedias
General works
840-848 Early through 1850 (Table B-BJ6)
851-858 1851- (Table B-BJ6a)
859 General special
Including special aspects of the subject as a whole
861.A-Z Special topics, A-Z
861.B86 Buttocks
861.C5 Comparative physiognomy
861.E3 Ear
861.E8 Eye
861.F66 Foot
861.I6 Intellect
861.M65 Moles
861.M7 Mouth
861.N7 Nose
Voice see BF637.V64
Phrenology
866 Periodicals. Serials
867 Societies
867.5 Dictionaries. Encyclopedias
868 History
Biography
869.A1 Collective
869.A3-Z Individual, A-Z
e. g.
869.C6 Combe, George
869.G3 Gall, Franz Josef

Phrenology
Biography
Individual, A-Z -- Continued
869.S6 Spurzheim, Johann Gaspar
General works
870 Early through 1870
871-878 1871- (Table B-BJ6a)
879 General special
Including special aspects of the subject as a whole
885.A-Z Special topics, A-Z
885.A5 Anti-phrenology
Including controversial literature
885.A6 Application
885.B5 Bible and phrenology
885.C5 Children and phrenology
885.C6 Christianity and phrenology
Crime and phrenology see HV6059
885.M4 Medical aspects
885.O2 Occult phrenology
885.R3 Religion
885.T3 Teaching and phrenology
Graphology. Study of handwriting
Cf. Z40+ Writing, autographs, penmanship
889 Periodicals. Societies. Serials
889.5 Dictionaries. Encyclopedias
General works
890 Early through 1850
891-898 1851- (Table B-BJ6a)
901 General special
Including special aspects of the subject as a whole
905.A-Z Special topics, A-Z
905.A3 Adolescents
Astrology see BF1729.G72
905.C44 Celebrities
905.C5 Children
905.C6 Conflict
905.C7 Crime and criminals
Criminals see BF905.C7
905.D7 Drawing
905.D77 Drug abusers
905.I47 Inferiority complex
905.I5 Intelligence testing
905.J87 Jury selection
905.L68 Love
905.M3 Marriage
905.M43 Medicine
905.P4 Personnel management

Graphology. Study of handwriting
Special topics, A-Z -- Continued
905.P57 Poets
905.P6 Political and war prisoners
905.P63 Politicians
Psychiatry see RC473.G7
905.S34 Self-perception
905.S4 Sex
905.S5 Signatures
905.S74 Stress
War prisoners see BF905.P6
905.W4 Wills
905.W65 Women
908 The hand
Palmistry. Chiromancy
Popular works
910-918 Early through 1850 (Table B-BJ6)
921-928 1851- (Table B-BJ6a)
935.A-Z Special topics, A-Z
935.C3 Celebrities' hands
935.C5 Children's hands
935.C75 Crime and criminals
935.F55 Fingerprints
935.G4 Gesture
935.L67 Love
935.M35 Mate selection
935.M4 Medicine
935.N3 Nails
935.S48 Sex
935.V6 Vocational guidance
935.W65 Women's hands
940.A-Z Biography of palmists, A-Z
e. g.
940.H3 Hamon, Louis ("Cheiro")
990 Curiosa. Miscellanea

Parapsychology
Psychic research. Psychology of the unconscious
Cf. BF638+ New Thought
Cf. BF1251+ Spiritualism, exclusively
Periodicals. Serials
Including periodicals in occult sciences
1001 English
1002 French
1003 German
1004 Italian
1005 Spanish and Portuguese
1006 Scandinavian
1008.A-Z Other, A-Z
Societies
1009 General works
1010 American
1011 English
1012 French
1013 German
1014 Italian
1015 Spanish and Portuguese
1018.A-Z Other, A-Z
1021 Congresses
1023 Collected works (nonserial)
(1024) Yearbooks
see BF1001+
1024.5 Directories
1024.6 Information services
1024.65 Computer network resources
Including the Internet
1025 Dictionaries. Encyclopedias
Biography
Cf. BF1127.A1+ Hypnotism
Cf. BF1281+ Mediums
1026 Collective
1027.A-Z Individual, A-Z
History
1028 General works
1028.5.A-Z By region or country, A-Z
Report of commissions, investigations, etc.
1029 General works
1030.A-Z Special cases. By name of case, A-Z
e. g.
1030.B6 Borley rectory
1031-1038 General works (Table B-BJ6a)
1040 General special
1040.5 Study and teaching. Research

Psychic research. Psychology of the unconscious -- Continued

1041 Joint debates and discussions

1042 Controversial works against spiritualistic and occult

1045.A-Z Special topics, A-Z

1045.A34 Adjustment (Psychology)

1045.A44 Akashic records

1045.A48 Altered states of consciousness

(1045.A6) Animals

see QL785.3

1045.A65 Anthropology and parapsychology

1045.A74 Archaeology and parapsychology

1045.A78 Art and parapsychology

Breathing see BF1045.R46

1045.C45 Children and parapsychology

1045.C6 Color

1045.C7 Criminal investigation

1045.D42 Decision making

1045.D67 Double

1045.D76 Drugs

1045.E65 Equipment and supplies

1045.F68 Fourth dimension

1045.G46 Geography and parapsychology

1045.I58 Interpersonal relations

1045.K37 Karma

1045.L35 Language and parapsychology

1045.L7 Love

1045.M44 Medicine and parapsychology

Cf. RZ400+ Mental healing

1045.M46 Memory

1045.M55 Military aspects

Cf. UB275+ Psychological warfare

1045.N4 Near-death experiences

Cf. BF1063.D4 Deathbed hallucinations

1045.N42 Near-death experiences in children

1045.O43 Older people

1045.P5 Philosophy and parapsychology

1045.P55 Plants

Including individual and groups of plants

1045.R43 Readings

1045.R46 Respiration

1045.S33 Science and parapsychology

1045.S44 Self-actualization

1045.S46 Self-defense

1045.S48 Sex

1045.S83 Success

1045.S84 Suffering

Surgery see RZ403.P75

Psychic research. Psychology of the unconscious
Special topics, A-Z -- Continued
1045.T43 Teenagers
1045.T55 Time travel
1045.W65 Women
Cf. BF1275.W65 Women and spiritualism
1045.Y63 Yoga
Hallucinations. Illusions
1048 Early through 1800
1051-1058 1801- (Table B-BJ6a)
1063.A-Z Special topics, A-Z
1063.D4 Deathbed hallucinations
Cf. BF1045.N4 Near-death experiences
1063.M6 Mirage
Sleep. Somnambulism
Cf. BF723.S45 Child psychology
Cf. BF1111+ Hypnotism
Cf. BF1321+ Trance states
Cf. QP425+ Physiology of sleep
Cf. RA786+ Personal hygiene
1068 Early through 1800
1071 1801-
1073.A-Z Special topics, A-Z
1073.P65 Position, Sleep
1073.S58 Sleep talking
Dreaming
Cf. BF175.5.D74 Psychoanalysis
Cf. BL65.D67 Religion
Cf. QP426 Physiology
Cf. RC489.D74 Psychotherapy
1074 Periodicals. Societies. Serials
General works
1075 Early through 1800
1078 1801-
Popular works. Dream books, etc.
1080-1088 Early works through 1800 (Table B-BJ6)
1091-1098 1801- (Table B-BJ6a)
1099.A-Z Special topics, A-Z
1099.A54 Anima. Animus
1099.B5 Biblical dreams
1099.C53 Children
1099.C55 Children's dreams
1099.C58 Churches
1099.D4 Death
1099.D47 Deserts
1099.E53 End of the world
1099.F34 Family

Dreaming
Special topics, A-Z -- Continued
1099.F57 Fire
1099.F69 Foxes
1099.H47 Heroes
1099.I58 Interpersonal relations
1099.L35 Language and languages
1099.L6 Lotteries
1099.L82 Lucid dreams
1099.N53 Nightmares
1099.P75 Problem solving
Psychoanalysis see BF175.5.D74
1099.R4 Dream recall
1099.R6 Royalty, British
1099.S36 Self-realization
1099.S4 Sex
1099.S73 Snakes
1099.S76 Spiritual healing
1099.T43 Teenagers' dreams
1099.T73 Trees
1099.W37 Water
1099.W65 Women's dreams
Visions
1100 Early through 1800
1101-1108 1801- (Table B-BJ6a)
Hypnotism. Animal magnetism. Odylic force. Biomagnetism. Mesmerism. Subliminal projection
Cf. BF1628.3 Radiesthesia
Cf. RC490+ Therapeutic use of hypnotism
Cf. RZ430 Mesmerism as a system of healing
1111-1118 Periodicals. Societies. Serials (Table B-BJ6a)
1119 Congresses
1121 Collected works (nonserial)
1125 History
Biography
1127.A1 Collective
1127.A3-Z Individual, A-Z
e. g.
1127.B5 Bishop, Washington Irving
1127.M4 Mesmer, Franz Anton
1128 Reports of commissions, investigations, etc.
1129.A-Z Special cases. By name of case, A-Z
General works
1131-1138 Early through 1870 (Table B-BJ6a)
1141-1148 1871- (Table B-BJ6a)
1152 General special
Including special aspects of the subject as a whole

BF

Hypnotism. Animal magnetism. Odylic force. Biomagnetism. Mesmerism. Subliminal projection -- Continued

1156.A-Z Special topics, A-Z

Autosuggestion see BF1156.S8

1156.C3 Catalepsy

1156.D4 Death

1156.E2 Education and hypnotism

1156.E5 Emotions and hypnotism

1156.F6 Folk psychology and hypnotism

1156.I53 Imagination and hypnotism

1156.O2 Odylic force

1156.P4 Personal magnetism

1156.P44 Personality and hypnotism

Psychotherapeutics see RC490+

1156.R45 Regression

1156.S55 Silva Mind Control

Cf. RZ403.S56 Mental healing

1156.S6 Social influence of hypnotism

1156.S7 Stage hypnotism

1156.S8 Suggestion. Autosuggestion

1156.S83 Susceptibility

Telepathy. Mind reading. Thought transference

General works

1161 Early through 1870

1171 1871-

1175 Coincidence. Synchronicity

Multiple consciousness. Dissociation of personality see RC569.5.M8

Spiritualism. Communication with discarnate spirits

For works not treating exclusively of spiritualism see BF1031+

For controversial works against the spiritualists see BF1042

Periodicals. Serials see BF1001+

1228 Societies

Cf. BF1009+ Psychic research

Cf. BX9798.S7 Christian denominations

1231 Congresses

Cf. BF1021 Psychic research

1235 Collected works (nonserial)

Cf. BF1023 Psychic research

1241 History

Cf. BF1028+ Psychic research

1242.A-Z By region or country, A-Z

Reports of commissions, investigations, etc. see BF1029+

General works

1251-1258 Early through 1880 (Table B-BJ6a)

Spiritualism. Communication with discarnate spirits
General works -- Continued
1881-
English and American
1261 1881-1950
1261.2 1951-
1262 French
1263 German
1264 Italian
1265 Spanish and Portuguese
1266 Russian and other Slavic
1268.A-Z Other, A-Z
1272 General special
Including special aspects of the subject as a whole
1275.A-Z Special aspects, A-Z
1275.A5 Anarchism and spiritualism
1275.A8 Atheism and spiritualism
1275.B5 The Bible and spiritualism
1275.C3 Catholic Church and spiritualism
1275.C4 Christian Science and spiritualism
1275.C5 Christianity and spiritualism
1275.D2 Death and spiritualism
1275.E4 Education and spiritualism
1275.E8 Ethics of spiritualism
1275.F3 Faith cure and spiritualism
1275.F7 Freemasons and spiritualism
1275.G85 Guides
1275.I5 Insanity and spiritualism
1275.I58 Literature and spiritualism
1275.M3 Marriage and spiritualism
1275.S3 Science and spiritualism
1275.S44 Self-realization and spiritualism
1275.S55 Soul and spiritualism
1275.S6 Spirit obsession
Spiritual healing and spiritualism see BF1275.F3
1275.T5 Theosophy and spiritualism
1275.W3 Watseka wonder
1275.W65 Women and spiritualism
Including women's rights and spiritualism
1277 Special persons: Attitude, belief, relation to spiritualism
e. g.
1277.A1 Collective
1277.L5 Lincoln, Abraham
Cf. E457.2 Biography
Mediumship. Psychometry. Channeling

Spiritualism. Communication with discarnate spirits
Mediumship. Psychometry. Channeling -- Continued
Biography and reminiscences of spiritualists, mediums, clairvoyants, etc. Cases
Cf. BF1241 History

1281 Collective
1283.A-Z Individual, A-Z
e. g.
1283.D3 Davenport brothers
1283.D44 De Benneville, George
1283.D45 Denis, Léon
1283.D5 Doyle, Arthur Conan
1283.F7 Fox sisters
1283.H7 Home, Daniel Dunglas
1283.P3 Palladino, Eusapia
1283.P6 Piper, Leonora E.
1283.Z9 Anonymous persons
General works
1286 English
1288 Other (not A-Z)
Exposures of mediums see BF1042
Spirit messages, inspirational records, etc.
Including writings by "spirit authors"
1290 Collected works (nonserial)
Including writings by two or more "spirit authors"
Individual "spirit authors"
1291-1298 Early through 1880 (Table B-BJ6a)
1301-1308 1881- (Table B-BJ6a)
1311.A-Z Special, A-Z
1311.A2 Ackley, H.A.
1311.A5 Alphabet and symbols (Spirit)
1311.A55 Anne Boleyn
1311.A57 Antonio de Padova, Saint
1311.A6 Apollonius of Tyana
1311.A7 Aronne, Maurizio
1311.A8 Atlantis
1311.B3 Barrett, Sir W.F.
1311.B4 Benson, R.H..
1311.B5 The Bible
1311.B57 Black Foot, Chief, d. 1877
1311.B6 Blasco Ibáñez, Vincente
1311.B65 Blavatsky,. Helene P.
1311.B66 Blum, Robert, 1807-1848
1311.B67 Bolívar, Simón
1311.C34 Carnegie, Andrew
1311.C35 Castro Alves, Antonio de
1311.C37 Caterina da Siena, Saint

Spiritualism. Communication with discarnate spirits
Mediumship. Psychometry. Channeling
Spirit messages, inspirational records, etc.
Special, A-Z -- Continued

1311.C48 Churchill, Winston, Sir
1311.D38 David, King of Israel
1311.D43 Dennis, Stephen Christopher
1311.D6 Dogs
1311.E4 Eddy, Mary Baker
1311.E43 Egypt
1311.E45 Egyptian language (Ancient)
1311.E46 Elijah (Biblical prophet)
1311.E47 Eliot, T.S.
1311.E5 Emerson, R.W.
1311.E7 Ericson, W.F.
1311.E75 Essenes
Evil see BF1311.G63
1311.F25 Fachiri, Adila
1311.F3 Faraday, Michael
1311.F47 Fetus
1311.F67 Francesco d'Assisi, Saint
1311.F7 Franklin, Benjamin
1311.F73 Franklin, John, Sir
1311.F77 Fryer, Charles Henry
1311.F8 Future life
1311.G35 Garcia, Jerry
1311.G5 Gibran, Kahlil
1311.G56 Glastonbury Abbey
1311.G6 God
1311.G63 Good and evil
1311.G68 Grant, U.S.
1311.G7 Great Britain
1311.H3 Hafed, Prince of Persia
1311.H37 Harry, 1862-1899
1311.H65 Holmes, Jesse Herman
1311.H8 Hugo, Victor
1311.H88 Hyslop, J.H.
1311.I5 Inheritance
1311.J25 James, William
1311.J3 Jansenius, Cornelius, Bp.
1311.J5 Jesus Christ
1311.J8 Julian, the Apostate
1311.J85 Jupiter (Planet)
1311.K5 Kingsley, Charles
1311.L25 Language
1311.L3 Lawrence, T.E.
1311.L33 Lemuria

Spiritualism. Communication with discarnate spirits
Mediumship. Psychometry. Channeling
Spirit messages, inspirational records, etc.
Special, A-Z -- Continued

1311.L35	Lennon, John
1311.L4	Life
1311.L43	Life on other planets
1311.L45	Lincoln, Abraham
1311.L5	Little, Rolf
1311.L6	Love
1311.L75	Lucretius Carus, Titus
1311.L8	Luther, Martin
1311.M4	Mars (Planet)
1311.M42	Mary, Virgin
1311.M45	Mathewson, Alonzo P.
1311.M5	Mercury (Planet)
1311.N4	Neptune (Planet)
1311.O8	Owen, G.V.
1311.P3	Parker, Theodore
1311.P34	Paul, the Apostle, Saint
1311.P4	Peacock, A.E.L.
1311.P47	Piergili, Renato
1311.P5	Pinnegar, Eira G.
1311.P6	Pluto (Planet)
1311.P67	Prayers
1311.P7	Prehistoric man
1311.P75	Prophecies
1311.P83	Pueblo Indians
1311.R33	Red Snake
1311.R35	Reincarnation
1311.R4	Revelation
1311.R5	Roosevelt, Theodore
1311.R85	Running Bear
1311.S25	Saint-Germain, comte de
1311.S3	Saturn (Planet)
1311.S4	Science
1311.S45	Sex
1311.S5	Shakespeare, William
1311.S53	Shelley, P.B.
1311.S6	Sprague, Clarissa A.
1311.S63	Stead, W.T.
1311.S67	Stoddard, Wilbur
1311.S7	Stowe, Harriet (Beecher)
1311.T3	Taber, Helen
1311.T62	Tolstoy, Leo
1311.T8	Twardy, Gottlieb
	Unborn children see BF1311.F47

Spiritualism. Communication with discarnate spirits
Mediumship. Psychometry. Channeling
Spirit messages, inspirational records, etc.
Special, A-Z -- Continued
1311.U5 United States history
1311.V3 Valentino, Rudolph
1311.V4 Venus (Planet)
1311.W3 Wakamussen, H.K.
1311.W4 Wells, H.G.
1311.W5 Wilde, Oscar
1311.W53 Wilson, Woodrow
1311.X38 Xavier, Francisco Côndido
1313 Spirit art
Including art work by "spirit artists"
1315 Spirit music
Including music by "spirit composers"
Sensory and motor automatism. Extrasensory perception
1321 General works
Telepathy see BF1161+
Clairvoyance
1325 General works
1335 Crystal gazing
1338 Clairaudience
1339 Retrocognition
1341 Precognition
1343 Automatic writing. Planchette. Ouija board
Including automatic communication in general
1347 Automatic drawing and painting
1352 Trance utterance
Cf. BF1290+ Spirit messages, inspirational records, etc.
1353 Polyglot mediumship. Xenoglossy
Spirit photography see BF1381
1371 Physical phenomena of spiritualism. Telekinesis. Psychokinesis
Special topics
1375 Raps. Table moving
1378 Materialization
1380 Phonotapes and spirit messages
1381 Spirit photography
1382 Telephones and spirit messages
1383 Dematerialization
1385 Levitation
Slate writing see BF1343
1386 Teleportation
1389.A-Z Other special topics, A-Z
1389.A7 Astral body. Astral projection

Spiritualism. Communication with discarnate spirits
Physical phenomena of spiritualism. Telekinesis.
Psychokinesis
Special topics
Other special topics, A-Z -- Continued

1389.A8 Aura, halo, nimbus, etc.
Cf. BP573.A8 Theosophy
1389.D57 Disappearances
Halo see BF1389.A8
Nimbus see BF1389.A8
1389.R45 Remote viewing
1389.T7 Transfiguration

Occult sciences
Periodicals. Serials see BF1001+
1404 Congresses
1405 Collected works (nonserial)
1407 Dictionaries. Encyclopedias
Biography
Cf. BF1597+ Biography of magicians and Hermetic philosophy
Cf. BF1679.8.A1+ Biography of astrologers
1408 Collective
1408.2.A-Z Individual, A-Z
1409 Directories
1409.5 Relation to science
General works
1410 Early through 1800
1411-1418 1801- (Table B-BJ6a)
History
General works see BF1410+
By period
1421 Ancient
1425 Medieval
1429 Modern
1434.A-Z By region or country, A-Z
1439 General special
Including special aspects of the subject as a whole
Controversial works see BF1042
1442.A-Z Special topics, A-Z
1442.B63 Bodies of man
1442.C35 Candles
1442.C53 Chakras
1442.C76 Crystal skulls
Including psychic aspects of specific crystal skulls, e.g. Mitchell-Hedges skull
1442.C78 Crystals
1442.D43 Death
1442.E77 Essences and essential oils
Gems see BF1442.P74
1442.G73 Grail
1442.H64 Holy Lance
1442.L53 Light body
1442.M34 Mandala
1442.M36 Mass
1442.P47 Perfumes
1442.P74 Precious stones. Gems
1442.Q35 Quartz
Rays, Seven see BF1442.S49
1442.S49 Seven rays

	Special topics, A-Z -- Continued
1442.S53	Sex
1442.V68	Vowels
	Ghosts. Apparitions. Hauntings. Haunted places
	Cf. GR580 Folklore
1444	Dictionaries. Encyclopedias
	General works
1445	Early through 1800
1451-1458	1801-1880 (Table B-BJ6a)
1461-1468	1881- (Table B-BJ6a)
1471	General special
	Including special aspects of the subject as a whole
1472.A-Z	By region or country, A-Z
1473.A-Z	Cases, A-Z
1474	Haunted castles
1474.3	Haunted cemeteries
1474.4	Haunted hospitals
1474.5	Haunted hotels
	Haunted houses
1475	General works
	By region or country see BF1472.A+
1476	Haunted lighthouses
1476.4	Haunted morgues
1477	Haunted parsonages
1477.2	Haunted plantations
1477.3	Haunted prisons
1477.5	Haunted theaters
1478	Haunted universities and colleges
1481	Apparitions of the living
	Cf. BF1161+ Telepathy
1483	House spirits. Hobgoblins
	Cf. BF1473.A+ Cases of hauntings
	Cf. BF1555 Possession, obsession
1484	Animal ghosts
	Cf. GR825+ Animal lore
	Cf. QL88.5 Living fossils
1486	Sea specters
	Cf. GR910 Folklore of the sea
	Cf. PN57.F6 Flying Dutchman
	Demonology
	Cf. BL480 Religious doctrines in general
	Cf. GR525+ Folklore
1501	Collected works (nonserial)
1503	Dictionaries. Encyclopedias
1505	History
	By period
1508	Ancient

Demonology
History
By period -- Continued
1511 Medieval
1514 Modern
1517.A-Z By region or country, A-Z
e. g.
1517.F5 France
1517.G7 Great Britain
General works
1520-1528 Early through 1800 (Table B-BJ6)
1531-1538 1801- (Table B-BJ6a)
1543 General special
Including special aspects of the subject as a whole
Satanism. Devil worship, etc
General works
Early through 1800
1546 English
1547 Other
1801-
1548 English
1549 French
1550 Other
1552 Elemental spirits. Genii. Elves. Fairies. Gnomes
Cf. GR549+ Folklore
1553 The "evil eye"
Cf. GN475.6 Anthropology
1555 Possession. Obsession
Cf. BF1227.2+ Spiritualism
Cf. BL53+ Psychology of religion
Cf. BR110+ Psychology of Christian religious experience, etc.
1556 Incubi. Succubi. Vampires
Cf. GR830.V3 Vampires (Folklore)
1557 Familiar spirits
1558 Incantations. Evocations. Grimoire
Cf. GR540 Folklore
1559 Exorcism of demons
Cf. BX2340 Catholic Church
1561 Talismans. Amulets, charms, etc.
Cf. BL2227.8.A45 Shinto amulets and talismans
Cf. BP190.5.A5 Islamic amulets and talismans
Cf. GR600+ Folklore
1562 Evil houses, stone walls, etc
Witchcraft
Cf. BP605.W53 Wicca
1562.5 Periodicals. Societies. Serials

Witchcraft -- Continued
1562.7 Congresses
1563 Collected works (nonserial)
1563.5 Terminology. Nomenclature
General works
1565 Early through 1800
1566 1801-
By period
1567 Ancient
1569 Medieval (General)
Special with countries see BF1573+
1571 Modern
1571.5.A-Z Special classes of persons, A-Z
1571.5.C64 College students
1571.5.G39 Gays
1571.5.M45 Men
1571.5.T44 Teenagers
1571.5.W66 Women
1572.A-Z Special topics, A-Z
1572.B44 Beltane
1572.B63 Body image in women
Calendar see BF1572.F37
1572.C68 Covens
1572.D43 Death
1572.D73 Dreams
1572.F35 Family
1572.F37 Fasts and feasts
1572.H34 Halloween
1572.H35 Handicraft
1572.L35 Lammas
1572.L6 Love
1572.M35 Marriage
1572.M37 Masks
1572.M46 Menopause
1572.P43 Plants
1572.P73 Prayers
1572.R4 Recipes
1572.S28 Sabbat
1572.S4 Sex
1572.S65 Spiritual healing
1572.W35 Walpurgis Night
By region or country
United States
General works
1573.A2 Early works through 1800
1573.A3-Z 1801-
1575 New England: Salem, etc.

Witchcraft
By region or country
United States
New England: Salem, etc. -- Continued
1576 Modern works
1577.A-Z Other regions, A-Z
e. g.
1577.P4 Pennsylvania
1578.A-Z Special cases, A-Z
For New England see BF1575
Other regions or countries
Under each 1-number country:

.A2	*Early works through 1800*
.A5-.Z4	*1801-*
.Z7	*Special. By date*

1581 Great Britain
1582 France
1583 Germany
1584.A-Z Other, A-Z
Under each Cutter-number country:

.xA2	*Early works through 1800*
.xA5-.xZ4	*1801-*
.xZ7	*Special. By date*

Magic (White and Black). Shamanism. Hermetics. Necromancy
1585 Periodicals. Societies. Serials
1586 Congresses
1587 Collected works (nonserial)
1588 Dictionaries. Encyclopedias
1589 History
1591-1595 By period
1591 Ancient
1593 Medieval
1595 Modern
Biography of magicians and hermetic philosophers
1597 Collective
1598.A-Z Individual, A-Z
e. g.
1598.A4 Agrippa von Nettesheim, Heinrich Cornelius
1598.A5 Albertus Magnus
1598.C2 Cagliostro, Alessandro (Giuseppe Balsamo)
1598.C6 Constant, Alphonse
1598.D5 Dee, John
1598.D86 DuQuette, Lon Milo
1598.H6 Hermes Trismegistus
1598.K44 Kelly, Edward
Lévi, Eliphas see BF1598.C6
1598.L5 Lilly, William

Magic (White and Black). Shamanism. Hermetics. Necromancy
Biography of magicians and hermetic philosophers
Individual, A-Z -- Continued
Luria, Isaac ben Solomon see BM525.L83+
Nostradamus (Michel de Notredame) see BF1815.N8
1598.P2 Paracelsus
Cf. B785.P2+ Biography as a philosopher
Cf. R147.P2 Biography as a physician
1598.S3P2 Saint-Germain, comte de
1598.S32 Schröder, Friedrich Joseph Wilhelm
1598.S92 Syberg, Johan Hendrik van, b. 1696
1598.V32 Vaughan, Thomas
General works
1600-1608 Early through 1800 (Table B-BJ6)
1611-1618 1801- (Table B-BJ6a)
Including works on modern Hermetic philosophy
1621 General special
Including special aspects of the subject as a whole
1622.A-Z By race, ethnic group, or country, A-Z
For ancient and medieval see BF1591+
1622.C5 Chinese
1622.M6 Mexican
1623.A-Z Special topics, A-Z
1623.A45 Alphabet
1623.A53 Angels
1623.A55 Animals
Astral body see BF1389.A7
Astrology see BF1729.M33
1623.B53 Bible
Cf. BS680.M3 Magic in the Bible
1623.C2 Cabala. Cabalistic works
1623.C26 Candles
1623.C47 Christian patron saints
1623.C5 Cities and towns
1623.C6 Color symbolism
1623.C7 Correspondences
1623.D35 Dancing
1623.D74 Drugs
1623.D76 Drum
1623.E55 Enochian magic
1623.F55 Finance, Personal
1623.F64 Food
1623.G37 Gardens
Goddesses see BF1623.G63
1623.G63 Gods. Goddesses
1623.H35 Happiness
1623.H67 Households. Home

Magic (White and Black). Shamanism. Hermetics. Necromancy
Special topics, A-Z -- Continued

1623.H85 Huna
1623.I52 Incense
1623.L6 Love
Magic wands see BF1626
1623.M37 Martinism
1623.M43 Medicine wheels
1623.M47 Metamorphosis
1623.M57 Mirrors
1623.M66 Moon
1623.N3 Names
1623.N35 Nature
Numerology see BF1623.P9
1623.O8 Oriental order of initiation
Personal finance see BF1623.F55
1623.P5 Plants
1623.P75 Protection magic
1623.P9 Pythagorean numbers. Numerology
Including symbolism of numbers and letters
1623.R6 Rituals
1623.R7 Rosicrucians
1623.R74 Rotas-Sator square
1623.R89 Runes
Sanctuaries see BF1623.T45
1623.S35 Science
1623.S4 Sex
1623.S5 Sigils
1623.S55 Soap
1623.S57 Sound
1623.S6 Sphinxes
1623.S63 Spiritual healing
1623.S73 Stars
1623.S8 Sun
1623.S9 Symbolism
Symbolism of numbers see BF1623.P9
1623.T45 Temples. Sanctuaries
1623.T47 Tetragrammaton
1623.T56 Theurgy
1623.V7 Vril
Wands see BF1626
1623.Y64 Yoga
1626 Magician's wands. Magic wands
1628 Divining rod. Dowsing for precious metals, water, etc
1628.3 Radiesthesia
Alchemy see QD13; QD23.3+
Astrology

	Astrology -- Continued
1651	Periodicals. Societies. Serials
1651.3	Congresses
1651.5	Directories
1655	Dictionaries. Encyclopedias
1661	Collected works (nonserial)
	History
1671	General works
	By period
1674	Ancient
1676	Medieval
1679	Modern
	Biography
1679.8.A1	Collective
1679.8.A2-Z	Individual, A-Z
	General works
1680-1688	Early through 1800 (Table B-BJ6)
1690-1698	1801-1880 (Table B-BJ6)
1701-1708	1881-1970 (Table B-BJ6a)
	1971-
1708.1.A1-.A3	Polyglot
1708.1.A4-Z	English and American
1708.2	French
1708.3	German
1708.4	Italian
1708.5	Spanish and Portuguese
1708.6	Russian and other Slavic
1708.8.A-Z	Other, A-Z
1711	General special Including special aspects of the subject as a whole
1713	Controversial works against astrologers
1714.A-Z	By ethnic group, religion, or country, A-Z
1714.A37	African American
1714.A6	Arabic
1714.A75	Asian
1714.A86	Assyro-Babylonian
1714.B35	Balinese
1714.B65	Bon (Tibetan religion)
1714.B7	Buddhist
1714.B8	Burmese
1714.C44	Celtic
1714.C5	Chinese
1714.E39	Egyptian
1714.H5	Hindu
1714.I49	Indian
1714.I5	Indic
1714.I7	Iranian

Astrology
By ethnic group, religion, or country, A-Z -- Continued
1714.I84 Islamic
1714.I87 Italian
1714.J28 Jaina
1714.J3 Japanese
1714.J35 Javanese
1714.J4 Jewish
1714.K5 Khmer
1714.K6 Korean
1714.L36 Lao
1714.M34 Malaysian
1714.M35 Mandaean
Maya see F1435.3.A8
1714.M6 Mongolian
1714.N4 Nepalese
(1714.O7) Oriental
1714.P65 Polish
1714.R6 Roman
1714.R86 Russian
1714.S55 Sinhalese
1714.S58 Slavic
1714.S65 Spanish
1714.T3 Tantric
1714.T34 Taoist
1714.T5 Thai
1714.T53 Tibetan
1714.V53 Vietnamese
1714.Z65 Zoroastrian
1715-1729 Special topics
1715 Tables of declinations, etc.
Houses
1716 General works
Individual houses
1716.28 Eighth house
1717 Ascendant
Aspects
1717.2 General works
1717.22.A-Z Special asects, A-Z
1717.22.Q55 Quindecile
Astrological geomancy see BF1779.A88
1717.23 Dispositors
1717.25 Electional astrology
1717.27 Esoteric astrology
1717.28 Essential dignities
1717.3 Heliocentric astrology
1717.5 Horary astrology

	Astrology
	Special topics -- Continued
1718	Medical astrology
1718.5	Midheaven
1719	Natal astrology
1720	Mundane astrology
1720.5	Predictive astrology
1721	Bible and astrology
1723	Lunar influences. Moon
1724	Planetary influences
1724.2.A-Z	Individual planets, A-Z
1724.2.C48	Chiron (Minor planet 2060)
1724.2.J87	Jupiter
1724.2.M37	Mars
1724.2.M45	Mercury
1724.2.N45	Neptune
1724.2.P4	Pluto
1724.2.S3	Saturn
1724.2.U7	Uranus
1724.2.V45	Venus
1724.2.V84	Vulcan
	Stars
1724.3	General works
1724.4.A-Z	Individual stars, A-Z
1724.4.S57	Sirius
1724.5	Asteroids
1725	Cyclic law. Periodicity
	Zodiac. Signs of the zodiac
1726	General works
(1726.3)	Houses see BF1716
	Individual signs
1727	Aries
1727.2	Taurus
1727.25	Gemini
1727.3	Cancer
1727.35	Leo
1727.4	Virgo
1727.45	Libra
1727.5	Scorpio
1727.6	Sagittarius
1727.65	Capricorn
1727.7	Aquarius
1727.75	Pisces
	Triplicities
1727.8	General works
1727.9.A-Z	Individual triplicities, A-Z

Astrology
Special topics
Zodiac. Signs of the zodiac
Triplicities
Individual triplicities, A-Z -- Continued
1727.9.A37 Air signs
1727.9.E27 Earth signs
Horoscopes
1728.A2 General works
1728.A3-Z Individuals and families, A-Z
1728.B47 Berkowitz, David Richard, 1953-
1728.F53 Ficino, Marsilio, 1433-1499
1728.G64 González, Felipe
1728.G84 Guicciardini, Francisco, 1483-1540
1728.H6 Himmler, Heinrich
1728.H65 Hitler, Adolf, 1889-1945
1728.K46 Kennedy family
1728.L4 Leonardo da Vinci
1728.L52 Lincoln, Abraham
1728.L6 Louis, Dauphin of France, 1661-1711
1728.N2 Napoleon I
1728.N34 Nehru family
1728.N58 Nixon, Richard Milhous
1728.O5 Onassis, Jacqueline Kennedy
1728.P4 Pedro, Prince of Brazil, 1712-1714
1728.P74 Presley, Elvis, 1935-1977
1728.P87 Putin, Vladimir Vladimirovich, 1952-
1728.W56 Windsor, House of
1728.2.A-Z Special groups, A-Z
1728.2.C44 Celebrities
1728.2.G39 Gay men
1728.2.G54 Gifted persons
1728.2.N38 National socialists (Germany)
Nazis (Germany) see BF1728.2.N38
1728.2.N62 Nobel prize winners
1728.2.P74 Presidents
1728.2.S7 Statesmen
1728.2.S9 Supervisors
1728.2.W66 Women
1728.3 Animals
1729.A-Z Other special topics, A-Z
1729.A25 Accidents
1729.A37 Agriculture
1729.A45 Alcoholism
1729.A52 America
1729.A68 Archetypes
1729.A7 Architecture

Astrology
Special topics
Other special topics, A-Z -- Continued
Astrological geomancy see BF1779.A88
1729.A87 Authorship
1729.B4 Birth control
1729.B45 Birthdays
1729.B5 Birthplaces
1729.B7 Breath
1729.B73 Brothers and sisters
1729.B75 Building
1729.B8 Business. Business cycles
Cats see BF1728.3
1729.C43 Child development
1729.C45 Child rearing
1729.C47 Childbirth
1729.C64 Contests
1729.C67 Counseling
1729.C73 Creative ability
1729.C75 Crime
1729.D4 Death
1729.D5 Diet
1729.D73 Dreams
1729.E34 Eclipses
(1729.E4) Electional astrology
see BF1717.25
1729.F35 Family
1729.F48 Finance, Personal
1729.F5 Fingerprints
Four temperaments see BF1729.T46
1729.F7 French Revolution
1729.G3 Gambling
1729.G35 Gardening
1729.G4 Gems
Geomancy see BF1779.A88
1729.G45 German history
1729.G53 Gifts
1729.G64 Golf
1729.G72 Graphology
1729.H37 Harness racing
Health see BF1729.H9
1729.H57 History
1729.H66 Homosexuality
1729.H9 Hygiene. Health
Cf. BF1729.D5 Diet
Cf. BF1729.P44 Physical fitness
1729.I54 India

Astrology
Special topics
Other special topics, A-Z -- Continued

1729.L6 Love. Marriage
Marriage see BF1729.L6
1729.M33 Magic
1729.M45 Men
1729.M453 Mental illness
1729.M46 Metals
1729.M47 Meteorology
1729.M52 Middle age
1729.M54 Military art and science. War
1729.M68 Moving, Household
1729.M8 Murder
1729.M9 Mythology
1729.N3 Names
1729.N85 Numerology
1729.O25 Occupations
Personal finance see BF1729.F48
Pets see BF1728.3
1729.P44 Physical fitness
Cf. BF1729.H9 Health
1729.P45 Physiognomy
1729.P5 Plants
1729.P6 Politics
1729.P73 Prayers
1729.P8 Psychology
1729.P83 Psychotherapy
1729.R37 Reincarnation
1729.R4 Religion
Relocation see BF1729.M68
1729.R85 Runes
1729.S34 Science
1729.S38 Self-realization
1729.S4 Sex
Sisters and brothers see BF1729.B73
1729.S6 Speculation (Commerce)
1729.S64 Spiritual life
1729.S88 Success
1729.S92 Sunspots
1729.T44 Teenagers
1729.T46 Temperament. Four temperaments
1729.T73 Travel
1729.U5 United States history
1729.V63 Vocational guidance
War see BF1729.M54
1729.W64 Women

Astrology
Special topics
Other special topics, A-Z -- Continued
1729.Y64 Yoga
Oracles. Sibyls. Divinations
1745 Collected works (nonserial)
1750-1758 General works. History (Table B-BJ6)
1761 Ancient
1762 Ancient Orient
Including Assyria, Babylonia, etc.
1765 Greece
1768 Rome
1769 Sibylline books
1770.A-Z Other ancient countries, A-Z
1771 Medieval
1773 Modern
1773.2.A-Z By region or country, A-Z
1775 Popular superstitions
1777 Omens. Signs. Auguries
Including prodigies, annus mirabilis, etc.
1778 Good luck and bad luck
1778.5 Divination cards
1779.A-Z Other special, A-Z
1779.A4 Alphabet
1779.A53 Angels
1779.A88 Astrological geomancy
1779.C56 Coins
1779.C6 Comets
1779.C64 Cowries
1779.D65 Dominoes
Extraterrestrials see BF1779.L5
1779.F4 Feng shui
Cf. SB454.3.F45 Gardens and gardening
1779.I4 Ifa
1779.L5 Life on other planets. Extraterrestrials
1779.L6 Lot, Choice by
1779.P45 Pendulum
1779.P76 Proverbs
1779.R86 Runes
1779.S32 Scapulimancy
1779.S74 Stones
1779.T73 Trees
1779.V38 Vāstu
1779.W43 Weather
1779.W7 Writing
Seers. Prophets. Prophecies
For visions see BF1100+

Seers. Prophets. Prophecies -- Continued
1783 Periodicals. Societies. Serials
1785 Collected works (nonserial)
1786 Dictionaries
1790-1798 General works. History (Table B-BJ6)
1801 Ancient
1805 Medieval
1809 Modern
1812.A-Z By region or country, A-Z
1815.A-Z Biographies and prophecies of individual seers, A-Z
Under each (in addition to the normal subarrangement for biography):
.xA26-.xA269 Individual prophecies. By title
e. g.
1815.B8 Brothers, Richard
1815.B8A26-.B8A269 Individual prophecies. By title
1815.C2 Campbell, Duncan
1815.C2A26-.C2A269 Individual prophecies. By title
1815.H5 Hermann von Lehnin
1815.H5A26-.H5A269 Individual prophecies. By title
1815.N8 Nostradamus (Michel de Notredame)
1815.N8A26-.N8A269 Individual prophecies. By title
1815.S5 Shipton, Ursula (Mother Shipton)
1815.S5A26-.S5A269 Individual prophecies. By title
Fortune-telling
Cf. BF910+ Palmistry
Cf. BF1080+ Dream books
1845 Collected works (nonserial)
General works
1850-1858 Early through 1800 (Table B-BJ6)
1861-1868 1801- (Table B-BJ6a)
1874 General special
Including special aspects of the subject as a whole
Special topics
Cartomancy. Fortune-telling by cards
1876 Early works through 1800
1878 1801-
1879.A-Z Special topics, A-Z
1879.A7 Astrology and cards
1879.T2 The Tarot
Cf. GV1295.T37 Card games
1881 Fortune-telling by tea and coffee cups
1891.A-Z Other special topics, A-Z
1891.A54 Animals
1891.B5 Birds
1891.B54 Birthdays
1891.B64 Bones

Fortune-telling
Special topics
Other special topics, A-Z -- Continued

1891.B66 Books
1891.B7 Breath and breathing
1891.C48 Chinese characters
1891.C64 Colors
1891.D5 Dice
Dreams see BF1080+
1891.F5 Fingerprints
1891.F55 Flames
Flowers see BF1891.P56
1891.M28 Magic mirror
1891.M3 Magic square
1891.M33 Mah-jong
1891.M65 Moles (Skin)
1891.N3 Names, Personal
1891.N8 Numbers
1891.P56 Plants. Flowers
1891.P74 Precious stones
1891.Q6 Quotations
1891.R85 Runes
1891.S38 Scarabs
1891.S4 Seals (Numismatics). Signets
Signets see BF1891.S4
1891.S48 Shells
1891.W4 Wheel of Pythagoras

Miscellaneous
Including works that bridge the occult, mythological, and traditional areas of religion
Cf. BP605.A+ Religious beliefs and movements

1995 Periodicals. Societies. Serials
1997.A-Z Biography, A-Z
1999 General works

Human-alien encounters. Contact between humans and extraterrestrials
Including alien abduction
Cf. CB156 Influence of extraterrestrial life on human civilization
Cf. QB54 Extraterrestrial life
Cf. TL789+ Unidentified flying objects

2050 General works
2055.A-Z Special topics, A-Z
2055.C65 Consciousness
2055.G73 Grays
2055.M45 Men in black

	Aesthetics
1-8	Periodicals. Serials (Table B-BJ6a)
11-18	Societies (Table B-BJ6a)
19	Congresses
21-28	Collected works (nonserial) (Table B-BJ6a)
	Philosophy. Methodology. Relation to other topics
39	General works
41	Special methods
	Aesthetics and religion see BL65.A4
	Aesthetics of music see ML3845
	Theory of visual arts see N61
	Theory of literature see PN45+
56	Dictionaries. Encyclopedias
61	Study and teaching. Research
62.A-Z	By region or country, A-Z
	Under each country: .x General works; .x2 Individual institutions. By place, A-Z
81	History
83	Origins
85	Comparative aesthetics
	Ancient
90	Collected works (nonserial)
91	General works
95	General special
	Orient
101	General
102	Special
	Egypt
105	General
106	Special
	Greece
108	General
109	Special
	Rome
115	General
116	Special
131	Medieval
136	General special
137	Byzantine
151	Modern
161-168	16th century (Table B-BJ6a)
171-178	17th century (Table B-BJ6a)
181-188	18th century (Table B-BJ6a)
191-198	19th century (Table B-BJ6a)
201-208	20th century (Table B-BJ6a)
220	Juvenile literature

221.A-Z	By region or country, A-Z
	Under each country:
	.x — *General works. History*
	.x15A-.x15Z — *Local, A-Z*
	By period
	.x2 — *Through 1800*
	.x3 — *1801-*
	.x4A-.x4Z — *Aesthetic philosophers, A-Z*
	e. g.
221.F8-.F84	France
221.G3-.G34	Germany
221.G7-.G74	Great Britain
221.I8-.I84	Italy
221.U5-.U54	United States
301.A-Z	Special topics, A-Z
	Aesthetic object see BH301.O24
301.A55	Animism
301.A7	Art for art's sake
301.A77	Attitude
301.A94	Avant-garde
301.B53	Black
301.C36	Camp (Style)
301.C4	Charm
301.C6	Color
301.C7	The comic
301.C75	Consumption (Economics)
301.C84	Creation
301.C88	Cruelty
301.C92	Culture
(301.D46)	Depth (Philosophy). Profundity
301.D5	Dilettantism
301.E45	Emotivism
301.E58	Environment
	Eros see BH301.L65
301.E77	Espionage
301.E8	Experience
301.E9	Expressionism
301.F3	Fantastic
301.F6	Form
	Cf. N7429.7+ Visual arts
301.G7	Grace
301.G73	Grief
301.G74	Grotesque
301.H3	Harmony
301.H36	Head
301.H4	The heroic
301.I3	Ideals

Special topics, A-Z -- Continued

301.I52 Image
301.I53 Imagination
301.I55 Imitation
301.I65 Influence
301.I7 Irony
301.J8 Judgment
301.K5 Kitsch
301.L3 Landscape
301.L65 Love. Eros
301.M25 Machinery
301.M3 Man
Cf. BD450 Philosophical anthropology
301.M35 Mathematics
301.M4 Metaphor
Cf. P301.5.M48 Metaphor (General)
301.M47 Mimesis
301.M54 Modernism
301.M6 Movement
301.M9 Myth
301.N3 Nature
301.N48 New and old
301.N67 Nostalgia
301.O24 Object, Aesthetic
Ocean see BH301.S4
301.O35 Odors
Old and new see BH301.N48
301.O75 Originality
301.P3 Particularity
301.P45 Physiological aspects of aesthetics
301.P53 The picturesque
301.P64 Politics
301.P67 Positivism
301.P69 Postmodernism
301.P78 Psychological aspects of aesthetics
301.Q34 Quality
301.R42 Realism
301.R43 Relativity
301.R46 Repetition
301.R47 Representation
301.R5 Rhythm
301.S4 Sea. Ocean
301.S43 Seduction
301.S46 Senses and sensation
301.S5 Situation
301.S65 Space
301.S68 Structuralism

Special topics, A-Z -- Continued

301.S69	Subjectivity
301.S7	The sublime
301.S8	Symbolism
301.S9	Symmetry
301.T7	The tragic
301.T77	Truth
301.U5	Ugliness
301.V85	Vulgarity
301.W43	Wealth
301.W56	Wine
	Woman see HQ1219+
301.W65	Wonder

Ethics
Periodicals. Serials
1 American and English
2 French and Belgian
3 German
4 Italian
5 Spanish and Portuguese
8.A-Z Other languages, A-Z
Societies
10.A-Z International societies and movements, A-Z
e. g.
Moral re-armament
10.M6 General works
10.M62A-.M62Z Local groups. By name, A-Z
11-18 General (Table B-BJ6a modified)
11.A4-Z American and English
e. g.
11.P3 Pathfinders of America
19 Congresses
Collected works (nonserial)
21.A1 Polyglot
21.A3-Z English
22 French
23 German
24 Italian
25 Spanish and Portuguese
26 Russian and other Slavic
28.A-Z Other, A-Z
37 Philosophy. Methodology. Relation to other topics
41 Relation to speculative philosophy
42 Relation to rhetoric
43 Relation to logic
44 Relation to language
45 Relation to psychology. Morale
45.5 Relation to cognitive science. Philosophy of mind
46 Relation to aesthetics (Art, literature, etc.)
47 Relation to religion and the supernatural
49 Relation to teaching
51 Relation to history and sociology
52 Relation to anthropology and culture
52.5 Relation to agriculture
53 Relation to economics
55 Relation to law and politics
57 Relation to science
Cf. Q175.35+ Scientific ethics
58 Relation to biology
59 Relation to technology

Philosophy. Methodology. Relation to other topics -- Continued
60 Relation to astronautics
63 Dictionaries. Encyclopedias
Cf. BJ1199 Christian ethics
Study and teaching. Research
66 General works
68.A-Z Individual schools, A-Z
69 Comparative ethics
History
Cf. BJ1001+ General works
71-78 General works (Table B-BJ6a)
84.A-Z Special topics, A-Z
84.E5 Ends and means
Means and ends see BJ84.E5
By period
101 Ancient
107.A-Z Special topics, A-Z
107.H8 Humanity
111 Orient
115 Far East
By region or country
China and Japan
Cf. BL1790+ Chinese religions
Cf. BL2220 Japanese religions
116 Collected works (nonserial)
117 General works, history
118.A-Z Special topics, A-Z
118.F54 Filial piety
118.F6 Fortitude. Hara
Hara see BJ118.F6
118.L68 Loyalty
India
Including ethics of modern India
Cf. BL1100+ Hinduism
Cf. BL1300+ Jainism
Cf. BL1500+ Parseeism
Cf. BL2000+ Religions of India
Cf. BQ1+ Buddhism
121 Collected works (nonserial)
122 General works, history
123.A-Z Special topics, A-Z
123.A45 Ahimsa

History
By period
Ancient
Orient
Far East
By region or country -- Continued
125.A-Z Other Far East regions or countries, A-Z
Under each country:
.x Collected works (nonserial)
.x2 General works, history
.x3 Special topics, A-Z
.x3F54 Filial pietry
Near East
130 General works
By region or country
Egypt
Cf. BL2420+ Religions of Egypt
131 Collected works (nonserial)
132 General works, history
133.A-Z Special topics, A-Z
Assyria-Babylonia
Cf. BL1620+ Religion
136 Collected works (nonserial)
137 General works, history
138.A-Z Special topics, A-Z
Persia. Iran
Including ethics of modern Iran
Cf. BL1500+ Zoroastrianism
Cf. BL2270+ Religions of Persia
141 Collected works (nonserial)
142 General works, history
143.A-Z Special topics, A-Z
Hebrews see BJ1279+
149.A-Z Other Near East regions or countries, A-Z
Under each country:
.x Collected works (nonserial)
.x2 General works, history
.x3 Special topics, A-Z

Greece and Rome
Including Greek ethics (General)
160 Collected works (nonserial)
161 General works
171.A-Z Special topics, A-Z
171.A82 Asceticism
171.C6 Conscience
171.E7 Escape
171.F54 Filial piety

History
By period
Ancient
Greece and Rome
Special topics, A-Z -- Continued

171.H35 Happiness
171.I76 Irony
171.P5 Piety
Piety, Filial see BJ171.F54
171.R4 Responsibility
171.V55 Virtue

By period
First period (to about 450 B.C.)
181 Collected works (nonserial)
182 General works, history, etc.
183.A-Z Special topics, A-Z
For list of topics, see BJ171.A+
184.A-Z Ethical philosophers, A-Z
Subarrange each philosopher by Table B-BJ19

Second period (to about 300 B.C.)
191 Collected works (nonserial)
192 General works, history, etc.
193.A-Z Special topics, A-Z
For list of topics, see BJ171.A+
194.A-Z Ethical philosophers, A-Z
Subarrange each philosopher by Table B-BJ19

Greco-Roman. Roman ethics
211 Collected works (nonserial)
212 General works, history, etc.
213.a-Z Special topics, A-Z
For list of topics, see BJ171.A+
214.A-Z Ethical philosophers, A-Z
Subarrange each philosopher by Table B-BJ19 unless otherwise indicated
Cutter numbers listed below are provided as examples
For the distinction in use between classes BJ and PA, see note in the record for B165+
214.B5-.B7 Bryson, Neo-Pythagorean (Table B-BJ19a)
214.C5-.C7 Cicero (Table B-BJ19a)
Cf. B550+ Philosophy
214.H6-.H8 Hierocles of Alexandria (Table B-BJ19a)
214.P6-.P8 Plutarch (Table B-BJ19a)
Cf. B600+ Philosophy
214.S3-.S5 Seneca (Table B-BJ19a)
Cf. B615+ Philosophy

221-224 Alexandrian and early Christian

History
By period -- Continued
231 Medieval
251.A-Z Special topics, A-Z
251.A37 Akrasia
255.A-Z Ethical philosophers, A-Z
Subarrange each philosopher by Table B-BJ19 unless otherwise indicated
Abelard
255.A2 Collected works (nonserial)
255.A25 Separate works
255.A3 Biography and criticism
255.T3-.T5 Thomas Aquinas (Table B-BJ19a)
Cf. B765.T5+ Philosophy
271 Renaissance
281.A-Z Special topics, A-Z
281.E56 Emotions
285.A-Z Ethical philosophers, A-Z
Subarrange each philosopher by Table B-BJ19
285.C5-.C7 Coornhert, Dirk Volkertszoon (Table B-BJ19a)
285.M5-.M7 Melanchthon (Table B-BJ19a)
Cf. B785.M4+ Philosophy
Modern (1700-)
301-308 General works (Table B-BJ6a)
By period
311 18th century
315 19th century
319 20th century
320 21st century
324.A-Z Special topics, A-Z
324.A88 Autonomy
324.C48 Character
324.F54 Filial piety
324.M64 Moral development
324.P67 Postmodernism
324.R4 Religion
324.S44 Self
324.S96 Sympathy
324.V35 Values
324.V66 Voodooism
324.W66 Work
324.W68 Worth
By region or country
351-354 United States (Table B-BJ20)
401-404 Canada (Table B-BJ20)
411-414 Latin America (Table B-BJ20)
421-424 Mexico (Table B-BJ20)

History
By period
Modern (1700-)
By region or country
Latin America -- Continued

431-434 Central America (Table B-BJ20)
441-444 West Indies (Table B-BJ20)
451-454 South America (Table B-BJ20)
461-464 Argentina (Table B-BJ20)
471-474 Bolivia (Table B-BJ20)
481-484 Brazil (Table B-BJ20)
491-494 Chile (Table B-BJ20)
501-504 Colombia (Table B-BJ20)
511-514 Ecuador (Table B-BJ20)
521-524 Guianas (Table B-BJ20)
531-534 Paraguay (Table B-BJ20)
541-544 Peru (Table B-BJ20)
551-554 Uruguay (Table B-BJ20)
561-564 Venezuela (Table B-BJ20)
591-594 Austria (Table B-BJ20)
595-598 Bulgaria (Table B-BJ20)
601-604 Great Britain (Table B-BJ20)
651-654 Scotland (Table B-BJ20)
701-704 France (Table B-BJ20)
751-754 Germany (Table B-BJ20)
Including West Germany
756-759 East Germany (Table B-BJ20)
761-764 Czechoslovakia. Czech Republic. Slovakia (Table B-BJ20)
801-804 Greece (Table B-BJ20)
805-808 Hungary (Table B-BJ20)
811-814 Italy (Table B-BJ20)
821-824 Low Countries (Table B-BJ20)
831-834 Netherlands (Holland) (Table B-BJ20)
841-844 Belgium (Table B-BJ20)
847-850 Poland (Table B-BJ20)
851-854 Russia. Soviet Union (Table B-BJ20)
861-864 Scandinavia (Table B-BJ20)
871-874 Denmark (Table B-BJ20)
881-884 Norway (Table B-BJ20)
891-894 Sweden (Table B-BJ20)
901-904 Spain and Portugal (Table B-BJ20)
911-914 Spain (Table B-BJ20)
921-924 Portugal (Table B-BJ20)
941-944 Switzerland (Table B-BJ20)
951-954 Romania (Table B-BJ20)
961-964 Asia (Table B-BJ20)

History
By period
Modern (1700-)
By region or country
Asia -- Continued
965-968 China (Table B-BJ20)
969-972 Japan (Table B-BJ20 modified)
971.A-Z Special topics, A-Z
For other topics, see BJ324.A+
971.B8 Bushido
971.S4 Seppuku
971.S5 Shingaku
973-976 Korea (Table B-BJ20)
977.A-Z Other regions or countries, A-Z
For India see BJ121+
980 Africa
981.A-Z By region or country, A-Z
982.A-Z By ethnic group, A-Z
982.A38 Akan
982.B34 Baganda
General works, treatises, and textbooks
991 Latin
993 Elementary textbooks. Outlines, syllabi, etc.
995 General special
Including special aspects of the subject as a whole
English
General works
1001 Through 1700
1005 1701-1800
1006 1801-1860
1008 1861-1900
1011 1901-1960
1012 1961-
Elementary textbooks. Outlines, syllabi, etc.
1021 Early through 1800
1025 1801-
Cf. BJ1631+ Ethics for the young
1031 General special
Including special aspects of the subject as a whole
French and Belgian
General works
1051 Through 1700
1054 1701-1800
1057 1801-1860
1059 1861-1900
1063 1901-
Elementary textbooks. Outlines, syllabi, etc.

General works, treatises, and textbooks
French and Belgian
Elementary textbooks. Outlines, syllabi, etc. -- Continued
1075 Early through 1800
1077 1801-
1087 General special
Including special aspects of the subject as a whole
German
General works
1101 Through 1700
1104 1701-1800
1107 1801-1860
1111 1861-1900
1114 1901-
Elementary textbooks. Outlines, syllabi, etc.
1119 Early through 1800
1121 1801-
1125 General special
Including special aspects of the subject as a whole
Italian
General works
1131 Early through 1800
1132 1801-
1133 Elementary textbooks. Outlines, syllabi, etc.
1134 General special
Including special aspects of the subject as a whole
Russian and other Slavic
General works
1135 Early through 1800
1136 1801-
1137 Elementary textbooks. Outlines, syllabi, etc.
1138 General special
Including special aspects of the subject as a whole
Spanish and Portuguese
General works
1141 Early through 1800
1142 1801-
1143 Elementary textbooks. Outlines, syllabi, etc.
1144 General special
Including special aspects of the subject as a whole
Scandinavian and Icelandic
General works
1151 Early through 1800
1152 1801-
1153 Elementary textbooks. Outlines, syllabi, etc.
1154 General special
Including special aspects of the subject as a whole

General works, treatises, and textbooks -- Continued
Swiss
see BJ1051+; BJ1101+; BJ1131+
General works
1161 Early through 1800
1162 1801-
1163 Elementary textbooks. Outlines, syllabi, etc.
1164 General special
Including special aspects of the subject as a whole
1185.A-Z Other languages, A-Z
e. g.
1185.C5 Chinese
For ancient ethics see BJ116+
1185.D8 Dutch
Icelandic see BJ1151+
1185.J3 Japanese
For ancient ethics see BJ116+
1185.K3 Korean
Polish see BJ1135+
Portuguese see BJ1141+
Religious ethics
For the religious aspects of medical ethics see R725.55+
Cf. BJ47 Ethics and religion
1188 General works
Christian ethics
Cf. BS2415+ Teachings of Jesus
Cf. BS2417.E8 Teachings of Jesus
Cf. BS2545.E8 New Testament ethics
1188.5 Periodicals. Serials
1188.7 Societies
1189 Congresses
1190-1198 Collected works (nonserial) (Table B-BJ6)
1199 Dictionaries. Encyclopedias
1200 Study of Christian ethics. Historiography. Methodology
History
1201-1208 General works (Table B-BJ6a)
By period
1212 Early Christian and patristic
1217 Medieval
Modern
1221 Through 1700
1224 1701-1800
1227 1801-1900
1231 1901-
1238.A-Z Special topics, A-Z
For Golden rule see BJ1278.G6
Psychiatry see BJ1238.P78

Religious ethics
Christian ethics
History
Special topics, A-Z -- Continued
1238.P78 Psychology. Psychiatry
Including psychoanalysis
General works, treatises, and advanced textbooks
Early through 1800
1240 Latin
1241-1248 Other languages (Table B-BJ6a)
1801-
1249 Catholic works
1250 Orthodox Eastern works
1250.5 Other Eastern churches' works
1251-1258 Other (Table B-BJ6a)
1261-1268 Elementary textbooks. Outlines, syllabi, etc. (Table B-BJ6a)
1275 General special
1278.A-Z Special, A-Z
1278.A3 Rules for right living and conduct from the teachings of Christ
1278.C66 Conscience
1278.D58 Divine commands
1278.E64 Epikeia
1278.F45 Feminism. Feminist ethics
1278.F86 Fundamental option
1278.G6 Golden rule
1278.L53 Liberty
1278.P47 Personalism
1278.P68 Power
Preaching, Ethics of see BV4235.E75
1278.P73 Priority
1278.P76 Probabilism
1278.R43 Reason
1278.S37 Scruples
1278.S44 Self-esteem
1278.5.A-Z Ethical philosophers, A-Z
Jewish ethics
1279 Collected works (nonserial)
1280 General works
By period
1281 Ancient. Pre-Christian
Cf. BS1199.E8 Old Testament ethics
1282 Medieval
Modern
1283 Through 1800
1284 1801-1900

Religious ethics
Jewish ethics
By period
Modern -- Continued

1285	1901-2000
1285.2	2001-
1285.5.A-Z	Special movements, A-Z
1285.5.M8	Musar movement
1286.A-Z	Special topics, A-Z
1286.A6	Altruism
1286.A64	Anger
1286.A88	Autopsy
1286.C5	Charity
1286.C66	Conscience
1286.E47	Empathy
	Ethical wills see BJ1286.W59+
	Falsehood and truthfulness see BJ1286.T7
	Fellowship see BM720.F4
1286.F67	Forgiveness
1286.G64	Golden rule
1286.G73	Gratitude
1286.H85	Humanitarianism
1286.H87	Humility
1286.K5	Kindness
1286.L3	Law
1286.L54	Life
1286.O73	Oral communication
1286.P38	Patience
1286.R4	Reconciliation
1286.R47	Respect for others
1286.S33	Secrecy
1286.S44	Self-respect
1286.S55	Silence
1286.T7	Truthfulness and falsehood
	Wills, Ethical
1286.W59	Collections
1286.W6A-.Z6	Individual. By maker
1286.W6Z8-.Z89	History and criticism
1287.A-Z	Ethical philosophers, A-Z
	Subarrange each philosopher like BJ1287.M6+ unless otherwise specified
	Aboab, Isaac, 14th cent.
1287.A15	Original text. By date
1287.A152	Translations. By language, A-Z, and date
1287.A153	Selections. By date
1287.A1532	Translations. By language, A-Z, and date
1287.A154	Biography, criticism, etc.

	Religious ethics
	Jewish ethics
	Ethical philosophers, A-Z -- Continued
	Maimonides, Moses, 1135-1204 see BJ1287.M6+
	Moses ben Maimon, 1135-1204
1287.M6	Collected works (Original language)
1287.M62A-.M62Z	Translations (Collected). By language, A-Z
1287.M63A-.M63Z	Separate works, A-Z
1287.M64	Biography. Criticism
1287.Z9	Anonymous works
1288	Bahai ethics
1289	Buddhist ethics
1289.3	Confucian ethics
1290	Jaina ethics
1290.3	Rastafarian ethics
1290.5	Sikh ethics
1290.8	Taoist ethics
1291	Islamic ethics
	Cf. BP134.E8 Ethics of the Koran
1292.A-Z	Special classes, groups, etc., A-Z
	Children see BJ1292.Y6
1292.S3	Scholars
1292.W6	Women
1292.Y6	Youth. Children
1295	Zoroastrian ethics
	Evolutionary and genetic ethics
	Including Monistic ethics
1298	History
	General works
1301-1308	Early through 1860 (Table B-BJ6a)
1311-1318	1861- (Table B-BJ6a)
1321-1328	Elementary textbooks. Outlines, syllabi, etc. (Table B-BJ6a)
1335	General special
	Including special aspects of the subject as a whole
1340	Existential ethics
1360	Humanist ethics
	Positivist ethics
1365	History
1371-1378	General works (Table B-BJ6a)
1385	General special
	Including special aspects of the subject as a whole
1388	Socialist ethics
1390	Communist ethics (20th century)
1390.5	Study and teaching. Research
1392	Totalitarian ethics
1395	Feminist ethics

Special topics
For ethics of specific disciplines, see classes BL-Z, e.g., Professional ethics for teachers, LB1779
Good and evil
General works
1400 Early through 1800
1801-
1401 English
1402 French
1403 German
1404 Italian
1405.A-Z Other languages, A-Z
1406 Origin of evil. Depravity of human nature
1408 Value of evil
1408.5 Moral judgment
1409 Pain and suffering
1409.5 Death
Right and wrong
1410 Early works through 1800
1411-1418 1801- (Table B-BJ6a)
1418.5 Appropriateness
1419 Decision making
Truth and falsehood. Lying
Cf. BC171 Truth and error (Logic)
Cf. BD150+ Epistemology
1420-1428 General works (Table B-BJ6)
1429 Mental reservation
1429.3 Self-deception
1429.5 Secrecy
1430-1438 Compromise. Tolerance. Toleration (Table B-BJ6)
1440-1448 Casuistry (Table B-BJ6)
1450-1458 Duty. Obligation. Responsibility. Supererogation (Table B-BJ6)
1458.3 Normativity
1458.5 Authority
1459 Obedience
1459.5 Nonviolence. Violence
Freedom of the Will. Necessitarianism
Cf. BD411 Finite and infinite
Cf. BD530+ Teleology
Cf. BF620+ Freedom of the will (Psychology)
1460-1468 General works (Table B-BJ6)
1468.5 General special
1469 Power over life and death
1470 Self-realization
Cf. BP605.S35+ Self-Realization movement
1470.2 Need. Needs

	Special topics -- Continued
1470.5	Fame
1471	Conscience
1471.5	Guilt
1472	Intuition Including ethical intuitionism
1473	Emotivism
1474	Altruism and egotism. Self-interest and egoism
1474.5	Exploitation
1475	Sympathy. Compassion. Caring Cf. BF575.S9 Sympathy (Psychology)
1475.3	Humanitarianism
1475.5	Encouragement
1476	Forgiveness. Pardon
1477	Optimism and pessimism For pessimism and optimism see B829.A+
	Happiness and joy Cf. BF515 Pleasure and pain
1480-1486	General works (Table B-BJ6 modified)
1486.5.A-Z	Other languages, A-Z
1487	Sorrow and grief Cf. BJ1409 Pain and suffering
1488	Despair
1490	Revenge
1491	Hedonism and asceticism. Renunciation Including Eudaemonism and stoicism Cf. B2799.E85 Eudaemonism (Philosophy)
1492	Puritanism
1493	Active vs. meditative life
1496	The simple life. Simplicity
1498	Work. Labor and idleness. Leisure Cf. BF481 Psychology of work Cf. GV14+ Sociology of leisure Cf. HD4801+ Labor (Economics)
1499.A-Z	Other topics, A-Z
1499.B6	Boredom
1499.K3	Karma
1499.R4	Rest
1499.S5	Silence
1499.S65	Solitude
1500.A-Z	Other special topics in ethics, A-Z
1500.A59	Anxiety
1500.B47	Betrayal
1500.C63	Consequentialism
1500.C65	Contractarianism
1500.D68	Double effect
1500.E94	Expressivism

Special topics
Other special topics, A-Z
Golden rule see BJ1278.G6
1500.M42 Mean
Cf. BJ1533.M7 Moderation as a virtue
1500.M47 Merit
1500.M67 Moral realism
1500.N8 Nudity
1500.P7 Promises
1500.R37 Relativism
1500.R4 Reward
1500.S65 Speech
1500.T78 Trust
1500.W55 Wishes
Individual ethics. Character. Virtue
Including standards of conduct, etc.
Cf. BF638+ New thought, menticulture, etc.
Cf. BJ1545+ Practical and applied ethics
1518 Collected works (nonserial)
General works
1520 Early through 1800
1521-1528 1801- (Table B-BJ6a)
1531 General special
Including special aspects of the subject as a whole
1533.A-Z Special virtues, A-Z
Cf. BV4630+ Virtues (Christian life)
Cf. BV4635+ Theological virtues (Christian life)
1533.A4 Ambition
1533.B7 Brotherliness
1533.C37 Charm
1533.C4 Chastity
1533.C5 Cheerfulness
1533.C56 Comradeship
Conceit vs. self-respect see BJ1533.S3
1533.C58 Concord
1533.C6 Confidence
Considerateness see BJ1533.T45
1533.C67 Constancy
1533.C7 Contentment
1533.C74 Cooperativeness
1533.C8 Courage
1533.C9 Courtesy
1533.D49 Discipline. Self-control
1533.D5 Discretion
1533.E2 Economy. Thrift
1533.E82 Excellence
1533.F2 Fairness

Individual ethics. Character. Virtue
Special virtues, A-Z -- Continued

1533.F5 Filial piety
1533.F8 Friendship
1533.G4 Generosity. Sharing
1533.G6 Glory
Good workmanship see BJ1533.W6
1533.G8 Gratitude
1533.H47 Heroism
1533.H7 Honesty
1533.H8 Honor
Hospitality see BJ2021+
1533.H9 Humanity. Human life (Respect for sacredness of)
1533.H93 Humility
Industry see BJ1498
1533.I58 Integrity
1533.J9 Justice
1533.K5 Kindness
Love see BF575.L8
1533.L8 Loyalty
1533.M3 Magnanimity
1533.M7 Moderation
Cf. BJ1500.M42 Mean in ethics
1533.M73 Modesty
1533.N4 Neighborliness
1533.N6 Nobility
Cf. BJ1600+ Practical and applied ethics
1533.O73 Orderliness
1533.P3 Patience
1533.P36 Perfection. Perfectionism
1533.P4 Perseverance
1533.P5 Philanthropy
1533.P9 Prudence
1533.P95 Punctuality
1533.P97 Purity
1533.Q5 Quietude
1533.R4 Respect
1533.R42 Respect for persons
Self-assurance see BJ1533.S27
Self-confidence see BJ1533.S27
Self-control see BJ1533.D49
1533.S27 Self-reliance, self-assurance, self-confidence
1533.S3 Self-respect, self-esteem vs. conceit, over-estimation
1533.S4 Self-sacrifice
Sharing see BJ1533.G4
1533.S55 Sincerity
Sympathy see BJ1475

Individual ethics. Character. Virtue
Special virtues, A-Z -- Continued
1533.T45 Thoughtfulness
Thrift see BJ1533.E2
Tolerance. Toleration see BJ1430+
1533.W6 Workmanship, Good
1534 Vices
Cf. BV4625+ Sins and vices (Christian life)
1535.A-Z Special vices, A-Z
1535.A6 Anger
1535.A8 Avarice. Covetousness
1535.C2 Calumny
Covetousness see BJ1535.A8
1535.C7 Cruelty
1535.E57 Envy
1535.F25 Fanaticism
1535.F3 Fault finding
1535.F55 Flattery
1535.F6 Folly
1535.G6 Gossip
1535.H8 Hypocrisy
1535.I6 Improvidence
1535.I63 Indifferentism
1535.I65 Ingratitude
1535.J4 Jealousy
1535.L87 Lust
1535.L9 Luxury
1535.O28 Obstinacy
1535.P9 Pride
Profanity see BJ1535.S9
1535.R45 Resentment
1535.R5 Ridicule
1535.S4 Selfishness
1535.S6 Slander
1535.S7 Snobbishness
Stubbornness see BJ1535.O28
1535.S87 Superficiality
1535.S9 Swearing. Profanity
1535.W67 Worldliness
Practical and applied ethics. Conduct of life, etc.
Cf. BF638+ New Thought
Cf. BJ1518+ Individual ethics
Cf. BJ1801+ Social usages, etiquette
1545 Periodicals. Societies. Serials
For moral reform associations see HN54+
1546 Dictionaries. Encyclopedias
1547 History

BJ

Individual ethics. Character. Virtue
Practical and applied ethics. Conduct of life, etc. -- Continued
Biography
1547.4 Collective
1547.5.A-Z Individual, A-Z
Collected works (nonserial)
1548 General
1549 Classics
General works
1550-1558 Through 1700 (Table B-BJ6)
1561-1568 1701-1800 (Table B-BJ6a)
1801-1900
English and American
1571.A1 Early 19th century through 1860
1571.A2-Z 1861-1900
1572 French
1573 German
1574 Italian
1575 Spanish and Portuguese
1576 Russian and other Slavic
1578.A-Z Other, A-Z
1901-2000
English and American
1581 1901-1950
1581.2 1951-2000
1582 French
1583 German
1584 Italian
1585 Spanish and Portuguese
1586 Russian and other Slavic
1588.A-Z Other, A-Z
2001-
English and American
1589 2001-
1590 French
1591 German
1592 Italian
1593 Spanish and Portuguese
1594 Russian and other Slavic
1594.5.A-Z Other, A-Z
1595 General special
Including special aspects of the subject as a whole
1595.5 Philosophical counseling
1596 Twelve-step programs
For specific addictions, habits, or problems, see subclasses BF, HQ, HV, RB, or RC
For meditations see BL624.5

Individual ethics. Character. Virtue
Practical and applied ethics. Conduct of life, etc. -- Continued
1597 Works in the form of stories, ethico-pedagogical novels
1600-1608 The "gentlemen," the courtier, etc. (Table B-BJ6)
Women. Beauties of female character, etc. Charm
Cf. BJ1681+ the young woman
1609 Early through 1800
1610 1801
Success
Class here general works on success
For psychological studies of success see BF637.S8
For women see HD6050+
For success in business (General) see HF5386
English and American
1611 Through 1950
1611.2 1951-
1612 French
1613 German
1614 Italian
1615 Spanish and Portuguese
1616 Russian and other Slavic
1618.A-Z Other, A-Z
1631-1638 Ethics for children (Table B-BJ6a)
Cf. BJ1292.Y6 Islamic ethics
Cf. HQ750+ Eugenics. Child culture, study, etc.
1641-1648 Boys (Table B-BJ6a)
Cf. HQ41 Works for boys (Sex relations)
1651-1658 Girls (Table B-BJ6a)
Cf. HQ51 Works for girls (Sex relations)
1661-1668 Ethics for young men and young women (Table B-BJ6a)
1671-1678 Young men (Table B-BJ6a)
Cf. HQ36 Works for men (Sex relations)
1681-1688 Young women (Table B-BJ6a)
Cf. HQ46 Works for women (Sex relations)
1689 Symbolic works
1690 Ethics for middle-aged persons
1691 Ethics for older people. "Old age"
Cf. BV4580.A1+ Religious life
Cf. HQ1060+ Social groups
1695 Ethics of the body
Cf. RA773+ Personal hygiene
1697 Ethics of dress and toilet
Amusements, recreation, games, dancing, etc. see GV14+
Ethics of social groups, classes, etc.
Community, nation, race, etc. see HN1+
Domestic and family ethics see HQ503+
City morals see HT265

Ethics of social groups, classes, etc. -- Continued

Political ethics, citizenship, etc.

see class J

1725 Professional ethics

Social usages. Etiquette
Cf. CR3575+ Order of precedence
Cf. HV7925 Police etiquette
1801 Periodicals. Societies. Serials
1809 Collected works (nonserial)
1815 Dictionaries. Encyclopedias
1818 Forms, blanks, etc.
1821 History
1838 General special
Special aspects of the subject as a whole
1843 Satire, etc.
General works
American
1850 Collected works (Nonserial)
General works
1851 Early through 1800
1852 1801-1900
1853 1901-
1854 General special
Including special aspects of the subject as a whole
Special topics
1855 Social usages for men
1856 Social usages for women
1857.A-Z Other special topics, A-Z
1857.A37 African Americans
1857.B7 Boys
1857.C5 Children
1857.E8 Escort service
1857.F3 Family
1857.G5 Girls
Military, The see U750+
1857.N8 Nurses
1857.S5 Sick, The
1857.S75 Students
1857.Y58 Young adults
1857.Y6 Young women
1858 Washington, D.C.
1859.A-Z Local, A-Z
British
Including Canada, etc.
1870 Collected works (Nonserial)
General works
1871 Early through 1800
1872 1801-1900
1873 1901-
1874 General special
Including special aspects of the subject as a whole

General works
British -- Continued
Special topics
1875 Social usages for men
1876 Social usages for women
1877.A-Z Other special topics, A-Z
1877.B7 Boys
1877.C5 Children
1877.E8 Escort service
1877.F3 Family
1877.G5 Girls
Military, The see U750+
1877.N8 Nurses
1877.S5 Sick, The
1877.S75 Students
1879.A-Z Local, A-Z
French
1880 Collected works (Nonserial)
General works
1881 Early through 1800
1882 1801-1900
1883 1901-
1884 General special
Including special aspects of the subject as a whole
Special topics
1885 Social usages for men
1886 Social usages for women
1887.A-Z Other special topics, A-Z
1887.B7 Boys
1887.C5 Children
1887.E8 Escort service
1887.F3 Family
1887.G5 Girls
Military, The see U750+
1887.N8 Nurses
1887.S5 Sick, The
1887.S75 Students
1889.A-Z Local, A-Z
German
1900 Collected works (Nonserial)
General works
1901 Early through 1800
1902 1801-1900
1903 1901-
1904 General special
Including special aspects of the subject as a whole
Special topics

General works
German
Special topics -- Continued
1905 Social usages for men
1906 Social usages for women
1907.A-Z Other special topics, A-Z
1907.B7 Boys
1907.C5 Children
1907.E8 Escort service
1907.F3 Family
1907.G5 Girls
Military, The see U750+
1907.N8 Nurses
1907.S5 Sick, The
1907.S75 Students
1909.A-Z Local, A-Z
Italian
1920 Collected works (Nonserial)
General works
1921 Early through 1800
1922 1801-1900
1923 1901-
1924 General special
Including special aspects of the subject as a whole
Special topics
1925 Social usages for men
1926 Social usages for women
1927.A-Z Other special topics, A-Z
1927.B7 Boys
1927.C5 Children
1927.E8 Escort service
1927.F3 Family
1927.G5 Girls
Military, The see U750+
1927.N8 Nurses
1927.S5 Sick, The
1927.S75 Students
1929.A-Z Local, A-Z
Russian
1940 Collected works (Nonserial)
General works
1941 Early through 1800
1942 1801-1900
1943 1901-
1944 General special
Including special aspects of the subject as a whole
Special topics

General works
Russian
Special topics -- Continued
1945 Social usages for men
1946 Social usages for women
1947.A-Z Other special topics, A-Z
1947.B7 Boys
1947.C5 Children
1947.E8 Escort service
1947.F3 Family
1947.G5 Girls
Military, The see U750+
1947.N8 Nurses
1947.S5 Sick, The
1947.S75 Students
1949.A-Z Local, A-Z
Scandinavian
1960 Collected works (Nonserial)
General works
1961 Early through 1800
1962 1801-1900
1963 1901-
1964 General special
Including special aspects of the subject as a whole
Special topics
1965 Social usages for men
1966 Social usages for women
1967.A-Z Other special topics, A-Z
1967.B7 Boys
1967.C5 Children
1967.E8 Escort service
1967.F3 Family
1967.G5 Girls
Military, The see U750+
1967.N8 Nurses
1967.S5 Sick, The
1967.S75 Students
1969.A-Z Local, A-Z
Spanish and Portuguese
1980 Collected works (Nonserial)
General works
1981 Early through 1800
1982 1801-1900
1983 1901-
1984 General special
Including special aspects of the subject as a whole
Special topics

	General works
	Spanish and Portuguese
	Special topics -- Continued
1985	Social usages for men
1986	Social usages for women
1987.A-Z	Other special topics, A-Z
1987.B7	Boys
1987.C5	Children
1987.E8	Escort service
1987.F3	Family
1987.G5	Girls
	Military, The see U750+
1987.N8	Nurses
1987.S5	Sick, The
1987.S75	Students
1989.A-Z	Local, A-Z
	Swiss (French) see BJ1880+
	Swiss (German) see BJ1900+
	Swiss (Italian) see BJ1920+
2007.A-Z	Other languages, A-Z

Under each:

.x	*Collected works (nonserial)*
	General works
.x1	*Early through 1800*
.x2	*1801-1900*
.x3	*1901-*
.x4	*General special (including special aspects of the subject as a whole)*
.x5-.x7	*Special topics*
.x5	*Social usages for men*
.x6	*Social usages for women*
.x7	*Other special topics, A-Z*
.x7B7	*Boys*
.x7C5	*Children*
.x7E8	*Escort service*
.x7F3	*Family*
.x7G5	*Girls*
.x7N8	*Nurses*
.x7S5	*Sick, The*
.x7S75	*Students*
.x9A-.x9Z	*Local, A-Z*

	Religious etiquette
2010	General works
	Christian etiquette. Church etiquette
2018	Catholic
2019	Protestant
	Cf. BV4000+ Pastoral theology

Religious etiquette -- Continued
2019.5.A-Z Other religions, A-Z
2019.5.B8 Buddhist etiquette. Temple etiquette
2019.5.I8 Islamic etiquette. Mosque etiquette
2019.5.J4 Jewish etiquette. Synagogue etiquette
Mosque etiquette see BJ2019.5.I8
Synagogue etiquette see BJ2019.5.J4
Temple etiquette see BJ2019.5.B8
2020 Social secretaries
Etiquette of clothing and dress
General and for women see TT507
For men see TT618
Etiquette of entertaining. Duties of host and hostess. Hospitality
Cf. GT3410+ Manners and customs
2021-2028 General works (Table B-BJ6a)
2038 Dinners, luncheons, etc.
2041 Table etiquette
Cf. TX851+ Dining-room service
2043 Dance etiquette
Etiquette of special occasions
Weddings
Cf. HQ745 Wedding ceremonies, planning, forms, etc.
2051-2058 General works (Table B-BJ6a)
2065.A-Z Special topics, A-Z
2065.B45 Best man
2065.R44 Remarriage
2065.T53 Thank-you notes
2065.W43 Wedding attendants
2071 Funerals
2075.A-Z Special topics, A-Z
2078.A-Z Other, A-Z
2078.B3 Bar mitzvahs. Bat mitzvahs
Card etiquette. Stationery
2081-2088 General works (Table B-BJ6a)
2092-2095 Special topics
2092 Wedding stationery
2095.A-Z Other special topics, A-Z
2095.B5 Birth announcements
2095.G5 Greeting cards
2095.M4 Memorial cards
Etiquette of letter-writing
2100 Early works through 1800
For Samuel Richardson's letters written to and for particular friends see PR3660+
2101-2108 1801- (Table B-BJ6a)
2115.A-Z Special topics, A-Z

Etiquette of letter-writing
Special topics, A-Z -- Continued
2115.C65 Condolence notes
2115.T45 Thank-you notes
Cf. BJ2065.T53 Wedding etiquette
Etiquette of conversation
Cf. BJ2195 Telephone etiquette
Cf. LC15 Conversation and culture
2120 Early works through 1800
2121-2128 1801- (Table B-BJ6a)
2137 Etiquette of travel
Special topics
2139 Airplane travel
2140 Bus travel
2141 Railway travel
2142 Ship travel
2144 Hotels
2147 Riding and driving
2151 Bicycling
2155 Automobiling
2156.A-Z Other special topics, A-Z
2183 Club etiquette
2187-2188 Special topics
2187 Women's clubs
Cf. HS2501+ Clubs
Cf. JF515 Manuals and rules of parliamentary procedure
2188.A-Z Other special topics, A-Z
Cf. HS467 Etiquette for Freemasons
Business etiquette. Office etiquette see HF5389+
Library etiquette see Z716.43
2195 Telephone etiquette

The Library of Congress discontinued use of Table B-BJ1 in 1999. The full subarrangements for those philosophers who had formerly been subarranged by Table B-BJ1 are now included in the main text of the classification schedule.

0	Periodicals. Societies. Serials
1	Dictionaries
	Collected works
2.A2	Original (vernacular) texts. By date
2.A3	Editions with commentary. By editor
2.A5	Partial editions, selections, etc. By editor or date
	Translations
	Subarrange by translator or date
	Including translations with original texts
2.A7	Greek
2.A8	Latin
2.A9-Z	Other languages, A-Z
	e. g.
2.E5	English
2.F5	French
2.G5	German
2.I5	Italian
2.S5	Spanish and Portuguese
3.A-Z	Separate works. By title, A-Z
	Subarrange each by Table B-BJ13
4	Spurious and apocryphal works
5	Indexes, outlines, paraphrases, etc.
6	Biography and memoirs (Table B-BJ14)
7	Criticism and interpretation
8.A-Z	Special topics, A-Z
	For examples of topics, see B398 , B491

TABLES

0.A1A-.A1Z	Periodicals. Societies. Serials
0.A16A-.A16Z	Dictionaries
	Collected works
0.A2	Original (vernacular) texts. By date
0.A3	Editions with commentary. By editor
0.A5	Partial editions, selections, etc. By date
	Translations
	Subarranged by translator or date
	Including translations with original texts
0.A7	Greek
0.A8	Latin
0.A9-Z	Other languages, A-Z
	e. g.
0.E5	English
0.F5	French
0.G5	German
0.I5	Italian
0.S5	Spanish and Portuguese
1.A-Z	Separate works. By title, A-Z
	Subarrange each by Table B-BJ13
2	Spurious and apocryphal works
3	Biography and memoirs. Criticism and interpretation (Table B-BJ14)
4.A-Z	Special topics, A-Z
	For examples of topics, see B398 , B491

0.A1A-.A1Z	Periodicals. Societies. Serials
0.A16A-.A16Z	Dictionaries
	Collected works
0.A2	Original (vernacular) texts. By date
0.A3	Editions with commentary. By editor
0.A5	Partial editions, selections, etc. By date
	Translations
	Subarranged by translator or date
	Including translations with original texts
0.A7	Greek
0.A8	Latin
0.A9-Z	Other languages, A-Z
	e. g.
0.E5	English
0.F5	French
0.G5	German
0.I5	Italian
0.S5	Spanish and Portuguese
1.A-Z	Separate works. By title, A-Z
	Subarange each by Table B-BJ13
2	Spurious and apocryphal works
3	Biography and memoirs. Criticism and interpretation (Table B-BJ14)

TABLES

	Collected works
.A3	Original texts. By date
.A35	Partial editions, selections, etc. By editor or date
.A4	Translations. By language, A-Z, and date
.A5-.Z68	Separate works. By title, A-Z Subarrange each by Table B-BJ13
	Biography, autobiography, criticism, etc.
.Z69	Dictionaries, indexes, concordances, etc.
.Z7A1-.Z7A19	Periodicals. Societies. Serials
.Z7A3	Autobiography. By date
.Z7A4	Letters. By date
.Z7A5	Speeches. By date
.Z7A6-.Z7Z	General works

	Collected works
.x date	Original texts. By date
.x1	Partial editions, selections, etc. By editor or date
.x2A-.x2Z	Translations. By language, A-Z, and date
.x3A-.x3Z7	Separate works, A-Z
	Biography, autobiography, criticism, etc.
.x3Z8-.x3Z99	Dictionaries, indexes, concordances, etc.
.x4A1-.x4A19	Periodicals. Societies. Serials
.x4A3	Autobiography, diaries, etc. By date
.x4A4	Letters. By date
.x4A5	Speeches. By date
.x4A6-.x4Z	General works

	Collected works
.x date	Original texts. By date
.x11	Partial editions, selections, etc. By editor or date
.x12A-.x12Z	Translations. By language, A-Z, and date
.x13A-.x13Z7	Separate works, A-Z
	Biography, autobiography, criticism, etc.
.x13Z8-.x13Z99	Dictionaries, indexes, concordances, etc.
.x14A1-.x14A19	Periodicals. Societies. Serials
.x14A3	Autobiography, diaries, etc. By date
.x14A4	Letters. By date
.x14A5	Speeches. By date
.x14A6-.x14Z	General works

	Translations are usually classified with the original language
0	Early works
	Including Latin and Greek
1.A1-.A3	Polyglot
1.A4-Z	English and American
2	French
3	German
4	Italian
5	Spanish and Portuguese
6	Russian and other Slavic
8.A-Z	Other, A-Z

Translations are usually classified with the original language

1.A1-.A3	Polyglot
1.A4-Z	English and American
2	French
3	German
4	Italian
5	Spanish and Portuguese
6	Russian and other Slavic
8.A-Z	Other, A-Z

(.A1)	Greek texts see PA4279.A75+ (Plato); PA3891+ (Aristotle)
(.A2)	Editions with commentary For textual criticism, see PA4279.A75+ (Plato); PA3891+ (Aristotle) For interpretive commentary see B-BJ7 .A9+
(.A3)	Selections, paraphrases, etc. see PA4279.A75+ (Plato); PA3891+ (Aristotle)
	Translations (with or without notes.) By language Subarrange by translator For translations with extensive commentaries see B-BJ7 .A9+
(.A4)	Latin see PA4280 (Plato); PA3895.A5 (Aristotle)
.A5	English
.A6	French
.A7	German
.A8A-.A8Z	Other languages, A-Z
.A9-.Z	Commentaries, interpretation, and criticism

TABLES

The Library of Congress discontinued use of Table B-BJ8 in 1999. Topics that had formerly been subarranged by this table are now subarranged by Table B-BJ9.

Add the appropriate number from this table to the first number of the classification number span to which the table applies

0	Collected works (nonserial)
1	General works, biography (Collective), etc.
2	General special
3.A-Z	Special topics, A-Z
3.F54	Finalism
3.F74	French philosophy
3.G3	German philosophy
3.H86	Humanism
3.O5	Ontology
3.P48	Phenomenology
3.P6	Positivism
3.R3	Rationalism
4.A-Z	Individual philosophers, A-Z Subarrange each by Table B-BJ5

Add the appropriate number from this table to the first number of the classification number span to which the table applies

0 Original texts. By date

1 Editions with commentary. By editor

2 Selections, paraphrases, etc. By date

3 Translations (with or without notes). By language and translator or date

Assign two Cutter numbers, the first for language, the second for translator

4 Commentaries, interpretation, and criticism (with or without translations)

1 Original texts. By date

2 Translations (with or without notes). By language and translator or date

Assign two Cutter numbers, the first for language, the second for translator

3 Commentaries, interpretation, and criticism (with or without translations)

.A3	Original texts. By date
.A4-.Z5	Translations (with or without notes). By language and translator or date Assign two Cutter numbers, the first for language, the second for translator
.Z7	Commentaries, interpretation, and criticism (with or without translations)

.A1	Original edition (texts). By date
.A2	Editions with commentary. By editor
.A3	Selections. By date
.A4A-.A4Z	Translations (with or without notes). By language, A-Z, and date
.A5-.Z	Commentaries, interpretation, and criticism (with or without translations)

.x date	Original texts. By date
.x15	Selections, paraphrases, etc. By date
.x2	Translations. By language, A-Z, and date
.x3	Commentaries, interpretation, and criticism (with or without translations)

.A1-.A19	Periodicals. Societies. Serials
.A3	Autobiography. By date
.A4	Letters. By date
.A5	Speeches. By date
.A6-.Z	General works

1	Collected works (nonserial)
2	General works, collective biography, etc.
3.A-Z	Special topics, A-Z For examples of topics, see B398 , B491
4.A-Z	Individual philosophers, A-Z Subarrange each by Table B-BJ5

1	Collected works (nonserial)
2	General works
3	General special Including special aspects of the subject as a whole
4.A-Z	Special topics, A-Z
4.A52	Analysis
4.A73	Aristotelianism
4.D5	Dialectical materialism
4.E5	Enlightenment
4.H43	Hegelianism
4.H84	Humanism
4.I3	Idealism
4.I8	Islamic philosophy
4.M27	Man
4.M3	Materialism
4.M4	Messianism
4.N46	Neo-Scholasticism. Neo-Thomism
4.P36	Pantheism
4.P6	Positivism
4.R66	Romanticism
4.S4	Semantics
4.V34	Values
5.A-Z	Individual philosophers, A-Z Subarrange each by Table B-BJ5

TABLE FOR SUBARRANGEMENT OF THE PHILOSOPHY OF ASIAN AND AFRICAN COUNTRIES (5 NUMBERS)

B-BJ17

0	Collected works (nonserial)
1	General works
2	General special
	Including special aspects of the subject as a whole
3.A-Z	Special topics, A-Z
3.B8	Buddhist philosophy
3.C6	Confucian philosophy
3.D43	Death
3.D5	Dialectical materialism
3.E55	Enlightenment
3.E9	Existentialism
3.H37	Harmony
3.H4	Heaven
3.H8	Humanism
3.I3	Idealism
3.I58	Introspection
3.L53	Life
3.M27	Man
3.M3	Materialism
3.N38	Naturalism
3.N45	Neo-Confucianism
3.O84	Other (Philosophy)
3.P7	Pragmatism
3.R4	Realism
3.S44	Self
4.A-Z	Individual philosophers, A-Z
	Subarrange each by Table B-BJ5

.x	Collected works (nonserial). General works. General special
.x2A-.x2Z	Special topics, A-Z
.x2B8	Buddhist philosophy
.x2C6	Confucian philosophy
.x2D5	Dialectical materialism
.x2E9	Existentialism
.x2H4	Heaven
.x2H8	Humanism
.x2I3	Idealism
.x2I58	Introspection
.x2M27	Man
.x2M3	Materialism
.x2N38	Naturalism
.x2N45	Neo-Confucianism
.x2P7	Pragmatism
.x2R4	Realism
.x3A-.x3Z	Individual philosophers, A-Z

TABLES

For the distinction in use between Classes BJ and PA, see note at B165+

.x Collected works (nonserial)

.x2 Separate works

.x3 Biography and criticism

For the distinction in use between Classes BJ and PA, see note at B165+

1	Collected works (nonserial)
2	Separate works
3	Biography and criticism

1 Collected works (nonserial)
2 General works. History
3.A-Z Special topics, A-Z
  For list of topics, see BJ324.A+
4.A-Z Ethical philosophers, A-Z
  Subarrange each by Table B-BJ19

(.x)	Original texts and Latin translations see PA4279+
.x2A-.x2Z	Translations. By language, A-Z, and date
.x3	Commentaries, interpretations, criticism

A

A priori (Epistemology): BD181.3
Abbagnano, Nicola, 1901-1990: B3611.A23+
Abbot, Francis Ellingwood, 1836-1903: B945.A26+
Abbt, Thomas, 1738-1766: B2632
'Abd al-Razzāq al-Qāshānī, d. 1330?: B748.A14+
Abduction
  Logic: BC199.A26
Abelard, Peter, 1079-1142: B765.A2+
Abhedānanda, Swami, 1866-1939: B5134.A22+
Abhinavagupta, Rajanaka: B133.A35+
Ability
  Child psychology: BF723.A25
  Infant psychology: BF720.A24
Ability testing: BF431+
Abnormalities of the will: BF635
Abraham ben David, ha-Levi: B759.A2+
Abramowski, Edward, 1868-1918: B4691.A2+
Absent-mindedness
  Psychology: BF323.A27
Absolute, The
  Ontology: BD416
  Philosophy
    German philosophy
      Fichte: B2849.A2
      Hegel: B2949.A28
      Schelling: B2899.A23
    Scottish philosophy
      Hamilton: B1428.A25
Abstraction
  Child psychology: BF723.A26
  Epistemology: BD235
  Philosophy
    English philosophy
      Berkeley: B1349.A2
    Greek philosophy
      Plato: B398.A25
  Psychology: BF443+
  Testing of
    Psychology: BF443.4+
Absurd (Philosophy): B105.A3
Abū al-Barakāt Hibat Allāh ibn 'Alī, fl. 1077-1164: B748.A2+
Abū al-Faraj 'Abd Allāh ibn al-Tayyib, d. 1043: B748.A245+
Abū Ḥayyān al-Tawḥīdī, 'Alī ibn Muḥammad, 10th cent.: B748.A25+
Academic achievement and personality: BF698.9.A3
Academy, The (Greek philosophy): B338
Accident
  Philosophy
    Greek philosophy
      Aristotle: B491.A24
Accidents
  Astrology: BF1729.A25
Achievement
  Child psychology: BF723.P365
Achievement motivation
  Child psychology: BF723.M56
Acintyabhedābheda: B132.A27
Ackley, H.A.
  Spirit messages: BF1311.A2
Acosta, Uriel, ca. 1585-1640: B3899.A3+
Acquisitiveness (Personality traits): BF698.35.A36
Acri, Francesco, 1834-1913: B3611.A3+
Act
  Logic: BC199.A28
  Philosophy: B105.A35
    French philosophy
      Descartes: B1878.A27
    German philosophy
      Hegel: B2949.A3
      Kant: B2799.A28
    Greek philosophy
      Aristotle: B491.A27
      Plato: B398.A3
    Medieval philosophy: B738.A37
Active intellect
  Philosophy
    Medieval philosophy: B738.S68
Active vs. meditative life (Ethics): BJ1493

Aggressiveness
  Child psychology: BF723.A35
  Psychoanalysis: BF175.5.A36
  Psychology: BF575.A3
Aging
  Psychology: BF724.55.A35
Agitation
  Psychology: BF575.A35
Agnosticism
  Philosophy: B808.A+
Agriculture and astrology: BF1729.A37
Agriculture and ethics: BJ52.5
Agrippa, Marcus Vipsanius: B535.A3+
Agrippa von Nettesheim, Heinrich Cornelius
  Occult sciences: BF1598.A4
Agrippa von Nettesheim, Heinrich Cornelius, 1486?-1535: B781.A3+
Agushewitz, Reuben: B945.A3+
Ahankara: B132.A43
Ahimsa
  Ethics
    Ancient Indic ethics: BJ123.A45
Aḥmad ibn al-Ṭayyib, al-Sarakhsī, d. 899: B748.A36+
Ai, Siqi, 1910-1966: B5234.A35+
Ailly, Pierre d', 1350-1420?: B765.A3+
Air signs (Astrology): BF1727.9.A37
Airplane travel
  Etiquette: BJ2139
Ajdukiewica, Kazimierz: B4691.A4+
Akan
  Ethics: BJ982.A38
Akashic records
  Psychic research: BF1045.A44
Akrasia
  Ethics
    Medieval: BJ251.A37
Akṣara: B132.A5
Alanus, de Insulis, d. 1202: B765.A346+
Albanian philosophy: B4851+
Albelda, Moses ben Jacob, 15th/16th cent.: B759.A333+
Albergamo, F. (Francesco), 1896-: B3611.A5+
Albert, Hans, 1921-: B3199.A39+
Alberti, Leon Battista, 1404-1472: B765.A35+
Albertus, de Saxonia, d. 1390: B765.A39+
Albertus magnus
  Occult sciences: BF1598.A5
Albertus, Magnus, Saint, 1193?-1280.: B765.A4+
Albinus: B535.A4+
Alcidamas, 4th cent. B.C.: B293.A2+
Alcinous: B535.A4+
Alcohol
  Psychological effect: BF209.A43
Alcoholism
  Astrology: BF1729.A45
Alcott, Amos Bronson, 1799-1888: B908.A5+
Alcuin, 735-804: B765.A6+
Alembert, Jean Le Rond d', 1717-1783: B1930+
Alexander, Hartley Burr, 1873-1939: B945.A5+
Alexander, of Aegae: B535.A5+
Alexander, of Aphrodisias: B535.A6+
Alexander, of Hales, ca. 1185-1245: B765.A7+
Alexander, Samuel, 1859-1938: B1618.A4+
Alexander technique
  Psychology: BF172
Alexandrian and early Christian philosophy: B630+
Alfarabi: B753.F3+
Alfred, of Sareshel: B765.A75+
Algerian philosophy: B5355+
Alhazen, 965-1039: B748.A39+
Alicea, Dennis: B1029.A55+
Alien abduction
  Occult sciences: BF2050+
Alien-human encounters: BF2050+
Alienation
  Philosophy: B808.2.A+
    French philosophy
      Rousseau: B2138.A55
    German philosophy
      Hegel: B2949.A5

André, Yves Marie, 1675-1764: B1939.A5+
Andronicus, of Rhodes: B535.A7+
Angels
  Divinations: BF1779.A53
  Magic: BF1623.A53
  Ontology: BD427
  Philosophy
    German philosophy
      Leibniz: B2599.A54
Anger
  Adolescent psychology: BF724.3.A55
  Child psychology: BF723.A4
  Ethics: BJ1535.A6
  Jewish ethics: BJ1286.A64
  Psychology: BF575.A5
Anima
  Dreaming: BF1099.A54
  Psychoanalysis: BF175.5.A52
Animal and human psychology: BF660+
Animal ghosts
  Occultism: BF1484
Animal magnetism
  Parapsychology: BF1111+
Animals
  Astrology: BF1728.3
  Child psychology: BF723.A45
  Expression of the emotions: BF593
  Fortune-telling: BF1891.A54
  Magic: BF1623.A55
  Philosophy: B105.A55
    German philosophy
      Nietzsche: B3318.A54
Animism
  Aesthetics: BH301.A55
  Philosophy: B808.6.A+
Animosity, Sexual (Psychology): BF692.15
Animus
  Dreaming: BF1099.A54
  Psychoanalysis: BF175.5.A53
Anne Boleyn
  Spirit messages: BF1311.A55
Annus mirabilis: BF1777
Anonymous Iamblichi, 5th/4th cent. B.C.: B293.A25+
Anscombe, G. E. M. (Gertrude Elizabeth Margaret): B1618.A57+
Anselm, of Laon, d. 1117: B765.A79+
Anselm, Saint, Archbishop of Canterbury, 1033-1109: B765.A8+
Anthropology
  Philosophy
    Greek philosophy
      Democritus: B299.A58
Anthropology and ethics: BJ52
Anthropology and parapsychology: BF1045.A65
Anti-phrenology: BF885.A5
Anticipation
  Philosophy: B105.E87
Antinomy
  Philosophy
    German philosophy
      Kant: B2799.A6
    Greek philosophy: B187.A6
Antipathy
  Child psychology: BF723.P75
Antiphon, of Athens: B293.A26+
Antisemitism
  Philosophy
    Danish philosophy
      Kierkegaard: B4378.A52
Antiseri, Dario: B3611.A64+
Antisthenes, ca. 445-ca. 360 B.C.: B293.A3+
Antonio de Padova, Saint
  Spirit messages: BF1311.A57
Antonovich, M. (Maksim), 1835-1918: B4238.A5+
Anus (Psychoanalysis): BF175.5.A55
Anxiety
  Adolescent psychology: BF724.3.A57
  Child psychology: BF723.A5
  Ethics: BJ1500.A59
  Infant psychology: BF720.A58
  Philosophy
    Danish philosophy
      Kierkegaard: B4378.A53
  Psychology: BF575.A6
Apel, Karl-Otto: B3199.A6+
Apollodorus, of Athens: B535.A8+
Apollonius, of Tyana: B536.A2+

Apollonius, of Tyana
  Spirit messages: BF1311.A6
Apologists (Alexandrian and early
  Christian philosophy): B635
Apologizing
  Psychology: BF575.A75
Aporia
  Philosophy
    Greek philosophy: B187.A66
Appartions
  Occultism: BF1444+
Appelbaum, David: B945.A66+
Apperception
  Intelligence testing: BF433.A6
  Philosophy
    German philosophy
      Kant: B2799.A7
  Psychology: BF321
Appleton, Charles Edward Cutts Birch,
  1841-1879: B1618.A7+
Application (Phrenology): BF885.A6
Applied psychology: BF636+
Appropriateness (Ethics): BJ1418.5
Apuleius: B536.A3+
Aquarius (Astrology): BF1727.7
Arabian and Moorish philosophers
  Medieval: B740+
Arabic astrology: BF1714.A6
Arabic logic, Medieval
  History: BC34+
Arabic philosophy (Influence on
  Medieval European thought): B723
Aranguren, José Luis L., 1909-1996:
  B4568.A7+
Arantes, Paulo Eduardo: B1044.A76+
Arata, Carlo: B3611.A73+
Arcesilaus: B536.A4+
Archaeology and parapsychology:
  BF1045.A74
Archetype (Psychoanalysis):
  BF175.5.A72
Archetypes (Astrology): BF1729.A68
Architecture
  Philosophy
    French philosophy
      Descartes: B1878.A73
Architecture (Astrology): BF1729.A7
Archytas, of Tarentum: B213
Ardao, Arturo: B1079.A72+
Ardigò, Roberto, 1828-1920: B3612
Arendt, Hannah, 1906-1975:
  B945.A69+
Argens, Jean Baptiste de Boyer,
  marquis d', 1704-1771: B1939.A6+
Argentine philosophy: B1030+
Argumentation
  Ancient Oriental logic: BC26.A6
  Logic: BC177
    History: BC21.A6
Aries (Astrology): BF1727
Aristippus, 435?-356? B.C.: B293.A7+
Aristocles, of Messene: B536.A47+
Ariston, of Chios: B536.A5+
Aristotle: B400+
  Influence on Medieval European
    thought: B725
Aristoxenus: B536.A6+
Armenian philosophy (Ancient):
  B149.2+
Armstrong, David Malet: B5704.A75+
Arnauld, Antoine, 1612-1694:
  B1824.A86+
Arnellos, Iōannēs G., 1870-1948:
  B3515.A75+
Arnobius, of Sicca: B650.A8+
Arnoldt, Emil, 1828-1905: B3199.A7+
Aronne, Maurizio
  Spirit messages: BF1311.A7
Art
  Philosophy
    Greek philosophy
      Aristotle: B491.A7
    Netherlands philosophy
      Spinoza: B3999.A7
  Spirit art: BF1313
Art and parapsychology: BF1045.A78
Art for art's sake: BH301.A7
Artificial life
  Ontology: BD418.8
Asaka, Gonsai, 1791-1860:
  B5244.A79+
Ascendant (Astrology): BF1717

Asceticism
  Ethics
    Greek and Roman ethics: BJ171.A82
  Philosophy
    Greek philosophy
      Plato: B398.A8
Asceticism and hedonism (Ethics): BJ1491
Ashino, Tokurin, 1696-1776: B5244.A85+
Asian Americans (Intelligence testing): BF432.A84
Asian astrology: BF1714.A75
Asian philosophy: B5000+
Aspasius: B536.A7+
Aspects
  Astrology: BF1717.2+
Assertiveness
  Child psychology: BF723.A74
  Psychology: BF575.A85
    Adolescent psychology: BF724.3.A77
Assessment
  Child psychology: BF722.3+
Assessment of personality: BF698.4
Association of ideas (Psychology): BF365+
Association tests: BF698.8.A8
Associationalism (Philosophy): B816.A+
Assyria-Babylonian philosophy: B145+
Assyro-Babylonian astrology: BF1714.A86
Asteroids
  Astrology: BF1724.5
Astrada, Carlos, 1894-: B1034.A8+
Astral body (Spiritualism): BF1389.A7
Astral projection (Spiritualism): BF1389.A7
Astrological geomancy (Divinations): BF1779.A88
Astrology and cards: BF1879.A7
Astrology and politics: BF1729.P6
Astrology, Buddhist: BF1714.B7
Astronautics
  Philosophy: B105.A75
Astronautics and ethics: BJ60
Ataraxia (Greek philosophy): B187.A8
Athanasius, Saint, Patriarch of Alexandria, d. 373: B653
Atheism
  Philosophy
    Italian philosophy: B3609.A8
Atheism and spiritualism: BF1275.A8
Atheism, Charge of
  Philosophy
    German philosophy
      Fichte: B2849.A8
Athenaeus, of Naucratis: B536.A75+
Athenagoras, 2nd cent.
  Philosophy: B654
Athīr al-Dīn al-Abharī, al-Mufaḍḍal ibn ʻUmar, d. 1265: B748.A56+
Atlantis
  Philosophy
    Greek philosophy
      Plato: B398.A85
  Spirit messages: BF1311.A8
Ātman: B132.A8
Atomic theory (Arabian philosophy): B745.A7
Atomism
  Cosmology: BD646
  Philosophy
    Greek philosophy: B193
      Democritus: B299.A86
    Indic philosophy: B132.A83
Attachment behavior
  Child psychology: BF723.A75
  Infant psychology: BF720.A83
  Psychology: BF575.A86
    Adolescent psychology: BF724.3.A84
Attention
  Child psychology: BF723.A755
  Infant psychology: BF720.A85
  Psychology: BF321
Attention-seeking
  Psychology
    Applied psychology: BF637.A77
Attentional and Interpersonal Style Inventory: BF698.8.A88
Atticus, Titus Pomponius: B536.A8+

Bashfulness
  Adolescent psychology: BF724.3.B36
  Child psychology: BF723.B3
  Psychology: BF575.B3
Basic Personality Inventory: BF698.8.B37
Basilides, fl. 117-140: B658
Bat mitzvahs
  Etiquette: BJ2078.B3
Bataille, Georges, 1897-1962: B2430.B3395+
Baṭalyawsī, ʻAbd Allāh ibn Muḥammad, 1052 or 3-1127: B753.B34+
Battaglia, Felice, 1902-1977: B3613.B35+
Bauch, Bruno, 1877-1942: B3209.B3+
Baudrillard, Jean, 1929-2007: B2430.B3397+
Baumeister, Friedrich Christian, 1709-1785: B2634
Baumgarten, Alexander Gottlieb, 1714-1762: B2637
Baumgarten, Arthur, 1884-1966: B3209.B36+
Bautain, L. (Louis), 1796-1867: B2192.B3+
Bax, Ernest Belfort, 1854-1926: B1618.B3+
Bayle, Pierre, 1647-1706: B1825
Beasley, Frederick, 1777-1845: B908.B3+
Beattie, James, 1735-1803: B1403.B5+
Beauty, Personal
  Child psychology: BF723.B37
Beauvoir, Simone de, 1908-1986: B2430.B34+
Beck, Friedrich Alfred, 1899-: B3209.B5+
Beck, Jakob Sigismund, 1761-1840: B2958
Beck, Lewis White: B945.B376+
Becker, Oskar, 1889-1964: B3209.B56+
Becoming
  Ontology: BD372
Becoming
  Philosophy
    Danish philosophy
      Kierkegaard: B4378.B43
Bede, the Venerable, Saint, 673-735: B765.B3+
Beginning
  Cosmology: BD638
  Philosophy
    German philosophy
      Hegel: B2949.B44
Behavior
  Sexual behavior (Psychology): BF692+
Behavior Assessment System for Children: BF722.35.B44
Behavior models, Human: BF39.3
Behavior modification
  Psychology
    Applied psychology: BF637.B4
Behavioral and Emotional Rating Scale: BF722.35.B46
Behavioral assessment (Psychological tests and testing): BF176.5
Behavioral psychology: BF199
Behaviorism (Psychology): BF199
Being, Attributes of (Ontology): BD352
Being (Ontology): BD331
Bekker, Balthasar, 1634-1698: B2545
Belarusian philosophy: B4756+
Belgian philosophy: B4151+
Belief
  Philosophy
    German philosophy
      Kant: B2799.B4
  Psychology of: BF773
Belief and doubt
  Epistemology: BD215
  Logic: BC199.B4
  Philosophy
    Scottish philosophy
      Hume: B1499.B4
Belinsky, Vissarion Grigoryevich, 1811-1848: B4238.B3+
Bellamy, Edward, 1850-1898: B945.B4+
Bello, Andrés, 1781-1865: B1084.B45+

Biofeedback training
  Psychology: BF319.5.B5
Biographical methods (Psychology):
  BF39.4
Biological aspects
  Personality: BF698.9.B5
Biological rhythms
  Psychology
    Applied psychology: BF637.B55
Biology and ethics: BJ58
Biomagnetism (Parapsychology):
  BF1111+
Biorhythm charting
  Psychology
    Applied psychology: BF637.B55
Birds
  Fortune telling: BF1891.B5
Birkman Method of Personality Testing:
  BF698.8.B47
Birth
  Ontology: BD443
  Premature birth
    Infant psychology: BF720.P7
Birth announcements
  Etiquette: BJ2095.B5
Birth control
  Astrology: BF1729.B4
Birth order
  Child psychology: BF723.B5
Birthdays
  Astrology: BF1729.B45
  Fortune-telling: BF1891.B54
Birthplaces (Astrology): BF1729.B5
Bishop, Washington Irving: BF1127.B5
Bitō, Jishū, 1747-1814: B5244.B38+
Black
  Aesthetics: BH301.B53
Black Foot, Chief
  Spirit messages: BF1311.B57
Black magic: BF1585+
Blacks
  Intelligence testing: BF432.N5
Blackwell, Antoinette Louisa Brown,
  1825-1921: B945.B5+
Blacky pictures test: BF698.8.B5
Blaga, Lucian, 1895-1961: B4825.B55+
Blakey, Robert, 1795-1878: B1574.B4+
Blasco Ibáñez, Vincente
  Spirit messages: BF1311.B6
Blavatsky, Helena P.
  Spirit messages: BF1311.B65
Blēsidēs, Thrasyboulos St.: B3515.B5+
Bloch, Ernst, 1885-1977: B3209.B75+
Blondel, Maurice, 1861-1949:
  B2430.B58+
Blum, Robert, 1807-1848
  Spirit messages: BF1311.B66
Blumbenberg, Hans: B3209.B83+
Bodies of man (Occult sciences):
  BF1442.B63
Bodin, Jean, 1530-1596: B781.B3+
Body
  Ethics of: BJ1695
  Human body
    Epistemology: BD214.5
    Philosophy: B105.B64
      German philosophy
        Nietzsche: B3318.H85
      Greek philosophy
        Plato: B398.B65
      Japanese philosophy: B5243.H84
Body and mind
  Philosophy: B105.M53
Body, Human
  Philosophy
    French philosophy: B1809.B62
Body image
  Psychoanalysis: BF175.5.B64
  Psychology
    Adolescent psychology:
      BF724.3.B55
    Child psychology: BF723.B6
    Differential psychology:
      BF697.5.B63
Body image in women
  Witchcraft: BF1572.B63
Body language
  Applied psychology: BF637.N66
  Psychology
    Child psychology: BF723.C57
Body schema
  Child psychology: BF723.B63
Body size and intelligence: BF433.B6

Boer, Theodorus de, 1932-: B4051.B62+
Boethius, d. 524
  Philosophy: B659
Boethius, of Dacia, 13th cent.: B765.B68+
Bofill, Jaime, 1910-1965: B4568.B63+
Böhme, Jakob, 1575-1624: B781.B6+
Bolingbroke, Henry St. John, Viscount, 1678-1751: B1355+
Bolívar, Simón
  Spirit messages: BF1311.B67
Bolivian philosophy: B1035+
Boltzmann, Ludwig, 1844-1906: B3209.B87+
Bolzano, Bernard, 1781-1848: B4805.B65+
Bon (Tibetan religion)
  Astrology): BF1714.B65
Bonald, Louis-Gabriel-Ambroise, vicomte de, 1754-1840: B2194.B4+
Bonatelli, Francesco, 1830-1911: B3613.B53+
Bonaventure, Saint, Cardinal, ca. 1217-1274: B765.B7+
Bonavino, Cristoforo: B3618
Bones
  Fortune-telling: BF1891.B64
Bonnet, Charles, 1720-1793: B1940+
Bontadini, Gustavo: B3613.B56+
Book collecting
  Philosophy
    Danish philosophy
      Kierkegaard: B4378.B66
Books
  Fortune telling: BF1891.B66
Books and reading
  Philosophy
    Danish philosophy
      Kierkegaard: B4378.B66
Boreas, Theophilos, 1870-: B3515.B6+
Boredom
  Ethics: BJ1499.B6
  Psychology: BF575.B67
    Adolescent psychology: BF724.3.B6
Borella, Jean: B2430.B5876+
Bori, Pier Cesare: B3613.B57+
Borley rectory: BF1030.B6
Bosanquet, Bernard, 1848-1923: B1618.B5+
Bosseut, Jacques Bénigne, 1627-1704: B1950+
Boström, Christopher Jacob, 1797-1866: B4480+
Botti, Luigi, 1879-: B3613.B6+
Boutroux, Émile, 1845-1921: B2194.B5+
Bouwsma, O.K.: B945.B6+
Bovillus, Carolus, 1479-1567: B781.B7+
Bowman, Archibald Allan, 1883-1936: B1618.B6+
Bowne, Borden Parker: B945.B7+
Boyle, Robert, 1627-1691: B1201.B43+
Boys
  Ethics: BJ1641+
Boys, Social usages for
  American: BJ1857.B7
  British: BJ1877.B7
  French: BJ1887.B7
  German: BJ1907.B7
  Italian: BJ1927.B7
  Portuguese: BJ1987.B7
  Russian: BJ1947.B7
  Scandinavian: BJ1967.B7
  Spanish: BJ1987.B7
Bradley, F. H. (Francis Herbert), 1846-1924: B1618.B7+
Bradwardine, Thomas, 1290?-1349: B765.B77+
Brāhmaṇas: B132.B7
Brahmanism
  Philosophy
    German philosophy
      Nietzsche: B3318.B73
Brain-damaged persons (Intelligence testing): BF432.B7
Brain-mind identity theory: B105.M55
Brainwashing: BF633
Branford, Benchara: B1618.B743+
Bräuer, Ernst Wasa, 1889-: B3210
Brazilian philosophy: B1040+

Breaking habits
  Psychology: BF337.B74
Breath
  Astrology: BF1729.B7
Breath and breathing
  Fortune-telling: BF1891.B7
Brentano, Franz Clemens, 1838-1917: B3212
Brentano, Margherita von, 1922-1995: B3213.B2+
Brescia, Giuseppe: B3613.B76+
Brightness perception
  Vision: BF241.7
Brinkley, Richard: B765.B78+
British royalty
  Dreaming: BF1099.R6
Brito, Raymundo de Farias, 1862-1917: B1044.B7+
Bröchner, H. (Hans), 1820-1875: B4353
Brockman, John, 1941-: B945.B745+
Brod, Max, 1884-1968: B3213.B4+
Brontë, Charlotte: BF416.B7
Brook Farm: B905
Brooke, Robert Greville, Baron, 1607-1643: B1201.B5+
Brotherliness
  Ethics: BJ1533.B7
Brothers and sisters
  Astrology: BF1729.B73
  Child psychology: BF723.S43
Brothers of Purity or Sincerity: B746
Brothers, Richard: BF1815.B8
Brown, Norman Oliver, 1913-2002: B945.B748+
Brown, Thomas, 1778-1820: B1405+
Browne, Peter, ca. 1666-1735: B1361
Browne, Thomas, Sir, 1605-1682: B1201.B6+
Brownson, Orestes Augustus, 1803-1876: B908.B6+
Brühlmann, Otto, 1883-: B3213.B6+
Bruliński, Władysław, 1915-: B4691.B76+
Brunner, Constantin, 1862-1937: B3213.B7+
Bruno, Giordano, 1548-1600: B783
Brunschvicg, Léon, 1869-1944: B2430.B75+
Buber, Martin, 1878-1965: B3213.B8+
Büchner, Ludwig, 1824-1899: B3215
Buddeus, Joannes Franciscus, 1667-1729: B2645+
Buddhism
  Philosophy: B162
    German philosophy
      Nietzsche: B3318.B83
Buddhist astrology: BF1714.B7
Buddhist ethics: BJ1289
Buddhist etiquette: BJ2019.5.B8
Buddhist logic, Ancient
  History: BC25+
Budé, Guillaume, 1468-1540: B784.B5
Buffier, Claude, 1661-1737: B1959.B7+
Buffon, Georges Louis Leclerc, comte de, 1707-1788: B1960+
Building
  Astrology: BF1729.B75
Bulaydī, Muḥammad ibn Muḥammad, d. 1762 or 3: B753.B82+
Bulgakov, Sergeĭ Nikolaevich, 1871-1944: B4238.B8+
Bulgarian philosophy: B4831+
Bullying
  Applied psychology: BF637.B85
Bunge, Carlos O. (Carlos Octavio), 1875-1918: B1034.B8+
Burge, Tyler: B945.B768+
Buridan, Jean, 1300-1358: B765.B84+
Burke, John Benjamin Butler, 1873-: B1618.B77+
Burke, Kenneth, 1897-1993: B945.B77+
Burlaeus, Gualterus, 1275-1345?: B765.B848+
Burmese astrology: BF1714.B8
Burmese philosophy: B5140+
Burns, Cecil Delisle, 1879-1942: B1618.B8+
Burski, Adam, 1560-1611: B4691.B87+
Burthogge, Richard, 1638?-ca. 1700: B1201.B7+
Burton, Asa, 1752-1836: B908.B7+

Cavell, Stanley, 1926-: B945.C27+
Cavendish, Margaret, Duchess of Newcastle: B1299.N27+
Celebrities
  Graphology: BF905.C44
  Horoscopes: BF1728.2.C44
Celebrities' hands (Psychology): BF935.C3
Celms, Teodors, 1893-1989: B4735.C44+
Celsus, Platonic philosopher, fl. 180: B538.C2+
Celtic astrology: BF1714.C44
Cemeteries, Haunted: BF1474.3
Ceretti, Pietro, 1823-1884: B3614.C3+
Cerf, Walter, 1907-2001: B945.C37+
Certeau, Michel de: B2430.C365+
Certification
  Psychologists: BF80.8
Certitude
  Epistemology: BC171
  Logic: BC171
Chaadaev, P. I͡A. (Petr I͡Akovlevich), 1794-1856: B4238.C47+
Chakras (Occult sciences): BF1442.C53
Chalybäus, Heinrich Moritz, 1796-1862: B2967.C52+
Chan, Jo-shui, 1466-1560: B128.C26+
Chance
  Child psychology: BF723.C4
  Cosmology: BD595
  Philosophy
    Greek philosophy
      Democritis: B299.C47
Chang, Shih, 1133-1180: B128.C28+
Chang, Tai-nien: B5234.C4492+
Chang, Tsai, 1020-1077: B128.C31+
Chang, Tung-sun, 1886-: B5234.C4496+
Chang, Yuan-fu: B5234.C45+
Change
  Logic: BC199.C47
  Ontology: BD373
  Philosophy
    Indic philosophy: B132.C52
  Psychology: BF471
Change
  Psychology
    Applied psychology: BF637.C4
Channeling: BF1281+
Channing, William Ellery, 1780-1842: B908.C4+
Chao, Jui, 8th cent.: B128.C33+
Character
  Ethics: BJ324.C48, BJ1518+
  Psychology: BF818
    Child psychology: BF723.C43
Charisma (Personality traits): BF698.35.C45
Charity (Jewish ethics): BJ1286.C5
Charm
  Aesthetics: BH301.C4
  Virtues: BJ1533.C37
  Women: BJ1609+
Charms
  Demonology: BF1561
Charron, Pierre, 1541-1603: B785.C5+
Chartier, Émile, 1868-1951: B2430.C49+
Chasdai ben Abraham Crescas: B759.C4+
Chastity
  Ethics: BJ1533.C4
Chattopadhyaya, Debiprasad: B5134.C47+
Cheerfulness
  Ethics: BJ1533.C5
Chelpanov, Georgiĭ Ivanovich, 1862-1936: B4238.C55+
Ch'en Hsien-chang, 1428-1500: B128.C346+
Ch'en, Liang, 1143-1194: B128.C347+
Cheng: B127.C48
Ch'eng, Chung-ying, 1935-: B5234.C495+
Ch'eng, Hao, 1032-1085: B128.C358+
Cheng, Hsüan, 127-200: B128.C359+
Ch'eng, I, 1033-1107: B128.C36+
Cheng, Kuan-ying, 1842-1922: B5234.C52+
Cheng, Xuanying, fl. 631-655: B128.C377+

Cohen, Jacques Judah, 1883-: B1618.C65+
Cohen, Morris Raphael, 1880-1947: B945.C5+
Cohn, Jonas, 1869-1947: B3216.C76+
Coimbra, Leonardo, 1883-1936: B4598.C6+
Coincidence
  Parapsychology: BF1175
  Psychoanalysis: BF175.5.C65
Coins
  Divinations: BF1779.C56
Coleridge, Samuel Taylor, 1772-1834: B1583
College students
  Witchcraft: BF1571.5.C64
Colleges, Haunted: BF1478
Colli, Giorgio: B3614.C56+
Collier, Arthur, 1680-1732: B1366.C6+
Collingwood, R. G. (Robin George), 1889-1943: B1618.C7+
Collins, Anthony, 1676-1729: B1367
Colombian philosophy: B1050+
Colonna, Egidio, Archbishop of Bourges, ca. 1243-1316: B765.C6+
Color
  Aesthetics: BH301.C6
  Fortune-telling: BF1891.C64
  Memory: BF378.C7
  Philosophy: B105.C455
    Greek philosophy: B187.C62
  Psychic research: BF1045.C6
  Psychology: BF789.C7
Color hearing (Psychology): BF497
Color music (Psychology): BF497
Color pyramid test: BF698.8.C6
Color symbolism (Magic): BF1623.C6
Color vision
  Child psychology: BF723.C55
Colored audition (Psychology): BF497
Colorni, Eugenio: B3614.C58+
Columbus test: BF698.8.C64
Combe, George: BF869.C6
Comets
  Divinations: BF1779.C6
Comic, The
  Aesthetics: BH301.C7
Comic, The
  Philosophy: B105.C456
    German philosophy
      Nietzsche: B3318.C64
    Greek philosophy
      Plato: B398.C63
Commands (Logic): BC199.C5
Commitment
  Psychology: BF619
Common sense (Philosophy): B105.C457
Commonplace book: B1340+
Communication
  Psychology: BF76.7+
    Adolescent psychology: BF724.3.C6
    Applied psychology: BF637.C45
    Child psychology: BF723.C57
    Infant psychology: BF720.C65
Communication and Symbolic Behavior Scales: BF722.35.C63
Communication and Symbolic Behavior Scales Developmental Profile: BF722.35.C63
Communication of information
  Philosophy: B52.66+
Communication with discarnate spirits (Parapsychology): BF1227.2+
Communist ethics (20th century): BJ1390
Communities
  Philosophy: B105.C46
    German philosophy
      Kant: B2799.C66
Comparative ethics: BJ69
Comparative philosophy: B799
Comparative physiognomy: BF861.C5
Comparative psychology: BF660+
Comparetti, Piero Milani: B3614.C6+
Comparison
  Child psychology: BF723.C58
  Epistemology: BD236
  Psychology: BF446
Compassion
  Ethics: BJ1475
Compensation (Philosophy): B105.C47

Compensation (Psychology): BF337.C65
Competence
  Child psychology: BF723.P365
Competition
  Adolescent psychology: BF724.3.C63
  Child psychology: BF723.C6
  Psychology
    Applied psychology: BF637.C47
Complexity (Philosophy): B105.C473
Comprehension
  Child psychology: BF723.C64
  Philosophy
    German philosophy
      Kant: B2799.C78
  Psychology: BF325
Comprehensive Test of Nonverbal Intelligence: BF432.5.C67
Compromise
  Ethics: BJ1430+
Computer applications
  Psychological tests: BF176.2
Computer models and simulation (Psychology): BF39.5
Computer network resources
  Parapsychology: BF1024.65
  Philosophy: B52.68
  Psychology: BF76.78
Comradeship
  Ethics: BJ1533.C56
Comrey Personality Scales: BF698.8.C66
Comte, Auguste,1798-1857: B2200+
Comte-Sponville, André: B2430.C635+
Conceit vs. self-esteem
  Ethics: BJ1533.S3
Concept
  Philosophy
    German philosophy
      Hegel: B2949.C49
Concepts
  Logic: BC199.C55
  Philosophy
    English philosophy
      Berkeley: B1349.C6
Conceptualism (Medieval philosophy): B731
Conceptualization
  Psychology: BF443+
  Testing of
    Psychology: BF443.4+
Concord
  Ethics: BJ1533.C58
Concord school of philosophy: B905
Concrete operations
  Child psychology: BF723.C645
Concrete, The
  Ontology: BD332
  Philosophy
    German philosophy
      Hegel: B2949.C5
Condillac, Étienne Bonnet de, 1714-1780: B1980+
Conditionals (Logic): BC199.C56
Conditioned and unconditioned (Ontology): BD411
Conditioned response
  Psychology: BF319+
Condolence notes
  Letter-writing etiquette: BJ2115.C65
Condorcet, Jean-Antoine-Nicolas de Caritat, marquis de, 1743-1794: B1990+
Conduct of life
  Ethics: BJ1545+
  Psychology
    Applied psychology: BF637.C5
Confession
  Psychology: BF634
Confidence
  Ethics: BJ1533.C6
Conflict
  Adolescent psychology: BF724.3.C65
  Child psychology: BF723.C647
  Graphology: BF905.C6
Conflict of opposites (Dialectical materialism): B809.833
Confucian ethics: BJ1289.3
Confucian philosophy: B127.C65
  East Asian philosophy: B5168.C6
Confucius: B128.C72+
Conjuring deceptions: BF493.C7
Conrad-Martius, Hedwig, 1888-1966: B3216.C77+

Contradiction
  Philosophy
    German philosophy
      Hegel: B2949.C64
    Greek philosophy
      Aristotle: B491.C65
Contrariety
  Philosophy
    Greek philosophy
      Aristotle: B491.O64
Contrast (Philosophy): B105.C54
Control
  Psychology: BF608+
    Older people: BF724.85.C66
Control, Agency, and Means-Ends
  Interview: BF722.35.C65
Control and age: BF724.55.C66
Control by others
  Psychology: BF632.5
Convention (Philosophy): B809.15.A+
Conversation, Etiquette of: BJ2120+
Conway, Anne, 1631-1679:
  B1201.C553+
Conybeare, William Daniel, 1787-1857:
  B1369
Cooperativeness
  Child psychology: BF723.C69
  Ethics: BJ1533.C74
Coping Response Inventory:
  BF335.5.C66
Corbin, Henry: B2430.C65+
Córdoba, Fernando de, 1422-1486:
  B785.C7+
Cornelius, Hans, 1935-: B3216.C78+
Correspondences (Magic): BF1623.C7
Cosmic harmony: BD645
Cosmogony
  Philosophy
    Egyptian philosophy: B142.C6
Cosmography
  Philosophy
    Greek philosophy
      Plato: B398.C66
Cosmology: BD493+
  Korean philosophy: B5253.C66
  Philosophy
    Arabian philosophy: B745.C6
Cosmology
  Philosophy
    Assyro-Babylonian philosophy:
      B147.C68
    Chinese philosophy: B127.C68
    German philosophy
      Hegel: B2949.C8
      Kant: B2799.C8
    Greek philosophy: B187.C7
      Plato: B398.C67
    Indic philosophy: B132.C67
    Jewish philosophy: B157.C65
Cosmopolitanism
  Philosophy
    German philosophy
      Kant: B2799.C82
Cotti, Claude: B2430.C66+
Cotton, John: B869.C5+
Counseling
  Astrology: BF1729.C67
  Psychology
    Applied psychology: BF636.5+
  Religious aspects: BF636.68
Counseling and psychoanalysis:
  BF175.4.C68
Counseling, Philosophical (Ethics):
  BJ1595.5
Counseling psychology: BF636.5+
Counterfactuals (Logic): BC199.C66
Courage
  Ethics: BJ1533.C8
  Philosophy
    Greek philosophy
      Aristotle: B491.C67
      Plato: B398.C69
  Psychology: BF575.C8
    Child psychology: BF723.C694
Cournot, A. A. (Antoine Augustin), 1801-
  1877: B2258.C6+
Court and courtiers
  Ethics: BJ1600+
  Philosophy
    French philosophy
      17th century: B1818.C6
Courtesy
  Ethics: BJ1533.C9
Cousin, Victor, 1792-1867: B2260+

Coutrot, Jean, 1895-1941: B2430.C67+
Couturat, Louis, 1868-1914:
  B2430.C68+
Covens
  Witchcraft: BF1572.C68
Covetousness
  Ethics: BJ1535.A8
Cowries (Divinations): BF1779.C64
Crantor: B557.C4+
Crates, ca. 360 B.C.-ca. 280 B.C.:
  B557.C5+
Crathorn, 14th cent.: B765.C7+
Creation
  Aesthetics: BH301.C84
  Philosophy
    Egyptian philosophy: B142.C6
    German philosophy
      Schelling: B2899.C74
    Greek philosophy
      Aristotle: B491.C7
    Indic philosophy: B132.C73
    Italian philosophy
      Rosmini Serbati: B3648.C7
Creative ability
  Astrology: BF1729.C73
  Philosophy: B105.C74
    German philosophy
      Kant: B2799.C84
  Psychology: BF408+
    Adolescent psychology:
      BF724.3.C73
    Child psychology: BF723.C7
    Older people: BF724.85.C73
Creative ability and personality:
  BF698.9.C74
Creative processes
  Psychology: BF408+
Creativity
  Philosophy: B105.C74
    German philosophy
      Kant: B2799.C84
Creativity and intelligence: BF433.O7
Creighton, James Edwin, 1861-1924:
  B945.C8+
Crescas, Hasdai: B759.C4+
Cresson, André, 1869-1950:
  B2430.C7+
Creuz, Friedrich Karl Casimir, Freiherr
  von, 1724-1770: B2651
Crime
  Astrology: BF1729.C75
  Graphology: BF905.C7
  Palmistry: BF935.C75
Criminal investigation
  Parapsychology: BF1045.C7
Criminals
  Graphology: BF905.C7
  Palmistry: BF935.C75
Crises
  Philosophy: B105.C75
Criterion (Epistemology): BD182
Critical philosophy
  Psychology: BF41
Critical psychology: BF39.9
Critical theory
  Philosophy
    German philosophy: B3183.5
Critical thinking
  Philosophy: B809.2.A+
  Psychology
    Child psychology: BF723.C5
Criticism
  Philosophy: B809.3.A+
    Russian philosophy
      19th and 20th centuries:
        B4235.C7
  Psychology
    Applied psychology: BF637.C74
Croatian philosophy: B4846.31+
Croce, Benedetto, 1866-1952:
  B3614.C7+
Cross-cultural counseling
  Psychology: BF636.7.C76
Crowding
  Environmental psychology:
    BF353.5.C74
Crozier, John Beattie, 1849-1921:
  B1618.C8+
Cruelty
  Aesthetics: BH301.C88
  Ethics: BJ1535.C7
Crusius, Christian August, 1715-1775:
  B2654

Demetrius, the Cynic: B557.D28+
Democritus: B295+
Demonology
  Occultism: BF1501+
Demopoulos, P.N.: B3515.D4+
Denis, Léon: BF1283.D45
Dennett, Daniel Clement: B945.D39+
Dennis, Stephen Christopher
  Spirit messages: BF1311.D43
Deontic logic: BC145
Dependency (Psychology): BF575.D34
Depravity of human nature (Ethics): BJ1406
Deprivation
  Child psychology: BF723.D4
  Middle age: BF724.65.L66
  Psychology: BF575.D35
Depth (Philosophy): B105.D37
Derrida, Jacques: B2430.D48+
Desanti, Jean Toussaint: B2430.D485+
Descartes, René, 1596-1650: B1830+
Description
  Philosophy: B105.D4
  Psycholinguistics: BF463.D47
Descriptive psychology: BF39.8
Deserts (Dreaming): BF1099.D47
Design and purpose (Cosmology): BD530+
Desire
  Philosophy: B105.D44
    French philosophy
      Rousseau: B2138.D47
    German philosophy
      Hegel: B2949.D47
    Greek philosophy
      Plato: B398.D47
    Indic philosophy: B132.D48
    Netherlands philosophy
      Spinoza: B3999.D4
  Psychology: BF575.D4
Desmond, William, 1951-: B1626.D47+
Despair
  Philosophy
    Danish philosophy
      Kierkegaard: B4378.D47
  Psychology: BF575.D45
Despair (Ethics): BJ1488
Dessoir, Max, 1867-1947: B3216.D25+
Destutt de Tracy, Antoine Louis Claude, comte, 1754-1836: B2000+
Determination (Personality traits): BF698.35.D48
Determinism
  Philosophy: B105.D47
    English philosophy
      Locke: B1298.F73
    Greek philosophy: B187.D47
Deubler, Konrad, 1814-1884: B3216.D295+
Deussen, Paul, 1845-1919: B3216.D3+
Deutinger, Martin, 1815-1864: B3216.D4+
Deutsch, Eliot: B945.D397+
Developmental psychology: BF712+
Developmental Test of Visual Perception: BF241.5.D48
Devil worship (Occult sciences): BF1546+
Dewey Color System: BF698.8.D49
Dewey, John, 1859-1952: B945.D4+
Dhamārī, Manṣur Suleiman, 15th cent.: B759.D53+
Dharma: B132.D5
Dharmakīrtī, 7th cent.: B133.D48+
Di Marzio, Cornelio: B3636.M36+
Diagoras, of Melos: B305.D2+
Dialectic
  Philosophy: B105.D48
    Arabian philosophy: B745.D48
    Danish philosophy
      Kierkegaard: B4378.D5
    German philosophy: B2748.D53
      Fichte: B2849.D5
      Hegel: B2949.D5
      Kant: B2799.D47
      Nietzsche: B3318.D5
      Schelling: B2899.D5
      Schleiermacher: B3098.D5
    Greek philosophy: B187.D5
      Aristotle: B491.D5
      Plato: B398.D5
      Socrates: B318.D53
    Indic philosophy: B132.D6
    Modern philosophy: B809.7.A+

Dialectical materialism
  Philosophy: B809.8
    American philosophy: B944.D5
    French philosophy
      20th century: B2424.D5
Dicaearchus, Messenius, 4th cent. B.C.: B557.D345+
Dice
  Fortune-telling: BF1891.D5
Dicta philosophorum (Arabian philosophy): B745.D5
Diderot, Denis, 1713-1784: B2010+
Diet
  Astrology: BF1729.D5
Dietrich, von Freiberg, ca. 1250-ca. 1310: B765.D3+
Dietzgen, Joseph, 1828-1888: B3216.D6+
Difference
  Philosophy: B105.D5
    Modern philosophy: B809.9.A+
Differential Ability Scales: BF432.5.D49
Differential Aptitude Tests: BF432.5.D53
Differential psychology: BF697+
Dignāga, 5th cent.: B133.D65+
Dilemma (Logic): BC185
Dilettantism (Aesthetics): BH301.D5
Dilthey, Wilhelm, 1833-1911: B3216.D8+
Ding an sich
  Epistemology: BD211
  Philosophy
    German philosophy
      Kant: B2799.D5
Dingler, Hugo, 1881-1954: B3217.D3+
Dinners
  Etiquette: BJ2038
Dio, Chrysostom: B557.D35+
Diodorus Cronus, 4th cent. B.C.: B557.D4+
Diogenes, d. ca. 323 B.C.: B305.D4+
Diogenes, of Apollonia, 5th cent. B.C.: B215
Diogenes, of Oenanda: B557.D56+
Diogenes, the Stoic: B557.D6+
Dionysius Areopagita: B667.D4+
Disappearances (Spiritualism): BF1389.D57
Disappointment
  Child psychology: BF723.D47
  Psychology: BF575.D57
Disasters (Reaction to)
  Child psychology: BF723.D5
  Psychology: BF789.D5
Discarnate spirits, Communication with: BF1227.2+
Discipline
  Child psychology: BF723.D54
  Ethics: BJ1533.D49
Discretion
  Ethics: BJ1533.D5
Discursive psychology: BF201.3
Diseases of the will: BF635
Disjunction
  Logic: BC199.D56
Disorders of the memory: BF376
Disorders of the will: BF635
Disposition
  Ontology: BD374
Disposition (Philosophy): B105.D56
Dispositors
  Astrology: BF1717.23
Dissymmetry (Philosophy): B105.D57
Distinction
  Philosophy
    Medieval philosophy: B738.D5
Distraction
  Philosophy: B105.D58
Distraction (Psychology): BF323.D5
Distress
  Infant psychology: BF720.D58
Divination cards
  Occult sciences: BF1778.5
Divinations: BF1745+
Divine commands
  Christian ethics: BJ1278.D58
Divining rod: BF1628
Divining wand: BF1628
Division
  Ontology: BD390
  Philosophy
    Greek philosophy
      Plato: B398.D58

Eilschov, Frederik Christian, 1725-1750: B4341.E5+
Einsiedel, August von, 1754-1837: B2967.E5+
Elation (Psychology): BF575.E5
Elean-Eretrian school: B274
Eleatics (Greek philosophy): B196
Electional astrology: BF1717.25
Electra complex
  Psychoanalysis: BF175.5.E45
Electronic behavior control: BF210
Electronic data processing
  Philosophy: B54
  Psychological tests: BF176.2
  Psychology: BF39.5
    Study and teaching: BF79.5
Elemental spirits (Demonology): BF1552
Elgin, Catherine Z., 1948-: B945.E4+
Elijah (Biblical prophet)
  Spirit messages: BF1311.E46
Eliot, John: B876.E3+
Eliot, T.S.
  Spirit messages: BF1311.E47
Ellis, Havelock, 1859-1939: B1626.E4+
Elster, Jon, 1940-: B4445.E47+
Elves: BF1552
Elzenberg, Henryk, 1887-1967: B4691.E58+
Embarrassment
  Adolescent psychology: BF724.3.E45
  Child psychology: BF723.E44
  Psychology: BF575.E53
Emerson, Ralph Waldo
  Spirit messages: BF1311.E5
Emotion (Psychology): BF511, BF531+
Emotional conditioning (Psychology): BF319.5.E4
Emotional contagion: BF578
Emotional intelligence: BF576+
Emotional intelligence testing: BF576+
Emotional Judgment Inventory: BF576.8.E56
Emotional problems
  Child psychology: BF723.E598
Emotions
  Adolescent psychology: BF724.3.E5
Emotions
  Child psychology: BF723.E6
  Ethics
    Renaissance: BJ281.E56
  Infant psychology: BF720.E45
  Japanese philosophy: B137.E46
  Philosophy: B105.E46
    African philosophy: B5315.E45
    Asian philosophy: B5015.E45
    German philosophy
      Kant: B2799.E5
      Nietzsche: B3318.E46
    Greco-Roman philosophy: B511.5
    Greek philosophy
      Plato: B398.E45
    Indic philosophy: B132.E45
    Medieval philosophy: B738.E46
    Modern philosophy: B815.A+
    Netherlands philosophy
      Spinoza: B3999.E5
    Scottish philosophy
      Hume: B1499.E45
  Psychology: BF511
    Older people: BF724.85.E56
Emotions and hypnotism: BF1156.E5
Emotions and language: BF582
Emotions and personality: BF698.9.E45
Emotivism
  Aesthetics: BH301.E45
  Ethics: BJ1473
Empathy
  Jewish ethics: BJ1286.E47
  Psychology: BF575.E55
    Child psychology: BF723.E67
Empedocles: B218
Empirical logic: BC80+
Empirical verification
  Epistemology: BD212.5
Empiricism
  Philosophy: B816.A+
    English philosophy
      Mill: B1608.E6
Employment surveys
  Psychology: BF75
Encounter (Epistemology): BD185
Encouragement
  Ethics: BJ1475.5

Encouragement
  Psychology
    Applied psychology: BF637.E53
End of the world
  Dreaming: BF1099.E53
Ends and means
  Ethics: BJ84.E5
Engagement (Philosophy): B105.E5
Engel, Johann Jacob, 1741-1802: B2657
Engels, Friedrich, 1820-1895: B3224.E6+
English philosophy: B1111+
  Influence on 18th century German philosophy: B2628.E5
Enlightenment
  Philosophy
    English philosophy: B1302.E65
    French philosophy
      18th century: B1925.E5
    Greek philosophy (Modern): B3511.E54
    Italian philosophy: B3595.E54
      Rosmini Serbati: B3648.E54
    Latin American philosophy: B1008.E5
    Renaissance philosophy: B802
    Russian philosophy
      17th and 18th centuries: B4215.E5
      19th and 20th centuries: B4235.E5
    Scottish philosophy
      18th and 19th centuries: B1402.E55
Enneagram (Personality traits): BF698.35.E54
Enoch ben Solomon al-Ḳusṭanṭini, fl. 1370: B759.E56+
Enochian magic (Magic): BF1623.E55
Entailment (Logic): BC199.E58
Entertaining
  Etiquette: BJ2021+
Enthoven, Raphaël: B2433.E58+
Enthusiasm
  Philosophy
    Greek philosophy
      Early: B200.E5
  Psychology: BF575.E6
Enthymeme (Logic): BC185
Entity (Ontology): BD336
Environment (Aesthetics): BH301.E58
Environmental psychology: BF353
Envy
  Ethics: BJ1535.E57
  Philosophy
    Greek philosophy: B187.E5
  Psychology: BF575.E65
Epictetus: B560+
Epicureanism (Greco-Roman philosophy): B512
Epicurus: B570+
Epikeia (Christian ethics): BJ1278.E64
Epiphanism
  Philosophy: B817.A+
Epistemics
  Ancient Oriental logic: BC26.E64
  Logic: BC21.E64
  Philosophy: B820.3.A1+
Epistemology
  Philosophy
    German philosophy
      Kant: B2799.K7
Epistemology and ethics: BD176
Epistemology and evolution: BD177
Epistemology and sociology: BD175+
Equality
  Philosophy
    Greek philosophy: B187.E6
Equilibrium (Logic): BC199.E7
Equipment and supplies
  Psychic research: BF1045.E65
  Psychology: BF80
Erasmus, Desiderius, d. 1536: B785.E6+
Erdmann, Johann Eduard, 1805-1892: B3225
Eribon, Didier: B2430.E75+
Ericson, W.F.
  Spirit messages: BF1311.E7

Experience
Philosophy
German philosophy
Hegel: B2949.E87
Kant: B2799.E9
Italian philosophy: B3561.E95
Experiential learning (Psychology): BF318.5
Experiential research (Psychology): BF76.6.E94
Experiential world inventory: BF698.8.E9
Experimental psychology: BF180+
Expertise and memory: BF378.E94
Explanation (Epistemology): BD237
Explanatory style (Psychology): BF698.9.E95
Exploitation
Ethics: BJ1474.5
Expression
Philosophy: B105.E95
Netherlands philosophy
Spinoza: B3999.E9
Expression of the emotions: BF585+
Animals: BF593
Children: BF723.E6
Humans: BF591
Expressionism
Aesthetics: BH301.E9
Expressivism
Ethics: BJ1500.E94
Extension
Logic: BC199.E93
Philosophy
French philosophy
Malebranche: B1898.E95
Extinction (Psychology): BF319.5.E9
Extrasensory perception
Spiritualism: BF1321+
Extraterrestrials
Divinations: BF1779.L5
Extraterrestrials and humans, Contact between: BF2050+
Extraversion
Personality traits: BF698.35.E98
Eye
Physiognomy: BF861.E8
Eye contact
Applied psychology: BF637.N66

F

Fabro, Cornelio: B3614.F136+
Face
Expression of the emotions: BF592.F33
Philosophy: B105.F29
Face perception
Infant psychology: BF720.F32
Face perception (Vision): BF242
Fachiri, Adila
Spirit messages: BF1311.F25
Fackenheim, Emil L.: B995.F33+
Factor analysis
Psychology: BF39.2.F32
Facts (Philosophy): B105.F3
Faggin, Giuseppe, 1906-1995: B3614.F1367+
Failure
Child psychology: BF723.F27
Psychology: BF575.F14
Fairies: BF1552
Fairness
Ethics: BJ1533.F2
Fairy Tale Test: BF698.8.F35
Faith
Epistemology: BD215
Philosophy
Arabian philosophy: B745.F26
Psychology: BF773
Faith cure and spiritualism: BF1275.F3
Falaquera, Shem Tov ben Joseph, ca. 1225-ca. 1295: B759.F3+
Falckenberg, Richard, 1851-1920: B3229.F2+
Fallacies (Logic): BC175
False alarms (Psychology): BF789.F29
Falsehood
Child psychology: BF723.T8
Philosophy
Greek philosophy: B187.T7

Falsehood and truthfulness
  Psychology
    Adolescent psychology: BF724.3.T78
Fame (Ethics): BJ1470.5
Familiar spirits (Demonology): BF1557
Family
  Astrology: BF1729.F35
  Dreaming: BF1099.F34
  Witchcraft: BF1572.F35
Family, Social usages for
  American: BJ1857.F3
  British: BJ1877.F3
  French: BJ1887.F3
  German: BJ1907.F3
  Italian: BJ1927.F3
  Portuguese: BJ1987.F3
  Russian: BJ1947.F3
  Scandinavian: BJ1967.F3
  Spanish: BJ1987.F3
Fan, Zhen, ca. 445-ca. 510: B128.F3+
Fanaticism
  Ethics: BJ1535.F25
  Psychology: BF575.F16
Fang, I-chih, 1611-1671: B5234.F32+
Fang, Tung-mei: B5234.F34+
Fantastic (Aesthetics): BH301.F3
Fantasy
  Child psychology: BF723.F28
  Psychoanalysis: BF175.5.F36
Fārābī: B753.F3+
Faraday, Michael
  Spirit messages: BF1311.F3
Fasts
  Witchcraft: BF1572.F37
Fate and fatalism
  Philosophy
    Arabian philosophy: B745.F3
    Greek philosophy: B187.F3
Father and child
  Child psychology: BF723.F35
Father and infant
  Infant psychology: BF720.F38
Father-separated children
  Child psychology: BF723.P33
Fatigue
  Mental fatigue: BF482
Fatigue
  Psychology: BF482
Fault finding
  Ethics: BJ1535.F3
Favorinus, of Arles, ca. 81-ca. 150: B577.F2+
Fear
  Ontology: BD440
  Psychology: BF575.F2
    Adolescent psychology: BF724.3.F34
    Child psychology: BF723.F4
    Infant psychology: BF720.F4
Feasts
  Witchcraft: BF1572.F37
Fechner, Gustav Theodor, 1801-1887: B3230+
Fechner's law: BF237
Fedorov, Nikolaĭ Fedorovich, 1828-1903: B4238.F4+
Feedback (Psychology): BF319.5.F4
Feeling
  Psychology: BF511
Feelings (Psychology): BF521
Feibleman, James Kern, 1904-: B945.F2+
Feijoo, Benito Jerónimo, 1676-1764: B4568.F4+
Femininity
  Philosophy
    German philosophy
      Nietzsche: B3318.F45
  Psychoanalysis: BF175.5.F45
Feminism
  Christian ethics: BJ1278.F45
  Philosophy
    French philosophy
      20th century: B2424.F45
Feminism and psychoanalysis: BF175.4.F45
Feminist ethics: BJ1395
  Christian ethics: BJ1278.F45
Feminist psychology: BF201.4
Feng shui (Divinations): BF1779.F4
Feng, Youlan, 1895-1990: B5234.F4+
Ferguson, Adam, 1723-1816: B1410+
Ferguson, James Henry: B945.F3+

Fischer, Karl Phil. (Karl Philipp), 1807-
  1885: B2974.F4+
Fischer, Kuno, 1824-1907: B3241
Fiske, John, 1842-1901: B945.F4+
Five agents (Chinese philosophy):
  B127.F58
Five-Factor Nonverbal Personality
  Questionnaire: BF698.8.F56
Flach, Werner, 1930-: B3244.F18+
Flake, Otto, 1880-1963: B3244.F2+
Flam, Léopold: B4159.F55+
Flames
  Fortune-telling: BF1891.F55
Flashbulb memory: BF378.F55
Flattery
  Ethics: BJ1535.F55
Flew, Antony, 1923-2010: B1626.F573+
Flonta, Mircea: B4825.F46+
Flowers
  Fortune-telling: BF1891.P56
Flusser, Vilém, 1920-1991: B1044.F57+
Fodor, Jerry A: B945.F63+
Folk psychology and hypnotism:
  BF1156.F6
Folly
  Ethics: BJ1535.F6
Fontenay, Elisabeth de: B2430.F66+
Fontenelle, M. de (Bernard Le Bovier),
  1657-1757: B2020+
Food
  Magic: BF1623.F64
  Philosophy: B105.F66
Foot (Physiognomy): BF861.F66
Force (Cosmology): BD652
Fordyce, David, 1711-1751:
  B1373.F67+
Forgetting: BF378.F7
Forgiveness
  Applied psychology: BF637.F67
  Ethics: BJ1476
    Jewish ethics: BJ1286.F67
  Philosophy
    Greek philosophy: B187.F67
Form
  Aesthetics: BH301.F6
  Logic: BC199.F6
Form
  Philosophy
    Greek philosophy: B187.F68
    Modern philosophy: B819.3+
Form perception
  Psychology: BF293+
Formalization of knowledge: BD258
Forms
  Philosophy
    Greek philosophy
      Aristotle: B491.F63
      Plato: B398.F57
Fortitude
  Ethics
    Ancient Chinese and Japanese
      ethics: BJ118.F6
Fortune
  Philosophy
    Greek philosophy
      Plato: B398.F6
Fortune-telling: BF1845+
Fortune-telling by cards: BF1876+
Fortune-telling by tea and coffee cups:
  BF1881
Foster children
  Psychology: BF723.F6
Foucault, Michel, 1926-1984:
  B2430.F72+
Fouillée, Alfred, 1838-1912: B2270.F6+
Foundationalism
  Epistemology: BD238.F68
Four beginnings and seven feelings
  thesis
  Korean philosophy: B5253.F68
Four picture Test: BF698.8.F6
Four temperaments
  Astrology: BF1729.T46
Fourth dimension
  Psychic research: BF1045.F68
Fox sisters: BF1283.F7
Foxes
  Dreaming: BF1099.F69
Fragility
  Psychology: BF575.F62

France
  Philosophy
    German philosophy
      Leibniz: B2599.F69
Francesco, da Prato, 14th cent.: B765.F55+
Francesco d'Assisi, Saint
  Spirit messages: BF1311.F67
Franchi, Ausonio: B3618
Francis, of Assisi, Saint, 1182-1226: B765.F6+
Franciscus, de Marchia, 14th cent.: B765.F65+
Franciscus, de Mayronis, ca. 1285-ca. 1328: B765.F66+
Franck, Adolphe, 1809-1893: B2270.F8+
Francke, Christian, b. 1549: B785.F73+
Frank, Adolf: B3244.F27+
Frank, Erich, 1883-1949: B3244.F28+
Frank, S. L. (Semen L͡iudvigovich), 1877-1950: B4238.F73+
Frankfurt school of philosophy: B3183.5
Franklin, Benjamin
  Spirit messages: BF1311.F7
Franklin, Benjamin, 1706-1790: B880+
Franklin, John, Sir
  Spirit messages: BF1311.F73
Franon, Frantz, 1925-1961: B1029.F35+
Franze, Paul Christian: B3244.F3+
Frazer, Alexander Campbell, 1819-1914: B1589.F7+
Frédault, Paul, 1850-: B2270.F86+
Fredegis, of Tours, d. 824: B765.F7+
Free logic: BC129
Free will
  Ethics: BJ1460+
  Philosophy
    Danish philosophy
      Kierkegaard: B4378.F68
    English philosophy
      Locke: B1298.F73
    French philosophy
      Voltaire: B2178.F9
    German philosophy
      Fichte: B2849.F7
Free will
  Philosophy
    German philosophy
      Hegel: B2949.F7
      Kant: B2799.F8
      Leibniz: B2599.F7
      Lotze: B3298.F7
      Schopenhauer: B3149.F7
    Greek philosophy: B187.F7
      Aristotle: B491.F68
      Plato: B398.F7
    Jewish philosophy: B757.F7
    Netherlands philosophy
      Spinoza: B3999.F8
    Swedish philosophy
      Boström: B4488.F7
Freedom
  Child psychology: BF723.A87
  Philosophy: B105.L45
    American philosophy: B861.L52
    Indic philosophy: B132.L53
    Modern philosophy: B824.4.A+
  Psychology: BF575.A88
Freedom of the will
  Ethics: BJ1460+
  Psychology: BF620+
Freemasons and spiritualism: BF1275.F7
Frege, Gottlob, 1848-1925: B3245.F2+
French literature, Knowledge of
  Philosophy
    Danish philosophy
      Kierkegaard: B4378.F7
French philosophy: B1801+
  Latin American philosophy: B-BJ9 3.F74
French Revolution
  Astrology: BF1729.F7
Fréret, Nicolas, 1688-1749: B2029.F74+
Freyer, Hans, 1887-1969: B3245.F3+
Friedlaender, Salomo, 1871-1946: B3245.F38+
Frieling test: BF698.8.F7
Friendship
  Adolescent psychology: BF724.3.F64
  Child psychology: BF723.F68

Gaultier, Jules de, 1858-1942:
  B2270.G35+
Gay men
  Horoscopes: BF1728.2.G39
Gays
  Witchcraft: BF1571.5.G39
Gehlen, Arnold: B3248.G38+
Geiger, Louis Bertrand, 1906-1983:
  B2430.G4+
Geijer, Erik Gustaf, 1783-1847:
  B4489.G4+
Gellner, Ernest: B1626.G44+
Gemelli, Agostino, 1878-1959:
  B3624.G4+
Gemini (Astrology): BF1727.25
Gemistus Plethon, George, 15th cent.:
  B785.P56+
Gemma, Cornelius, 1535-1579:
  B785.G38+
Gems
  Astrology: BF1729.G4
  Occult sciences: BF1442.P74
Genealogy
  Philosophy
    German philosophy
      Nietzsche: B3318.G45
    Modern philosophy: B819.5.A1+
General factor
  Intelligence testing: BF433.G45
Generalization (Epistemology): BD235
Generosity
  Ethics: BJ1533.G4
  Psychology: BF575.G44
Genetic epistemology
  Child psychology: BF723.C5
Genetic ethics: BJ1298+
Genetic logic: BC121
Genetic psychology: BF699+
Geneticism
  Philosophy
    English philosophy
      Berkeley: B1349.G4
Genii: BF1552
Genius
  Philosophy
    German philosophy: B3184
      Nietzsche: B3318.G46
Genius and heredity: BF418
Genius and mental illness: BF423
Genius and mental retardation: BF426
Gennadius II, Patriarch of
  Constantinople, ca. 1405-ca. 1472:
  B765.G39+
Genocide
  Philosophy
    Judaism: B5802.G46
Genovesi, Antonio, 1712-1769:
  B3598.G3+
Gentile, Giovanni, 1875-1944:
  B3624.G5+
Gentlemen, The
  Ethics: BJ1600+
Genua, Marco Antonio, 1491-1563:
  B785.G4+
Geography and parapsychology:
  BF1045.G46
Geometry
  Philosophy
    German philosophy
      Leibniz: B2599.G46
Geraldus, Odonis, 1285-1349:
  B765.G397+
Gérando, Joseph-Marie, baron de,
  1772-1842: B2270.G45+
Gerard, Alexander, 1728-1795:
  B1419.G47+
Gérard, Philippe Louis, 1737-1813:
  B2037.G4+
German history
  Astrology: BF1729.G45
German philosophy: B2521+
  Latin American philosophy: B-BJ9
    3.G3
German transcendental idealism:
  B2745
Gerratana, Valentino: B3624.G542+
Gershenzon, M. O. (Mikhail Osipovich),
  1869-1925: B4238.G5+
Gerson, Jean, 1363-1429: B765.G4+
Gersonides, 1288-1344: B759.L4+
Gessen, Sergeĭ Iosifovich, 1887-1950:
  B4238.G56+
Gestalt psychology: BF203

Gravina, Gianvincenzo, 1664-1718:
B3578.G74+
Grays
Human-alien encounters:
BF2055.G73
Great Britain
Spirit messages: BF1311.G7
Grebe, Wilhelm, 1897-: B3252.G68+
Grecian logic, Ancient
History: BC28+
Greco-Roman philosophy: B504+
Greece, Knowledge of
Philosophy
German philosophy
Hegel: B2949.G73
Greek ethics: BJ160+
Greek influences (German philosophy):
B2528.G73
Greek life and literature and Greek
philosophy: B178
Greek philosophy
Ancient: B165+
Influence on Arabian philosophy:
B744.3
Modern: B3500+
Green, Thomas Hill, 1836-1882:
B1630+
Greeting cards
Etiquette: BJ2095.G5
Gregory, of Nazianzus, Saint
Philosophy: B667.G5+
Gregory, of Nyssa, Saint, ca. 335-ca.
394
Philosophy: B667.G7+
Gregory, of Rimini, d. 1358: B765.G65+
Greinert, Willy: B3252.G7+
Grene, Marjorie, 1910-2009:
B945.G73+
Gri͡aznov, B.S. (Boris Semenovich),
1929-1978: B4238.G67+
Grief
Aesthetics: BH301.G73
Ethics: BJ1487
Philosophy
Renaissance philosophy: B780.G74
Grief
Psychology
Adolescent psychology:
BF724.3.G73
Child psychology: BF723.G75
Older people: BF724.85.G73
Grimaldi, Nicolas: B2430.G75+
Grimoire
Demonology: BF1558
Groethuysen, Bernhard, 1880-1946:
B3252.G8+
Groĭs, Boris: B4238.G72+
Grosseteste, Robert, 1175?-1253:
B765.G7+
Grot, N. I͡A. (Nikolaĭ I͡Akovlevich), 1852-
1899: B4240+
Grote, George, 1794-1871:
B1589.G75+
Grote, John, d. 1866: B1589.G8+
Grotesque
Philosophy
Renaissance philosophy: B780.G76
Grotesque (Aesthetics): BH301.G74
Grotius, Hugo, 1583-1645: B785.G7+
Group counseling
Psychology
Applied psychology: BF636.7.G76
Group Environment Scale:
BF698.8.G74
Grubbe, Samuel, 1786-1853:
B4489.G7+
Gruppe, O. F. (Otto Friedrich), 1804-
1876: B3254.G7+
Gruyer, L. A. (Louis Auguste), 1778-
1866: B4161
Gu, Yanwu, 1613-1682: B5234.G8+
Guattari, Félix, 1930-1992:
B2430.G78+
Guénon, René: B2430.G8+
Guicciardini, Francisco (Horoscopes):
BF1728.G84
Guides (Parapsychology): BF1275.G85
Guigo I, Prior of the Grande Chartreuse,
1083?-1136: B765.G77+
Guigues, du Chastel, 1083?-1136:
B765.G77+

Happiness
  Philosophy
    Danish philosophy
      Kierkegaard: B4378.H34
    German philosophy
      Kant: B2799.H36
      Schleiermacher: B3098.H35
    Greek philosophy: B187.H3
      Aristotle: B491.H36
    Medieval philosophy: B738.H3
  Psychology: BF575.H27
    Adolescent psychology: BF724.3.H35
    Child psychology: BF723.H37
    Older people: BF724.85.H35
Hara
  Ethics
    Ancient Chinese and Japanese ethics: BJ118.F6
Hardenberg, Friedrich, Freiherr von, 1772-1801: B3071
Haribhadrasūri, 700-770: B133.H37+
Harmony
  Aesthetics: BH301.H3
  Philosophy: B105.H37
    Greek philosophy
      Heraclitus of Ephesus: B224.H37
    Indic philosophy: B132.H37
Harness racing
  Astrology: BF1729.H37
Harris, William Torrey, 1835-1909: B945.H285+
Harrison, Frederic, 1831-1923: B1646.H2+
Harrison, Jonathan: B1646.H26+
Harrower inkblot test: BF698.8.H35
Harry, 1862-1899
  Spirit messages: BF1311.H37
Hartley, David, 1705-1757: B1375+
Hartmann, Eduard von, 1842-1906: B3270+
Hartmann, Nicolai, 1882-1950: B3279.H2+
Hartsen, F. A. (Frederik Anthony), 1838-1877: B4051.H4+
Hartshorne, Charles, 1897-2000: B945.H35+
Harvard school of philosophy: B944.H3
Harvey, Gideon, 1640?-1700?: B1201.H2+
Hashish
  Psychological effect: BF209.C3
Hate
  Psychology: BF575.H3
    Adolescent psychology: BF724.3.H38
    Child psychology: BF723.H38
Haunted castles: BF1474
Haunted cemeteries: BF1474.3
Haunted colleges: BF1478
Haunted hospitals: BF1474.4
Haunted hotels: BF1474.5
Haunted houses
  Occult sciences: BF1475+
Haunted lighthouses: BF1476
Haunted morgues: BF1476.4
Haunted parsonages: BF1477
Haunted places
  Occultism: BF1444+
Haunted plantations: BF1477.2
Haunted prisons: BF1477.3
Haunted theaters: BF1477.5
Haunted universities: BF1478
Hauntings
  Occultism: BF1444+
Hayashi, Ryōsai, 1807-1849: B5244.H37+
Haym, R. (Rudolf), 1821-1901: B3279.H3+
He, Xinyin, 1517-1579: B128.H48+
Head (Aesthetics): BH301.H36
Health
  Astrology: BF1729.H9
Hearing
  Philosophy
    Greek philosophy
      Aristotle: B491.E23
  Psychology: BF251+
Hearn, Lafcadio, 1850-1904: B945.H38+
Heaven
  Philosophy
    Chinese philosophy: B127.H4

Huet, Pierre-Daniel, 1630-1721:
  B1889.H7+
Hugging
  Psychology
    Applied psychology: BF637.H83
Hugh, of Saint-Victor, 1096?-1141:
  B765.H7+
Hugo, Victor
  Spirit messages: BF1311.H8
Hui, Shi, ca. 370-ca. 310 B.C.:
  B128.H95+
Huisman, Denis: B2430.H8+
Hulme, T. E. (Thomas Ernest), 1883-
  1917: B1646.H8+
Hülsen, August Ludewig: B3053.H55+
Human and extraterrestrials
  Contact between: BF2050+
Human behavior models: BF39.3
Human body
  Philosophy
    German philosophy
      Nietzsche: B3318.H85
Human geography and psychoanalysis:
  BF175.4.H84
Human life (Respect for sacredness of)
  Ethics: BJ1533.H9
Human nature, Depravity of (Ethics):
  BJ1406
Human potential movement:
  BF637.H85
Human rights
  Philosophy
    Greek philosophy
      Plato: B398.H85
Humanism
  Latin American philosophy: B-BJ9
    3.H86
  Philosophy: B105.H8
    American philosophy: B944.H85
    Chinese philosophy: B127.H8
    French philosophy
      Pascal: B1904.H86
    Greek philosophy
      Socrates: B318.H84
    Latin American philosophy:
      B1008.H8
    Medieval philosophy: B738.H8
Humanism
  Philosophy
    Modern philosophy: B821.A+
    Renaissance: B778
    Russian philosophy
      19th and 20th centuries:
        B4235.H85
    Spanish and Portuguese philosophy:
      B4515.H85
Humanist ethics: BJ1360
Humanistic counseling
  Psychology: BF636.7.H86
Humanistic psychology: BF204
Humanitarianism
  Jewish ethics: BJ1286.H85
Humanitarianism (Ethics): BJ1475.3
Humanities
  Philosophy
    German philosophy
      Nietzsche: B3318.H87
Humanities and psychoanalysis:
  BF175.4.H85
Humanity
  Ancient ethics: BJ107.H8
  Ethics: BJ1533.H9
Humans
  Expression of the emotions: BF591
Humboldt, Alexander von, 1769-1859:
  B3053.H6+
Humboldt, Wilhelm, freiherr von, 1767-
  1835: B3053.H7+
Hume, David, 1711-1776: B1450+
Humidity
  Psychology
    Environmental psychology:
      BF353.5.H84
Humiliation
  Psychology: BF575.H85
Humility
  Ethics: BJ1533.H93
  Jewish ethics: BJ1286.H87
Humor
  Philosophy
    French philosophy
      Rousseau: B2138.H95
  Psychology
    Child psychology: BF723.H85

Irony
Philosophy
Greek philosophy
Socrates: B318.I7
Irrationalism (Philosophy): B824.2.A+
Isidore, of Alexandria, 5th cent.: B672.I4+
Isidore, of Seville, Saint, d. 636: B672.I6+
Isidore, the Gnostic, Son of Basilides: B672.I7+
Islam
Philosophy
German philosophy: B2528.I85
Islamic astrology: BF1714.I84
Islamic ethics: BJ1291
Islamic etiquette: BJ2019.5.I8
Islamic logic, Medieval
History: BC34+
Islamic philosophers
Medieval: B740+
Isolation (Philosophy): B824.3.A+
Israeli, Isaac, ca. 832-ca. 932: B759.I8+
Israeli philosophy: B5055+
Italian astrology: BF1714.I87
Italian philosophy: B3551+
Item response theory
Psychology: BF39.2.I84
Itō, Jinsai, 1627-1705: B5244.I76+
Itō, Tōgai, 1670-1736: B5244.I86+
Iversen, Herbert, 1890-1920: B4395.I77+
Izoulet, Jean Bernard Joachim, 1854-1929: B2430.I9+
Izzat, 'Abd al-'Aziz, 1907-: B5344.I9+

J

Jackson, Frank, 1943-: B5704.J33+
Jackson Personality Inventory: BF698.8.J33
Jacobi, Friedrich Heinrich, 1743-1819: B3055+
Jacoby, Günther, 1881-1969: B3279.J15+
Jahn, Aegidius: B3279.J17+
Jaina astrology: BF1714.J28
Jaina ethics: BJ1290
Jaina philosophy: B162.5
Jakovenko, Boris V. (Boris Valentinovich), 1884-1949: B4249.J34+
James, Henry, 1811-1882: B921.J2+
James, William
Spirit messages: BF1311.J25
James, William, 1842-1910: B945.J2+
Jan, z Kluczborka, ca. 1355-ca. 1436: B765.J145+
Janicaud, Dominique, 1937-: B2430.J28+
Janke, Hans: B3279.J2+
Jankélévitch, Vladimir: B2430.J3+
Jansen, Bernard, 1877-1942: B3279.J27+
Jansenius, Cornelius, Bp.
Spirit messages: BF1311.J3
Japanese astrology: BF1714.J3
Japanese philosophy
Ancient: B135+
Modern: B5240+
Jaspers, Karl, 1883-1969: B3279.J3+
Javanese astrology: BF1714.J35
Jayarāśibhatta, 8th cent.: B133.J35+
Jayatīrtha, 14th cent.: B133.J37+
Jealousy
Ethics: BJ1535.J4
Psychology: BF575.J4
Adolescent psychology: BF724.3.J4
Child psychology: BF723.J4
Jean, de Jandun: B765.J15+
Jeanson, Francis, 1922-2009: B2430.J43+
Jedaiah ben Abraham Bedersi, ca. 1270-ca. 1340: B759.J43+
Jefferson, Thomas, 1743-1826: B885
Jen: B127.J4
Jen-tzu, 545-469 B.C.: B128.J44+
Jerusalem, Karl Wilhelm, 1747-1772: B3060.J3+
Jesus Christ
Philosophy
German philosophy
Hegel: B2949.J47

Jesus Christ (Spirit messages): BF1311.J5
Jewish astrology: BF1714.J4
Jewish ethics: BJ1279+
Jewish etiquette: BJ2019.5.J4
Jewish philosophy
  Ancient: B154+
  Medieval: B755+
Jews
  Intelligence testing: BF432.J4
  Philosophy
    French philosophy
      Diderot: B2018.J83
Jiao, Xun, 1763-1820: B5234.J536+
Jiva: B132.J58
Joad, C. E. M. (Cyril Edwin Mitchinson), 1891-1953: B1646.J7+
Joannes Phiuloponus: B673.J6+
Jobert, Antoine Claude Gabriel: B2275.J6+
Jodl, Friedrich, 1849-1914: B3279.J6+
Johannes de Siccavilla, ca 1215-1295: B765.J36+
Johannes, Scotus Erigena, ca. 810-ca. 877: B765.J3+
John, of Salisbury, Bishop of Chartres, d. 1180: B765.J4+
John of St. Thomas, 1589-1644: B4568.J64+
Johnson, Samuel: B876.J5+
Joint attention
  Apperception: BF323.J63
Jollien, Alexandre, 1975-: B4651.J65+
Jonas, Hans, 1903-1993: B3279.J66+
Jones, Henry, Sir, 1852-1922: B1646.J8+
Jones, John Robert, 1911-1970: B1646.J862+
Jordanian philosophy: B5060+
Joseph ben Jacob Ibn Ẓaddik, 1075-1149: B759.J5+
Jouffroy, Théodore, 1796-1842: B2280+
Joy
  Ethics: BJ1480+
  Psychology: BF575.H27
    Child psychology: BF723.J6
Joy (Psychoanalysis): BF175.5.J69
Juan, Chi, 210-263: B128.J83+
Judaism
  Philosophy
    Ancient philosophy: B154+
    French philosophy
      Diderot: B2018.J83
    German philosophy
      Hegel: B2949.J84
      Nietzsche: B3318.J83
    Modern philosophy: B5800+
    Netherlands philosophy
      Spinoza: B3999.J8
Judgment
  Aesthetics: BH301.J8
  Logic: BC181
  Philosophy
    German philosophy
      Kant: B2799.J8
  Psychology: BF447
    Adolescent psychology: BF724.3.J8
    Child psychology: BF723.J8
Julian, Emperor of Rome, 331-363: B674
Julian, the Apostate (Julianus, Apostata)
  Spirit messages: BF1311.J8
Jullien, François: B2430.J85+
Junge, Reinhard: B3279.J8+
Jupiter (Planet)
  Astrology: BF1724.2.J87
  Spirit messages: BF1311.J85
Jury selection
  Graphology: BF905.J87
Justice
  Ethics: BJ1533.J9
  Philosophy: B105.J87
    German philosophy
      Kant: B2799.J87
      Leibniz: B2599.J8
      Nietzsche: B3318.J87
    Greek philosophy
      Aristotle: B491.J87
      Early: B200.J8
      Plato: B398.J87
    Scottish philosophy
      Hume: B1499.J86
  Psychology: BF789.J8

Justice
Psychology
Adolescent psychology: BF724.3.J87
Justification
Epistemology: BD212
Justin, Martyr, Saint: B675

K

Kada, Azumamaro, 1669-1736: B5244.K23+
Kagan, M. S. (Moiseĭ Samoĭlovich): B4249.K29+
Kahn test of symbol arrangement: BF698.8.K3
Kaibara, Ekiken, 1630-1714: B5244.K25+
Kaibel, Franz, 1880-1935: B3279.K15+
Kairēs, Theophilos, 1784-1853: B3515.K3+
Kallen, Horace Meyer, 1882-1974: B945.K28+
Kambartel, Friedrich: B3279.K155+
Kames, Henry Home, Lord, 1696-1782: B1435
Kanellopoulos, Panagiōtēs, 1902-: B3515.K4+
Kang, Youwei, 1858-1927: B5234.K36+
Kanger, Stig: B4495.K35+
Kann, Albert: B3279.K2+
Kant, Immanuel, 1724-1804: B2750+
Kapila: B133.K38+
Karinskii, Mikhail Ivanovich, 1840-1917: B4249.K35+
Karma
Ethics: BJ1499.K3
Psychic research: BF1045.K37
Karsavin, L.P. (Lev Platonovich), 1882-1952: B4249.K37+
Kassner, Rudolf, 1873-1959: B3279.K25+
Kaufman Assessment Battery for Children: BF432.5.K38
Kaufman Brief Intelligence Test: BF432.5.K39
Kaufmann, Felix, 1895-1949: B3279.K29+
Kazakhstan philosophy: B4765.2+
Kearney, Richard: B945.K38+
Kearns, John T., 1936-: B945.K39+
Kelly, Edward
Occult sciences: BF1598.K44
Kemmerich, Max: B3279.K3+
Kennedy family (Horoscopes): BF1728.K46
Kenny, Anthony, 1931-: B1646.K46+
Kenyan philosophy: B5415+
Kevelson, Roberta: B945.K45+
Keyserling, Hermann, Graf von, 1880-1946: B3279.K4+
Khmer astrology: BF1714.K5
Khomi͡akov, A. S. (Alekseĭ Stepanovich), 1804-1860: B4249.K5+
Khuwārizmī, Muḥammad ibn Aḥmad, d. 997 or 8: B753.K47+
Kierkegaard, Søren, 1813-1855: B4370+
Kiho school (Korean philosophy): B5253.K53
Kilwardby, Robert, d. 1279: B765.K5+
Kim, Hyong-sok, 1920-: B5254.K498+
Kinder-Angst-Test: BF698.8.K5
Kindī, d. ca. 873: B753.K5+
Kindness
Ethics: BJ1533.K5
Kindness (Ethics)
Jewish ethics: BJ1286.K5
Kinetic family drawing test: BF698.8.K53
Kinetic-House-Tree-Person Technique: BF698.8.K55
Kingdom of God
Philosophy
German philosophy
Kant: B2799.K54
Kingsley, Charles
Spirit messages: BF1311.K5
Kirchmann, J. H. von (Julius Hermann), 1802-1884: B3279.K5+
Kireevskiĭ, Ivan Vasil'evich, 1806-1856: B4249.K56+

Liceti, Fortunio, 1577-1657: B3578.L5+
Lichtenberg, Georg Christoph, 1742-1799: B2681.L4+
Liebmann, Otto, 1840-1912: B3286.L5+
Life
  Conduct of: BF637.C5
  Jewish ethics: BJ1286.L54
  Ontology: BD430+
  Philosophy
    Chinese philosophy: B127.L55
    German philosophy
      Fichte: B2849.L5
      Kant: B2799.L5
    Greek philosophy: B187.L5
      Aristotle: B491.L5
    Indic philosophy: B132.L54
  Spirit messages: BF1311.L4
Life and death, Power over: BJ1469
Life, Artificial
  Ontology: BD418.8
Life change events
  Psychology
    Applied psychology: BF637.L53
Life on other planets: BD655
  Divinations: BF1779.L5
  Spirit messages: BF1311.L43
LIFO Survey: BF698.8.L54
Light
  Psychology: BF789.L53
Light body (Occult sciences): BF1442.L53
Lighthouses, Haunted: BF1476
Liiceanu, Gabriel, 1942-: B4825.L55+
Lilly, William (Occult sciences): BF1598.L5
Limentani, Ludovico, 1884-1940: B3634.L3+
Liminality (Psychoanalysis): BF175.5.L55
Limit (Logic): BC199.L54
Lincoln, Abraham
  Horoscopes: BF1728.L52
  Spirit messages: BF1311.L45
Lindemann, Hans Adalbert: B3286.L6+
Lindsay, James, 1852-1923: B1646.L6+
Lingis, Alphonso, 1933-: B945.L458+
Linguistics
  Philosophy
    German philosophy
      Wolff: B2728.L54
Lipps, G. F. (Gottlob Friedrich), 1865-1931: B3286.L7+
Lipps, Theodor, 1851-1914: B3287
Lipsius, Justus, 1547-1606: B785.L4+
Listening
  Philosophy: B105.L54
  Psychology: BF323.L5
Literature
  Philosophy
    German philosophy
      Nietzsche: B3318.L5
Literature and philosophy: B66
Literature and spiritualism: BF1275.I58
Lithuanian philosophy: B4741+
Litt, Theodor, 1880-1962: B3288.L54+
Little, Rolf
  Spirit messages: BF1311.L5
Liu, Chi, 1311-1375: B128.L57+
Liu, Chou, 514-565: B128.L58+
Liu, Hsiang, 77?-6? B.C.: B128.L586+
Liu, Tsung-chou, 1578-1645: B128.L59+
Liu, Xiaobo: B5234.L56+
Liu, Yin, 1249-1293: B128.L64+
Living, The, Apparitions of (Occult sciences): BF1481
Ljungström, Oscar, 1868-: B4495.L5+
Lledó Iñigo, Emilio: B4568.L54+
Llull, Ramón, 1232?-1316: B765.L8+
Locke, John, 1632-1704: B1250+
Locomotion
  Infant psychology: BF720.M69
Locus of control (Personality traits): BF698.35.L62
Lodge, Oliver, Sir, 1851-1940: B1646.L7+
Logic: BC1+
  Philosophy
    English philosophy
      Bacon: B1199.L6
      Mill: B1608.L6
    German philosophy
      Fichte: B2849.L6

Love
  Philosophy
    Russian philosophy
      19th and 20th centuries:
        B4235.L69
  Psychic research: BF1045.L7
  Psychoanalysis: BF175.5.L68
  Psychology: BF575.L8
    Adolescent psychology:
      BF724.3.L68
  Spirit messages: BF1311.L6
  Witchcraft: BF1572.L6
Lovejoy, Arthur O. (Arthur Oncken),
  1873-1962: B945.L58+
Lowber, James William, 1847-1930:
  B945.L6+
Lowde, James: B1299.L5+
Lowenfeld Mosaics: BF698.8.L6
Löwith, Karl, 1897-1973: B3299.L68+
Loyalty
  Ethics: BJ1533.L8
    Ancient Chinese and Japanese
      ethics: BJ118.L68
  Philosophy
    German philosophy: B2528.L7
Lu, Chia, ca. 216-ca. 172 B.C.:
  B128.L81+
Lu, Chiu-yüan, 1139-1193: B128.L83+
Lü, Kun, 1536-1618: B128.L85+
Lu, Shiyi, 1611-1672: B5234.L87+
Lü, Zuqian, 1137-1181: B128.L87+
Lucian, of Samosata: B577.L5+
Lucid dreams: BF1099.L82
Lucretius Carus, Titus: B577.L6+
Lucretius (Titus Lucretius Carus)
  Spirit messages: BF1311.L75
Ludowici, August: B3299.L8+
Luescher test: BF698.8.L8
Lugmayer, Karl, 1892-1972:
  B3299.L85+
Lunar influences
  Astrology: BF1723
Luncheons
  Etiquette: BJ2038
Luo, Qinshun, 1465-1547: B128.L94+
Lupasco, Stéphane, 1900-1988:
  B2430.L8+
Luporini, Cesare, 1909-1993:
  B3634.L7+
Lust
  Ethics: BJ1535.L87
Luther, Martin
  Spirit messages: BF1311.L8
Lutosławski, Wincenty: B4691.L83+
Luxury
  Ethics: BJ1535.L9
Lyco, of Troas: B577.L8+
Lying
  Ethics: BJ1420+
Lyotard, Jean François, 1924-1998:
  B2430.L96+
Lysergic acid diethylamide
  Psychological effect: BF209.L9

M

Ma, Yifu, 1883-1967: B5234.M32+
Macedonian philosophy: B4861+
Mach, Ernst, 1838-1916: B3300+
Machan, Tibor R.: B945.M26+
Macherey, Pierre: B2430.M22+
Machiavelli, Niccolò, 1469-1527:
  B785.M2+
Machiavellianism (Personality traits):
  BF698.35.M34
Machinery
  Aesthetics: BH301.M25
Machover Draw-a-Person Test:
  BF698.8.M24
MacIntyre, Alasdair C.: B1647.M12+
Mackaye, James, 1872-1935:
  B945.M24+
Mackie, J. L. (John Leslie):
  B5704.M33+
Mackintosh, James, Sir, 1765-1832:
  B1510+
Macmurray, John, 1891-1976:
  B1647.M13+
Macrobius, Ambrosius Aurelius
  Theodosius: B680.M3+
Macrocosms, History of the theories of:
  BD497
Mādhava, d. 1386: B133.M16+
Madhusūdana Sarasvatī: B133.M18+

Many-valued logic: BC126
Marcel, Gabriel, 1889-1973:
  B2430.M25+
Marciani, Armando: B3636.M26+
Marcion, of Sinope, 2nd cent.: B681
Marcus Aurelius: B579.2+
Marcuse, Herbert, 1898-1979:
  B945.M298+
Margaret Cavendish, Duchess of
  Newcastle, 1624?-1674: B1299.N27+
Marías, Julián, 1914-2005:
  B4568.M37+
Marijuana
  Psychological effect: BF209.C3
Marion, Jean-Luc, 1946-: B2430.M28+
Maritain, Jacques, 1882-1973:
  B2430.M3+
Mărjani, Shihabetdin, 1818-1889:
  B4249.M374+
Marriage
  Astrology: BF1729.L6
  Graphology: BF905.M3
  Witchcraft: BF1572.M35
Marriage and spiritualism: BF1275.M3
Mars (Planet)
  Astrology: BF1724.2.M37
  Spirit messages: BF1311.M4
Marsh, James, 1794-1842: B931.M3+
Marsh, James L.: B945.M37+
Marsilius, of Inghen, d. 1396: B765.M3+
Martensen, H. (Hans), 1808-1884:
  B4383
Martí, José, 1853-1895: B1029.M3+
Martin, of Alwick: B765.M332+
Martineau, James, 1805-1900:
  B1647.M2+
Martinetti, Piero, 1872-1943:
  B3636.M3+
Martinism
  Magic: BF1623.M37
Marty, Anton, 1847-1914: B4651.M3+
Marvelous, The, Psychology of: BF775
Marx, Karl, 1818-1883: B3305.M7+
Marxist philosophy: B809.8
  Philosophy
    French philosophy
      20th century: B2424.D5
Mary, Blessed Virgin, Saint
  Spirit messages: BF1311.M42
Marzio, Cornelio di: B3636.M36+
Masculinity
  Psychoanalysis: BF175.5.M37
Masks
  Witchcraft: BF1572.M37
Masnovo, Amato, 1876-1955:
  B3636.M3642+
Mass (Occult sciences): BF1442.M36
Mastri, Bartolomeo, 1602-1673:
  B3578.M36+
Mate, Reyes: B4568.M386+
Mate selection
  Palmistry: BF935.M35
Material falsity
  Philosophy
    French philosophy
      Descartes: B1878.M28
Materialism
  Philosophy
    Chinese philosophy: B127.M38
    English philosophy: B1133.M38
    French philosophy: B1809.M3
      18th century: B1925.M25
      Diderot: B2018.M3
    German philosophy: B3188
      18th century: B2628.M3
    Greek philosophy: B187.M28
      Democritus: B299.M37
    Medieval philosophy: B738.M3
    Modern philosophy: B825.A+
    Russian philosophy
      19th and 20th centuries:
        B4235.M3
Materialization (Spiritualism): BF1378
Maternal deprivation
  Child psychology: BF723.M35
  Infant psychology: BF720.M38
Mathematical logic: BC131+
Mathematical methods
  Psychology: BF39+
Mathematics
  Aesthetics: BH301.M35
  Philosophy
    Greek philosophy: B398.M3
  Psychology: BF456.N7

Mather, Cotton: B876.M2+
Mathewson, Alonzo P.
  Spirit messages: BF1311.M45
Mathieu, Vittorio: B3636.M3644+
Matrix Analogies Test: BF432.5.M36
Matsuzaki, Kōdō, 1771-1844: B5244.M38+
Matter
  Philosophy
    Arabian philosophy: B745.M33
    English philosophy
      Berkeley: B1349.M35
    French philosophy
      18th century: B1925.M3
    German philosophy
      Kant: B2799.M43
    Greek philosophy: B187.M3
      Aristotle: B491.M3
      Plato: B398.M35
  Structure of matter (Cosmology): BD646
Matter and form (Cosmology): BD648
Matter and motion (Cosmology): BD652
Mattheus, Aurelianensis, 13th cent.: B765.M36+
Maturation (Genetic psychology): BF710
Maturi, Sebastiano, 1843-1917: B3636.M367+
Maturity (Genetic psychology): BF710
Maudsley personality inventory: BF698.8.M3
Maugé, Francis: B2430.M36+
Maupertuis, 1698-1759: B2080+
Maximos, ho Ephesios, d. 372: B683
Maximus, of Tyre, 2nd cent.: B588
Maximus, the Greek, Saint, 1480-1556: B785.M298+
Maya: B132.M3
Mayer, Julius Robert von, 1814-1878: B3308
Maze learning (Intelligence testing): BF433.M3
Mazes (Intelligence testing): BF433.M3
Mazzoni, Jacopo, 1548-1598: B785.M3+
McCosh, James, 1811-1894: B925+
McDermott, John J. (John Joseph), 1932-: B945.M454+
McDowell, John Henry: B1647.M14+
McKeon, Richard (Richard Peter), 1900-1985: B945.M456+
McTaggart, John McTaggart Ellis, 1866-1925: B1647.M15+
Mead, George Herbert, 1863-1931: B945.M46+
Mean
  Ethics: BJ1500.M42
  Philosophy
    Greek philosophy
      Aristotle: B491.M36
Meaning
  Philosophy: B105.M4
    English philosophy
      Locke: B1298.M4
    Greco-Roman philosophy: B513
    Modern philosophy: B840.A1+
  Psycholinguistics: BF463.M4
  Psychology: BF778
  Psychology of meaning: BF778
Meaning, Psychology of: BF455+
Meaninglessness (Philosophy): B825.2.A+
Means and ends
  Ethics: BJ84.E5
Measures of Psychosocial Development: BF698.8.M35
Mechanical aptitude (Intelligence testing): BF433.M4
Mechanical logic: BC137+
Mechanical theories of the universe: BD553
Mechanism
  Philosophy
    French philosophy
      Descartes: B1878.M43
Mechanism (Cosmology): BD553
Medical aspects
  Phrenology: BF885.M4
Medical astrology: BF1718
Medicine
  Graphology: BF905.M43
  Palmistry: BF935.M4

Men, Social usages for
  Spanish: BJ1985
Menagias, Iōannēs, 1811-1870:
  B3515.M43+
Mencius: B128.M324
Mendelssohn, Moses, 1729-1786:
  B2690+
Menopause
  Witchcraft: BF1572.M46
Mensch, James R.: B945.M468+
Mental ability
  Child psychology: BF432.C48
  Psychology: BF431+
Mental fatigue (Psychology): BF482
Mental illness
  Astrology: BF1729.M453
Mental illness and genius: BF423
Mental imagery: BF367
Mental representation
  Psychology: BF316.6
    Child psychology: BF723.M43
Mental reservation (Truth and
  falsehood)
  Ethics: BJ1429
Mental retardation and genius: BF426
Menticulture: BF638+
Mentoring
  Psychology
    Applied psychology: BF637.M45
Menzer, Paul, 1873-1960: B3309.M38+
Mercury (Planet)
  Astrology: BF1724.2.M45
  Spirit messages: BF1311.M5
Merit
  Ethics: BJ1500.M47
Merleau-Ponty, Maurice, 1908-1961:
  B2430.M376+
Mersenne, Marin, 1588-1648:
  B1899.M4+
Merz, John Theodore, 1840-1922:
  B1647.M4+
Mescaline (Psychological effect):
  BF209.M4
Mesmerism (Parapsychology):
  BF1111+
Messer, August, 1867-1937:
  B3309.M4+
Messer, Max: B3309.M443+
Metals
  Astrology: BF1729.M46
Metamorphosis
  Magic: BF1623.M47
Metaphor
  Aesthetics: BH301.M4
  Philosophy
    Danish philosophy
      Kierkegaard: B4378.M48
    German philosophy
      Leibniz: B2599.M6
      Nietzsche: B3318.M4
    Greek philosophy
      Aristotle: B491.M38
Metaphysics: BD95+
  Philosophy
    American philosophy: B944.M47
    Arabian philosophy: B745.M4
    Chinese philosophy: B127.M48
    English philosophy
      Berkeley: B1349.M47
    French philosophy
      Descartes: B1878.M5
      Malebranche: B1898.M4
    German philosophy
      Hegel: B2949.M4
      Kant: B2799.M5
      Leibniz: B2599.M7, B2599.O7
      Nietzsche: B3318.M5
      Schelling: B2899.M48
      Wolff: B2728.M4
    Greco-Roman philosophy:
      B532.M48
    Greek philosophy
      Aristotle: B491.M4
      Early: B200.M45
      Plato: B398.M4
    Judaism: B5802.M48
    Medieval philosophy: B738.M47
    Netherlands philosophy
      Spinoza: B3999.M45
Metempsychosis (Ontology): BD426
Meteorology
  Astrology: BF1729.M47
Methodius, of Olympus, Saint, d. 311:
  B684.M3+

Methodology
Ethics: BJ37
Christian ethics: BJ1200
Philosophy: B53+
French philosophy
Pascal: B1904.M48
German philosophy
Hegel: B2949.M43
Kant: B2799.M514
Nietzsche: B3318.M54
Greek philosophy
Aristotle: B491.M45
Socrates: B318.M48
Psychology: BF38.5
Speculative philosophy: BD239.2+
Mexican philosophy: B1015+
Mexicans
Intelligence testing: BF432.M4
Meyer, Hans: B3309.M45+
Meyer-Kendall Assessment Survey: BF698.8.M38
Meyer, Michel, 1950-: B4165.M49+
Meyerson, Émile, 1859-1933: B2430.M4+
Michalski, Konstanty: B4691.M54+
Michelet, Jules, 1798-1874: B2331.M5+
Michelet, Karl Ludwig, 1801-1893: B3309.M5+
Michelstaedter, Carlo, 1887-1910: B3636.M49+
Michigan picture test: BF698.8.M44
Microcosms, History of the theories of: BD497
Middle age
Astrology: BF1729.M52
Psychological aspects: BF724.6
Middle-aged persons
Ethics: BJ1690
Midgley, Mary, 1919-: B1647.M47+
Midheaven
Astrology: BF1718.5
Midlife crisis (Psychology): BF724.65.M53
Mikhaĭlov, F. T. (Feliks Trofimovich): B4249.M52+
Miki, Kiyoshi, 1897-1945: B5244.M54+
Military art and science
Astrology: BF1729.M54
Military aspects
Parapsychology: BF1045.M55
Mill, James, 1773-1836: B1595+
Mill, John Stuart, 1806-1873: B1600+
Miller, John William: B945.M476+
Mīmāṃsā: B132.M5
Mimesis
Aesthetics: BH301.M47
Mimicry
Psychology: BF357
Mind
Ontology: BD418+
Philosophy
German philosophy
Kant: B2799.M52
Greek philosophy: B187.M55
Medieval philosophy: B738.S68
Philosophy of (Ethics): BJ45.5
Mind and body
Child psychology: BF723.M48
Philosophy: B105.M53
French philosophy
17th century: B1818.M56
Descartes: B1878.M55
Greek philosophy
Aristotle: B491.M5
Indic philosophy: B132.M54
Netherlands philosophy
Spinoza: B3999.M5
Scottish philosophy
Hume: B1499.M47
Psychology: BF150+
Mind-brain identity theory: B105.M55
Mind, Philosophy of
Philosophy
German philosophy
Hegel: B2949.M55
Mind reading (Parapsychology): BF1161+
Minnesota Multiphasic Personality Inventory: BF698.8.M5
Minucius Felix, Marcus: B684.M5+
Mīr Findariskī, Abū al-Qāsim ibn Mīrzā Buzurg, d. 1640?: B753.M57+

Montesquieu, Charles de Secondat, baron de, 1689-1755: B2090+
Monthaye, Gaston, 1871-: B2430.M67+
Mood
  Memory: BF378.M65
  Philosophy
    Danish philosophy
      Kierkegaard: B4378.M66
  Psychology: BF521
    Adolescent psychology: BF724.3.M64
Moon
  Astrology: BF1723
Moon (Magic): BF1623.M66
Moore, G. E. (George Edward), 1873-1958: B1647.M7+
Moorish philosophers: B740+
Moral and ethical aspects
  Counseling psychology: BF636.67
Moral development
  Child psychology: BF723.M54
  Ethics: BJ324.M64
Moral judgment (Ethics): BJ1408.5
Moral Re-Armament
  Ethics movement: BJ10.M6+
Moral realism: BJ1500.M67
Morale and ethics: BJ45
Moralists
  Philosophy
    French philosophy: B1809.M7
    Greco-Roman philosophy: B514
Mordinov, A. E. (Avksentiĭ Egorovich): B4249.M66+
More, Henry, 1614-1687: B1299.M6+
More, Thomas, 1565-1625: B785.M8+
Morelly, M.: B2100+
Moretti-Costanzi, Teodorico: B3636.M7+
Morgan, Conway Lloyd: B1647.M76+
Morgues, Haunted: BF1476.4
Morin, Edgar: B2430.M676+
Moroccan philosophy: B5360+
Morris, George Sylvester, 1840-1889: B945.M5+
Moses, of Narbonne, d. 1362: B759.M64+
Mosque etiquette: BJ2019.5.I8
Mother and child
  Child psychology: BF723.M55
Mother and infant
  Infant psychology: BF720.M68
Motion
  Philosophy
    Greek philosophy: B187.M6
      Aristotle: B491.M6
Motion perception (Vision): BF245
Motion pictures
  Psychology: BF789.M6
Motivation
  Adolescent psychology: BF724.3.M65
  Child psychology: BF723.M56
  Psychology
    Older people: BF724.85.M67
Motoda, Eifu, 1818-1891: B5244.M65+
Motoori, Noringa, 1730-1801: B5244.M67+
Motor ability
  Child psychology: BF723.M6
  Infant psychology: BF720.M69
  Psychology: BF295+
Motor ability and intelligence: BF433.M68
Motor ability testing
  Psychology: BF295.4+
Motor automatism (Spiritualism): BF1321+
Motor learning
  Psychology: BF295+
Motor skill learning
  Psychology: BF295+
Mou, Zongsan: B5234.M67+
Mounier, Emmanuel, 1905-1950: B2430.M69+
Mountains
  Psychology: BF789.M65
Mouth (Physiognomy): BF861.M7
Movement
  Aesthetics: BH301.M6
  Philosophy: B105.M65
    Danish philosophy
      Kierkegaard: B4378.M68
    German philosophy
      Kant: B2799.M68

N

Nagel, Thomas, 1937-: B945.N33+
Naigeon, Jacques André, 1738-1810: B2109.N3+
Nails (Palmistry): BF935.N3
Nakae, Toju, 1608-1648: B5244.N28+
Nakamura, Yūjirō, 1925-: B5244.N295+
Names
  Astrology: BF1729.N3
  Logic: BC199.N3
  Magic: BF1623.N3
  Memory: BF387.N34
  Personal names (Fortune-telling): BF1891.N3
  Philosophy
    Russian philosophy
      19th and 20th centuries: B4235.N36
Nammyŏng school: B5253.N36
Nancy, Jean-Luc: B2430.N36+
Napoleon I (Horoscopes): BF1728.N2
Narāqī, Muḥammad Mahdī ibn Abī Ẕarr, d. 1794 or 5: B753.N37+
Narcissism
  Adolescent psychology: BF724.3.N35
  Psychology: BF575.N35
Nardi, Bruno: B3636.N36+
Natal astrology: BF1719
Natanson, Maurice Alexander, 1924-: B945.N35+
National socialists (Germany)
  Horoscopes: BF1728.2.N38
Nations, Psychology of: BF751
Natoli, Salvatore: B3636.N38+
Natorp, Paul, 1854-1924: B3309.N2+
Natural sciences and psychology: BF64
Naturalism
  Philosophy
    American philosophy: B944.N3
    Germany philosophy: B3191
    Indic philosophy: B132.N3
    Modern philosophy: B828.2.A+
    Scottish philosophy
      Hume: B1499.N37
Nature
  Aesthetics: BH301.N3
  Environmental psychology: BF353.5.N37
Nature
  Magic: BF1623.N35
  Philosophy
    Arabian philosophy: B745.N38
    Chinese philosophy: B127.N3
    Danish philosophy
      Kierkegaard: B4378.N3
    East Asian philosophy: B5168.N38
    English philosophy
      Bacon: B1199.N38
    French philosophy
      Descartes: B1878.N3
    German philosophy: B2528.N38, B2748.N35
      Fichte: B2849.N37
      Hegel: B2949.N3
      Kant: B2799.N37
      Nietzsche: B3318.N3
      Schelling: B2899.N3
      Schopenhauer: B3149.N38
    Greek philosophy
      Aristotle: B491.N3
    Medieval philosophy: B738.N3
    Netherlands philosophy
      Spinoza: B3999.N34
    Renaissance philosophy: B780.N37
    Scottish philosophy
      Hobbes: B1248.N3
Nature and nurture
  Psychology: BF341+
Nature of reality (Ontology): BD331
Navy Computer Adaptive Personality Scales: BF698.8.N39
Nayrīzī, Najm al-Dīn Maḥmūd, d. ca. 1526: B753.N39+
Nazis (Germany)
  Horoscopes: BF1728.2.N38
Near-death experiences in children
  Psychic research: BF1045.N42
Near-death experiences (Psychic research): BF1045.N4
Necessitarianism
  Ethics: BJ1460+
Necessity
  Ontology: BD417

O

Ø

P

Plutarch: B600+
Plutarch, of Athens, d. ca. 431: B695
Pluto
  Astrology: BF1724.2.P4
Pluto (Planet)
  Spirit messages: BF1311.P6
Poetics
  Philosophy
    Arabian philosophy: B745.P64
Poetry
  Philosophy
    Greek philosophy
      Plato: B398.P6
Poets
  Graphology: BF905.P57
Polak, Leo, 1880-1941: B4095.P55+
Polanyi, Michael, 1891-1976: B945.P58+
Polarity
  Philosophy
    German philosophy
      Schelling: B2899.P58
    Modern philosophy: B830.5.A+
Polish astrology: BF1714.P65
Polish philosophy: B4687+
Political correctness
  Epistemology: BD175.5.P65
Political prisoners
  Graphology: BF905.P6
Political science and philosophy: B65
Politicians
  Graphology: BF905.P63
Politics
  Aesthetics: BH301.P64
Politics and astrology: BF1729.P6
Politics and ethics: BJ55
Politics and personality: BF698.9.P6
Poliziano, Angelo, 1454-1494: B785.P6+
Polo, Leonardo: B4568.P65+
Polyglot mediumship: BF1353
Polystratus: B605.P5+
Pomponazzi, Pietro, 1462-1525: B785.P8+
PONS test: BF698.8.P16
Popper, Karl R. (Karl Raimund), 1902-1994: B1649.P6+
Popular superstitions: BF1775
Porphyry, ca. 234-ca. 305: B697
Port, Kurt, 1896-1979: B3323.P59+
Porter, Noah, 1811-1892: B931.P5+
Portuguese philosophy: B4511+
Porzio, Simone, 1496-1554: B785.P86+
Pos, Hendrik Josephus, 1898-1955: B4095.P67+
Posidonius: B607.P2+
Position, Sleep (Parapsychology): BF1073.P65
Positive psychology: BF204.6
Positivism
  Aesthetics: BH301.P67
  Latin American philosophy: B-BJ9 3.P6
  Philosophy: B105.P6
    Belgian philosophy
      Modern: B4155.P66
    English philosophy
      19th and 20th centuries
        Earlier: B1568.5
        Later: B1616.P6
    French philosophy
      18th century: B1925.P6
      Comte: B2249.P6
    Germany philosophy: B3197
    Italian philosophy: B3605
    Latin American philosophy: B1008.P6
    Modern philosophy: B831.A1+
    Russian philosophy
      19th and 20th centuries: B4235.P67
    Spanish and Portuguese philosophy: B4515.P6
    Spanish philosophy: B4565.P65
Positivist ethics: BJ1365+
Possession, Demonaic: BF1555
Possessiveness: BD460.P67
Possessiveness (Personality traits): BF698.35.P67
Possibility
  Child psychology: BF723.P67
  Logic: BC199.P7

Primitivism
  Philosophy
    Germany philosophy: B3197.5
Principle (Philosophy): B105.P7
Prini, Pietro: B3636.P7+
Prior, A. N. (Arthur N.), 1914-1969:
  B5714.P74
Priority
  Ethics
    Religious ethics: BJ1278.P73
  Philosophy: B105.P73
    Greek philosophy
      Aristotle: B491.P75
Priscian, fl. ca. 500-530: B765.P75+
Prisoners of war (Psychology):
  BF727.P7
Prisons, Haunted: BF1477.3
Privacy
  Psychology
    Applied psychology: BF637.P74
Private language problem (Philosophy):
  B832.3.A+
Probabilism (Christian ethics):
  BJ1278.P76
Probabilities
  Philosophy
    Scottish philosophy
      Hume: B1499.P7
Probability (Logic): BC141
Problem solving
  Child psychology: BF723.P8
  Dreaming: BF1099.P75
  Psychology: BF449
Problems, Emotional
  Child psychology: BF723.E598
Process (Ontology): BD372
Proclus, ca. 410-485: B701
Procrastination
  Applied psychology: BF637.P76
Prodicus, of Ceos: B305.P7+
Prodigies: BF1777
Proença, Raul: B4598.P7+
Profanity
  Ethics: BJ1535.S9
Professional ethics: BJ1725
  Counseling psychology: BF636.67
Progress
  Philosophy
    English philosophy
      Bacon: B1199.P76
    Greek philosophy
      Plato: B398.P7
    Italian philosophy
      Rosmini Serbati: B3648.P74
Projection (Psychoanalysis):
  BF175.5.P68
Projective assessment of aging method:
  BF698.8.P76
Projective techniques (Personality
  testing): BF698.7
Promises (Ethics): BJ1500.P7
Proof (Logic): BC173
Prophecies
  Occult sciences: BF1783+
  Philosophy
    Jewish philosophy: B757.P7
  Spirit messages: BF1311.P75
Prophecy
  Philosophy
    Arabian philosophy: B745.P66
Prophets
  Occult sciences: BF1783+
Proportion
  Philosophy
    Greek philosophy
      Plato: B398.P75
Propositions (Logic): BC181
Prospective memory: BF378.P76
Protagoras: B305.P8+
Protection magic: BF1623.P75
Protestant etiquette: BJ2019
Proverbs
  Divinations: BF1779.P76
Prudence
  Ethics: BJ1533.P9
Przywara, Erich, 1889-1972:
  B3323.P8+
Psellus, Michael: B765.P8+
Pseudo-Dionysius, the Areopagite:
  B667.D4+
Pseudochromesthesia (Psychology):
  BF497

Rastafarian ethics: BJ1290.3
Rationalism
  Latin American philosophy: B-BJ9 3.R3
  Philosophy
    Chinese philosophy: B127.R37
    English philosophy: B1569
    Greek philosophy
      Plato: B398.R3
    Indic philosophy: B132.R3
    Modern philosophy: B833.A1+
    North African philosophy: B5338.R38
Rationalization (Psychology): BF337.R28
Ratramnus, monk of Corbie, d. ca. 868: B765.R16+
Ravaisson, Félix, 1813-1900: B2337
Ravasi, Elio: B3636.R3+
Raven's Progressive Matrices: BF432.5.R38
Rawls, John, 1921-2002: B945.R28+
Rayid method (Personality testing): BF698.8.R28
Raymond, George Lansing, 1839-1929: B945.R3+
Raymond, of Sabunde, d. 1436: B765.R2+
Rays, Seven (Occult sciences): BF1442.S49
Rāzī, Abū Bakr Muḥammad ibn Zakarīyā, 865?-925?: B753.R38+
Rāzī, Fakhr al-Dīn Muḥammad ibn ʻUmar, 1149 or 50-1210: B753.R4+
Re-evaluation counseling
  Psychology: BF636.7.R44
Reaction
  Philosophy: B834.A+
Reaction time
  Psychology: BF317
Reactions
  Psychology: BF317
Reading
  Psychology: BF456.R2
Readings
  Psychic research: BF1045.R43
Reale, Miguel: B1044.R43+
Realism
  Aesthetics: BH301.R42
  Philosophy
    American philosophy: B944.R4
    English philosophy: B1616.R3
    French philosophy
      20th century: B2424.R4
    Indic philosophy: B132.R4
    Medieval philosophy: B731
    Modern philosophy: B835.A+
Reality
  Philosophy
    German philosophy
      Kant: B2799.R35
  Psychoanalysis: BF175.5.R4
Reason
  Ethics
    Christian ethics: BJ1278.R43
  Philosophy
    Arabian philosophy: B745.R4
    French philosophy
      Pascal: B1904.R36
    German philosophy: B2748.R37
      Hegel: B2949.R25
      Schelling: B2899.R38
    Greek philosophy: B187.R35
      Aristotle: B491.R4
      Plato: B398.L85
    Medieval philosophy: B738.R42
    Scottish philosophy
      Hume: B1499.R4
    Spanish philosophy: B4565.R4
Reasoning
  Logic: BC177
  Philosophy
    French philosophy
      Descartes: B1878.R37
    Indic philosophy: B132.R415
  Psychology: BF442
    Adolescent psychology: BF724.3.R4
    Child psychology: BF723.R4
Recall of dreams: BF1099.R4
Recipes (Witchcraft): BF1572.R4
Recognition
  Philosophy: B105.R23

Science
  Philosophy
    Greek philosophy: B187.S32
  Spirit messages: BF1311.S4
Science and ethics: BJ57
Science and parapsychology: BF1045.S33
Science and philosophy: B67
  Medieval philosophy: B738.S55
Science and spiritualism: BF1275.S3
Scorpio (Astrology): BF1727.5
Scottish philosophy (Influence on American philosophy): B903
Scotus Erigena, Johannes, ca. 810-ca. 877: B765.J3+
Scruples (Christian ethics): BJ1278.S37
Scruton, Roger: B1649.S247+
Sea
  Aesthetics: BH301.S4
Sea specters (Occult sciences): BF1486
Seals (Numismatics)
  Fortune-telling: BF1891.S4
Searching behavior
  Child psychology: BF723.S2
Searle, John R.: B1649.S26+
Secondary function
  Psychology: BF323.S4
Secrecy
  Ethics: BJ1429.5
    Jewish ethics: BJ1286.S33
  Psychology
    Applied psychology: BF637.P74
Secret (Philosophy): BD401
Secrétan, Charles, 1815-1895: B2392
Secundus, of Athens, 2nd cent.: B614.S4+
Security
  Psychology: BF575.S35
    Child psychology: BF723.S22
Seduction
  Aesthetics: BH301.S43
  Applied psychology: BF637.S36
Seeds
  Philosophy: B105.S43
Seelye, Julius H. (Julius Hawley), 1824-1895: B931.S3+
Seers
  Occult sciences: BF1783+
Seillière, Ernest Antoine Aimé Léon, Baron, 1866-: B2430.S4+
Seixas, J. M. da Cunha (José Maria da Cunha), 1836-1895: B4598.C8+
Selectivity (Memory): BF378.S45
Self
  Ethics: BJ324.S44
  Medieval philosophy: B738.S57
  Ontology: BD438.5
  Philosophy
    African philosophy: B5315.S34
    Asian philosophy: B5015.S34
    Danish philosophy
      Kierkegaard: B4378.S4
    German philosophy: B2748.S44
      18th century: B2628.S34
      Kant: B2799.S37
      Nietzsche: B3318.S45
      Schleiermacher: B3098.S34
    Greco-Roman philosophy: B526
    Greek philosophy
      Plato: B398.S45
    Scottish philosophy: B1499.S45
  Psychoanalysis: BF175.5.S44
  Psychology: BF697+
    Child psychology: BF723.S24
    Infant psychology: BF720.S44
Self-acceptance
  Psychology: BF575.S37
Self-actualization
  Adolescent psychology: BF724.3.S25
  Psychic research: BF1045.S44
  Psychology
    Applied psychology: BF637.S4
    Middle age: BF724.65.S44
    Older people: BF724.85.S45
Self-assurance
  Ethics: BJ1533.S27
Self-confidence
  Ethics: BJ1533.S27
  Psychology: BF575.S39
Self-consciousness (Sensitivity)
  Psychology: BF575.S4
Self-control
  Child psychology: BF723.S25

Sex
  Magic: BF1623.S4
  Occultism: BF1442.S53
  Palmistry: BF935.S48
  Psychic research: BF1045.S48
  Psychoanalysis: BF175.5.S48
  Psychology
    Adolescent psychology: BF724.3.S4
    Child psychology: BF723.S4
    Older people: BF724.85.S48
  Spirit messages: BF1311.S45
  Witchcraft: BF1572.S4
Sex differences
  Philosophy
    German philosophy
      Kant: B2799.S47
  Psychoanalysis: BF175.5.S49
  Psychology: BF692.2+
    Adolescent psychology: BF724.3.S4
    Intelligence testing: BF433.S48
  Testing: BF692.3+
Sex role
  Infant psychology: BF720.S48
  Psychology: BF692.2+
    Adolescent psychology: BF724.3.S4
    Child psychology: BF723.S42
  Testing: BF692.3+
Sexism
  Psychoanalysis: BF175.5.S52
Sextus, Empiricus: B620+
Sexual animosity (Psychology): BF692.15
Sexual behavior (Psychology): BF692+
Shadow (Psychoanalysis): BF175.5.S55
  Child psychology: BF723.S425
Shaftesbury, Anthony Ashley Cooper, Earl of, 1671-1713: B1385+
Shakespeare, William
  Spirit messages: BF1311.S5
Shamanism: BF1585+
Shame
  Psychology: BF575.S45
Shang, Yang, d. 338 B.C.: B128.S47+
Shao, Yong, 1011-1077: B128.S51+
Sharing
  Child psychology: BF723.S428
  Ethics: BJ1533.G4
  Psychology: BF575.S48
Shaw, Charles Gray, 1871-1949: B945.S5+
Shcherbatskoĭ, F. I. (Fedor Ippolitovich), 1866-1942: B4259.S4337+
Shelley, P.B.
  Spirit messages: BF1311.S53
Shells
  Fortune-telling: BF1891.S48
Shen, Dao, 350?-275? B.C.: B128.S54+
Shestov, Lev, 1866-1938: B4259.S5+
Shields, Charles W. (Charles Woodruff), 1825-1904: B945.S6+
Shiffers, Evgeniĭ, 1934-1997: B4259.S546+
Shih, Jiao, ca. 390 B.C.-ca. 330 B.C.: B128.S58+
Shingaku (Japanese ethics): BJ971.S5
Shinkaruk, V. I. (Vladimir Illarionovich), 1928-: B4259.S55+
Shinto (Philosophy): B162.6
Ship travel
  Etiquette: BJ2142
Shipton, Ursula (Mother Shipton): BF1815.S5
Short-term counseling
  Psychology: BF636.7.S57
Short-term memory: BF378.S54
  Psychology
    Adolescent psychology: BF724.3.M46
    Child psychology: BF723.M4
Shpakovskiĭ, Anatoliĭ Ignat′evich, 1895-: B4259.S56+
Shpet, Gustav, 1879-1937: B4259.S566+
Shyness
  Child psychology: BF723.B3
Siamese twins and heredity: BF346.S5
Sibbern, Frederikl Christian, 1785-1872: B4389

Succubi
  Demonology: BF1556
Sudanese philosophy: B5400+
Suffering
  Philosophy: B105.S79
    Danish philosophy
      Kierkegaard: B4378.S84
    French philosophy
      Pascal: B1904.S8
  Psychic research: BF1045.S84
  Psychology: BF789.S8
    Child psychology: BF723.S78
    Older people: BF724.85.S92
Suffering and pain (Ethics): BJ1409
Sufficient reason
  Philosophy
    German philosophy
      Leibniz: B2599.S94
Suggestibility
  Child psychology: BF723.S8
Suggestion (Hypnotism): BF1156.S8
Suhrawardī, Yaḥyá ibn Ḥabash, 1152 or 3-1191: B753.S83+
Suicide
  Ontology: BD445
Sully, James, 1842-1923: B1667.S5+
Sully Prudhomme, 1839-1907: B2403
Sulzer, Johann Georg, 1720-1779: B2709.S6+
Summism
  Philosophy
    Medieval philosophy: B737
Sun
  Magic: BF1623.S8
Sun, Wanpeng: B5234.S99+
Sunspots
  Astrology: BF1729.S92
Superego (Psychoanalysis): BF175.5.S93
Supererogation (Ethics): BJ1450+
Superficiality
  Ethics: BJ1535.S87
Superman
  Philosophy
    German philosophy
      Nietzsche: B3318.S8
Supernatural and ethics: BJ47
Superstitions, Popular: BF1775
Supervenience
  Philosophy: B841.8.A+
Supervisors
  Horoscopes: BF1728.2.S9
Surfaces (Philosophy): B105.S85
Surprise
  Child psychology: BF723.S87
Susceptibility (Hypnotism): BF1156.S83
Suso, Heinrich, 1300?-1366: B765.S7+
Sustainable development
  Environmental psychology: BF353.5.S87
Svoboda, Emil, 1878-1948: B4805.S8+
Swearing
  Ethics: BJ1535.S9
Swedenborg, Emanuel, 1688-1772: B4468.S8+
Swedish philosophy: B4455+
Swieżawski, Stefan: B4691.S94+
Swiss philosophy: B4625+
Syberg, Johan Hendrik van (Occult sciences): BF1598.S92
Syllogism
  Philosophy
    Greek philosophy
      Aristotle: B491.S9
Syllogisms
  Ancient Oriental logic: BC26.S9
  Logic: BC185
    History: BC21.S9
Symbolic logic: BC131+
Symbolic play
  Infant psychology: BF720.P56
Symbolic profile test: BF698.8.S79
Symbolism
  Aesthetics: BH301.S8
  Child psychology: BF723.S94
  Magic: BF1623.S9
  Philosophy
    German philosophy
      Kant: B2799.S94
  Psychoanalysis: BF175.5.S95
  Psychology: BF458
Symmetry
  Aesthetics: BH301.S9

Symonds Picture Story Test:
BF698.8.S8
Sympathy
Ethics: BJ324.S96, BJ1475
Philosophy
Scottish philosophy
Hume: B1499.S9
Psychology: BF575.S9
Synagogue etiquette: BJ2019.5.J4
Synchronicity
Parapsychology: BF1175
Psychoanalysis: BF175.5.C65
Syncretism
Philosophy
Greco-Roman philosophy: B531
Synesius, of Cyrene, Bishop of Ptolemais
Philosophy: B703.S7+
Synesthesia (Psychology): BF495+
Synthetic sense (Psychology): BF299.S9
Syrian philosophy: B5050+
Syrianus: B703.S8+
Szondi test: BF698.8.S85

T

Taber, Helen
Spirit messages: BF1311.T3
Table etiquette: BJ2041
Table moving (Spiritualism): BF1375
Tacit knowledge
Psychology: BF317.5
Tagore, Rabindranath, 1861-1941: B5134.T27+
Tai, Chen, 1724-1777: B5234.T32+
Taine, Hippolyte, 1828-1893: B2405+
Tajikistan philosophy: B4796+
Takahashi, Fumi, 1901-1945: B5244.T26+
Takahashi, Sekisui, 1769-1848: B5244.T28+
Talebearing
Child psychology: BF723.T3
Talismans
Demonology: BF1561
Tanabe, Hajime, 1885-1962: B5244.T336+
T'ang, Chen, 1630-1704: B5234.T33+
Tang, Junyi, 1909-1978: B5234.T34+
Tang, Zhongyou, 12th cent.: B128.T34+
Tantric astrology: BF1714.T3
Tanzanian philosophy: B5425+
Tao
Philosophy
Chinese philosophy: B127.T3
Taoism (Philosophy): B162.7
Taoist astrology: BF1714.T34
Taoist ethics: BJ1290.8
Tarde, Gabriel de, 1843-1904: B2411
Tarot, The: BF1879.T2
Tasks of emotional development test: BF698.8.T3
Tassy, Edme, 1876-: B2430.T3+
Taste (Psychology): BF261
Tatian, ca. 120-173: B704.T3+
Tattling
Child psychology: BF723.T3
Tauler, Johannes, ca. 1300-1361: B765.T2+
Tauros, b. 105?: B626.T25+
Taurus (Astrology): BF1727.2
Taylor, A. E. (Alfred Edward), 1869-1945: B1669.T2+
Taylor, Brook, 1685-1731: B1390.T4+
Taylor, Charles, 1931-: B995.T3+
Taylor, Jeremy, 1613-1667: B1299.T3+
Taylor-Johnson Temperament Analysis: BF698.8.T35
Taylor, Mark C., 1945-: B945.T39+
Teachers, Logic for: BC161.T4
Teaching and ethics: BJ49
Teaching and phrenology: BF885.T3
Teaching and psychology: BF54
Teasing
Psychology
Applied psychology: BF637.T43
Techne (Philosophy): B105.T43
Plato: B398.T4
Technology and ethics: BJ59
Teenagers
Astrology: BF1729.T44
Parapsychology: BF1045.T43

Theodicy
  Philosophy
    German philosophy
      Kant: B2799.T45
      Leibniz: B2599.T38
Theodōrakopoulos, Iōannēs Nikolaou, 1900-: B3515.T45+
Theology
  Philosophy
    French philosophy
      Descartes: B1878.T45
    Greek philosophy: B187.T5
Theology and philosophy: B56
Theology and psychology: BF51
Theophrastus: B626.T3+
Theory
  Philosophy: B105.T52
    Greek philosophy: B187.T53
      Plato: B398.T53
    Modern philosophy: B842.A+
Theosophy and spiritualism: BF1275.T5
Thesis
  Ancient Oriental logic: BC26.T5
Thesis (Logic): BC21.T5
Theurgy
  Magic: BF1623.T56
Thiazinamium
  Psychological effect: BF209.T5
Thibon, Gustave, 1904-: B2430.T4+
Thing in itself
  Philosophy
    German philosophy
      Kant: B2799.D5
Thomae, Petrus ca. 1280-ca. 1340: B765.P4+
Thomas, à Kempis, 1380-1471: B765.T4+
Thomas, Aquinas, Saint, 1225?-1274: B765.T5+
Thomas, de Argentina, d. 1357: B765.T55+
Thomas, de Clivis, 14th cent.: B765.T56+
Thomas, Elystan: B1669.T5+
Thomas, John, M.A.: B1669.T57+
Thomasius, Christian, 1655-1728: B2605
Thöne, Franz, 1884-: B3346.T6+
Thoreau, Henry David, 1817-1862: B931.T4+
Though experiments: BD265
Thought
  Psycholinguistics: BF463.M4
  Psychology
    Older people: BF724.85.C64
  Psychology and age: BF724.55.C63
Thought and thinking
  Philosophy
    German philosophy
      Hegel: B2949.T48
  Psychology: BF441+
Thought transference (Parapsychology): BF1161+
Thoughtfulness
  Ethics: BJ1533.T45
Threat
  Psychology: BF575.T45
Three-dimensional personality test: BF698.8.T53
Three person test: BF698.8.T55
Thrift
  Ethics: BJ1533.E2
Tibetan astrology: BF1714.T53
Tiedemann, Dietrich, 1748-1803: B2715
Tierno Galván, Enrique: B4568.T5+
Tilgher, Adriano, 1887-1941: B3652.T55+
Timaeus, of Locri: B258.T4+
Time
  Cosmology: BD638
  Logic: BC199.T4
  Philosophy
    American philosophy: B944.T54
    Danish philosophy
      Kierkegaard: B4378.T5
    German philosophy: B2528.T56
      Hegel: B2949.T54
      Kant: B2799.T5
      Nietzsche: B3318.T5
    Greek philosophy: B187.T55
      Aristotle: B491.T5
      Heraclitus of Ephesus: B224.T56
      Plato: B398.T55

U

Ubaldi, Pietro: B3652.U2+
Udayanācārya: B133.U29+
Ueberweg, Friedrich, 1826-1871: B3351
Ueda, Shizuteru, 1926-: B5244.U29+
Ugandan philosophy: B5420+
Ugliness
  Aesthetics: BH301.U5
Ukrainian philosophy: B4751+
Ulrici, Hermann, 1806-1884: B3160+, B3354.U47+
'Umar ibn Sulaimān: B753.U8+
Umemoto, Katsumi, 1912-1974: B5244.U45+
Unamuno y Jugo, Miguel de, 1864-1936: B4568.U5+
Uncertainty
  Psycholinguistics: BF463.U5
Unconscious
  Psychology of the unconscious: BF1001+
Unconscious mind
  Psychology: BF315
Underachievement
  Psychology
    Applied psychology: BF637.U53
Understanding
  Philosophy
    German philosophy
      Kant: B2799.C78
  Psychology: BF325
Unger, Peter K.: B945.U54+
United States history
  Astrology: BF1729.U5
  Spirit messages: BF1311.U5
Unity
  Dialectical materialism: B809.833
  Philosophy
    English philosophy
      Berkeley: B1349.U6
    German philosophy: B2748.U55
Unity and plurality
  Ontology: BD394
Universals
  Philosophy: B105.U5
Universals
  Philosophy
    English philosophy
      Locke: B1298.U55
    Indic philosophy: B132.U54
Universities, Haunted: BF1478
Unknowable, The (Epistemology): BD211
Unrequited love
  Psychology: BF575.U57
Upamāna: B132.U62
Upham, Thomas Cogswell, 1799-1872: B931.U6+
Uranus (Planet)
  Astrology: BF1724.2.U7
Uruguay philosophy: B1075+
Ussher, Arland: B1669.U8+
Utilitarianism
  Philosophy
    English philosophy
      Berkeley: B1349.U8
    Modern philosophy: B843.A+
Uzbekistan philosophy: B4786+

V

Vacherot, E. (Etienne), 1809-1897: B2415
Vagueness
  Philosophy: B105.V33
Vagueness (Logic): BC199.V34
Vaihinger, Hans, 1852-1933: B3354.V48+
Vailati, Giovanni, 1863-1909: B3652.V33+
Vaiśeṣika: B132.V2
Valencia, Pedro de, 1555-1620: B785.V1138+
Valentino, Rudolph
  Spirit messages: BF1311.V3
Valentinus, 2nd cent.: B708.V3+
Valla, Lorenzo, 1407-1457: B785.V114+
Vallin, Georges: B2430.V33+
Valperga di Caluso, Tommaso, 1737-1815: B3598.V3+

INDEX

W

X

Xavier, Francisco Côndido
  Spirit messages: BF1311.X38
Xenocrates, of Chalcedon, ca. 396-ca. 314 B.C.: B626.X3+
Xenoglossy: BF1353
Xenophanes, ca. 570-ca. 478 B.C.: B258.X3+
Xirau, Joaquín, 1895-: B4568.X5+

Y

Yaḥyá ibn ʻAdī, ca. 893-974: B753.Y3+
Yamaga, Soko, 1622-1685: B5244.Y26+
Yamazaki, Ansai, 1618-1682: B5244.Y279+
Yan, Jun, 1504-1596: B128.Y23+
Yang, Jian, 1141-1226: B128.Y25+
Yang, Xianzhen: B5234.Y29+
Yatabe-Guilford personality test: BF698.8.Y3
Ye, Zigi, fl. 1378: B128.Y36+
Yen, Fu, 1853-1921: B5234.Y39+
Yen, Hui, 6th/5th cent. B.C.: B128.Y3664+
Yen, Ying, d. 500 B.C.: B128.Y393+
Yen, Yüan, 1635-1704: B5234.Y46+
Yi jing: B127.I2
Yin, Haiguang: B5234.Y5+
Yin, Wen, 350-284 B.C.: B128.Y55+
Yin-yang: B127.Y56
Yoga
  Astrology: BF1729.Y64
  Magic: BF1623.Y64
  Philosophy
    Indic philosophy: B132.Y6
  Psychic research: BF1045.Y63
Yōmeigaku (Japanese philosophy): B5243.Y6
Young adults, Social usages for American: BJ1857.Y58
Young men
  Ethics for: BJ1661+
Young women
  Ethics for: BJ1661+
Young women, Social usages for American: BJ1857.Y6
Youth
  Developmental psychology: BF724
  Islamic ethics: BJ1292.Y6
Yugoslav philosophy: B4841+
Yulingzi, 4th cent. B.C., 4th cent. B.C.: B128.Y8+

Z

Zambrano, María: B4568.Z34+
Zanotti, Francesco Maria, 1692-1777: B3598.Z3+
Zdziechowski, Marjan, 1861-1938: B4691.Z38+
Zeigarnik effect: BF378.I65
Zeller, Eduard, 1814-1908: B3391
Zeno, of Elea: B258.Z3+
Zeno, of Tarsus: B626.Z18+
Zeno, the Stoic: B626.Z2+
Zerahiah ben Isaac ben Shealtiel: B759.Z47+
Ziegler, Leopold, 1881-1958: B3393.Z7+
Ziegler, Theobald, 1846-1918: B3395
Zirm, Eduard Konrad: B3396.Z76+
Zodiac
  Philosophy
    Greek philosophy
      Plato: B398.Z63
Zodiac (Astrology): BF1726+
Zola, Émile: BF416.Z8
Zoroastrian astrology: BF1714.Z65
Zoroastrian ethics: BJ1295
Zubeldia y de Inda, Néstor de: B4568.Z75+
Zubiri, Xavier: B4568.Z8+
Zulliger test: BF698.8.Z8

GPO U.S. GOVERNMENT PRINTING OFFICE: 2012–372–396/40016